To Love, Honor, and Obey in Colonial Mexico

TO LOVE, HONOR, AND OBEY IN COLONIAL MEXICO

Conflicts over Marriage Choice, 1574-1821

PATRICIA SEED

STANFORD UNIVERSITY PRESS
Stanford, California

Stanford University Press
Stanford, California
© 1988 by the Board of Trustees of the
Leland Stanford Junior University

Printed in the United States of America

Original printing 1988
Last figure below indicates year of this printing:
04   03   02   01   00   99

CIP data appear at the end of the book

Published with the assistance
of Rice University

For Rachel

Acknowledgments

The Bibliographic Note (p. 309) outlines in detail the nature of my research and some of the difficulties involved in studying a mass of documents that are in some cases only roughly classified. By far the greatest part of my research was done in the National Archives (Archivo General de la Nación) of Mexico, and it is to this institution and its former director, Alejandra Moreno Toscano, and her successor, Leonora Ortíz, that I am most indebted. During the long years of my research, the entire staff of the archives was always helpful and interested.

To a lesser degree, but no less gratefully, I am indebted to the staffs of the Archivo General de Indias (Seville), the Archivo Histórico Nacional (Madrid), the Bibliotecas Nacionales of Madrid and Mexico, the British Museum, and the Hispanic Division of the Library of Congress. I am also grateful for the help I received from the Interlibrary Loan departments of the University of Wisconsin-Madison, Ohio University, the College of Charleston, and Rice University. Financial assistance for research in Mexico came from a Fulbright-Hays Dissertation Fellowship and the Social Science Research Council, and for research in Spain from the National Endowment for the Humanities and the College of Charleston (S.C.) Foundation. I also thank the Tinker Foundation.

Special thanks are also due to the past director of the Dirección de Estudios Históricos of the Instituto Nacional de Antropología e Historia, Enrique Florescano, who created and fostered intellectual excitement for a generation of young Mexican scholars and those of us fortunate to be associated with that enterprise during the late 1970's. In particular, I am indebted to my colleagues for two years in the Seminario de Historia Urbana who taught me a great deal about life in Mexico City not only in the late eighteenth and early nineteenth centuries but in the twentieth as well. And I owe an enormous debt of gratitude to Solange de Alberro and the members of the Seminario de Historia de Mentalidades who have listened with interest and enthusiasm since I first presented the results of this study to them in 1978. I would also like to thank Norris Pope of Stanford University Press for his unflagging interest and Shirley Taylor, copy editor *extraordinario*.

For helpful comments on earlier drafts of the manuscript I wish to thank John Chance, Ira Gruber, Thomas Haskell, and James A. Yorke, also Peter Smith and Thomas Skidmore, who read the original version as a doctoral dissertation. Molly Kelly and George E. Marcus have contributed a great deal toward turning this material into a book, and I am extremely grateful to both of them.

Additional thanks for assistance at other stages of research are also due to Alan Booth, Jorge Ceballos Loya, George Heltai, Richard Kagan, Rosario Parra, and the indispensable Roberto Beristáin of the AGN (Mexico).

P.S.

Contents

*To Love, Honor, and Obey
in Colonial Mexico*

Introduction: Romeo and Juliet in Mexico

 On the evening of September 16, 1591, in Mexico City, Gerónimo Valverde, the son of a wealthy Spanish merchant, was visiting his uncle. As they talked quietly with other relatives, Gerónimo's father suddenly stormed into the house, accompanied by a huge black slave. Drawing his sword on his son, the father and the slave forced Gerónimo into a small room and shackled his feet. Then the father took out a large padlock made specially in Flanders, fixed it to the door, and posted the slave outside to ensure that Gerónimo could not escape. When the uncle and the relatives demanded to know why he was treating his son like that, the father replied that Gerónimo wanted to marry Juana Herrera, the sixteen-year-old daughter of a rival merchant in the city. Vowing that he would never allow his son to marry against his will, the father turned on his heel and left.

Locked in the room, Gerónimo wrote the chief church judge of the city, telling of his imprisonment and his father's threats against him if he married. He pleaded with the judge to stop his parents from interfering and allow him to wed. The note was smuggled out, and Gerónimo's uncle took it to the church court early on the morning of September 17. After reading the note and hearing the uncle's story, the chief judge immediately ordered his prosecutor to find a royal police official and release Gerónimo. Church prosecutor and crown policeman together sought out Gerónimo's father to request politely that he hand over the key. He refused. In that case, the church prosecutor said, he would be excommunicated: he could never again attend Mass if he failed to hand over the key. Reluctantly the father gave him the key, but he still threatened to disinherit his son and persecute him until he dropped if he actually married Juana.

The prosecutor and the royal constable went immediately to the uncle's house where Gerónimo was held. Ordering the slave to stand aside, they struggled with the lock for some time before it came free. As they unchained Gerónimo, they asked if he still wanted to marry. Yes, he replied; not only have I promised to do so, but my confessor has charged my conscience with fulfilling my obligation to Juana. The prosecutor and the policeman immediately accompanied him to the church court, where the senior magistrate issued an order allowing Gerónimo to marry that same day. He did not even need to be married by his own priest, the judge said. The church was holding Juana in protective custody in another parish; the priest there could perform the ceremony. The record of the dispute ends here, with both Gerónimo and Juana under church protection, and the church judge's order for their marriage.[1]

The drama of Gerónimo and Juana, as recorded in detail by the notary of the church court in Mexico City, resembles that of another, more celebrated sixteenth-century pair of lovers—Shakespeare's Romeo and Juliet. The actors are the same: rival families whose son and daughter want desperately to marry. The central conflict is the same, between a young couple and their respective fathers who, because of the families' long-standing antagonism, are implacably opposed to a marriage. In both cases, persons sympathetic to the couple act as intermediaries: Juliet's nurse and Gerónimo's uncle. Perhaps surprisingly in both cases, a Catholic priest is willing to marry the couple without the knowledge of either set of parents. In Shakespeare's play Friar Laurence performs the ceremony; in real life in Mexico City the wedding was ordered by the principal church judge for the city of Mexico.

But along with these similarities and the similarity also of date— Gerónimo and Juana's story unfolded only a year or two before Shakespeare probably began to write *Romeo and Juliet*—there are some significant differences between the two stories.[2] The real-life Romeo did not murder a member of the rival clan and was not banished. The real-life Juliet was not threatened by her parents with marriage to someone she did not love. And Gerónimo and Juana's love did not end in tragedy. Why did they marry safely when the "star-cross'd lovers" were doomed? Two factors were critically important. Although Gerónimo's father had a long-standing feud with Juana's father, the rivalry was not shared by all members of either family, and so the Valverde-Herrera feud lacked the all-encompassing dimensions of the rivalry of the Montagues and the Capulets; in fact, a member of the Valverde clan assisted the young couple. The state of absolute enmity between Shakespeare's families rendered Romeo's murder of Tybalt and subsequent banishment inevitable, and meant separation from his beloved Juliet.

Second, the two stories were set in vastly different cultures. Shakespeare's, although set in Verona, actually refers to Elizabethan England; Gerónimo and Juana's drama unfolded in Mexico, a colony of Spain, England's principal rival in the sixteenth century. One important difference between England and the Spanish colony was the role played by the church. In Shakespeare's England, a friar could certainly do what Friar Laurence did—marry Romeo and Juliet secretly in his cell. But Friar Laurence was not an official of the established church, and he had no way of shielding the children from their parents' opposition, and specifically of preventing Juliet's father from forcing her to marry someone else. The chief ecclesiastical judge of Mexico City, on the other hand, was able to throw the weight of his office against the two fathers who opposed the match.[3] Faced with the institutional power of the church, the rival families were helpless, and so the Mexican Romeo and Juliet escaped to be married. Although they were wed in secret to keep their families from interrupting the ceremony, Gerónimo and Juana's legitimate union was made public shortly thereafter. Juliet's tragedy—that her parents did not know of her marriage to Romeo and tried to force her into marrying someone else—was, for the Mexican lovers, effectively forestalled by the Mexican church's disclosure.

What is striking about Juana and Gerónimo's story, then, is the independence and power of the church judge of Mexico City. He did not rule in favor of a wealthy and established merchant, but rather contradicted him and frustrated his wishes. Nor did he seek to play the impartial mediator between parent and child: instead he adopted a partisan role. Partisanship does not surprise, but the side he chose does. Why urge a boy to disobey his father and then openly abet his disobedience? Why throw the entire authority of the Catholic Church behind a young couple wishing to marry and thus alienate a powerful and influential member of the community? Juana Herrera's role was also significant. Because her family, too, was against the marriage, church officials took her from her home and placed her in safe custody, although that was an act of interference in parental rights over their children.

The case of Gerónimo and Juana was not an isolated case. Others similar to it occurred during the two hundred years of post-Conquest Mexican history. They represent a particular kind of conflict within the family, disputes concerning a couple's personal choice to marry in the face of opposition from members of their families. Although those in opposition were usually parents, they were sometimes other relatives, and occasionally masters opposing the marriage of their dependents, employees, servants, or slaves. In this study the term prenuptial disputes is used to refer generally to such situations. "Marriage oppositions" is used to refer to the various means employed to prevent a marriage—that is, any action, legal or illegal, designed to halt a planned marriage that has not yet taken place.[4]

Over the course of the colonial period, the reception accorded couples such as Gerónimo Valverde and Juana Herrera by both the authorities and public opinion was to change drastically. Nearly two hundred years later another merchant father, similarly enraged, seized his son and locked him up, to prevent his marrying the niece of a prominent royal bureaucrat. On this occasion, no royal police went immediately to the rescue, no church official ordered the secret marriage of the couple, and the son languished for several months on an estate outside Mexico City while his father persuaded officials of the royal court that as a father he had superior rights over his son's choice of a wife.[5] The difference between the situation of Gerónimo and Juana in 1591 and that of Manuel Fernández and Joaquina López in 1785 is profound. By 1785, mediation of marriage conflicts had been removed from the church's jurisdiction and appropriated by the state, parents were accorded a veto over their children's marriages, and the social values that had the effect of giving priority to the rights of children over those of parents had been substantially altered.

Although the differences between the two cases are striking, so too are the similarities. The actual conduct of Manuel's father differed little from that of Gerónimo's father almost two hundred years before. Their reasons for opposing the marriage were similar. The crucial transformation, therefore, did not take place in the behavior of parents in the intervening two hundred years. Rather it occurred in the mechanisms of social control—the church and state—and more profoundly in certain cultural beliefs and values pertaining to marriage and family that informed them.

In Mexico in the sixteenth and seventeenth centuries, parental authority and personal will in matters of marriage were contested ground, in both official and popular discourses. Although they presumed parental authority in the family, the institutions of social control, namely the church courts, clearly and consistently favored the choices of children over parental objections. Hispanic literature, both high and popular, of the period reveals a fundamental tension between an almost formulaic recognition of parental authority and equally frequent assertions of the precedence of the children's right to follow their own will and choose marriage partners purely on the basis of attachment. The public voice of the largely Hispanic community in colonial Mexico, registered in the testimony of sixteenth- and seventeenth-century prenuptial conflict cases, demonstrated surprisingly uniform support for the independent choice of children. But in the course of the colonial era, two changes occurred: a waning of the cultural forces that had provided normative support for the children's position in prenuptial conflicts, and the appearance of an unprecedentedly explicit affirmation of normative parental—and specifically patriarchal—control over marriage choices. Two intertwined processes were at work.

First, the values that provided affirmation for children became less compelling during the final years of the seventeenth century. This was followed in the mid-eighteenth century by the positive valuing of patriarchal control over marriage; in effect a doctrine of normative patriarchy emerged in opposition to the now declining support for the position of children. The institutions of social control—church and state—responded to the dissolving social consensus by modifying their policies. Therefore to understand how the situation of Gerónimo and Juana came to exist, as well as how attitudes and institutions changed to bring about the very different situation of Manuel and Joaquina, one must examine the role of church and state in colonial Mexico, and the evolution of three areas of cultural belief central to marriage and family: attitudes toward individual free will, love, and honor.

A commonly accepted view of colonial Latin American society is that post-Conquest institutions and values crystallized at the end of the sixteenth century and remained more or less stable until the middle of the eighteenth century, a period often referred to as the "mature colonial period" or the "baroque era." This book argues to the contrary, that the institutions of social control and cultural values of colonial Spanish society both altered significantly during this period. Beginning in the seventeenth century, the Catholic Church suffered a gradual loss of independence, and the basis of social prestige—the culture of honor—similarly altered. Because these changes occurred in ways that were neither dramatic nor arresting, they have tended to be overshadowed by a dominant historical judgment of a period of stability, if not equilibrium. This study demonstrates that the incremental and irregular pace of cultural and institutional change during this period had striking cumulative effects in the matter of marriage choice.

In spirit at least, this study also offers a revisionist contribution to the field of Western family history. The accepted view of the traditional family in Western Europe and its American colonies is that during the sixteenth and seventeenth centuries fathers controlled marriages often for considerations of gain, whether social, economic, or political. With the onset of capitalism in the eighteenth century, historians argue, greater emphasis on the individual allowed freedom of choice and permitted marriages for love.[6]

Since the publication of the formative works on the traditional family, several revisionist critiques have appeared, all of which in one way or another qualify the standard rigid version of traditional and modern family norms. Some of these have argued on philosophical grounds that the standard thesis is too congratulatory of the modern era.[7] Others, relying on contemporary sources, chiefly diaries, to show the existence of a greater degree of emotional responsiveness between parent and child than earlier studies predicated, have questioned the correspondence between stated norms and actual behavior of parents during the sixteenth, seventeenth, and eighteenth centuries. Still others have raised literary evidence, such as the tale of Romeo and Juliet, to show that marriage for love was not unknown in the early modern era.[8] This study aims at a different critique.

The concept of traditional control of marriage by parents in early modern Western Europe has been derived mostly from research on France and England, the Anglo-American colonies, and to a lesser extent Germany. What becomes evident from this study is that religious teachings and cultural attitudes toward parental control of marriage in these countries differed from those of the sixteenth- and seventeenth-century Hispanic world. Most Protestant sects and French Catholics required parental consent to marry; of the major Western European religions, only the Church of England and the Spanish Catholic Church did not. And of these two, only the Spanish Catholics created actual mechanisms to protect freedom of marital choice, supplying both moral and institutional support to couples whose parents, guardians, or relatives sought to block their marriage plans. In other words, in Spain and Spanish America, parental consent to marriage was not part of what historians have labeled traditional society; in fact, what was traditional there looks on the surface very much like the effect of the modern faith in individualism in matters of marital choice.[9]

Because this work belongs to a revisionist trend, and revisionist works are often read (rightly or wrongly) as trying to make their challenges to more established views complete reversals rather than careful qualifications, it is important to clarify what I am, and what I am not, arguing about patriarchy in New Spain. Patriarchalism was a powerful and persuasive ideology in society at large, but it was not monolithic. It was the dominant metaphor for a variety of hierarchies in the colonial era that were organized upon the principle of patrons and clients and cut across social and ethnic boundaries. Within the family itself, the strongest expression of patriarchy was in the father's control of his children's property until they married. But in some contexts of family life, other principles existed that not only qualified patriarchy but even made such behavior anomalous in terms of the society's articulated norms. Such is the case with the prenuptial disputes treated in this study. Here, not patriarchy, but a qualified paternalism was expected of parents, and their authority was limited by doctrinal and cultural support for the freedom of children to choose their spouses. What looks like a very modern

configuration of parent-child relations in terms of collective attitudes was embedded within a traditional society that otherwise has
exemplified the characteristic of patriarchal institutions.

Ironically, in Hispanic America the ideological changes accompanying the initial stages of capitalism were what finally brought
patriarchy in the authoritarian sense to bear on parent-child relations
concerning marriage. The values that accompanied early capitalism,
interacting with other independent changes, stimulated the cultural
elaboration of patriarchal control of marriage at the expense of the
socially sanctioned prerogative of couples. It was only with the later
development of industrial capitalism in the nineteenth and twentieth centuries that the relatively recent appearance of normative patriarchy in marital matters ebbed. Modern culture did not over-
whelm the timeless or the tradition of centuries; one era merely
worked complex changes on the conditions of another. Thus this
book argues for a more studied view of the impact of capitalism on
family life, as well as for an appreciation of the cultural variability
of the so-called "traditional" early modern European family.

The other kind of contribution this study makes to family history
is methodological. Heretofore, much of the research into cultural
attitudes in the early modern era toward children, marriage, and
family relationships has depended upon an examination of the
largely religious prescriptive literature along with the writings,
published and unpublished, of a small number of elite families.[10] In
analyzing cultural beliefs in a broader range of society, historians
have for the most part relied on another type of source, demographic records. From their information on births and marriages,
historians have attempted to deduce, sometimes very creatively, underlying attitudes and social values. Recently several historians have
adopted the anthropological method of examining folklore and rit-
uals for the social values of nonliterate people.[11]

The common aim of most of these studies has been to establish
the dominant trains of thought or discourses about family life. But
objections can be raised to each of these approaches. To what extent
does the diary of one person (that of Ralph Josselin, for example) or
the correspondence of one family represent the feelings and beliefs
of a whole culture, or even a whole class? In the instance when a
group of diaries is available for study, they are still only a handful,
representing only the literate elite, and are the records of persons

who in the very act of writing about their children were more likely to have wished to describe positive relationships. It may be that in many (perhaps even a majority) of the countless other unrecorded families, relationships between parents and children were more problematic, neglectful, or troubled. One cannot easily determine whether or not the attitudes toward the family as revealed in existing correspondence or diaries were dominant within the culture.[12]

Demographic analyses, on the other hand, are valuable reconstructions of conduct, but the motivation for the behavior they record remains a matter of conjecture: such guesses usually can be expected to reflect contemporary cultural expectations rather than those of cultures distant in time. The actual feelings and attitudes that determined the conduct of people of another era and culture remain obscure.[13] Some historians have usefully pursued different types of documentation—seventeenth-century patient records, for example—in order to avoid the biases of strictly elite records, wisely avoiding the tendency to establish these records as reflecting dominant ideas.[14] Collections of folklore offer a novel and interesting way of analyzing social trends, but they are rarely reliable historical materials for periods earlier than the nineteenth century, when most such collections were made. And as with elite documentation, the question of dominant ideas or discourses is often difficult to determine.

The final usual body of information, religious and literary evidence, has been challenged on grounds both of its elite provenance and of its failure to reflect the actual behavior of most people.[15] Questioning the relationship of prescriptive literature to behavior can be a useful corrective to ungrounded generalizations about society on the basis of a few religious texts, but it is unanswerable in an empirical sense. Studies of any body of documentation can be used to support almost any hypothesis about past behavior, since our knowledge of past conduct is always incomplete and partial.

The method of this book is to focus on what I should like to call the problem of language—the history of change in socially constituted meanings of words, concepts, and language. To this end I have employed both literary and religious prescriptive writing, not to describe behavior but as a means of establishing the range of socially constituted meanings as understood and expressed in a given historical period. In some historical periods the dominant discourses are apparent in the literature itself, but often in a fragmented and sometimes mutually contradictory form. Therefore to establish the ascendant attitudes it is often necessary to turn away from the sometimes confusing set of meanings established in literature and doctrinal works and look instead at the language that is expressed in the conflicts within families over marriage choices. A careful study of the language used by the families in these disputes as well as of the language and responses of church officials can help to establish whether or not certain sets of meaning were dominant in a given period. Obviously, since the church officials were by virtue of their office inclined to impose their views upon the society, there was no question of the way in which their ideas were dominant. But even within this framework the predominant sets of ideas vary over time, from periods of a reigning set of ideas to periods when these ideas were under siege. Even when the discourses were being contested, however, it was still possible to establish the relationship among discourses.

In this study, the problem of change, which Hayden White has correctly pointed out as one of the weakest points of studies of discourses,[16] is examined by looking at shifts in the meanings of words such as "love," "will," "honor," and *patria potestad* (the authority of fathers) within the context of conflicts over marriage choices. It is also examined by analyzing the changes and shifts in the discourse of officials within the dominant institutions, evident in their gradual modification of practices as well as in a growing impreciseness in their use of language. It is by tracing shifts in the socially constituted meanings of language that this book illustrates historical change in attitudes and values.

The records upon which this study is based—detailed descriptions of prenuptial disputes recorded by an institution, the Catholic Church—describe the conduct and reflect the fundamental attitudes of parents and children from a broader range of society than merely the literate.[17] They also establish the dominant interpretations and the range of submerged or conflicting interpretations of the roles of parents and children in marriage choices. Even though the language is filtered through the requirements of the institution, much of what is recorded is snippets or summaries of hundreds of conversations that took place between ordinary parents and children. It is true that these records exist for only the top half of colonial Mexican society, which characteristically resided in urban areas, but even so they are far more representative of that society than the works of the extremely small number of literate persons who are usually the source of information in studies of attitudes in family history. Records like these, if examined not merely for the information they provide about the institution, as is most commonly done,[18] but also for the social attitudes and values articulated therein, can provide a far broader and more representative access to attitudes toward the family and marriage than has been possible in the past.

The book is divided into three parts. Part I, Chapters 1–5, examines prenuptial disputes, similar to Gerónimo and Juana's, that were resolved by church intervention in ways that protected and even encouraged the personal choices of both men and women regarding marriage partners. During the period 1574–1689, the independent actions of young couples such as Juana and Gerónimo were supported by cultural norms, and parental opposition was treated as illicit by the judicial authorities. This period is the chronological basis of the first part of the book, 1574 being the date of the first extant documentation on marriage conflicts, and the year 1689 marking the first significant increase in the number of marriages parents were able to prevent.

Part II, Chapters 6–9, describes the social changes that led to the emergence of a cultural discourse that approved of rigid patriarchal control over children's marriages. Part III, Chapters 10–13, discusses the consequences of the changes in cultural discourse examined in Part II for the major institutions of social control, the church and the royal bureaucracy. It was not just that the church and state traded places in resolving prenuptial disputes; rather, there was a significant turn away from the cultural values that had for so long supported individual choice in marriage. Specifically, the favoring of patriarchal authority in marriage choices seemed linked to a positive valuing of economic power and considerations of status, which had only recently begun to inform the major institutions of social control. A concluding chapter places the findings of this study in a comparative context with those of scholarship of the same period in other European societies.

The sources for this study are diverse. Decrees of ecclesiastical councils, papal bulls, and canonical commentaries were investigated to identify the formal Catholic doctrines on marriage. Catechisms, confessional manuals for priests, and popular religious literature were consulted to determine how the church's formal teachings were understood and interpreted as guides for concrete action. The basic cultural attitudes toward marriage, love, and honor were studied in both popular religious literature and the drama and prose of Spain's Golden Age. The backbone of this study, however, consists of the actual records of prenuptial disputes that took place in the colony of New Spain.

The geographical area from which the prenuptial disputes are drawn is the archdiocese of Mexico, which in colonial times embraced the highly populated central region of the Spanish colony of New Spain. About three-quarters of the documentation originated in Mexico City itself; the remainder came from urban areas outside the city.

Two types of records form the documentary base of the study. The first and largest category is that of ordinary marriage applications, which were made by every couple who wanted to marry and were the first official step toward marriage. Every couple had to appear before the local priest (or simply his notary in the larger parishes) to declare that both parties were free to marry and intended to do so. Often couples were accompanied by witnesses who were prepared to swear to the truth of the statements. It was in the course of these ordinary applications that couples informed church officials in their own words of any opposition to their wedding, and it is from these first applications that most of the evidence concerning marriage conflicts originates. A second and much smaller body of documentary evidence consists of the records of lawsuits and formal appeals to church officials to halt or permit marriages. Such cases represent only a small fraction of the incidents of opposition and tended to involve only the wealthiest families, who could afford such actions.

In addition to reading nearly all the surviving marriage license applications for Mexico City of the colonial period (approximately 16,000 applications), I examined a major portion of the approximately 300 extant formal lawsuits over prenuptial disputes for the archdiocese of Mexico during the colonial period. For the final period covered by the study, when the church ceded its control over prenuptial disputes to the crown, I examined the appeals to the central royal court in the viceroyalty of New Spain, called the Audiencia of Mexico. Although its jurisdiction extended beyond the boundaries of the archdiocese, the Audiencia was the secular unit that corresponded most closely to the archdiocesan one.

Although this study is based on careful, detailed reading of a large number of cases, only a few can be presented in the body of the text and only the most significant points are illustrated with actual cases. The remaining cases are summarized, either statistically or in the Notes.

PART ONE

The Early Colonial Period
1574-1689

CHAPTER I

The Mexican Background

 When Hernán Cortés and his small band of Spaniards came to the shores of Mexico in 1519, they brought with them not only soldiers and sailors, nobles and artisans, but the history, culture, and tradition of the Iberian peninsula. For 301 years after Cortés captured Mexico City, that vast territory formerly governed by native tribes and empires was ruled by a foreign power that imposed its own religion, government, and cultural tradition, that of the Crown of Castile and León. To understand how New World prenuptial conflicts took shape, it is necessary to know what the Old World brought to the New in the way of religious and cultural beliefs about marriage and how the special conditions of the New World affected those beliefs.

For much of the sixteenth and seventeenth centuries, the marital ideals, practices, and aspirations of the couples and families in this study reflect explicitly Spanish social mores and customs which were played out by a society that included not only Spaniards but Indians, slaves, and racially mixed persons. The boundaries that defined these racially distinct groups were maintained during these first two colonial centuries with relatively little incidence of interracial marriage. The conflicts that arose from marriages within these groups were regulated by a Spanish institution, the Catholic Church, that operated with a surprising degree of independence from the crown in enforcing Spanish religious and cultural ideas about marriage relationships and in adjudicating conflicts over marriage choice. Although both Spanish society and its relation to state and church power would begin to be transformed in the latter part of the seventeenth century, Hispanic customs and culture provided the significant background against which the conflicts surveyed in this book took place.

The peninsular mores and customs imported to and imposed upon the New World underwent subtle shifts in emphasis which often reinforced their Hispanic character. The basic outlines of food preferences, superstitions, folklore, and material culture in Spanish America were established by a process anthropologist George Foster has labeled "culture crystallization"—the rapid selection of Hispanic traits and adaptation to new conditions by means of conscious and unconscious choices made during the highly fluid initial decades of contact.[1] During this early period, certain elements of Spanish culture, particularly of southern and western Spain, since the great proportion of the migrants came from Andalucia, the Castiles, and Extremadura, became distilled and fixed in the mixture of colonial and indigenous society; at the same time, the ethical and moral beliefs of Spanish society crystallized into a rather homogeneous version by the consolidation of a single ethnic and privileged social category of "Spaniard" in the New World. Moral judgments related to a fundamental conviction of Spanish superiority were intensified by comparison with indigenous attitudes. The conquerors' encounters with Aztec human sacrifice, idol worship, and sexual conduct, customs characterized by Cortés as "horrible and abominable," served to solidify and reinforce Spanish assumptions about the superiority of their civilization, their religion, their government, and their cultural beliefs.[2]

For most of the great number of Spaniards who emigrated to the New World, there were still strong physical and emotional bonds with the Old World; their hearts, habits of mind, and ambitions remained in Spain, and the frequent passage of men back and forth across the Atlantic—particularly the leadership of colonial society—served to reinforce these bonds. During the greater part of the sixteenth and seventeenth centuries, aspirations for status, power, and influence were shaped by the standards of Castile. One way to judge the extent of this tie to Spain is the inclination of Spanish migrants not to remain in the New World, as would migrants in the nineteenth century, but rather to return home. Successful conquistadors

faced a quandary: the New World promised a lucrative but often uncertain future, the Old a certain yet circumscribed existence. It has
been estimated that among early conquerors, as many as half returned home.[3]

Even the successful Spaniards who stayed still aspired to the rewards of Spain. A lucky emigrant would send money home to acquire the status symbols of the peninsula—a coat of arms, the habit
of one of the honorific military orders, even a title of nobility. One
not so lucky would still send home money to build a house, perhaps
one with a big garden full of fruit trees and animals, and thus ame-
liorate his standard of living.[4] Still others aspired to become members of the Spanish nobility or add economic heft to their existing
titles. The original conquerors were not from the high nobility—
those who bore titles such as count or duke. Although many aspired
to such titles, only a few, like Cortés who became the Marquis of
the Valley of Oaxaca, were so rewarded. In the decades after the
conquest, second sons and less wealthy members of the titled Spanish nobility sailed across the Atlantic hoping to strengthen their position at home with the legendary gold of the Indies. Like many others who set across the ocean in search of fortune, most of them were
disappointed. But unlike those others, they had a semblance of a position to return to in Spain, and many did return.[5]

The royal officials and governors who arrived in the New World
kept in close contact with friends and relatives back in Spain, sending a stream of missives with instructions on how to promote their
careers and position at court. As one governor wrote to his wife,
such advancement was merited, since "for similar things and of less
service others have been given principalities," adding that for such
services "it is customary . . . to found entails and noble houses."[6]
The status and privileges he aspired to were, as always, focused on
Spain.

Many of the merchants and traders who arrived in the New
World represented transatlantic commercial networks with head-
quarters in Seville. Their status was inferior to those of the merchants of Seville, upon whom they were dependent for advancement and for a steady stream of goods, and their primary responsibility, as they were constantly reminded, was to maintain a
steady stream of payments back across the ocean.[7] Spain, and par-

ticularly Seville, was the nerve center of commerce with the Indies, and a position in Seville was the aspiration of merchants in the New World.[8]

Even when they found attractions in the New World, most of the new arrivals still thought of Spain as home—it was the focus of their thoughts, their ambitions, and their hearts. One of the early judges of the court of New Spain wrote to a friend: "This is the best land warmed by the sun. There is nothing wrong with it but being so far from the Guadalquivir [in his hometown of Seville]."[9] A priest, by his own description "very gray and fat," contemplating his retirement and weighing the choice of settling on a farm in the New World or returning to Spain, wrote his sister, "Surely my desire is not to die here, but where I was born."[10] The typical Spanish migrant did not bid adieu to his native shore with such finality as did many of his English counterparts.

By 1580, roughly the starting point for this study, this pattern changed. Conquest society had come to an end. All the settled areas of the New World had been conquered, and most of the unpromising lands, from arid northern Mexico to the steamy Amazon jungles, had at least been explored. The basic social institutions—the church and royal bureaucracies—were well established, and the wars and turmoil that accompanied the Conquest were largely over. By the close of the sixteenth century, many of the Spaniards who arrived in New Spain were contemplating staying to "buy properties and possessions and marry here, intending not to see Spain again."[11] But the emotional and physical connection of Spaniards to the Old World was to remain central for decades to come.

One reason for this continuity was that the leadership of colonial social institutions continued to be recruited from the Old World. At the summit of colonial society was the viceroy, who was either a member of the high nobility in Spain or a close relative of such a family.[12] Also often Spanish, but from less distinguished families, were the judges of the high court or Audiencia. The archbishop, the head of the church, was almost invariably from Spain, as were the members of his entourage, who often received positions within the New World ecclesiastical bureaucracy. Although these high bureaucrats and churchmen often had to adjust to the realities of the New World, their training, concepts, and cultural baggage were those of the Iberian peninsula.

The same was true of the merchants who dominated trade in the New World. By the early seventeenth century, the dominant merchants in New Spain were no longer the local representatives of Sevillan operations but were instead entrepreneurs working on their own, men who had established their own New World companies to buy up European merchandise. These men were Iberian-born, however, and remained so until the end of the colonial period.[13]

Throughout the colonial period, the majority of the books and plays read and performed in the New World were of Spanish origin. And until the middle of the seventeenth century, all the major New World writers and dramatists had lived in both Spain and the Indies; Mexican-born Juan Ruíz de Alarcón grew up in the New World but wrote all his major plays in Spain. Not until the second half of the seventeenth century, when the Golden Age was waning in Spain, were there major writers, such as Carlos Sigüenza y Góngora and Sor Juana Inés de la Cruz, who had no experience of the Old World.[14]

The discovery of the New World and its treasures gave Spaniards an unparalleled opportunity for social advancement and economic gain. They were not always successful, but the dream kept young men coming across the Atlantic for generations. These migrants and their largely invisible cultural baggage reinforced Hispanic beliefs throughout the colonial period. And since the ranks of immigrants provided the leadership of colonial commerce, religion, and government, they were often in the position to impose Hispanic values.

The Spaniards who did stay, and who received large grants of Indian labor or invested in large estates and mines, wanted to see themselves as part of an international gentry, equal in prestige to *hidalgos* in Spain. But the Spanish aristocracy refused to acknowledge the colonials as equals and were especially contemptuous of their descendants, known as creoles. As early as the second half of the sixteenth century, Spanish aristocrats were characterizing the American-born offspring of Spaniards as lazy, racially inferior, mentally deficient, and physically degenerate. Overt acknowledgment of such prejudice diminished in the early seventeenth century, but it was still sufficiently evident to arouse in the American-born Spanish an insistence on equality with the European Spaniards that betrayed an underlying anxiety that they were not indeed equal.[15] As Immanuel Wallerstein has more generally observed: "The capitalist farmers of the semi-periphery would have gladly thought of themselves as part of an international gentry class. They willingly sacrificed local cultural roots for participation in 'world' cultures. But to constitute an international class they needed the cooperation of . . . the core states, and this was not forthcoming."[16]

The Spanish-inspired aspirations, the desire for status in Old World terms, were, of course, played out in the New World against a background very different from that of Spain. In New Spain the population was far from being racially homogeneous, and the presence of large numbers of Indians and smaller numbers of black slaves meant that traditional Hispanic categories of status would have to be adapted to the New World conditions; in other words, Old World status distinctions acquired a racial tinge.

The Indian population of central Mexico at the time of the Conquest was approximately five to ten million. Within less than a hundred years the number had dropped to only one million,[17] but despite this devastating population loss, the Indians remained numerically dominant for virtually the entire colonial period. For most of the period, they were chiefly engaged in agricultural pursuits, either on their own land or as laborers on land owned by Spaniards. Those who went to the cities worked as unskilled laborers or in the retail sale of fruit and vegetables; Indian women were also widely employed as domestic servants. All Indians were obliged to pay a poll tax (tribute) that went to sustain both the government in Spain and a small group of Spaniards known as the *encomenderos*.

For the Spanish in Mexico, the presence of this large Indian population altered one of the fundamental distinctions of status in Spain, that between noble and plebeian. In Spain, the category of plebeian was identified with manual, largely agricultural, labor, and plebeian inferior status was reinforced by the payment of a poll tax from which nobles were exempted. In Mexico, the Indians, who were with few exceptions manual agricultural laborers, became the plebeians; except for a small group of Indian leaders who were classed as "noble," all Indians were subject to tribute. The Spanish category of plebeian was thus displaced on to them. The Indians' position as a conquered, hence subject, people further strengthened this association.

The consequence of this large category of "plebeian" Indians was a widespread belief in the fundamental equality of all Spaniards in the New World. (The ideological expression of this equality was the concept of honor, which is discussed in Chapter 4.) Even though the conviction of fundamental equality among Spaniards in the face of New World racial diversity had a considerable element of self-delusion about it, it remained influential through the end of the colonial period. Alexander von Humboldt, at the end of the colonial era, described it as the conviction that any white man had of his innate superiority in the face of overwhelming numbers of social inferiors.[18] Any Spaniard was able to envision himself as a member of the superior group and underplay ideas of social distinction that existed within the Spanish community. Not only did Spaniards believe themselves to be fundamentally equal, but in their equality all came to establish closer distinct linkings to nobility.

In Spain the status of noble had provided a series of privileges to a small minority, roughly 10 percent of the population. Not only were nobles exempt from payment of a poll tax (tribute), but also they could not be imprisoned for debt, and they were allowed to bear arms. It was hardly surprising that the elimination of the noble-plebeian distinction among New World Spaniards was regarded by many as an entirely worthwhile change. As Juan Solórzano would later put it, "This distinction [between noble and plebeian] does not exist in the New World, nor is it suitable for such a distinction to be introduced."[19] And indeed, the security of a tiny minority white population ruling over masses of Indians would not be helped by accentuating inequalities of wealth and power within this minority.

Spanish ideas about the status of the third racial group, the blacks, were also based on a condition of society. Whereas the Indians were primarily identified with agriculture, the blacks came to the New World as slaves of the Spanish population. They worked for the Spaniards as domestic servants in the large cities, as craftsmen and laborers on the sugar plantations, and as laborers in the silver mines and estates. From a legal standpoint, the blacks in Mexico had the fewest privileges of any of the racial groups, and they performed some of the most exhausting manual labor. On the other hand, the black population, uprooted from its native customs and cultures, of necessity quickly absorbed much of the language and customs of the Spaniards, while retaining some distinctive African traits.

Spanish attitudes toward blacks reflected the tension between antipathy and attraction. As slaves, the blacks occupied a social space inferior to the plebeian Indians, but since as a group they were more familiar with Spanish ways, they were at the same time more intimate with the Spaniards and more of a threat. Because they were apt to rebel against the conditions of their enslavement, their close residential proximity to Spaniards in the cities made them a more direct potential danger to the Spanish population than an Indian rebellion in a remote community. On the other hand, black and mulatta women particularly in urban areas were able to enter into relationships with wealthy Spaniards for which they were well rewarded financially. Because of their familiarity with Spanish customs, urban blacks were more likely to appear in prenuptial conflicts than the Indians, who lacked such knowledge.

This tripartite division within colonial society of Spaniard, Indian, and black echoed the peninsular division of status among nobles, plebeians, and slaves.[20] Only in the New World, however, did all ethnic Spaniards consider themselves noble, see the Indians as plebeian, and the blacks as slaves. Thus in the New World, without fundamental alteration, Spanish categories of status came to represent racial difference.

What would eventually disturb this fundamentally stable status system was the growth of a large group of people classified in intermediate racial groups. The racially mixed inhabitants, denominated *castas*, included the offspring of black and white parents, called mulattoes; of white and Indian parents, called *mestizos*; and of black and Indian parents, to whom no single term was applied. The mestizos, mulattoes, and black Indians themselves intermingled and produced descendants of even greater racial mixture, part Indian, part Spanish, part black. No distinctive name has ever been widely applied to these later descendants; they were usually simply called *castas*. For the first two centuries of Spanish colonial rule this intermediate group remained relatively stable and small, primarily because of the pattern of interracial sexual contact. A considerable amount of interracial sexual contact existed, but the castas, owing to prejudice rather than to laws prohibiting intermarriage, were the product of miscegenation that occurred only occasionally in marriage and largely outside it.[21] Nonmarital unions, especially concubinage between Spanish men and black, racially mixed, and Indian women, were the principal factor in creating this small but distinctive intermediate group in the sixteenth and seventeenth centuries; in those centuries mestizo and mulatto were synonymous with illegitimate.[22]

The system of Hispanic status distinctions laid over racial differences was thus maintained in marriage throughout the sixteenth and seventeenth centuries: Spaniards married Spaniards, Indians Indians, and blacks blacks; or by parallel with the traditional language of Spanish status, noble married noble, plebeian plebeian, and slave slave. Since most racially mixed people were incorporated into the status categories of one or the other parent, for a long time those actually classified as castas remained a small minority of the population. Castas were socially invisible.

Beginning in the second half of the seventeenth century this racially mixed population began to grow and increasingly participate in legitimate marriage. By the middle of the eighteenth century castas made up 21 percent of the population of the archdiocese, and at the close of the colonial period, roughly a quarter (25.4 percent) of the total population of New Spain was racially mixed.

The growing numbers of castas became an intermediate group in nearly every sense. Although they were exempt on the one hand from the slavery of the blacks, and generally exempt on the other hand from the poll tax levied on the Indian population, they failed to enjoy the economic position and political status of Spaniards. Often, their occupations were related to those of their parent groups: they worked as artisans in the large cities, as muleteers, as foremen on estates in rural areas. Their women worked as seamstresses, cooks, washerwomen, and domestic servants.[23] Some of these castas were part of the Indian communities, others were more closely affiliated with their fathers' Spanish world.[24] As their numbers increased through marriage in the eighteenth century, the castas provoked significant changes in the system of marriages in colonial society.[25] However, during the first period of this study—the sixteenth and seventeenth centuries—castas were few in number, and they played a very small role in prenuptial conflicts; relatively few conflicts involved interracial marriage.

Although marriage between racial groups remained rare during the first two centuries of Spanish rule in Mexico, the incidence of marriage in the different racial groups varied greatly, and along racial lines. The incidence of marriage, as opposed to less formal

unions, also followed racial lines in colonial Mexico. During the sixteenth and seventeenth centuries, marriage was most common
among the Spaniards, the most prosperous and secure group in colonial society, and least common among blacks and castas. The Indians, exempted by the church from the relatively higher fees
charged other racial groups and subject to closer supervision by
priests, married almost as frequently as Spaniards.[26]

Prenuptial conflict predictably emerged in those groups who
were most likely to marry, but the Indians were a significant exception. Separated by language and custom from Spaniards, they were
less likely to be cognizant of Spanish marriage practices and more
likely to follow the traditions of their own communities. If church
officials participated in mediating disputes over marriage within the
Indian community, they failed (with rare exceptions) to keep written records of their intervention. Thus the records primarily document conflicts among Spaniards, secondarily those among Hispanicized blacks and castas, who were well acquainted with, and
aspired to, the Hispanic ideal of marriage.

Blacks, who in the first century and a half of colonial rule were
still for the most part slaves, were less likely to be able to marry, because of highly imbalanced sex ratios, short life expectancies, and
owner indifference or opposition. That blacks and castas were less
likely to marry is borne out in the high illegitimacy rate that characterized these two groups. Baptismal records from the central parish of Mexico City in the second half of the seventeenth century, for
example, show that 50 percent of the children of black and mixed
race parentage were illegitimate.[27]

Black and casta marriages were underrepresented by about half
in the prenuptial conflicts. Excluding Indian marriages, between 33
and 40 percent of the marriages in Mexico City involved blacks or
castas, but only approximately 20 percent of the recorded conflicts
originated with this group.[28] (Race was omitted and unascertainable
for at least one spouse in over 20 percent of the cases.) Since marriage was a ceremony intimately integrated into Catholic doctrine
and Hispanic culture, the aspirants to church marriage who appear
in the prenuptial conflicts therefore represent the most thoroughly
Hispanicized and catechized of the blacks and castas, rather than
those castas tied closely to the Indian communities or recent arrivals
from Africa who retained their own ideas about marriage.

In socioeconomic terms, conflicts over marriage choice emerged in the middle and upper levels of colonial Mexican society. Merchants, royal bureaucrats, landowners, and professionals make up about half the families in the first period of this study; humbler people—artisans, muleteers, domestic servants, and slaves—the remaining half. Comparing these proportions with the city population as a whole, we find that these groups, with the exception of the slaves, roughly correspond to the upper half of colonial society.[29] By no means were only the very richest people involved in prenuptial conflicts, but most of those who were had some property or a trade. Further evidence that the parties were relatively prosperous can be found in the fact that half of the men and 16 percent of the women were able to sign their names, however crudely, to the marriage license applications.

There are several reasons why the middle and upper levels of colonial society would feature in the records of marriage oppositions. The first concerns the nature of marriage itself in colonial Mexico. Marriage was undertaken relatively infrequently among the very poor of colonial society (except in Indian communities): more common was the practice of simply living together, in colonial Mexico called "concubinage." Of course no records were made of any opposition. If parents opposed a match, the couple could simply leave town and live together elsewhere without marrying; in their hometowns they could be prosecuted for concubinage.[30]

For those with some property to inherit, opposition by parents was potentially a more serious issue. Running away was not feasible for members of the upper half of society since the couple would lose the financial support that meant the difference between poverty and comfort. Failure to marry would also deprive any children of their rightful inheritances from their grandparents and perhaps condemn them to a life of penury. Rebellion against parents thus carried the implication of greater loss for the more privileged, and therefore the resolution of conflicts over marriage choice became particularly critical for them.

In other respects, prenuptial conflicts appear to mirror marriages. Nearly 11 percent of all the conflicts were between American-born Spaniards (creoles) and peninsular Spaniards, and roughly 11 percent of the marriages in Mexico City in the seventeenth century were between these two groups. Similarly, 2 percent of the conflicts and 2 percent of the marriages originated with Portuguese-Spanish marriages. Disputes stemming from interracial marriages by Spanish men were 4 percent of the total, roughly what they were generally in Mexico City during the seventeenth century, and conflicts over interracial marriages by Spanish women were less than 2 percent of the total, once again close to the number of such marriages during this period. Nearly 40 percent of the conflicts were strictly between American-born Spaniards, as were a third of the marriages.

The disputes that emerged over marriage in colonial Mexico resulted from private conflicts, but they were subject to public jurisdiction. Marriage in colonial Mexico was not simply a personal, private bond between a man and a woman nor even a bond uniting families within a society, but a bond regulated by the institutions of social control. Therefore both marriages and the conflicts they provoked were subject to the intervention of an institution.

For most of the colonial period, the principal institution ensuring the enforcement of a combination of ecclesiastical and Spanish traditions from the Old World regarding marriage was the Catholic Church. The church determined the minimum qualifications of age, examined the degree of kinship between the spouses, and registered and legitimized marriages. To a slight extent, the regulations on marriage were altered to address the special needs of the newly converted Indian population.[31] For the Spanish and casta population, the regulations and traditions enforced for marriages and prenuptial conflicts were those of the Old World.

Since the Catholic Church regulated marriage in colonial Mexico, it also regulated prenuptial conflicts. What was perhaps most distinctive about ecclesiastical regulation of prenuptial disputes for most of the colonial period was its independence of royal authorities. Although the crown was in a position to exercise greater control of ecclesiastical personnel in the New World than it could in Spain itself, its control was limited by practical political and historical considerations. Indeed, the most remarkable feature of its New World regulation of marriage (and prenuptial conflicts) was the extent to which the church exercised control independent of royal officials. The explanation of this unusual independence is rooted in the history of the Iberian peninsula.

The political unification of the area now called Spain was initiated by the marriage in 1469 of Isabella of Castile and Ferdinand of Aragón. But the union of Castile and Aragón, territories as politically diverse as their histories would lead one to expect, imposed no new uniform political structures on the formerly separate political jurisdictions: each retained its own *fueros*, standards and systems of justice, political order, militia, and even coinage.[32] The problem of governing such a diverse political unit posed an enormous challenge to the new rulers, and part of the solution was found in a new use of religion.[33]

In fact, Catholicism was virtually the only common bond between the peoples of the unified kingdoms of Castile and Aragón. It is therefore not surprising that the crown turned to religion in its search for unity. Both the expulsion of the Jews from Spain at the end of the fifteenth century and the dispersion and later expulsion of the Moors in the sixteenth and early seventeenth centuries were attempts to achieve political unity by creating religious homogeneity. For Isabella and Ferdinand and their Hapsburg successors, Catholic orthodoxy and loyalty to the crown were one and the same.[34]

The belief in the identity of religious orthodoxy and political loyalty led to the creation of the Inquisition. This institution, dedicated to the preservation of Catholic orthodoxy by a network of spies and the power to imprison, to torture and, in effect, to condemn to death, was only ostensibly religious in character; its true purpose was political. In the Old World its targets were primarily converted Jews (called New Christians). In the New World, where there were very few New Christian settlers, the Inquisitors had relatively few targets to pursue. The Indians were completely exempt from its probings, so that left only the Spaniards, blacks, and castas subject to the dreaded investigations.

Despite the restricted role of the Inquisition, the Catholic Church remained an important ally of the crown in governing the New World. Without either a standing army or a reliable bureaucracy, the crown used the church to ensure fundamental loyalty to the crown, believing that maintaining religious orthodoxy would ensure political loyalty. The relationship between church and crown in Spain and her colonies has often been described as that of two equal and mutually dependent partners, symbolized by the two swords, Church and Crown.[35] Spanish government officials referred to the "two heads, ecclesiastical and secular," or to the "two jurisdictions, spiritual and temporal." As one seventeenth-century Spanish official put it succinctly, "Government depends on both," that is, on Church and on Crown.[36]

This mutual dependence gave rise to a complex political and economic relationship. Royal officials, for example, collected tithes for the church but retained a portion of the funds for the crown. The crown received income from a variety of other ecclesiastical sources, and in turn paid salaries to a number of local priests. On the other hand, ecclesiastical wealth became a major source of credit to be tapped by the crown when faced with extraordinary expenses. Politically, the crown controlled appointments to posts in the ecclesiastical hierarchy in the New World, a system known as the *Patronato real*, or royal patronage.[37]

Royal nomination to posts in the ecclesiastical hierarchy, technically called "presentation," was potentially the most important method of controlling the church. The king retained the power to appoint New World bishops, while the viceroy in New Spain could fill ecclesiastical benefices below the rank of bishop.[38] But the Hapsburgs never fully exploited the opportunity to control the church hierarchy. Instead, in the sixteenth century the crown appointed men who would serve as moral examples to the populace, and in the seventeenth century, men with high social standing and political influence.[39]

For the most part, the actual regulation of marriage and prenuptial conflicts, including the authority to enforce ecclesiastical rules or to make exceptions in individual cases, rested in the hands of the bishops, who were appointed by the crown. In practice, however, the bishops generally delegated the daily decision making to the vicars general and rarely intervened. The vicar general was responsible solely to the bishop and was free of interference from royal officials.

The Hapsburg crown never attempted to control either the procedures or the substance of ecclesiastical decision making regarding prenuptial conflicts, relying instead on appeals to royal courts by especially aggrieved parties. But since appeals were made only on individual initiative and lacked general guidelines or procedures, they were relatively rare. Thus the church's judicial regulation of marriage and the conflicts it provoked not only was carried out without direct royal supervision but also was largely free of appeals to royal courts. By contrast, in Catholic France during the same century royal courts directly exercised authority over prenuptial conflicts, and proceedings in church courts were subject to frequent intervention by royal officials.[40]

The ecclesiastical courts in New Spain that decided such issues as conflicts over marriage choice were also largely free of supervision by Rome. By agreement with the Pontiff, the crown arranged that appeals from ecclesiastical courts in New Spain be made to the nearest diocesan court; in case of an appeal of that decision, the court of last resort would be another diocesan court in New Spain. No appeals from New Spain to Rome were permitted.[41]

All this meant that the Spanish crown exercised little direct control over prenuptial disputes in Mexico for most of the colonial period. It regulated appointment and removal of ecclesiastical personnel, and occasionally it reviewed judicial decisions, but it did not set policy for the church nor did it interfere in its ordinary operations.[42] In matters of doctrine and belief, such as marriage and conflicts over marriage choice, the Catholic Church was virtually sovereign for most of the period.[43]

The teachings of the Catholic Church on marriage revolved around two central points: the sacramentality or sacred character of marriage, and the importance of personal will in creating the marriage bond. These church doctrines, and especially the concept of will, are discussed in the following chapter.

CHAPTER 2

Will

Of the three basic cultural attitudes inherited from Spain that shaped the course of the church's intervention in co-lonial prenuptial conflicts, the most striking was that of the importance of individual will. In the case of Juana and Gerónimo, their affirmation that they wished to marry each other of their own free will galvanized ecclesiastical officials to order Gerónimo's father to stand aside while they freed his son. The doctrine of individual consent to marry was critical in Catholic tradition in establishing normative support for allowing the child, not the parents, to make the decision regarding marriage. The doctrine of free will set the limits of parental authority—what parents could and could not do to change a child's wishes—and in particular condemned the use of force. These beliefs were rooted in Catholic teachings and Hispanic culture of the sixteenth century.

Given the significance of the Catholic Church's role in prenuptial disputes in colonial Mexico, it is necessary to understand what his-torical forces underlay the character of its intervention in prenuptial conflicts. Chief among these is the transformation of the church's doctrines on marriage that occurred in the middle of the sixteenth century at the Council of Trent (1545–63). In response to the Prot-estant challenges to Roman Catholic hegemony in Europe, the Council of Trent was called to redefine key elements of Catholic doctrine so as to provide a uniform and effective rejoinder to Prot-estant criticism.

Luther and Calvin had rejected most of the sacraments instituted by the Catholic Church, including the sacrament of marriage: Protestant reformers considered marriage a matter that secular leaders should regulate.[1] Catholic response to this attack focused on two questions. First, the church sought to reestablish marriage as a sacrament. This was an important question, for denying the sacramentality of marriage indirectly threatened the jurisdiction of the ecclesiastical courts over marriage. Consequently three of the canons issued by the Council of Trent affirmed the sacramentality of marriage and the church's exclusive jurisdiction over marriage; one of these excommunicated anyone who failed to uphold this doctrine. Another canon specifically attacked the Protestant belief that regulation of marriage belonged in secular hands by challenging the authority of civil magistrates over marriage.

The second focus of the Catholic response was the question of predestination and its opposite, free will. Catholicism and Protestantism had, of course, evolved from the same Christian tradition—the same texts, the same commentaries, the same Bible—but their interpretations were vastly different. The Lutheran and Calvinist doctrine that man was saved by faith stressed one part of this common tradition, that of predestination. The Catholic Church, drawing upon the identical texts, took the opposite position, a stance more favorable to free will. There was nothing in Catholic tradition that made this position inevitable; the works of the church fathers could be read to support either position. What led the church to affirm free will at Trent was simply organizational necessity—the need to provide a coherent counterpoint to the Protestant position on predestination. As Antonio Gramsci characterized a similar conflict, "The two Churches . . . posed questions which are principles of distinction and internal cohesion for each side, but it could have happened that either of the Churches could have argued what in fact was argued by the other."[2]

This organizational need to stress free will produced a renewed Catholic emphasis on the necessity of the parties' freely given consent to a marriage. Individual consent was already well established in Catholic tradition as the essential condition for a valid marriage; the Council of Trent not only reiterated its importance, it also went further than had earlier Catholic tradition in defining the exercise of free will. Canon 9 of the Council's session on marriage stated that no civil authority could use penalties (disinheritance, for example)

or threats to force a couple to marry. Chapter 1 contained the remarkable affirmation that children had a right to marry of their own
free will and therefore did not require parental consent. Here again,
both these positions arose from the Catholic reaction to Luther and
Calvin. These Protestants granted civil authorities the right to regulate all aspects of marriage; therefore the Catholics denied civil au-
thorites this right. Protestants said marriage contracted without the
consent of parents was invalid; therefore the Catholics affirmed the
contrary.[3] Thus with regard to the choice of a marriage partner, Catholicism found itself in the curious position of supporting the
rights of the individual over the dictates of authority—a general
philosophical proposition usually associated with Protestantism.

Catholic teachings on the sacred character of marriage were an
important element of the doctrine of free will. Since the essential
condition of marriage was the freely given consent of the couple,
the individual's right to make his or her own choices in marriage was
therefore also held to be sacred. This meant that the exercise of parental authority in marriage was at best ambiguous and at worst
morally wrong if it forcibly prevented the exercise of free will.
When Gerónimo and Juana declared that they wished to marry of
their own free will, thus giving evidence of a sacred intention, their
choice became worthy of the church's protection from parental
opposition.

The Council of Trent's decrees regarding the exclusive jurisdiction of church courts over marriage and the absence of a requirement for parental consent were not arrived at without dissent. A vocal minority favored mandatory parental consent, and fought for
making such a requirement part of church rules at the Council.
They were defeated, however, and no requirement for parental consent was approved.[4]

Once passed, Trent's decrees met with a variety of fates in the
hands of the European powers. The decree eliminating parental
consent was, in fact, not promulgated in the Protestant countries for
fear that other aspects of its wording would nullify marriages between Protestants, and its reception in the Catholic countries was
uneven.[5] In France, beside Spain the premier Catholic nation of
Western Europe, Henry III not only refused outright to receive the
decree but issued laws mandating parental consent for marriage under civil law. When some bishops complained, the crown only

slightly relented: in 1579, Henry allowed marriages without parental consent, in accord with Catholic doctrine, but defined such marriages as rape, for which the penalty was death.[6] The intent of the Council of Trent was subverted by civil law and ecclesiastical opposition to parental consent rendered impotent.

The French position requiring parental consent to marriage choices bore a greater resemblance to Protestant doctrine than to Catholic. Nearly all Protestant sects supported the priority of parents' wishes in marriage decisions over those of their children; most required parental consent for marriage. Only the Anglicans remained aloof from this trend, retaining traditional Catholic emphasis on individual consent in keeping with their tendency to strike a middle course between Protestantism and Catholicism.

Beyond this customary Protestant requirement, the extent of parental control of marriage varied from sect to sect. The Hutterites gave young people virtually no room for choice: instead the elders of the community selected three acceptable candidates from which the person seeking to marry might choose a spouse.[7] Martin Luther and most of the other Protestant leaders stressed that children should obey their parents even if a marriage were contrary to what the child wanted or needed, because the rights of parents took priority over those of children. Such attitudes were in keeping with the broader Protestant emphasis on the authority of parents, especially fathers, in the family, and its glorification of the patriarchal family.[8]

This celebration of parental control over marriage did not occur in Catholic Spain. The Catholic Spanish kings did not obstruct the marriage laws issued at Trent but embraced them. The decrees of Trent overrode medieval civil legislation requiring parental permission for a daughter's marriage and curtailed parents' capacity to disinherit children for marrying against their wishes.[9] Hence, in accord with the decrees of Trent, marriage without parental consent was valid in Spain and her New World colonies, and parental consent was not necessary for marriage.

Even though the necessity of parental consent to marriage had been denied at Trent, however, the conflict between individual wishes and obedience was still not resolved because the Council did not rule on the extent to which parents could exert control over marriage. Was it preferable, for example, to follow one's own inclination in choosing a marriage partner, or should one be guided by what one's parents wanted? Could parents force a child to marry someone of their choosing by invoking the Fourth Commandment, "Honor thy father and thy mother"? What was at stake was more than a question of canon law. The fundamental issue was who should choose a marriage partner, child or parent. European Catholics differed profoundly on the significance and role of parents in marriages, and on the extent to which children should be allowed to follow their own inclinations.

The leading German, Italian, French, and Portuguese church jurists of the late sixteenth century argued in favor of parental authority: unless they were ordered to marry unjustly, children had to bow to their parents' wishes.[10] But the vast majority of Spanish canonists, led by one of Spain's greatest authorities on marriage, Tomás Sánchez, argued that children, not parents, had priority in the selection of a marriage partner. The only exception to this rule was if the parents had grave cause to reject a child's choice. (Sánchez gave as examples of grave cause reasons of state and the establishment of peace between warring territories, exceptions applicable only to the royal family.)[11]

Few sixteenth-century Spanish canonists writing after Trent disagreed with Sánchez, and most of those who did were expatriates who held ecclesiastical positions in Italy and Germany, and who were therefore isolated from post-Tridentine Spanish society. The proponents of the majority, and indeed the dominant, position included Juan Gutiérrez, author of the most widely used contemporary handbook of legal practice; Basilio Ponce de León, an Augustinian and chancellor of the influential University of Salamanca; Francisco Vitoria, founder of modern international law; and Diego de Covarrubias, one of the preeminent Spanish thinkers of the period and later president of the governing body of Castile.[12] The bulk of the Hispanic Catholic establishment after Trent came down clearly on the side of choice, and favored the right of young people over that of parents to choose marriage partners. The Spanish position was not advocated by canonists in other European countries until the eighteenth century.[13]

The attitudes of the Spanish Catholic theologians were not simply those of the higher reaches of canon law; they were informed not only by religious doctrine but also by widely held Spanish cultural values. Popular religious writings—treatises, catechisms, confessional guides for priests—often reflected a belief that children, not parents, had priority in the choice of a marriage partner. As with the canonists, only a minority espoused the view that children should follow their parents' wishes.[14] More often, moralists not only acknowledged the independent will of the child, but frequently enjoined parents to respect this independent will in matters such as marriage, and they went further than canon lawyers in explaining why they espoused the children's cause in the selection of what was called a "state" in life.

According to the author of one popular moral treatise, a son or daughter had the right to choose his or her state in life—marriage or celibacy. For this purpose, he explained, God removed sons and daughters from subjection to their parents. Children were generally constrained to obey their parents, but they were not obliged to do so in the choice of a marriage partner. Furthermore, he argued, God Himself specifically removed children from subjection to their parents when it came to marriage.[15]

A guide for confessors written by a mid-seventeenth-century clergyman called parental selection of a state for their offspring "ignorance and foolishness." This cleric made it clear why parents should not interfere: the choice of a state in life should be left to God. "If Our Lord picks them [children] to be priests or nuns or married persons, He will give them what they need to achieve these states. He is all-powerful and will grant them a liking for it [the state] so that it will give them pleasure." A child's likes and preferences for a particular state were a God-given indication of the child's aptness for that state.[16] Most Protestant teachings regarded such preferences as evidence of the child's own willful desires, not promptings of the deity. In these Spanish Catholic teachings, however, parents, like all human beings merely mortal, did not enjoy the right to contradict what was God-given—namely, individual will and individual preference.

This support for the exercise of free will in marriage was general in the popular confession manuals of the period. One widely circulated seventeenth-century Spanish manual, written by Enrique Villalobos, said, "Parents cannot force their children to marry, nor impede [veto] their marriages, because in this matter they are sui juris."[17] Children were responsible for their actions in marrying; they were independent of their parents.

Parents had an obligation to provide children with what was financially necessary to enter a state, but their role was clearly limited: "First, give them a state at the right time [age]: second, the state should be the one to which the son or daugher is inclined, not the one that appeals to the parents or that they would like." Parents were not to give a state in life at their own whim or to fulfill their own desires. "The state that parents should give their children should be their [the children's] own choice and not at the mercy and election of the parents."[18]

Not only were the limitations of parental authority clearly defined, but the consequences for failing to consider the children's wishes were painted in the darkest terms by popular religious writing. One cautionary tale describes a daughter who, when she is not given her state in life, runs away and is murdered by the Indians. Another story warns domineering parents of the consequences of their behavior: a father says, "If a daughter of mine does not marry except when and to whom I wish, I will cut off her legs," and within a year his daughter becomes pregnant, to the scandal of society and the dishonor of her parents.[19] The burden of these fables is that parents who disregard their children's own wishes will ultimately themselves be hurt by their selfishness.

Other sixteenth-century Spanish writers point out the unhappy consequences a young woman suffers by marrying a man who does not want to marry her: such a man would refuse to touch her, and would probably leave his home every evening for the arms of someone else. An enforced marriage was unlikely to make a daughter happy.[20] The consequences of forcing daughters into marriages are clearly illustrated by the tale of Gerarda, in Lope de Vega's *La discreta enamorada*, who is constrained to marry against her wishes by her noble parents. The marriage is so unhappy that she contemplates suicide, but eventually she runs off with a handsome young man to lead a licentious existence. The moral is clear: forcing a marriage on a daughter could lead not only to her unhappiness and ruin but also to disgrace for her family.

As the preceding examples illustrate, regard for individual inclinations in the choice of a marriage partner was not limited to the formal canonical literature of the era. Since these ideas were embedded in Spanish cultural attitudes, similar ideas were echoed by the popular literature of the late sixteenth and early seventeenth centuries—Spain's literary Golden Age. In a play by Lope de Vega, the foremost Spanish dramatist of the age, a daughter whose father is trying to force her into a marriage says, "Pardon, but this is not / obedience; moreover it is not just / . . . To take a state is reasonable . . . / but ruled and guided by one's own inclination."[21] One's own inclination took precedence over obedience to parents in the choice of a marriage partner. Cervantes, the greatest prose writer of the age, put it even more succinctly: "The laws of forced obedience oblige us to do a great deal; but the force of liking obliges us even more." Obedience to parents, Cervantes acknowledged, was a central obligation in most matters, but when choosing a state in life or marrying, the wishes and dislikes of the person involved were a more important consideration.[22]

While emphasizing a young person's right to oppose a parent's imposed choice, the dramatists also made the point that marriage for love was preferable to obedience to parents. In Lope de Vega's *Nadie se conoce*, one character remarks, "To obey my father is just, but who is enough against Love, if God is love and to the opposite I am ordered"[23]—that is, to marry for love is an even higher duty than obedience to parents, because God is Love. Affirmations of this sort were rarely heard elsewhere in Western Europe during this period.[24]

In sixteenth-century Spain, therefore, the dominant religious teachings were buttressed by a cultural conviction that young people should have the right to choose their own marriage partners even over the objections of their parents. Cultural and religious beliefs showed limited support for the idea of parental control over marriage and suggested moreover that God Himself was on the side of children: a young person's inclination was a manifestation of God's plan for that person. Parents were mortal beings, who therefore lacked authority to interfere with what God had created, or with His plans for a young person.

Such beliefs partly explain why a case such as the Mexican Romeo and Juliet occurred. In sixteenth-century Spain, unlike most of Western Europe, the dominant attitudes of society viewed parental control of marriage as human interference in God's design. Therefore Gerónimo's father had neither the moral nor the cultural authority to interfere with his son's marriage; the church, accordingly, would not back him because it considered parental authority less important than Gerónimo and Juana's wish to marry.

Support for this position was by no means universal; some Golden Age authors and church canonists favored greater parental authority over marriage.[25] But they stopped short of supporting parental vetoes of marriage partners, and, unlike their Protestant counterparts, they did not go so far as to celebrate parental authority, nor do they appear to have expressed the dominant viewpoint on this matter within the church or Hispanic society.

The church's protection of Gerónimo and Juana also stemmed from a second condition related to the exercise of free will in marriage. In its redefinition of church doctrine on marriage, the Council of Trent called activities obstructing the exercise of matrimonial liberty "unjust interference," rendered in Spanish by the phrase *impedir maliciosamente*.[26] It did not make clear, however, what it meant by unjust or malicious interference, and this lack of precise definition left Catholic churchmen from different lands free to interpret "malicious" intervention in terms of their own cultures. As interpreted by the Catholic clergymen of colonial Mexico, malicious interference originated almost exclusively in the actions of parents, guardians, other relatives, or employers of the couple who unreasonably tried to prevent a marriage from occurring.

Force: The Other Side of Will

As Catholic theologians and canonists in the years after Trent sought to establish more precisely what was meant by malicious or unjust actions by parents, they turned to the conditions that inhibited free will. To do so, they went back to the medieval tradition of nullifying marriages that were contracted under any threat of mutilation, imprisonment, loss of honor, privation of goods, reduction to slavery, or "considerable torment."[27] This tradition, however, carried new implications in sixteenth-century Spanish society. Since freedom to marry without parental consent had been clearly established at Trent and accepted in Spain, it followed that parents specifically could not use such means to coerce their children to marry, or to prevent them from marrying.

This position differed profoundly from that of Western European Protestantism. In general, Protestant moral literature showed little respect for the individual will of the child.[28] Protestant teachings on whether children should be allowed to choose their own marriage partners followed this same tradition. Some Protestant leaders openly sanctioned the use of force—with the intention of breaking a child's will—to compel acceptance of unwanted marriage partners.[29] Even those who, like Luther, did not condone force in these circumstances nevertheless failed to support any institutional guarantee or protection against violence. Luther furthermore failed to condemn parental violence to prevent or veto a marriage.[30]

By contrast, sixteenth-century Spanish Catholicism set stringent limits on parental authority over the choice of a marriage partner: parents might only persuade, counsel, or show by precept that they wanted a child to marry a particular person, or that they wished to dissuade a child from a choice independently made. The great conservative theologian of the era, Tomás Sánchez, even found excessive pleading and psychological pressure by parents to be morally wrong. Persuasion and example were acceptable means of dissuading children from marrying, psychological or physical coercion was not.[31]

Nor was this attitude confined to the higher levels of Hispanic Catholicism. One popular seventeenth-century Spanish confession manual said: "[Parents] can persuade them [children] with gentle means, without fear, nor force. . . . They cannot compel them . . . nor can they use words of punishment."[32] Threats to refuse a son or daughter an inheritance or assertions that a child must enter the religious life because an estate could not be divided were wrong.[33]

Another moral treatise set similar limits. Parents could counsel and advise but could not impose their own wishes: "Parents should direct children prudently and gently toward the best; but if the children [merely] choose well even though it may not be the best, the parents may not violate their will."[34] In other words, a parent's dislike for a particular person was not sufficient reason for rejecting that person as a child's marriage partner. Parents might express their own likes and dislikes but they were morally bound not to exceed these limits. By the standards of Hispanic society, therefore, parents were not supposed to exercise *any* degree of coercive control over their offspring's choice of a spouse. That was, in both religious and cultural terms, the child's own responsibility. The limits on parental authority over marriage choices were thus carefully circumscribed, and despotic control by fathers was condemned.

The actual reports of prenuptial disputes in colonial Mexico show how seriously this belief was taken: cultural attitudes clearly supported the idea that young people seeking to marry were expressing their individual free will and that parental authority in this sphere was at best debatable, at worst immoral when it became coercive.

In two-thirds of all prenuptial conflicts brought before church officials in Mexico City between 1574 and 1689, couples and their advocates alleged excessive coercion. The acts of coercion ranged from threats of murder, disgrace, and imprisonment to jailing and actual attempts at murder; they included not only outright force but also the use of excessive persuasion, such as constant pleading.[35] It must be noted that only happy endings appear in the records; undoubtedly other parents who plotted to murder their children and potential in-laws were successful.

Threats alone were regarded as malicious interference in matrimonial choices, as in the following case. In the years after the flood of 1629 that inundated the city of Mexico, Juan Galván de Segovia, then in his early thirties, became a friend of a family named Velasco and frequently visited their home. There he became acquainted with Antonia, the family's teen-age daughter. Over the course of time, her mother and Juan had a falling out, perhaps over financial issues, which eventually led to their becoming sworn enemies. Naturally Juan was asked to refrain from visiting the home. Juan, however, had by this time fallen in love with Antonia and had asked her to marry him; she had agreed. In November 1640 a close relative of Antonia's mother asked her if she would consent to her daughter's marriage to Juan. The mother became furious, saying she would kill her daughter before she allowed her to marry Juan. Furthermore, she detailed how she would carry out her threat: she would thrust Antonia's head between two mattresses and suffocate her. Aghast at what they considered the unreasonable objections and excessive reaction of Antonia's mother, Antonia's maternal aunt and uncle espoused the cause of the young couple. For three months they tried to persuade the mother to agree to the marriage, but to no avail. Finally Juan and Antonia went before the ecclesiastical court and asked to be married quietly. The aunt and uncle lent their support, saying that the frequency of Juan's visits to the Velasco house had given rise to rumors in the neighborhood that the two had engaged in sexual relations. They further testified that the mother's hatred of the young man reflected only her own prejudices and had nothing to do with his suitability as a husband for the daughter. Because of the mother's clear intent to do physical harm to Antonia, they also suggested that the marriage take place without notice. Church officials agreed, and on January 28, 1641, ordered the marriage of Juan Galván de Segovia and Antonia Velasco.[36] It is noteworthy that not only the church but her own sister found the mother's attempt at intimidation unjust.

A number of parents did more than threaten; they took action. The following case illustrates a flare-up of violent tempers on both sides. In 1629, Simon Nieto, a twenty-six-year-old Spanish merchant from Aranjúez, wanted to marry a twenty-five-year-old creole widow from Mexico City named Doña Sebastiana Sándoval. Both families reacted to the news of the impending wedding with explosive anger. On June 5, 1629, Nieto's father stormed into the home of a friend of the son's, swearing that if Simon dared to marry Sebastiana he would sue his son for 8,000 pesos or would have him arrested and sentenced to serve eight years in one of His Majesty's fortresses. Another witness heard Simon's father threaten both to send him to the penal colony in the Philippines and to pummel him personally. As if such intimidation were not enough, on the Saturday night after his father burst into the friend's home, a band of hired thugs set upon Simon and managed to wound him on the hand and chest. They would have killed him but the knife broke on his sternum.

Sebastiana's parents reacted with equal violence. They execrated her savagely, threatening to burn her or wall her up alive before seeing her married to Simon. Sebastiana fled her parents' home for that of her first cousin. Her mother found her a few days later and tried to drag her, clawing and pulling, from the house. Several hours later Sebastiana and Simon appeared before the ecclesiastical judge of Mexico City seeking protection. After hearing from Sebastiana and Simon as well as from persons who had witnessed the vicious vituperation of both sets of parents, the church judge ordered the pair to be married secretly that same day.[37] The source of this intense mutual hatred between the Nietos and the Sándovals was never disclosed.

The horror and dismay the witnesses felt in this case make clear the degree to which force in such instances was condemned by their culture: witnesses were willing to intervene to stop the violence, and were eager to testify about what they clearly considered unjust interference in marriage.

Other cases show similar reactions by relatives, friends, or even unrelated parties. One mother was stopped from choking her daughter to death on the streets of Mexico City by passersby who showed no reluctance to intervene in this family matter to save the daughter's life.[38] Another young man was chased by his fiancée's sword-brandishing brother through the corridors of the Hospital of Our Lady until an onlooker took pity on the young man and managed to hide him from his would-be executioner.[39] One afternoon in 1628 six armed riders appeared at the residence of twenty-one-year-old Ana María Vargas, banged on the door, and shouted that she would die before her fiancé, Alonso Delgado, could enjoy her. Galloping toward the church of San Pablo, they encountered Alonso and gave chase. Alonso managed to elude his pursuers by slipping into a patio while his friends and neighbors came out and swarmed around the horsemen, forcing them to retreat. The next morning a parade of witnesses from the neighborhood appeared in church court to testify to the danger Alonso and María faced.[40] The willingness of friends, family, neighbors, and even passersby to intervene on behalf of young couples demonstrates that these matters were *public* concerns: the actions of those opposing the matches violated commonly held norms and values.

The extent to which parental force was condemned by other members of the community can also be seen from cases in which parents attempted to bypass the ecclesiastical system and use the criminal courts against their offspring. Often, when parents called out the police to arrest their children, neighbors and in some cases even landlords hid the couple and helped them reach the safety of the ecclesiastical court. When the mother and brothers of his fiancée threatened to kill him, friends of thirty-year-old José Enríquez hid him on the rooftops of their houses.[41] When the father of Toluca resident María González refused to heed the entreaties of prominent local citizens to allow his daughter to marry, María's older brother helped her leave home and escorted her to Mexico City, where she was able to marry.[42] When the brother of Juana Zamora denounced her to royal authorities for living with her fiancé, neighbors warned the pair of their impending arrest and concealed them until they could safely walk to the church court to be married.[43] The actions of the ecclesiastical court were, of course, of great consequence in ensuring that marriages took place, but the keystone was the support from family and community members who shared in the cultural values condemning violence and threats against persons choosing marriage partners.

Not only force, such as the attempt on the life of Simon Nieto and the attack by Sebastiana's mother, provoked an automatic response: threats of another order elicited a similar reaction. The Hispanic antipathy to coercion extended to the intimation of disgrace, for in a society in which honor was a central concern, disgrace was the equivalent of social death.[44]

In 1641, a nineteen-year-old apprentice merchant named Nicolas Fernández Ortega wanted to marry Doña Francisca Tolosa. Nicolas's employer was not pleased by the match, but more important, neither was Francisca's domineering mother. She wanted to pick her daughter's mate herself, and had vowed to numerous acquaintances that if her daughter married against her wishes, she would cut off the daughter's hair, or even suffocate her. Francisca's mother did not actually make good her threats, but her conduct was regarded as malevolent by both the ecclesiastical authorities and those who testified on Francisca's and Nicolas's behalf. To cut off a person's hair was a serious matter, for it was a traditional Spanish method of dishonoring: honor was symbolically associated with the head (an association that persists to the present day in such gestures as removing a hat as a sign of respect). To prevent Francisca's mother from acting, church officials permitted the couple to marry secretly.[45]

Less severe forms of coercion were also common. Many times relatives or guardians simply locked the offending persons away, depriving them of food, or transported them to another residence, including convents upon occasion, where they were held incommunicado. Luisa Dualde, the daughter of an influential peninsular family, was locked up by her mother in the home of a pastry-maker in order to prevent her from marrying her Andalucian countryman, Pedro Ruíz. On the afternoon of the feast of the Assumption, Luisa was allowed on the balcony of the pastry-maker's home and managed to catch the attention of Diego Ramírez, a neighbor who had witnessed her promise to marry Pedro. She told him that she was being held against her will and asked him to find Pedro to help rescue her.[46] As in the foregoing threats of violence, disgrace, and murder, her incarceration was brought to the attention of the religious authorities, who responded with the speed the witnesses' indignation and sense of urgency demanded.

From the evidence of the cases, it is clear that the Hispanic belief in the importance of individual will in marriage, and its corollary, the condemnation of the use of force to prevent a marriage, were not drawn from the dusty books of canon law or even popular literature but were cultural norms shared broadly in Spanish colonial society. Those who assisted couples against unjust interference ranged from humble artisans to wealthy and influential citizens, and many of them had little or nothing to gain from their support of a couple. They were willing to testify before a priest or church court judge or even intervene physically, if necessary, to uphold these norms about will and force and prevent the arbitrary exercise of paternal power. Limits on the exercise of paternal power over marriage choices were thus enforced in the first instance by members of the community. And these social norms were sustained by the Catholic Church, the primary institution to exercise authority over marriage during this period.

CHAPTER 3

Love

Why were Gerónimo and Juana, the Mexican Romeo and Juliet, so eager to marry each other? Their motives were not mentioned in the case, and indeed there are many possibilities: desire to be independent of a domineering parent, a moral obligation, even love. Although we can never know Gerónimo's and Juana's motivations, we can learn more generally about the culturally accepted motives for marriage, and about Hispanic beliefs concerning love, so central for the question of marriage.

Catholic doctrine emphasized the right of the individual to exercise free will in marrying, because such intentions were a manifestation of God's wishes for the world. "Will" was the word that denoted individual intentions; the popular gloss on the term was "love." Love was the expression of will, and since will was a manifestation of divine intention, this popular understanding lent young people in conflict with parents great normative support.

Spanish cultural beliefs about motives for marriage were sometimes articulated in the prenuptial disputes, but rarely elaborated. One reason for this is their very transparency to other members of society. There was no need to explain these notions at length: the vast complex of beliefs, shared by members of the culture, could be referred to with a single phrase or word. It is only to the modern mind that such ideas are obscure. Our culture, our code words, and our values are different.

Since detailed information about the cultural beliefs of sixteenth- and seventeenth-century Hispanic society does not emerge from the prenuptial conflicts themselves, it must be sought elsewhere. It is in the popular religious literature, novels, and plays of the era that we can find clues to the meaning of the code words and the values that are so glancingly mentioned but so profoundly influential. To understand the cultural system behind the conflicts, two aspects of sixteenth-century Hispanic society must be understood: the prevailing attitudes toward marriage for love, and its opposite, marriage for money. We are not trying to define actual motives for marrying of any given person; rather, we want to determine the cultural expectations of the period.

What sentiments did the people themselves voice about their preferences? Few of those whose marriage plans are described in these cases mentioned their motives because the issue being joined in the prenuptial conflicts was individual choice, not the reasons for the choice. Young men and women may have married to be free of parental domination, or to secure the fortune of an heir or heiress, or even for love, but it is impossible to know how many married for these or other reasons, for the reasons were not expressed. What can be shown, however, is how couples chose to explain their marriages, and the language in which their motives were discussed.

The only reason mentioned by couples for their desire to marry was the development of a mutual feeling of attachment, but they did not use the word love, *amor*. They used the phrases "to my liking" (*de mi gusto*) or "attachment and will" (*afiliación y voluntad*) to describe their feelings for each other. The use of the words "liking" and "attachment" to describe the emotional connection do not sound odd to modern ears, but why choose the word "will"? [1] The answer lies in the popular cultural Spanish conception of love, which can be illustrated by the literature of the Golden Age and by the popular moralists of the sixteenth and seventeenth centuries.

In sixteenth-century Spain there existed a variety of conceptions of love. Love of God, of neighbor, of country and homeland, of parents and friends all had their content defined and often their theological significance defined as well. For heterosexual relationships, however, there existed a tension between conflicting ideas of the relationship between love and will, one inherited from a medieval tradition Spain shared with the rest of Western Europe, the other a more recent and distinctively Spanish development. The medieval tradition of courtly love stressed the idea of love as an inescapable and enslaving passion.[2] When love struck, the will became enslaved, and the whole being was bound to love regardless of the consequences. The twelfth-century *Roman de Troie* (later translated into Castilian) described the imprisoning effects of love on the will: "He cannot have enjoyment / whom love has prisoner / such is the care of love." This tradition persisted in the literature of the Golden Age and is particularly apparent in tales of adulterous love, love that violated the social and moral standards of the period.[3]

In the sixteenth century, however, another set of attitudes about love and will emerged, related to the increasing dominance of the teachings of Thomas Aquinas in Spanish intellectual life. Thomistic philosophy stressed individual free will. In the *Summa Theologica*, Aquinas describes the soul as composed of three elements, the rational, the sensitive, and the vegetative. To the rational element of the soul, the *anima intellectiva*, belong three faculties, memory, understanding, and will; will was part of the rational faculty of man. "Love, concupiscence, and the like can be understood in two ways," Aquinas wrote. "Sometimes they are taken as passions. . . . They may, however, be taken in another way . . . [as] *acts of the will*."[4]

In expressing approval of marriage for love, the Golden Age writers who dealt most frequently with this theme often associated love with the action of the will. Both Lope de Vega and Cervantes made this relationship quite clear. In Lope de Vega's play *Enmendar un daño a otro* Don Juan says, "What loves is the will."[5] Cervantes described love as partly an act of volition in his early novel *La Galatea*. Love, Cervantes said, had three components: *memory*, "which serves only to treasure and protect what the eyes regard, *understanding* [which] scrutinizes and knows the value of that which it loves well, and the *will* which allows both memory and understanding to be so occupied"[6]—the same faculties Aquinas ascribed to the rational element of the soul. Of critical importance in Cervantes's schema is the action of the will: it was seen as the active force that permitted one to love. Love, in other words, was not necessarily a blind driving passion but a force subject to one's individual free will.

This new attitude is reflected in the psychological advice offered by sixteenth-century moralists. Pedro Luján, author of *Matrimonial Colloquies*, suggested that a young woman wishing to exercise her will and stop loving someone should throw herself into exhausting physical activities, distract herself with good books, and, when thoughts of the young man inevitably occurred, concentrate on his faults—his thinness, his limp, his bad family, his drinking, or his gambling.[7] Luján addressed his advice to women because they had fewer outside diversions and therefore needed more help in breaking away from a relationship that had ended. In this new vision, human beings were not slaves of their emotions but could exercise their free will by choosing to love or not to love.[8]

The repetition of the word "will" in connection with what dramatists and moralists described as the central component of love argues that the cultural understanding of love in sixteenth-century Spain was based on a belief in one's capacity to control emotions or passions. When seventeenth-century Mexican couples described their feelings toward each other as attachment and will, they were using culturally accepted terms to describe an emotional attachment appropriate to that time.

The connection drawn by Hispanic writers between love and will was consonant with ecclesiastical definitions of the need for free will to be exercised regarding the choice of a marriage partner. The decrees of the Council of Trent and the popular religious literature of sixteenth- and seventeenth-century Spain all exhorted parents to respect the independent will of the child in marriage. Church officials in colonial Mexico did not intervene in prenuptial conflicts in order to defend love, but the defense of love, however indirect, did not conflict with religious conceptions of marriage.

Why did the couples not use the word *amor*, which sometimes appeared in sixteenth- and seventeenth-century confession manuals and moral tracts, to describe their feelings toward one another? Even today the phrase *te amo*, literally "I love you," is eschewed by Mexican couples as stiff and awkward, in favor of *te quiero*, literally "I want you." The popularity of "liking" and "attachment and will" among seventeenth-century couples in preference to *amor* may similarly have been due to the latter term's perceived awkward formality. Another possible explanation stems from the other connotations of the word. While the singular form *amor* was used in a formal context to mean the deeply felt attachment between people of opposite sex, the plural form, *amores*, in seventeenth-century Mexican Spanish meant sexual lust. The term *mujer enamorada* signified a woman who publicly engaged in repeated sexual activity, not a woman in love.[9] Sexual lust was, of course, strictly frowned upon as a motive for marriage, or indeed for any form of impulsive action, so couples articulating their feelings may have purposely avoided any association with the concept of love as lust or an enslaving passion. But love that was chosen (attachment and will) was freely asserted by the couples, since it was the culturally appropriate way to affirm a licit emotional union.[10]

Although literary sources at times painted love, especially the illicit sexual or adulterous variety, as a blind passion, they also often exalted love for what were termed "honest ends," or marriage, as worthy and well chosen. Beginning with the late fourteenth century Catalan classic *Tirant lo Blanc*, marriage for love was a common theme of Iberian chivalric novels.[11] The most famous and widely read of all Spanish novels of chivalry was *Amadis of Gaul*, in which the hero Amadis falls in love with and marries the heroine in the first of four books and then becomes separated from her but remains loyal. The theme is marriage for love and monogamy within marriage.[12] Cervantes in *Don Quixote* satirizes the excesses of *Amadis*, but he praises marriage and presents throughout the work characters who renounce family, homeland, religion, and fortune in order to marry for love.[13] He treated the same theme in several of his exemplary novels as well as in his last novel, *Persiles y Sigismunda*.[14]

Equally important for examining popular sixteenth- and seventeenth-century Spanish conceptions of love is the work of the dramatist Lope de Vega. Like Shakespeare for England, Lope set the artistic standards for the Spanish theater. He was a prolific writer, and he had the good fortune to write for the theater at a time when it was a popular rather than an aristocratic pastime. With his enormous gifts, he became the most acclaimed Spanish playwright of his day. Perhaps as a result, Lope's plays, even more than the literature of Cervantes, reflected popular ideas of the late sixteenth and early seventeenth centuries. The majority of his plays were comedies, and the majority of his romances had happy endings. For Lope, and probably for his public as well, the happy ending of love was inevitably marriage. Ginés in *Lo fingido verdadero* says, "The comedy will not end, except in marriage," and adds, "There is no true love if it is not in marriage."[15] In another play, a character remarks, "The greatest good that comes to be / on earth has arrived / in being always in love / a man of his wife." Like Cervantes, Lope approvingly depicted young women who sacrificed everything and young men who risked both parental anger and the loss of fortune in order to marry for love.[16]

Mexican-born Golden Age playwright Juan Ruíz de Alarcón y Mendoza shared the vision of his Spanish contemporaries. In his play El examen de los maridos, a wealthy woman places the pretenders to her hand in a contest. The heroine at one point says, "To love for inclination / is genuine ease." The drama closes with a debate between the two principal contenders for her hand. They must argue whether it is better for her to marry a man she loves but who has a defect, or to marry a flawless man whom she does not love. The winning discourse, acclaimed by all who witness the contest, is that of the man who advocates marrying for love. And so she does, after a final plot twist.[17]

Calderón's play La dama duende (The Phantom Lady, 1629) tells of a widow's rebellion against her brothers who try to keep her from loving whom she pleases. The heroine is locked up by her brothers, but she escapes her incarceration and falls in love with a guest in the house whose apartments she visits secretly, like a phantom. She is eventually liberated from her brothers to marry the man she loves.[18]

Support for love as a legitimate reason to marry was not limited to the Golden Age dramatists and novelists. Authors of sixteenth-century confession manuals painted marital love in glowing colors. One of the most widely used mid-sixteenth-century confession manuals included the love of husband and wife for each other in a list of the valid forms of love.[19] Seventeenth-century confession guides described the love between spouses as a constant emotion guiding their thoughts and behavior toward each other. A popular moralist depicted the desired relationship between husband and wife in the following terms: "What spouses should most try to procure is that they love each other greatly, because if love walks within all things go well. Such love is firm, long-lasting, and steady and although life may be full of difficulties, love is the permanent thing that remains."[20] Literary and religious works cannot reveal how often people married for love, but they can and do tell us much about the cultural values of the era.

The positive discussion of marriage for love in popular Spanish writing was in some ways unique in seventeenth-century Europe. Praise of marital love is absent, for example, from religious writings in Catholic France. Of the eighteen catechisms published there between the close of the Council of Trent and the end of the eighteenth century, only one recommends love in marriage, and this lone exception makes its appearance only at the end of the eighteenth century.[21] Spanish Catholic catechisms, on the other hand, frequently exalt marriage for love throughout this period.

In England, praise of marriage for love can be found in a variety of sources from Anglican and Puritan writings to popular plays.[22] Much of this writing, however, particularly that of the Puritans, mentioned only the right of men to marry for love, neglecting women altogether.[23] The Spanish religious and cultural tradition, on the other hand, not only assumed that men could marry for love but gave special attention to the fate of women who wanted to do so, because women faced potentially greater difficulties in realizing their desires. Calderón's *La dama duende* and Ruíz de Alarcón's *El examen de los maridos* both supported the right of women to marry for love. In the plays of Lope de Vega, tragedy unfolded when a woman could not marry the man she loved, comedy when she did. And as many critics have shown, this popular Hispanic dramatist especially championed the right of women not only to choose whom they were to marry but also to marry for love.[24] The literary and religious works of sixteenth- and seventeenth-century Spain thus reflected approval of marriage for love that was more qualified in similar literature elsewhere in Europe. Lending special support to the ideal of marriage for love in Spain was the belief that love was the personal expression of the religious doctrine of free will.

Interest: The Opposite of Love

The same Spanish cultural values that supported marriage for love condemned marriage for economic, political, or social gain. There are a variety of indicators of this antipathy to marriage for gain, beginning with the statements by the couple and their witnesses in the prenuptial disputes themselves. No would-be spouse in these cases ever acknowledged that the motive for marriage was money, or a desire to escape parental domination or political ambition. The young men pursuing heiresses almost certainly sought financial gain, and the viceroy's gentleman-in-waiting who married the widow of an influential political figure hoped to move up in the world. But their silence about the acquisitiveness or ambition that undoubtedly moved them suggests that it was disreputable to express or acknowledge such motives.[25]

The absence of normative support for motives of gain was a major theme throughout sixteenth-century Spanish-American culture. The sixteenth-century Hispanic attitude toward money was one of ambivalence. Torn between valuing the riches to be won in the colonies and a cultural and religious tradition that vilified gain as a motive for human action, Spaniards bowed to the tremendous moral power of the tradition and remained silent. Their unworthy motives were impossible to acknowledge.

In questions of marriage the prohibition against acknowledging motives of gain was quite evident. The writers, moralists, and dramatists of the Golden Age disapproved of marriages for social, political, or economic gain, or, as a sixteenth-century writer would put it, for "interest." A mother in one of Lope de Vega's plays (*La mala casada*) tries to marry her daughter to a wealthy man. She asserts that money will buy happiness, but the daughter remains unconvinced. In another play (*La niña de plata*) a father wants his son to marry a wealthy woman, and the son complains of his father's preoccupation with "vile fortune." Lope's criticism of marriages for gain can go deeper. In *Amigo hasta la muerte*, one character says to his beloved, "To marry at your displeasure with that rich stranger is to sell you for money, and not at a fair price."

Writers of popular moral guides also illustrated the negative consequences of making matches in order to improve political or social position. A famous sixteenth-century moralist pointed out that parents seeking to marry a son or daughter up the social ladder would acquire an insufferable son- or daughter-in-law, one who would then look down on the family he or she had joined.[26] Such statements cannot disclose how often parents attempted to make such matches, but they do tell us that the leading and most widely circulated Spanish writers and dramatists were sharply critical of such activity.[27]

In the colonies, these attitudes were particularly striking. On the one hand, the young men who came to the New World were certainly looking to advance themselves. Yet on the other hand, their motives were normatively questionable, rarely overtly acknowl-

edged, and frequently condemned, especially by clerics. The social
norms that condemned their greed played a prominent role in the
widespread disparagement of marriages for gain.

Cases

Passions, or the emotions prompting human actions, are tricky
issues for the historian. The twentieth-century observer has to be
careful about attributing motives to the seventeenth-century inhabitants of New Spain across cultural space and three centuries of
time, as if we today had some superior psychological insight.[28] An
understanding of the passions that gave rise to sixteenth- and
seventeenth-century marriage oppositions must rest primarily with
those directly involved as well as with observers in the neighborhood, family, or wider community whose reports are unquestion-
ably those of the culture and the era.

In prenuptial disputes during the early Mexican colonial period
the motives for opposing a match are characterized by the couple
and their friends, relatives, and neighbors who frequently volun-
teered to testify. Each of these reports represents a slightly different
perspective, based on the witness's own experience of the events.
They vary slightly in language and emphasis, but they share a common theme—that the action being undertaken was unjust and un-
warranted.

Their accounts afford a glimpse of what ordinary people labeled
unjust motives for their relatives and neighbors in preventing a
match. They further indicate significant popular antipathy to motives perceived as malicious in a wide variety of circumstances. And
in those cases in which parents and children were at odds, they illustrate the credibility of the idea that parental motives were not always in their children's best interests but on the contrary often represented the personal aims and desires of the parents themselves.

Of the motives for opposing a marriage that witnesses considered discreditable, the most frequently mentioned was "interest."
About a third of all cases alleging unjust interference in the choice
of a marriage partner between 1580 and 1689 were related to the idea
that it was disreputable to marry for money, or to allow monetary
considerations to interfere with the choice of a spouse. Parents who
used the threat of disinheritance to prevent a marriage were subject

to condemnation, as were also those who objected on grounds that a mate was insufficiently wealthy.[29]

In 1640, in the provincial town of Huachinango, twenty-year-old Nicolás Vargas became engaged to María Carvallo. María's mother and stepfather, however, conspired to impede the match. Their motives were not hard to discern. María's father had died, her mother had remarried, and María's inheritance had passed into the hands of her stepfather. Under Spanish law, María was entitled to receive her share of her father's estate when she married. Her stepfather did not want to lose the money, the fruits of which he had been enjoying, so he refused to allow María to marry Nicolás. Nicolás sought assistance from the ecclesiastical court in Mexico City. With support from two friends, a mule train owner and the town's sixty-year-old notary public, he let the court know that in an effort to persuade her stepfather to change his mind, he and María had become sexually intimate about six months before. The preparations for his plea had been carefully laid: the priest of Huachinango was consulted as to what to do in the case, and citizens of sufficient stature in the community, such as the notary public, were asked to help by traveling to Mexico City and serving as witnesses, stating their knowledge of the families and people involved as well as their opinions of the motives of María's mother and stepfather.

The vicar general of the archdiocese, the bishop's representative, decided without any hesitation in favor of Nicolás and María. The day after the formal presentation was made he issued an order that the priest of Huachinango first ascertain privately that María wanted to marry Nicolás, then unite the couple immediately and without any publicity. In this fashion the vicar general prevented the stepfather's greed from interfering with the couple's wishes to marry. The evidence of extended sexual involvement was a further factor in his decision, since disclosure of María's loss of virginity would dishonor her and damage her reputation. Although the vicar general by allowing the marriage acted in accord with the prescriptions of religious authority, the conviction underlying his decision—that trying to hold on to an inheritance was morally wrong—was shared by the church, the notary public, and the other citizens of Huachinango who lent their support to the suit. Their testimony clearly expressed the Hispanic cultural tradition, which not only placed great value on the public reputation of Spanish women, but also considered a desire to hold on to an inheritance a malicious motive for trying to prevent a marriage.[30] Such outright greed was the motive of many parents, tutors, and guardians in control of considerable inheritances (10.5 percent of all cases), for under Spanish law they were obliged to surrender any funds in their control upon a charge's marriage.

In a reversal of the generations, a smaller number of sons and sons-in-law, as well as distant relatives of wealthy and childless widows and widowers, threatened their elders when a proposed remarriage imperiled their chances of a substantial inheritance. Sebastian Gago de Aspeita was a thirty-six-year-old merchant and widower who wanted to marry forty-year-old Mariana Gutiérrez de Salas, a widow. Mariana was a woman of means, and her sons and two sons-in-law, themselves established merchants, opposed her remarriage probably because they were counting on her capital for themselves. A silversmith and the administrator of the city's hospital testified that the opposition was unreasonable, and church officials allowed the couple to be married secretly.[31] In another case two ambitious young men who had married a childless widow's niece and cousin, respectively, in hopes of inheriting her substantial estate, objected violently to her remarriage. María de Tavira, however, had powerful friends who were happy to see her remarry, and with their assistance she pressed her case successfully and married her widower.[32]

Objections to marriages based on economic inequality provoked a hefty number of oppositions (18.5 percent of all cases). Most involved wealthy parents or other relatives who opposed the marriages of their offspring because the intended spouse was not sufficiently wealthy. Francisca García and Pedro de Neiva were a young Spanish couple who wanted to be married in Mexico City in 1629. Francisca came from a poor family, and Pedro's rich father had refused his consent: he said that he would never agree to a marriage unless the girl brought him "many ducats." Adding an incentive to his threatened disapproval, Pedro's father let it be known that he had a considerable sum to hand over if his son should choose to marry a wealthy woman. But Pedro still wanted to marry Francisca. To prevent the father's pecuniary ambitions from standing in the way of a legitimate marriage, church officials granted Francisca and Pedro the right to marry secretly.[33]

Other parents were more subtle in their approach than Pedro de
Neiva's father but nevertheless made it clear they would not tolerate
any but the wealthiest of in-laws. Juan Adame de Montemayor
came to the New World from Spain to work as his uncle's clerk and
at twenty-one fell in love with the thirty-year-old widow of a notary public. Juan's uncle was disgusted by his nephew's interest in a
woman who would not bring vast amounts of capital to the family
business, and he let this, as well as his willingness to use his economic muscle to impede the marriage, be known. Fortunately a
great many people were willing to testify to the desirability of the
marriage and to the uncle's unreasonable insistence on marrying
money, so the two were united.[34]

Other forms of "interested" behavior condemned by community and family in colonial Mexico were manifested in the masters'
oppositions to servants' and slaves' marriages (10.5 percent). At
stake was not money but the income earned or services provided by
the slave or servant. In 1621 a tailor opposed the marriage plans of
a skillful young seamstress in his employ, for if she were to wed she
would no longer work for him.[35] Slaveowners were often reluctant
to allow their slaves to marry the slaves of other masters for fear of
losing their services. In 1640, two Angola-born slaves, Anton and
Cristina, wanted to marry. Cristina's master wanted her to wed one
of his own slaves rather than Anton, who served another man, and
to prevent her marriage, he locked her up and prepared to send her
to the mines in Pachuca. Just as she was about to be taken away,
Cristina managed to escape and fled to the protection of the
church.[36] Similarly, several parents and guardians tried to retain the
domestic services of daughters and wards for their own comfort,
and in one instance a father refused to allow his son to marry because
he wanted his cheap labor in the family bakery.[37]

The denunciation of economic motives by friends and relatives
of the marrying couples provides evidence that sixteenth- and
seventeenth-century Hispanic society considered such interference
in marriage unjust. Like the general condemnation of economic
motives by colonial society, the witnesses' disapprobation failed to
keep parents from acting, but it did establish normative principles
that permitted others to intervene and thwart the parents' ambitions. The moral censure of such motives thus contributed to the

normative support for the wishes of children over those of their parents or other relatives.

A second group of unreasonable designs, stemming from personal or social aims of the parents, was also condemned by community members, friends, and relatives. Some of those who refused to agree to marriages of their offspring were domineering parents who sought to control every aspect of their children's lives. Others desired to cement friendships or had sentimental reasons for promoting a particular marriage. Still others, for personal reasons, wanted their son or daughter to marry someone other than the child's chosen partner, or preferred their sons to become priests or their daughters nuns. In all, about 8 percent of parents fell into this category.

In the oppositions to marriage explored here, two characteristics stand out. First, marriages were obstructed for a variety of motives, and no single aim came close to being a majority. The largest single category was differences of wealth between the two parties, which were raised in 18.5 percent of the cases. Motives of gain, more generally understood, constituted one-third of all instances of unjust interference but were far from a majority. The motivations for behavior were so complex and varied that they cannot be reduced to a single category.

Second, the motives that led parents or others to oppose marriages remained relatively stable over time. The desire to hold on to an inheritance, to have a son or daughter marry money, to retain the services of a servant—all were present at the end of the colonial period as much as at the beginning. What changed in the intervening years was not the motives of parents but the social and cultural attitudes toward their ambitions.

A modern observer might be surprised that a traditional society would allow freedom of choice in marriage and permit marriage for love. Such marriages are frequently portrayed as disruptive of the social structure because they unite persons of different social and economic backgrounds and can disrupt a family's plans for economic or political advancement.[38] Did freedom of choice and marriage for love have this impact on colonial society?

The evidence of the conflict cases indicates that heads of families who desired to hold on to inheritances could be thwarted by the nuptial intentions of their offspring. Don Gerónimo Vargas was the heir to an entail. His father, who remarried before he died, had left the entail to his widow until his son married or came of age. At the age of twenty-two, three years short of his majority, Don Gerónimo announced that he was going to marry a Spanish girl named Doña Catalina Villalobos. The stepmother, realizing that she would lose the income from the entail if this marriage took place, tried to force Gerónimo into marrying her own sister's daughter. Gerónimo resisted, since he not only wanted to marry Catalina but also desired to be rid of his stepmother. With the assistance of friends and the ecclesiastical court, Gerónimo overcame the opposition of his stepmother and married Catalina.[39] If parents and elders were to retain the management of the inheritances or fortunes they had accumulated, they had to be able to control the matrimonial choices of their offspring. When their wishes were frustrated by their children's matrimonial preferences, the Catholic courts, and the cultural and moral imperatives of the era, attempts to create fortunes through the manipulation of marriages were made immeasurably more difficult.

This handicap to increasing fortunes was one of the reasons for the small number of dynasties established in the colonial period. There were a variety of more conventional reasons as well—infertility, spendthrift heirs, the vicissitudes of the business cycle—but families who retained their wealth for several generations were the exception rather than the rule.[40] Dynastic families did not become common until the late eighteenth and early nineteenth centuries.[41]

Why did Spanish society in the New World accept or tolerate economically unequal marriages or those that thwarted dynastic ambitions? The answer lies partly in the powerful moral critique that labled intentions of gain as unjustifiable. An additional and even more compelling reason for accepting such marriages lay in one of the other major cultural traditions of Hispanic society, honor.

CHAPTER 4

Honor

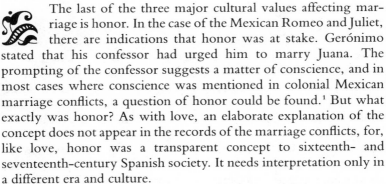

The last of the three major cultural values affecting marriage is honor. In the case of the Mexican Romeo and Juliet, there are indications that honor was at stake. Gerónimo stated that his confessor had urged him to marry Juana. The prompting of the confessor suggests a matter of conscience, and in most cases where conscience was mentioned in colonial Mexican marriage conflicts, a question of honor could be found.[1] But what exactly was honor? As with love, an elaborate explanation of the concept does not appear in the records of the marriage conflicts, for, like love, honor was a transparent concept to sixteenth- and seventeenth-century Spanish society. It needs interpretation only in a different era and culture.

Honor is perhaps the most distinctive of all Spanish cultural traits. From the medieval laws known as the *Partidas* through the literature of the Golden Age, the theme was repeatedly sounded that honor was the supreme social virtue. The spell of honor and its ascendancy over the Spanish are mirrored in an often-quoted remark by Lope de Vega: "The cases of honor are the best [for theater] / because they move all people powerfully." It was more important than love ("Honor should be preferred to any love") and more essential than money. One character exclaims, "O vile fortune! What are you worth without honor?" Another remarks, "What honor is you know; / that with it fortune and life are not equal to it." Honor was worth fighting for, and dying for: as Cervantes summed up several centuries of tradition, "The man without honor is worse than dead."[2]

Two aspects of honor were critical in the prenuptial conflicts of colonial Mexico: the sexual honor of Spanish women and the sacredness of a pledge or promise in the code of honor. The concept of honor was a complex social code that established the criteria for respect in Hispanic society; it meant both the esteem a person had for himself and the esteem that society had for him. This double reliance on self-knowledge and the opinions of others gave honor a precarious footing that did not pass unnoticed. In *Porfiar hasta morir* one of Lope de Vega's characters remarks ironically, "Among all the nations / the Spaniard's value / bases all his honor / in others' opinions." Because honor was a public as well as a private question, and public opinion was the ultimate arbiter of individual honor, one had to defend one's reputation.[3]

Whether based on self-respect or public opinion, honor could have two distinct meanings. In the words of a Calderón scholar, "Honor can mean the outward dignity conferred by rank, pride in the superiority of birth; public respect. . . . Honor can also mean integrity, and the recognition of integrity by the world at large. This is an idea which represents honor more as the expression of the moral worth of the individual." These two meanings of honor can be summed up in the dual concepts of honor = precedence (status, rank, superior birth) and honor = virtue (moral integrity).[4] In the sixteenth and seventeenth centuries, honor was generally considered an attribute of the well-born, but its principal manifestation was through virtuous conduct.[5]

Virtue was both the way honor was manifested and its principal justification. The prevailing conception of honor as moral integrity or virtue was reflected in the literature of the Golden Age. "Honor never rests / except on virtue, its own center / like a ship upon the sea." "Most noble is honor when acquired / by arms or letters; it gilds the coats of arms, / and even more noble is that [blazón] which virtue decorates." Cervantes frequently repeated the phrase "True nobility consists in virtue" and stressed the priority of virtue over status and lineage. "An ounce of good reputation is worth more than a pound of pearls."[6] To define honor as a consideration of property in colonial New Spain is simply anachronistic: in the sixteenth and seventeenth centuries the connection between honor and property was not made.

The virtue Cervantes celebrated was a category of conduct that had different requirements in those centuries for men and women. For men, maintaining honor implied a willingness to fight, to use force to defend one's reputation against those who would impugn it. Cowardice led to a precipitous loss of honor. As a result, honor created significant meanings for male conduct on the battlefield, in commerce, and in other areas of life. For women, the defense of honor as virtue was tied to sexual conduct. Before marriage, honorable conduct meant the appearance of chastity; afterward, fidelity. If made public, sexual relations before or outside of marriage would demolish a woman's honor and her reputation.[7]

More important than private morals in this Spanish code was the lack of public disclosure. This meant that, more than anything else, maintaining honor signified preserving appearances once virtue had been lost. In this fashion one of the great ironies of the era was created. Iberian Spanish society with its strict prohibitions on premarital sexual activity had the highest levels of pregnancies outside of marriage in Western Europe, twice and even four times as high as in other European countries of the same era. Spanish women in the New World followed the pattern of their European cousins, having extraordinarily high numbers of births outside of marriage, significantly higher than even their European counterparts.[8]

Sexual honor, although the preserve of women, also concerned men. A man could be dishonored by the public disclosure of the sexual activities of a sister or wife, and it was imperative for both men and women that such indiscretions should not be revealed. This gender-based concern for sexual honor, so characteristic of societies on the rim of the Mediterranean, was central to marriage in colonial Mexico.

Colonial society's principal response to the loss of sexual honor (virtue) was to cover up or to remedy the loss of virtue as quickly and as quietly as possible. Spanish society refused to subject the person who had lost honor to public shame and humiliation, since public embarrassment was worse than death. To subject a woman to public shame, moreover, would humiliate not just her but her entire family. High levels of illegitimacy required parents and family to cooperate to preserve the illusion of chastity in spite of social reality. Consequently family, royal officials, and the church worked together to prevent public disclosure of the Spanish woman's loss of virtue. The protection of feminine sexual honor was, indeed, one of the very few social values that enjoyed nearly universal respect and consideration, and it followed that, in marriage conflicts, protecting a young woman's reputation was accorded precedence over the wishes of parents. Together with attitudes toward love and will, this valuing of sexual honor lent greater normative support to young people's desire to marry than to parental control. The possible loss of feminine honor was mentioned in nearly half of all the prenuptial conflicts of the sixteenth and seventeenth centuries.

Since a woman's reputation could be damaged by public disclosure of a premarital pregnancy, in such cases church officials deemed it necessary for her to be married secretly and without delay.[9] Parental interference, such as trying to prevent a son from marrying a woman he had seduced, or, less likely, hindering a daughter from marrying the man who had taken her virginity, was condemned as malicious. And since a woman's reputation could be destroyed by even the appearance of impropriety, public disclosure of evening visits to a woman's home was seen as scandalous and was therefore sufficient reason for church, neighbors, and relatives to intervene to protect a woman's honor.

One Wednesday evening in the summer of 1644, Pedro de Agüero, scion of a wealthy Mexico City family, was visiting his fiancée's house when a man hired by his father to prevent the marriage entered the house and attacked Pedro. The girl's family lived in rented rooms in a large house shared by several other families, all of whom were aroused by the sound of clashing swords. The alcalde of the criminal court was summoned to the scene to stop the fight, thereby causing an even greater scandal and commotion in the neighborhood. To keep public disclosure of Pedro's late-evening visit from damaging his fiancée's honor, church officials allowed the two to marry immediately and in private. Witnesses to the disturbance appeared on behalf of the couple, their intent being to protect the reputation of Pedro's fiancée from the appearance of her misconduct to the rest of her neighborhood.[10]

The importance of not disclosing feminine loss of honor was a potent weapon in the hands of young men and women seeking to force a parent's hand. Don Diego Andelo Montezuma, a descendent of the Aztec emperor Montezuma's daughter and a member of one of the most litigious clans of the sixteenth and seventeeth centuries, was a powerful, domineering figure who sought to manipulate the matrimonial alliances of his offspring for his own benefit. He made arrangements for his eldest son's marriage without regard for the son's wishes. But Diego, aged thirty, and his younger brother Antonio, aged twenty-three, were enamoured of the two daughters of Juan Velásquez, who resided in the nearby town of Coyacán. Fed up with their father's insistence that they marry to suit him, and having probably secured the consent of their fiancées' father, the brothers eloped with the two Velásquez daughters just before Mardi Gras in 1676. The four stayed together in Mexico City for two weeks before Juan Velásquez appeared to take his daughters back to Coyacán. As soon as Lent had drawn to a close, the two couples appeared in church court and asked to be married secretly, because of the danger that Don Diego would prevent the nuptials and, above all to redeem the honor of the two Velásquez girls, who had lost their virginity to the brothers Montezuma. To protect the sexual honor of these young Spanish women, church officials granted the request for secret marriages.[11] The planned double elopement was a successful strategy to force the marriages despite parental opposition.

In addition to the protection of feminine sexual honor, another critical aspect of marriage conflicts in which honor was the issue was the need to keep one's spoken promises. For all its preoccupation with notarizing transactions, Hispanic society of the sixteenth century was, like most other European societies of the period, largely illiterate. Consequently oral commitments and verbal promises were the basic medium of everyday commerce and exchange. The reliability of such verbal promises was founded on knowledge of the other person, and particularly on an awareness of the extent to which he was honorable. A serious spoken commitment was referred to in the Spanish of the period as a "word of honor," or sometimes in a more abbreviated form as simply "my word." In Tirso de Molina's *El burlador de Sevilla*, Don Gonzalo asks, "Will you fulfill your word as a gentleman?" To which Don Juan replies, "I have honor and fulfill my promises because I am a gentleman."

Keeping promises was an essential element of the code of honor. In a world that relied at least as much on verbal contracts as on written ones, a spoken promise was a solemn commitment.

The definition of honorable conduct as abiding by one's word extended to fulfilling promises to marry. Both men and women acknowledged the requirement: because most betrothals in sixteenth- and seventeenth-century Mexico were verbal (changes would come later) rather than written,[12] young women had to rely on the honor of men to fulfill their commitments. Such pledges were, after all, expressions of individual will. In this way honor was tied to the central doctrine on marriage. According to orthodox Catholic theology, will was the basis of marriage, and love was the cultural interpretation of will. Honor was the social expression of will. To keep one's vow to marry was an important element of honor, valued by both men and women, and it reinforced the significance of personal choice in marriage. Honor, even more than will and love, made it incumbent upon young people to act upon their personal choices, expressed as promises.

As is true for all central social values, there was also a system of enforcement. If a man was unwilling to marry a woman to whom he had pledged himself—a relatively rare occurrence in the seventeenth century as compared with the eighteenth—and if sexual relations had taken place, the young woman's father and brothers were the first line of defense. When male family members were lacking or were ineffectual in seeing that the marriage took place, the institutions of church and crown could be rallied on a young woman's behalf.[13]

The considerable social weight given to enforcing betrothals followed by sex was apparent in the actions of secular officials. Notified of a complaint, royal officials and local police were swift to respond. Young men by the dozens were arrested and imprisoned without bail for having taken the virginity—that is, the sexual honor—of young women.[14] After their arrest, offenders were given the opportunity either to marry or to be transported to the Philippines to work on the king's fortresses. A great many, but not all, chose to marry, but certainly the severity of the punishment for breaching the code of honor contributed to the relative infrequency of such violations.

Clearly, the family, church, and crown were interested not only in protecting feminine sexual honor but in enforcing one of the basic tenets of the code of honor, the need to fulfill spoken promises. When offenders in cases of seduction chose to marry, church officials both enforced the promise to marry and helped to protect the honor of the young women by allowing marriage to take place secretly, and without prenuptial publicity. If any publicity was ordered, it took place after the marriage, so that no stain of dishonor could cling to the match.

The same set of forces could be mobilized to ensure that the promise to marry could be fulfilled in cases when an engagement followed by sex was opposed by a third party such as a parent. As the following example shows, ecclesiastical officials played an even more powerful role than secular officials in enforcing honor. Relations between Don Fernando Andrade Montezuma and the family of María de Castro were tense in the summer of 1628. María and Don Fernando wanted to marry, but there was considerable hostility to the match from María's mother and brothers. In the autumn of 1628 the pair decided to elope. María left her mother's home, met Fernando at a previously arranged rendezvous, and there lost her virginity. He then took her to the home of one of his relatives, where the couple stayed together for nearly a week. When mother and daughter met again, María attempted to persuade her mother that she had to marry Don Fernando because she had lost her honor to him; but the mother's dislike of Don Fernando exceeded her concern for her daughter's reputation, and she was unmoved by her daughter's argument.

That night, at the mother's instigation, Don Fernando was attacked and wounded by María's brothers. When Don Fernando still refused to renounce his pledge to marry María, the mother, realizing that knives were not enough to stop him, lodged a criminal complaint against him for rape. He was arrested by the royal criminal court the next day. From his jail cell, Don Fernando sent word to the church court that he was imprisoned and in danger of his life for having tried to marry María de Castro. That Monday, the church court judge heard Don Fernando's testimony and evidence from two of his friends; María was also summoned to give her version of the events. She corroborated Fernando's story in detail, and affirmed that she still very much wanted to marry him. On the following day the church gave permission for the pair to be united in secret.[15] Because of the church's authority over marriage, ecclesiastical officials were able to counter even criminal proceedings against young couples seeking to marry.[16]

In addition to the common cultural motivation, shared by family and state as well, in seeing that promises were fulfilled, church officials had other reasons for protecting honor that stemmed from ecclesiastical tradition. The promise to marry had historically occupied a significant place in church law. Engagement was known technically in canon law as spousals, the promise of future marriage. During the medieval period, little distinction had been been made between a promise of future marriage—engagement—and an immediate intent to marry. Several important medieval canonists held that if an engagement was followed by sex between the partners, the couple was legally married, even though they had only made a promise to marry in the future. Although this doctrine was rejected as official church policy in the fourteenth century, in the popular mind, the idea that marriage began when a promise to marry was followed by sexual intercourse persisted for generations. The engagement was customarily seen as the occasion for the initiation of sexual relations between the couple, so if a man broke off an engagement after sexual relations, the woman was dishonored.[17]

Sixteenth-century canon law retained the solemnity and importance of promises to marry from the earlier medieval period. According to church law, an engagement created a permanent bond between a couple that could be broken only for a very limited number of serious reasons.[18] As a result of this ecclesiastical tradition, in addition to the cultural emphasis on the importance of promises and protecting feminine sexual honor, the spoken promise to marry was seen as a serious, indeed a binding, commitment, worthy of enforcement by church officials.

A final consideration in the church's actions to enforce marriage promises is likely to have been the high levels of illegitimacy in Spanish colonial society. The large numbers of couples avoiding marriage and having children out of wedlock suggest that perhaps church officials were more than willing to assist couples who showed some eagerness to marry.

The importance of honor as virtue in sixteenth- and seventeenth-century prenuptial conflicts thus had both cultural and religious origins. Its paramount position in the Spanish value system gave the greatest normative support to the efforts of persons to marry spouses of their own choosing. By engaging in sexual relations, or simply promising to marry, young people could force their elders to accept marriages they would have otherwise opposed. The need to protect a woman from loss of reputation and the requirement that men honor their verbal promises to marry were both powerful tools in the hands of young people seeking to force their parents to accept their choice of a spouse. In the eighteenth century this powerful weapon of honor as virtue would be lost.

Honor as Status: The Counterpoint to Virtue

The second dimension of honor, honor as status or precedence, failed to attain the normative power of honor as virtue during the sixteenth and seventeenth centuries. Evidence of this can be found in the conflict between these two often mutually contradictory claims. To church officials was it more important to protect the reputation of a poor Spanish girl (and thus of her family as well) if she were seduced by the scion of a wealthy family, or should her seducer's family be allowed to preserve their status brushing aside the girl's (and her family's) honor?[19] From the conflict cases for these centuries, the answer was consistent and unequivocal: provided both families were honorable, sexual virtue took precedence over status regardless of the relative social standing of the families. Because honor as virtue was more highly valued than honor as wealth or status in these circumstances, marriages across boundaries of wealth and status were not only permitted but approved.

Fostered by the system of freedom of choice in marriage, and protected by society's insistence upon honor as virtue, marriages between persons of disparate social origins were not wholly forbidden in seventeenth-century Mexico. Almost one-third of the opposed marriages (N = 389) crossed economic or social barriers. Twelve percent of the conflicts arose when there was a disparity of wealth or income between the two parties, 10 percent when creoles wished to marry peninsulars (frequently a matter of economic disparity as well), 2 percent from Portuguese-Spanish unions, and 2 percent from marriages between persons of different social status. An additional 6 percent arose from interracial marriages, also enforced against family wishes.

Was the sexual honor of Spanish women so important that the need to maintain it could override social and economic concerns? To an extent, yes, but a more complete answer lies in the fact that sixteenth- and seventeenth-century Spanish society had a different conception of social equality. Honor, the virtuous reputation of men and women, was to some extent independent of wealth and status. It presupposed a certain social standing—one could not easily be a tribute payer and have honor, for example—but it did not require great wealth or high position. A man or woman could lose a fortune and still maintain a reputation for honor; the picaresque novels illustrate this in the satiric figure of the poverty-stricken hidalgo who disdains manual labor but preserves his honorable appearance, and thus his honor. The concept of equality among Spaniards in the sixteenth century was based on a belief in the equality of honor as manifested in virtuous conduct rather than on similarities of wealth, income, or social status. As long as respect and reputation were maintained, any Spaniard, male or female, had a fundamental claim to equality with any other Spaniard in society.

The resulting insistence that families be treated equally because of the equality of honor is reflected in the marriage conflicts. In a substantial number of cases, the persons wishing to marry, or the witnesses who took their part, specifically cited equality of honor as a reason why the church should intervene to protect a marriage. In 18 percent of all cases, it was alleged that the marriage was being interfered with because the opposing family disliked the difference in economic position between the two families; in 2.3 percent of the cases, differences in social position were alleged to be the cause.

What is most important about these conflicts is not the fact that families opposed marriages because of differences of wealth or prestige, but rather who it was who mentioned the differences, and why. Invariably, it was the party of lesser wealth and status, the party seeking to marry, who made the observation that economic and social disparities existed between the two families. The opposing families themselves almost never mentioned their motives, for declaring objections of that sort was not supported by the cultural norms of colonial society. An heir or heiress and a poor but honorable Spaniard were not thought of as being unequal in any significant sense;

they were considered to be fundamentally similar in possessing honor. To oppose their marriage on the grounds of economic or social differences was seen as malicious interference, and was regarded as good reason for the church to take action.

The supremacy of honor as virtue in the Spanish value system was most apparent when honor came into conflict with claims of requirements for similarity of economic and social position in marriages. Parents who alleged these requirements were held to be in violation of society's norms. For the sixteenth and seventeenth centuries, the more important consideration was a reputation for sexual virtue.

The social consequences of the sixteenth- and seventeenth-century adherence to honor as virtue were particularly devastating for certain types of ambitions. Because the cultural ideology of honor placed a greater value on being faithful to promises than on an economic similarity between marriage partners, it forced young men who seduced women of lower social or economic standing to accept their marital responsibilities. As a result, numerous well-to-do parents were compelled to accept the less wealthy sons- and daughters-in-law who were their offspring's choices. In other words, the requirements of honor forced families to acquiesce in a kind of social integration that they would not have deliberately undertaken. Society's esteem for sexual honor made such resignation unavoidable: accepting an economically unequal marriage was a better alternative than submitting a woman and her family to public disgrace.

Protection of feminine sexual reputation for virtue was a primary cultural concern, surpassing even claims of social status and economic privilege. The classic illustration of this is to be found in one of the largest categories of marriage conflicts: those in which parents opposed the marriage of a child to a poorer partner despite evidence of a sexual relationship.[20]

Juana Moreno came from a comfortably circumstanced Spanish family in Mexico City. Her father wanted her to marry a wealthy man, preferably someone twice her age who had an established fortune. In this respect he resembled the fathers that Lope de Vega criticized as wanting "to sell their daughters for money." Juana, who was only fifteen, wished to marry Juan de Monguiar, who was closer to her own age and had no particular fortune. Her father was not to be swayed, so Juana and Juan took matters into their own hands. After pledging formally to marry, they set off for Chapultepec and along the way entered an unoccupied house in a cul-de-sac, where they initiated sexual relations. A young girl from the neighborhood peered in the window. In view of Juana's loss of sexual honor, which was publicly exposed by the inquisitive girl, Juana's father had no choice—he had to allow the pair to marry secretly despite his hopes of a wealthier husband.[21]

Two considerations determined the resolution of this case. First, the father's desire for his daughter to marry money contradicted prevailing cultural values, as the testimony of the couple's witnesses made clear. Second, the critical choice in this case was, as in all the cases like it, between the demands of sexual honor on the one hand and the father's opposition on the other. The need to protect the woman from public disclosure of her loss of honor took precedence over the father's ambitions.

A related but not identical source of opposition was concern for perceived social prestige. Although these distinctions were ill-defined even by the participants themselves and accounted for only 2.3 percent of the total, nonetheless several Spanish families turned up their noses when their daughters chose to marry artisans—weavers and shoemakers—on the grounds that artisans lacked social standing. But these families, too, were forced into accepting in-laws of lesser status.[22] Considerations of different social status received no more privileged response than those of economic difference.

Marriages were enforced that crossed boundaries of race also. Why did the Catholic Church support interracial marriages, against the wishes of parents, and why was this action tolerated by society? Only 6 percent of all marriage conflicts forced Spanish families to accept in-laws of a different race,[23] but even this small number was significant because they demonstrated the inability of the Mexican aristocracy to maintain absolute racial boundaries. The margins were permeable, though few were able to pass through.

Most commonly, unwilling families were forced to accept a member's long-term concubine of another race as a legitimate spouse. In November 1682, in the town of Texcoco, a Spaniard named Cristóbal Jiménez de la Chica attempted to marry Doña Gerónima Hernández. Cristóbal was poor, unable even to pay the church's fees for marriage, but his brothers and other relatives were quite arrogant. They declared that Doña Gerónima, a mestiza, was not their brother's equal and said they would halt the marriage, something they had done in the past. This time, however, Cristóbal persisted, and with the help of the church he succeeded. Cristóbal was hardly a callow youth. He was forty-eight years old, and had lived with Gerónima for twenty-two years and had had eight children with her. Neither the long duration of Cristóbal's commitment to Gerónima nor the existence of their children had swayed his family from their racial prejudice.[24]

On March 15, 1633, Tomás Rivera y Portes finally asked the church court to help him carry out his pledge to marry María de Berrica, the castiza with whom he had been living for four years. The obstacles to the marriage were considerable. Several of Tomás's relatives had made menacing statements, and his brother Diego had even threatened to kill him if he attempted to wed María. The threat had been so serious that Tomás had fled the city and had made his way clandestinely to the church court. The court permitted him to marry María in secret that very day. The Rivera family was clearly not going to be very happy with the marriage, but there was nothing further they could do.[25] Certainly many families did not welcome dark-skinned former concubines with open arms, but the children were legitimized by this process and gained the right to inherit their family's fortune, and thus given an entrée to the social level of their fathers, despite being racially mixed.

Enforcing interracial marriage is understandable from a number of different perspectives. First, the number of such marriages by Spaniards was relatively small during the sixteenth and seventeenth centuries. Most interracial sex took place outside of wedlock, and the men who desired to marry their concubines were few. The relationships thus formalized were generally of long duration, were not likely to be terminated in the near future, and generally had resulted in the creation of a family with several offspring. Why men such as Tomás Rivera y Portes decided to marry their long-term concubines was rarely explained. One old peninsular man remarked that he was moved to marry his black housekeeper out of gratitude and affection for the devotion she had shown him for ten years; in other instances a father's attachment to his young heirs may well have been the motive.[26] In any case, these marriages were so few that they posed little threat to society as a whole, and they conformed to the socially accepted pattern of interracial liaisons, between a Spanish male and a darker female. Furthermore, because living in a sexual union outside marriage was a mortal sin, and because these longstanding unions offered little prospect of such reformation and termination, the church sometimes performed such marriages for what was called "the service of God"—that is, to rescue the man's immortal soul from eternal damnation.

Like the allegations of motives of concern for economic position or social status, objections based on racial difference were also labeled unjust interference in the choice of a spouse. In most of the instances of interracial marriage by Spaniards, it was the couple themselves or their witnesses who pointed to the families' racial attitudes as examples of malicious interference. Only rarely did a parent attempt to maintain that such a difference constituted a legitimate cause for opposition, and such claims were unsuccessful.[27]

The conflict between freedom of choice in marriage and the desire of families for socially or economically advantageous unions certainly did exist in colonial Mexico, and was an issue in one-third of all marriage conflicts. Marriages between apparently unequal persons were tolerated, partly because they were few in number, partly because the social need for marriage as a remedy for lost honor was seen to outweigh social or economic differences, and partly also because the fundamental ideology of social equality was that of equality of honor, not prestige or money. Love and honor could not only coexist, they could complement each other.

Honor, love, and will—three central Spanish social values—together provided normative support for the position of children seeking to marry in Spanish colonial society. Ecclesiastical teachings emphasized the operation of free will in the sacred context of marriage and deemphasized the role of parents. Love was the cultural understanding of the operation of individual will, and approval of marriage for love in popular culture strengthened the hand of young people. Finally, honor provided the social mechanism for the expression of free will in marriage. Upholding a promise and protecting feminine reputations both enjoyed greater support from the prevailing cultural norms than considerations of parental authority or social and economic differences. What is left to discuss are the ways in which the Catholic Church in colonial Mexico went about intervening to enforce and fulfill these cultural values.

CHAPTER 5

The Role of the Church

When prenuptial conflicts were brought to the ecclesiastical courts, church officials had three techniques available to re-solve them. Sometimes one technique sufficed. In other cases, such as that of Gerónimo and Juana, the Mexican Romeo and Juliet, all three were used together.

Juana was removed from her home by church officials and placed with another family, a procedure called *depósito*, or temporary cus-tody. Because Gerónimo's father had locked him up, the "secular arm," the royal police, was called to force his father to release him to church custody. Finally, the two were united in a secret marriage. Of these three techniques—temporary custody, use of the secular arm, and secret marriage—the most commonly used was secret marriage. From 1574, the date of the earliest surviving records of the ecclesiastical court of the archdiocese of Mexico, until 1689, well over a century later, and despite numerous changes of arch-bishops, vicars general, and chief judges, the ecclesiastical courts consistently permitted secret marriages for one principal reason: un-just interference by relatives, guardians, or employers in matrimo-nial plans.[1] Secret marriage was allowed in nearly two-thirds of all conflicts in this period. In canon law the practice was referred to as dispensation of the banns.[2]

The banns of marriage were then and are now a kind of prenup-tial publicity, made mandatory for Catholic marriage by the Coun-cil of Trent: an announcement from the pulpit, on three successive feast days, that two people, mentioned by name, intend to marry.

Members of the parish are required to disclose any information that might prevent the couple from marrying. If no one has come forward after three announcements have been made, the couple can be married. However, the Council of Trent in making publication of the banns mandatory, at the same time granted bishops the authority to dispense with the banns as they saw fit.[3] It was this authority that church officials of colonial Mexico used to intervene when the couple and their friends and relatives alleged that parents were unjustly interfering in their marriage plans. Dispensing with the banns meant in fact that the couple were married immediately and in secret, with only the priest and two witnesses present. In some instances, dispensation was granted when it was feared that even notifying a parent would lead to unjust interference.

In 1584 in the city of Mexico, a poor Spanish orphan named Luisa de Ávila became engaged to a wealthy muleteer named Pedro Hernández. The banns for the pair's impending nuptials were first announced on the last Sunday of August. Upon hearing the announcement, three of Pedro's married sisters decided that something had to be done to prevent the unequal marriage. They informed their acquaintances that they intended to write their father in Acapulco, anticipating that notification would bring a prompt halt to the union. Church officials were quicker, however. Rather than wait for the father to find out his son's intentions, they dispensed with the banns of marriage and allowed Pedro and Luisa to be married immediately and in secret, before the news could reach Pedro's father in Acapulco. Dispensation not only protected a couple from the violence that might be used to prevent their marriage, but also served as a way of avoiding formal prior notification of parents, other relatives, or guardians known to oppose the match.[4]

Church officials granted the request of nearly all couples who sought dispensation of the banns because of opposition by relatives. The exceptions largely fell into two categories: cases in which the witnesses failed to corroborate the couple's allegations of unjust interference, and cases in which the church suspected the existence of a condition, such as incest or bigamy, that canon law admitted as sufficient reason to forbid a marriage.[5] In such instances the officials ordered the announcements made in the ordinary manner.

The technique of secret marriage was extensively used, even when the marriage conflicted with an arrest order or jail sentence handed down by a royal court. Pedro León was a Mexico City tailor. In July 1631 he and Juana Zamora, a thirty-five-year-old widow, decided to marry and began living together. Her brother, adamantly opposed to her remarriage, denounced her sexual misconduct to the royal authorities. The pair fled from their home and were in hiding with various friends and relatives when they heard that an order for their arrest had been issued by the royal authorities. They made their way to the ecclesiastical court and, with the support of virtually their entire neighborhood, including one member of a lay religious organization, they asked the church to allow them to marry secretly. The authorities granted their request, thus nullifying the royal arrest order.[6] Secret marriages were granted on other occasions to young couples who had already been arrested. Since the criminal complaints in such matters were usually for illicit sexual relations, the church's action also removed the cause for the criminal charges.[7]

By authorizing secret marriages, church officials not only overturned arrests ordered by the secular political authorities but also countered the influence of Audiencia judges and upon occasion even the viceroy himself. On June 5, 1631, Don Fernando de la Mota y Portugal approached the chief judge of the ecclesiastical court in Mexico City and asked for dispensation of prenuptial publicity for his marriage to Doña Catalina Ruíz. It was an extraordinary request: Don Fernando's brother was Don Cristóbal Mota y Portugal, secretary of the Audiencia and one of the most powerful men in New Spain. Since Cristóbal did not care for Fernando's intended mate there was a chance that the high court secretary would try to prevent the marriage by withholding the 400 pesos a year that he was obliged to pay Fernando from their father's estate. If the marriage took place, the law required the stipend be paid. The church judge, more concerned with matrimonial liberty than with the displeasure of a royal court official, ordered the marriage to take place without any publicity that very day.[8] Church officials intervened on other occasions to allow secret marriages, without the viceroy's knowledge and against his wishes, of that august official's own gentlemen- and ladies-in-waiting.[9] It is indicative of the independence of the seventeenth-century church in marriage matters that it was able to take such steps.

Generally, secret marriage was sufficient, but sometimes the secular arm or temporary custody had to be used to prevent families from maliciously hindering a match. If relatives or other persons opposing a marriage detained the person wishing to marry and appeared unlikely to release him or her even at the request of church officials, as in the case of Gerónimo and Juana, additional assistance was called in. When Ana de Rua refused to allow her stepdaughter Sebastiana out of the house because she wanted to retain the girl's domestic services, church officials sent the royal police to Sebastiana's aid. Similarly, when the uncle of Madrid-born Eugenia Suárez cut off her hair and locked her up in his house for attempting to marry, church officials called out the royal police to rescue her.[10] This freedom to use the royal police to enforce ecclesiastical orders was a courtesy extended by law to church officials throughout Spanish America. Although it was invoked infrequently for incidents of marriage opposition (less than 7 percent of all cases), it was critical to the church's success, for unless the church could force the most recalcitrant families into compliance, all its moral authority would be for naught. The assistance of the royal police against involuntary incarceration was the key not only to preventing harm but also to the successful conclusion of marriage.

Temporary custody, or *depósito* (from the·Latin word *depositus*), means a trust or a bond, originally signifying the temporary placement of property in trust (as a deposit). In medieval ecclesiastical writing, the term was used to refer to temporary guardianship of people, as in the practice of separating a young couple who had eloped in order to ascertain whether the young woman had consented to elope of her own volition.[11] By church tradition, a woman who had eloped was placed in temporary custody with an unrelated family for three days so that she could freely contemplate the step she was about to undertake. At the end of the three-day period she was brought to the church court to swear whether her intent to marry was unchanged and her elopement was voluntary.

The practice of seclusion was designed to ensure that a woman's freedom to marry would not be interfered with by the man she had eloped with, and it also prevented interference by her own family. In 1633, Juan Rodríguez and Doña Gerónima Muñoz eloped from Queretaro to escape the opposition of her father, a prominent citizen. Upon arriving in Mexico City, the couple went promptly to the ecclesiastical judge, who ordered Gerónima placed in temporary custody in the home of a local merchant. When asked after the customary three days why she came to Mexico City, she told the judge, "I have come to this city in order to marry Juan Rodríguez because in my hometown my father prevented us from marrying." When asked whether Juan took her by force from her parents' home or in any way coerced her, she replied: "Juan Rodríguez did not forcibly remove me from my home, nor has he in any way compelled me. I left my parents' house voluntarily in order to marry him, and my statement now is made without pressure or compulsion from anyone." The statement that she had acted of her own free will allowed the church judge to order her immediate, secret marriage to Juan.[12]

The action of the ecclesiastical judge in Gerónima Muñoz's case was by no means unusual. A woman who eloped was offered the opportunity to be placed in the temporary custody of someone she knew if that was possible, or else with as prominent a citizen as could be persuaded to take her. During the custodial period, neither the man with whom she eloped nor anyone connected with her family was allowed to have contact with her.

As with Juan Rodríguez and Gerónima Muñoz, Mexican church judges often ordered secret marriages for eloping couples.[13] This additional action was based on the assumption that elopement invariably meant the loss of sexual honor, a matter to be remedied with as much haste as possible. Such secret marriages also were a way of soothing family feelings. The code of honor required a woman's family to take action against the man who had taken their daughter or sister; if the pair was legally married, honor was preserved and there was no further need for retribution, revenge, or bloodshed. Peace was thus maintained.

Temporary custody was never a frequent recourse of church officials, and it was used most often in prenuptial disputes as a form of special protection for women who had not eloped, in cases in which it was decided that, for various reasons, the woman needed safeguarding.[14] If a woman was being threatened with physical harm and also being prevented from appearing in church court, the royal police were sent to her aid and temporary custody was ordered.[15] The royal police were called upon to force the recalcitrant family to release her into church control; temporary custody was used to protect her until the marriage could take place. Mexican church officials not only adopted ecclesiastical tradition and the innovations of Trent, but also applied them to a situation that Hispanic culture labeled unjust, namely the malicious interference of parents, guardians, or employers in the choice of a marriage partner.

The details of cases in which ecclesiastical officials unhesitatingly intervened to allow marriages against the wishes of the highest officials, or nullified orders for criminal prosecution, reveal the scope of the Mexican church's independent power over marriage. But the church's actions in nearly all the conflicts would have been impossible without the help and support of friends, neighbors, prominent members of the community, and others who brought the young couples to court, hid them from relatives or royal policemen, and testified on their behalf. Without such assistance, the church could not have intervened and the couples could not have prevailed. The enthusiasm of the witnesses, even in the face of high-ranking disapproval, makes it clear that ecclesiastical intervention was not merely a defense of a purely religious doctrine. Rather, in intervening, church officials were enforcing the normative cultural beliefs of the era.

Armed with the backing of the crown, and the active support of the population it served, the Catholic Church exercised a powerful dominion over prenuptial conflicts. Over 92 percent of the conflicts that came before ecclesiastical judges between 1580 and 1689 were resolved not for the parents but *in favor of the couple*, a stunning percentage by any measure. More importantly, it was the action of church courts that ensured these favorable results for couples. Most of these outcomes were achieved through the use of a single ecclesiastical response, dispensation of banns ensuring secret marriages. Over three-quarters of the resolutions in favor of the couple were effected by secret marriage alone. Almost 10 percent of the favorable resolutions were obtained by the additional assistance of the royal police and temporary custody. In the remaining cases, church officials simply ordered the marriage to proceed in the customary manner, while, for example, ordering a slaveowner not to take the person marrying out of the city.[16]

Exceptional Cases

Although the church had great power to intervene, it was not omnipotent. Excluding the cases in which the outcome could not be determined because paper had deteriorated or pages were missing, ecclesiastical intervention was unsuccessful in slightly over 7 percent of the cases.[17] The couples in these cases did not fail to marry because the church supported parental authority; on the contrary, church officials in those exceptional cases assisted the couple. But for a variety of reasons ecclesiastical aid was insufficient or came too late. In a few instances, the woman changed her mind after getting to know the man better, or decided that she would rather not risk parental displeasure.[18] More often, however, pressure had been brought to bear on one of the parties to such an extent that he or she desisted from efforts to marry. In some cases the young woman was so intimidated that she denied knowing the young man even though several highly reputable witnesses had been present when the couple promised to marry and had sworn this before the ecclesiastical judge.[19]

On other occasions, ecclesiastical intervention failed because the church was unable to execute its orders, as when one of the principals had been moved beyond the reach of its jurisdiction, usually by being shipped out of town.[20] Not all such cases, however, resulted in the prevention of a marriage. One persistent young man searched for nearly two years before finding, and eventually marrying, the woman whose parents had uprooted her in order to prevent their union.[21] Miscellaneous reasons prevented other marriages. Only in two instances were royal courts looked to overturn the decision of the church courts on procedural grounds, and in both cases the final outcome of the dispute is unclear. The rarity of this sort of intervention suggests that extraordinary personal pressure on the couple rather than institutional action impeded marriages.[22]

The final significant factor in preventing marriages was insufficient assistance from the church, which was most marked in cases involving blacks, castas, servants, and slaves. Opposition by slaveowners and servants' masters gave rise to only 8 percent of the conflicts, yet nearly 30 percent of all the prevented marriages fall into this category. Similar discrepancies are evident when the church's record is examined by race. Creole and peninsular Spanish males make up 74 percent of the total men whose matrimonial aims were contested, but only 40 percent of those whose marriages were prevented; similarly, Spanish women make up 68 percent of those whose marriages were opposed but only 24 percent of those whose marriages were halted. On the other hand, fewer than a quarter of all contested marriages involved only blacks, Indians, or persons of mixed race, yet these accounted for 40 percent of the prevented marriages.[23]

Church officials did not ignore pleas for help from couples of mixed race, blacks, or Indians, but they did tend to pursue remedies less vigorously and to be less diligent about ensuring enforcement than they would have been if the couple had been Spanish. In one case, for example, Leonor de Mendoza, a slave, and Tomás Ortega appeared in church court and began procedures to marry. Leonor's master received news of the planned marriage, marched to the powder mill where Tomás worked, and locked him up, even though Tomás was another man's slave. Leonor turned to the church court for help. Church officials sided with her, ordering her master to bring Tomás to church court, and issuing an excommunication decree against the master or anyone else who interfered with the marriage.[24] Had the pair been Spanish rather than slaves, church officials would probably have sent the royal police to release Tomás rather than opt for the relatively weak and less effectual excommunication threat. Leonor was doubly handicapped because ordering out the royal police probably required payment of a fee; a slave woman was less likely than even a poor Spanish woman to have access to such funds.

Church officials were similarly indifferent when the conflict originated from a black or mulatto family. Matias Lisea was an extraordinary man. A free black, he not only was able to sign his name, something most Spaniards could not do, but also was a master cartwright in a time when laws and guild regulations usually prevented mulattoes and blacks from qualifying as master craftsmen. Matias was enamored of eighteen-year-old Felipa Concepción, a free mulatta who worked as a servant for the nuns of the convent of Valvanera. The first banns were published in January 1686. For reasons that were never disclosed, Felipa's parents opposed her marriage to the master cartwright and asked her employers, the nuns of Valvanera, to keep her in the convent. An ecclesiastical notary was dispatched to the convent on January 10 to ask Felipa if she wished to marry. She said no, but asked to be allowed to leave the convent, and was released the following day.[25] No effort was made to allow Felipa time in a neutral home to think over her decision, although church officials would certainly have taken such an action if Felipa had been Spanish rather than mulatto.

This is not to say that slaves and servants were totally unprotected by church officials, since several mulatto and black slaves were given assistance to marry against the wishes of their masters.[26] Individual examples illustrate that the church was not blind to the abuse of power by slave owners or masters. But the odds against a couple seeking to marry in the face of an owner's opposition were vastly greater than they were against two Spaniards facing opposition from relatives or guardians.[27]

Parental Stratagems in Extremis

The actions of the Catholic Church in premarital disputes were not only consistent, but also highly effective in preventing parents from exercising a veto over their children's choice of a marriage partner. Lacking both normative cultural support and institutional assistance, those who opposed marriages had to go to extreme lengths in order to make their protests in any kind of formal manner. Since appeal to secular authority was unlikely, those seeking to counter a successful appeal to the church authorities were forced to work within the framework established by the church. Such protests were no more likely to be successful than the usual sort of opposition, but they are instructive on several counts. By their very excessiveness they illustrate the extent to which parental selection or veto of a spouse lacked a compelling moral authority in this first period. Furthermore, they foreshadow the kind of case that would become significantly more common during the period of development of normative patriarchy.

Attempts to use the legal machinery of the church to prevent a marriage were made in fewer than 3 percent of all marriage conflicts. The primary reason is quite simple: since the church was more likely to side with the couple, parents seeking to halt marriages undoubtedly avoided the church courts because they knew they were likely to lose. A second reason for the failure to petition the church was related to the nature of church intervention. Eliminating prenuptial publicity meant that opposers did not know the marriage was about to be performed. Consequently there was no opportunity to petition the court until *after* the marriage had already occurred.

Yet in spite of the long odds and the lack of opportunity, a small number of opposers did appeal to the church courts to prevent marriages. They based their petitions upon an obscure area of canon law.

The grounds upon which the church could consider challenges to the validity of a marriage were known as *impediments*. These were classified into two categories, depending on the degree of gravity that canonists attached to the problem. A "prohibitive" impediment was a relatively minor charge; it did not prevent marriage but merely rendered transgressions subject to a fine or imposition of a spiritual penalty. The more serious category of impediments was labeled "diriment" by canonists. A diriment impediment was of sufficient consequence to nullify a marriage even after it had been consummated and children born. If discovered before the marriage was contracted, a diriment impediment resulted in the church's permanently forbidding the marriage to take place.[28] Since the church had exclusive jurisdiction over marriage, there could be no appeal from such a decision to secular authorities. In the sixteenth, seventeenth, and early eighteenth centuries the only means of using the church to obstruct a marriage was to uncover the existence of a diriment impediment. Claims that such a barrier existed thus became the principal legal strategy used in attempting to stave off a wedding. Success was by no means automatic, however.

Locating a valid reason for the church to forbid a marriage was made exceedingly difficult by the very nature of the diriment impediments. Both the theory and the definitive list of impediments were promulgated mainly between the eleventh and thirteenth centuries, a result of the establishment of exclusive church jurisdiction over marriage.[29] The impediments themselves were the end product of historical evolution, a gradual accretion of layers of Mosaic, Germanic, and Roman law, the major cultural sources of Western Christendom.[30] In codifying the list of impediments, medieval canonists for the most part concentrated on reconciling the mutually contradictory aspects of each of these three cultural traditions. In addition, they made the impediments consistent with the religious tradition which by the twelfth century had established marriage as consensual and indissoluble.[31]

One category of impediments, requiring the active consent of the couple, was effectively a means by which someone could escape from a marriage arranged or forced upon him by his parents or others.[32] It was thus not a category to which parents seeking to prevent a marriage would have recourse.[33] The remaining categories, known as "incapacities," included impotence, having entered the priesthood, having made solemn vows of chastity, possessing another living spouse, being under the age of puberty, or not being Catholic.[34] Most of these were matters of record that could be disclosed by witnesses. More important, it would be nearly impossible for such evidence to be manufactured or invented by relatives opposing a marriage because they desired to hold on to an inheritance or because they disliked the family of the boy or girl. So only four of these incapacities—being under age, impotence, having made private vows of chastity, and having a living spouse—were ever invoked by those seeking to obstruct marital union.

A second group of incapacities referred to a person's qualifications to marry the intended spouse and included such diverse causes as consanguinity, affinity (roughly the bond between in-laws), spiritual kinship (more popularly known as *compadrazgo*, resulting from sponsorship in a sacrament), crime (the murder of one party's spouse, or adultery with a promise to marry as soon as the spouse died), and public honesty (public engagement to another close relative of the intended present spouse).[35] A final incapacity was clandestinity, or failure to observe the public formalities of marriage. Clandestinity was the only diriment impediment established after the thirteenth century, the only major innovation in the fundamentally medieval list of prohibitions.[36]

It was uphill work for those opposing marriages to conform their objections to these categories of medieval canon law. One of the few clashes resulting from an attempt to use the diriment impediments to halt a marriage illustrates the difficulty parents faced in trying to use the authority of the church to obstruct a marriage for social or economic reasons before 1730. In 1674 a young man, José María Esquivel, appeared in ecclesiastical court and stated that his father opposed his marriage because the father wanted him to become a priest. He said that his father had threatened to remove him from the city if he carried through with his intention to marry. The ecclesiastical judge dispensed with the banns and allowed them to marry immediately. As was usual, the couple was ordered not to consummate the union until after the postnuptial banns had been read.

These were customarily announced after the marriage on three successive feast days so that if a diriment impediment was found to exist, the marriage could be nullified without the additional compli-
cation of offspring.[37] During the week after the marriage, the banns
were read from the pulpit of José María's parish. Hearing of them,
José María's father hastened to enter a plea for the nullification of his
son's marriage on the grounds that a diriment impediment existed.
The grounds he used to argue his case were at once novel and designed to show irrefutably that the son should have been a priest instead of a husband: José María, the father alleged, was impotent and
would thus never be able to consummate his marriage, much less procreate.[38]

This singular excuse produced consternation in both medical and
ecclesiastical circles. Canon law had been designed to deal with allegations from the woman that her husband was impotent, not with
allegations from a parent.[39] And because José María had been born
with an irregularity in the male organ, to which was added a childhood injury that had left him with a scar on the underside of the pe-
nis, debate arose within the medical community as to whether he
could in fact have sexual relations.[40]

The actual presence of such physical irregularities, combined
with the father's resistance to the marriage, produced a case that
was, in the judgment of all whose opinion was consulted, highly irregular. The father protested that he was not hostile to the marriage
but was merely trying to inform the judge ("para ynformar el animo
de Vmd.") of a matter the truth of which was evident ("aquí se
manifeste la verdad del hecho"). Yet the existence of less drastic and
less public alternatives to the father's formal opposition—a private
examination could have been made by the family, for example, or
the young woman merely forewarned that her husband might not
be able to have a normal sex life—clearly gave the lie to the father's
claims.[41] According to José María, the father's interest in having him
enter the priesthood arose from his desire to retain the substantial
property that he would have to hand over to him, upon his marriage, from his deceased mother's estate. It seems certain that the father's desire for gain motivated this singular case in the ecclesiastical
court records of Mexico.[42]

The debate first centered on the correct procedures to be followed. After several solutions had been raised and debated by law-

yers for both sides, the ecclesiastical judge's legal adviser suggested a remedy that had originated in the thirteenth century: that a visual inspection of the young man and his ability to perform be made by experts.[43] José María was notably reluctant to undergo such an examination—which his lawyer kept referring to as these "dishonest investigations"—but was ordered under penalty of a one-hundred-gold-peso fine to appear before an examining board composed of the head of the medical tribunal and six of the most eminent physicians and surgeons in New Spain.[44]

Attempts were made on two separate afternoons for nearly two hours each, both occasions witnessing the use of every aphrodisiac then known, including hot baths, but without success. The report of these examinations detailed the young man's physical condition and described with great sympathy his futile efforts to achieve an erection under such trying circumstances.[45] In spite of José María's failures, a majority of the physicians and surgeons reported that the defect in the young man's organ would not prevent him from procreating.

The conviction with which the eminent doctors rendered their opinion suggests that they were relying on other evidence than that of the dismal trial. Assurance of José María's ability to ejaculate could have come only from José María himself, specifically from his descriptions of either masturbation or sexual activity with other women. The physicians probably quizzed him in detail about his prior sexual experience and found sufficient reliable evidence to pronounce him potent. But the real problem lay in convincing the ecclesiastical judge. Masturbation was a sin called pollution, and previous sexual activity was a sin called fornication. The physicians had to decide how to convince a churchman that the young man was potent without accusing him of the ecclesiastical equivalent of a felony. Not surprisingly, their reports contain unequivocal assertions based only on their status as experts, citing no sources of information and giving no basis for their opinions.[46]

Although these apparently unfounded asseverations aroused the suspicion of the church's legal counselor, José María's lawyer argued that impotence as a valid ground for dissolving a marriage must consist in the inability to procreate, not in the irregular appearance of the organ. This argument, accompanied by the young man's later declaration that his wife was pregnant, led to the overruling of the counselor's opinion by the chief court judge.[47] This clergyman declared that a valid marriage existed, since in his opinion no diriment impediment, as defined by canon law, could be proved.

It is as important to note what was not said as well as what was said in this case. The father did not voice his real motives as the reasons why the church should hear his objections. He made no claim for his authority over his son's actions, but kept his entire argument within the bounds of canon law. The final decision, as well as the language of the evidence, was based entirely on ecclesiastical definitions of impediments to marriage, not on the social merits or moral validity of the father's opposition.

José María's father's attempt to use the canonical impediment of impotence was unsuccessful. His efforts illustrate the virtual impossibility of fitting opposition to a marriage based on social or economic considerations into the categories permitted by canon law. In using the impediment of impotence, the father hoped to embarrass his son into renouncing the marriage. The son by persevering managed to overcome the opposition to his marriage. Those seeking to obstruct marriages on other grounds, such as social and racial inequality, were similarly stymied by the church's insistence on the primacy of canon law over secular concerns.

In one such instance, dating from 1628, Catalina Salguero, a Spanish resident of the silver-mining town of Zacualpa, protested to the judge of the regional religious court that her son was about to marry the mestiza servant of a prominent local citizen. Catalina launched a two-pronged attack on the nuptials. First she stated that Isabel, the servant, was already married. Then she added a second point, alleging that the marriage was prejudicial to her, the mother, because the servant girl was "very base and my son is an hidalgo and nobleman, and they are different [racial] conditions." Few of those resisting marriages confessed their profane motives for opposition. Catalina's candor, however, had no effect either on procedures or on the outcome. Church officials ignored her objections based on the secular category of social and racial differences and devoted their time instead to investigating the claim of Isabel's prior marriage. After an extensive inquiry they found nothing to support the mother's contention that the marriage would be bigamous. The final decision is missing from the case, but there was no indication that Catalina Salguero's protest disrupted her son's matrimonial plans.[48] To the seventeenth-century church, claims of secular or profane differences, including those of social and racial disparity, were beside the point. Only the religious requirements of canon law were relevant.

The only diriment impediment in canon law not of medieval origin was that of clandestinity, or abduction, which was formulated at the Council of Trent. By formulating the impediment, the Council hoped to achieve two purposes: to ensure that the proper formalities—presence of a priest and witnesses—be observed in marriage, and that the consent given before witnesses be given freely and without pressure. This was originally construed to mean that if a young woman eloped, it could be assumed that the man she eloped with had put pressure on her to do so. If proof could be given that he *had* placed undue pressure on her, he could be permanently prohibited from marrying her.[49] This impediment could also be raised when a couple had engaged in premarital intercourse away from the parental domicile. Since eloping couples were usually attempting to evade family opposition, it is not surprising that the opposing families raised clandestinity as an objection more frequently than any other category of church prohibition.[50] But because church officials relied on the word of the woman that she had or had not consented to the loss of her honor, those parents bent on stopping a marriage by arguing abduction were frustrated by a daughter's declaration that she had willingly participated in the sexual act: in Mexican church courts it was not the parents' testimony that was relevant in determining whether a canonical barrier existed to marriage but only that of the couple. Consequently, clandestinity was no more likely to be a successful strategy than the other canonical impediments.[51]

Mexican ecclesiastical officials interpreted clandestinity as a defect in the woman's capacity to grant valid consent to marriage. By contrast, French royal law after 1579 defined clandestinity or abduction to mean the use of force against the parents' dominion over their daughter. Any elopement in France, therefore, could be charged with the impediment of clandestinity and the marriage invalidated.[52] The Mexican ecclesiastical courts customarily did not adhere to the French definition, and Hispanic Catholic theologians, led by Tomás Sánchez, held that such an interpretation was incorrect because parental permission was nowhere a church requirement for marriage.[53] It is worth noting that the conception of the impediment of abduction in the minds of Mexican clergymen derived from their belief in the primacy of sexual honor, whereas that of French officials stemmed from a belief in the supremacy of parental authority. The cultural conception of the authority of parents over marriage choices could not have been more different.

Because of the church's exclusive focus on canon law criteria for judging marital suitability, obstructors rarely made mention of the underlying social causes—racial inequality, social differences, the desire to hold on to a family inheritance—when using church courts to impede matrimonies. When mention was made of such profane matters, it was usually done by the couples or their allies in an effort to convince the church that those who were trying to prevent the marriage were motivated by base, ignoble, and fundamentally irreligious considerations. The rhetoric of racial inequality and social difference did not belong to the opposers except in a submerged or covert fashion. Adherence to the church's rules for rhetoric regarding marriage by even the obstructors is evidence of the degree to which marriage was the church's province during the sixteenth and seventeenth centuries.

It has been said that the ruling ideas of an era are those of the dominant class. Does the church's exclusive use of medieval theory to decide issues of concern to the Mexican ruling class contradict this claim? The resolution of this anomaly resides in the complexity of colonial reality, both in the dominance of a religious world-view in the minds of seventeenth-century middle and upper class Mexicans and in the historical position of the Catholic Church. The respect in which the church was held is illustrated by the fact that parents, guardians, and relatives undertook the arduous task of proving the existence of a diriment impediment. Their acceptance of the terms of argument of canon law indicates that they recognized the legitimacy of the Catholic Church's authority to decide family conflicts, even when that authority could not be invoked readily on their own behalf. This period can thus be described as a hegemonic one for the Catholic Church—one in which its basic tenets and principles were accepted by Spanish families even when they conflicted with personal or material interests. Only when this regard deteriorated was the church's hegemony over marriage imperiled.

A second striking feature of these cases is the fact that none of the parents made an explicit argument for parental authority in marriage questions; in spite of their enormous difficulty in contending with the ecclesiastical machinery, they never protested the church's lack of support for parental authority. Those who saw their servants, wards, and relatives married secretly (and against their wishes) by the Catholic Church also largely resigned themselves to accepting ecclesiastical actions. It is important that even those holding the power in colonial families accepted the church's right to decide disputes over a potential marriage partner during this period. The absence of claims for parental authority and the lack of protest against the church's action further indicate the extent to which normative support for parental control of marriage was lacking during this first period of colonial Mexican history.

The strategies that appeared absurd in the sixteenth and seventeenth centuries—the tortured arguments about canonical impediments—would be resorted to frequently in the eighteenth century. As parents increasingly came to protest their offspring's marriages openly, they began to use the canonical impediments as a means of arguing that parental objections to marriage should also be considered a barrier to matrimony. The evolution of a doctrine of normative patriarchy, however, was a slow, gradual process, and it is this transition that will be examined in Part II.

PART TWO

The Transitional Period
1690-1779

CHAPTER 6

Changing Attitudes Toward Honor

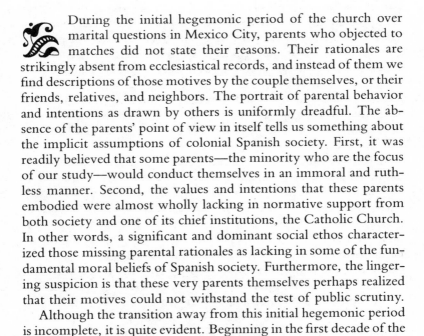 During the initial hegemonic period of the church over marital questions in Mexico City, parents who objected to matches did not state their reasons. Their rationales are strikingly absent from ecclesiastical records, and instead of them we find descriptions of those motives by the couple themselves, or their friends, relatives, and neighbors. The portrait of parental behavior and intentions as drawn by others is uniformly dreadful. The absence of the parents' point of view in itself tells us something about the implicit assumptions of colonial Spanish society. First, it was readily believed that some parents—the minority who are the focus of our study—would conduct themselves in an immoral and ruthless manner. Second, the values and intentions that these parents embodied were almost wholly lacking in normative support from both society and one of its chief institutions, the Catholic Church. In other words, a significant and dominant social ethos characterized those missing parental rationales as lacking in some of the fundamental moral beliefs of Spanish society. Furthermore, the lingering suspicion is that these very parents themselves perhaps realized that their motives could not withstand the test of public scrutiny.

Although the transition away from this initial hegemonic period is incomplete, it is quite evident. Beginning in the first decade of the eighteenth century the voices of parents appear at first contesting the moral aspersions cast on their conduct by their offspring and proclaiming the morality or nobility of their own ambitions to control marriage choices. These first attempts of parents to justify their

motives in conflict with those of their offspring mark the beginning
of a significant effort to challenge the assumptions about immorality
in an earlier period. Although during the first period only a min-
iscule fraction of all conflicts ever escalated to the stage of a formal
lawsuit, this trend would not continue. As parents grew increasingly convinced of the integrity of their own position, they became
willing to expose their motives to public disclosure, confident that
their attitudes would not be readily scorned as they might have been
in an earlier age.

The resulting cacophony of voices in eighteenth-century marriage conflicts is strikingly different from the apparent univocity of
the sixteenth and seventeenth centuries. What had once been condemned by church, couple, and community without opposition by
parents had become noisily contested ground, parents and children
each proclaiming their own version of morality and social priorities.
Caught in the middle of a raging debate over the extent of parental
authority over marriage choices, church officials sat back and
watched a previous social consensus dissolve. Matters that had once
been dispatched by the stroke of a clergyman's pen became the subject of endless contention and ceaselessly mounting reams of paper.
What underlay the appearance of parental voices was a questioning
of definitions of morality and upright conduct, ideas that had been
clear in an earlier age.

In the final third of the seventeenth century, attitudes toward sexual honor began to change in ways that would significantly affect
ecclesiastical protection of couples. The shifts, most of which occurred between 1670 and 1730, were gradual rather than sudden.
During those years, alterations in two separate but related aspects of
sexual honor undermined support for couples. First, the increasing
participation of black and casta women in marriage lessened the urgency of protecting Spanish women's premarital reputations and
thus undermined an important reason for ecclesiastical intervention
in prenuptial disputes. Second, the act that gave force to the maintenance of honor as sexual virtue—the solemn promise, or "word
of honor" as it was called in Spanish—began to lose its power to
compel men to marry. As men became increasingly willing to go
back on their word, church officials could no longer be certain that
a mutually binding promise preceded sexual relations, and so they
were unable to intervene rapidly and confidently to enforce a prom-

ise to marry against parents' wishes. Church and state responded in different ways, but by 1730 both had retreated from their long-standing policies of protecting and enforcing honor. Without vigorous ecclesiastical and royal assistance in both enforcing promises and protecting reputations for honor, couples lost a powerful means for compelling parents to accept their marriage partners.

The first dimension of honor that figured in the church's policy of protecting couples was the ideal of protecting feminine sexual honor. Seventeenth-century church officials were eager to marry couples secretly to shield women and their families from the disgrace of public disclosure of the loss of virginity before marriage. In the final years of the seventeenth century, however, a change in the marital practices of non-Spaniards may have contributed to an increasing perception by status-conscious Spaniards of a need to alter their adherence to the protection of feminine sexual virtue.

The Spanish society that laid such stress on the importance of sexual honor believed profoundly that "honorable" conduct was the exclusive preserve of the upper levels of society. Honor was available to everyone within that upper level without regard to income or status, and it was the characteristic that distinguished them from the racially mixed population. In Spain, the possession of honor distinguished the nobility from the peasants and tribute payers; in the New World, having honor was the ideological key to separating Spaniards from the Indians and slaves. The special protection afforded the reputation of Spanish women (and their families) in colonial New Spain maintained the boundary between Spaniards and non-Spaniards—this despite a Spanish illegitimacy rate that was vastly higher than among continental Europeans.

Social convention from the time of the Conquest had permitted Spanish men to have nonmarital liaisons with darker women, despite the periodic protests of priests or reform-minded royal officials. Slaves often found it difficult to contract marriages, so the children of black women were frequently born out of wedlock. As a result, marriage was comparatively less frequent and the disgrace of public illegitimacy was more common among black and casta women than among Spanish women. Perhaps more importantly, it was normatively believed that pregnancy outside of marriage was the province of black and casta women, while it was similarly believed that virginity was the rule among Spanish women.

But in the late seventeenth century the incidence of marriage among black and casta women rose sharply, so that it approximated the frequency of marriage among Spanish women. What had always been true of Spanish women—relatively high marriage rates and relatively low levels of illegitimacy—began to be true of casta women as well.[1] The process tended to break down the perceived differences of behavior among the races that adherence to the code of honor had implicitly depended upon. The decline of one of the principal rationales for granting special protection to Spanish women's reputations—the link between racial superiority and adherence to a code of honor—may have also contributed to diminishing the salience of the whole complex of attitudes and beliefs about honor among Spaniards in the New World, which was founded upon the related ideals of virtuous women and appropriate behavior in men.

The increasing doubts about the wisdom of protecting Spanish women's reputations were manifested in a shift in the division of labor between church and state. In the 1670's and 1680's, royal officials were becoming increasingly passive and indifferent in response to church requests for assistance in prenuptial conflicts. By the 1690's this assistance was virtually halted except for symbolic gestures in urban areas and occasional use in rural communities. Royal officials thus withdrew one of the forms of support that historically had been available to the church when there had been a breach of honor.[2]

In 1690, church officials made their own response to the changing social significance of honorable sexual conduct by discontinuing the practice that had traditionally shielded Spanish women from public disclosure of their sexual activities and thus their loss of honor: granting secret marriages. Before 1690, two-thirds of all couples who faced family opposition had been protected by secret marriages. Nearly half of those marriages had involved some kind of prior sexual activity acknowledged by the parties. After 1690, secret marriage was available to protect the honor only of Spanish women at the very summit of the colonial elite.[3] For example, Doña Tomasa de Loro was described as the daughter "of honorable people of notable conduct and nobility." Her soon-to-be-apparent pregnancy would publicly proclaim her fall from honor, and her disgrace would be even greater if there was poorly timed premarital publicity. These facts were conveyed to church authorities in the language characteristic of the time: "If she were not to marry, disgrace, damage, scandal, and discredit would result because she will not be able to hide the signs of her fragility."[4] "Fragility" was the common term for having given in to the desires of the flesh, the word implying that control over the sexual impulse was "fragile" and thus easily broken. Given Tomasa's social standing and her pregnancy, church officials allowed her to marry without publicity.

To sustain secret marriages on a wide scale meant full confidence in the ideal of protecting Spanish women's honor. Restricting the availability of secret marriage to elite women suggests a more cynical view, that only the reputations of the elite deserved protection, even though the conduct of elite women was as suspect as that of their less well-to-do sisters. For the remainder of the colonial period secret marriage was largely reserved for influential families, and especially for those connected to the church.[5]

After 1690, most Spanish women who lost their honor found the glare of publicity shining on their unmarried state, since church officials no longer dispensed with the banns of marriage. Instead of having their transgressions covered up, Spanish women were forced to endure public knowledge of their activity. There was less charity toward peccadillos in the new approach, and more emphasis on punishment.

At the same time, however, church officials continued to adhere to their customary practices having to do with the other aspect of honor—promise keeping. Through the 1730's, the church was still insisting that men fulfill their promises to marry women they had seduced, and it persisted as well in ordering marriages against the wishes of parents, especially if the woman was pregnant.[6]

In a world that relied as much on verbal contracts as on written agreements, a spoken promise was a solemn commitment. To pledge one's word was tantamount to enactment. Failure to fulfill a promise risked a man's reputation, since his word and his honor were interchangeable. In the latter part of the seventeenth century, this link between the worth of a man and his word of honor became less reliable. Whereas in the early part of the seventeenth century suits over promises to marry and the invention of excuses were extremely rare, men who had promised to marry women now appeared in church courts to invent pretexts and excuses for their behavior.[7] Before 1670, men who sought to evade the promise to marry were strongly pressured by church authorities to marry, and usually then acknowledged their responsibility.[8] Such acknowledgments were to become increasingly infrequent in the decades that followed.

The first formal lawsuit over a promise to marry was heard in 1671. José, the son of a well-to-do Mexico City family had become engaged to Doña Teresa Trejo, the daughter of a town councilman, despite his parents' opposition. After a year had passed, Doña Teresa's mother asked the fiancé to fulfill his promise. Appearing before the church court judge, José said that he had set a year's limit on the promise to marry, and it had expired. (Hispanic custom traditionally had allowed the termination of engagements if a formal time limit had been set for their expiration.) However, it soon became apparent that this statement was only a pretext, since the José tried another tactic, suggesting this time that the supposedly expired engagement be extended for another three years. Remarking that José's statements were full of malice and prejudicial to a woman of considerable social standing, the judge ordered him arrested.[9] Rather than admitting that his parents were pressuring him to retract his promise, José devised a series of subterfuges, grounded in the language of canon law. This willingness to argue that some unstated condition had been attached to the promise marked the start of a fundamental change in men's attitudes toward promise keeping, a key element in the code of honor. Although not a direct assault on the position of the couple in prenuptial disputes, the declining reliability of marriage promises would have significant consequences for the couples involved. The institutions of social control, the church and the state, would eventually be persuaded that they could no longer depend upon the spoken promise in order to enforce the decision to marry.

Throughout the seventeenth century the obligation to carry out marriage promises had been enforced by both royal and ecclesiastical officials. The state imprisoned men and exiled them to the Philippines for failing to marry women they seduced under promise of marriage; if the man chose to marry rather than be exiled, the church stepped in to marry the pair. Royal officials were the first to respond to the declining sense of obligation associated with promise keeping. In the last third of the seventeenth century they lessened the punishment for seduction: three-year jail terms rather than lengthier exile became common. And whereas previously men were jailed indefinitely until they were sentenced or decided to marry, now they were sometimes released on bail for such an offense. Predictably, reducing the criminal penalties further hastened the decline in the importance of marital promises.[10]

The position adopted by the secular authorities elicited considerable sympathy among the clergy. By the last third of the seventeenth century, church officials had come to realize that marriages made under threat of exile were rarely successful. These men rarely remained with their spouses, and if they did, they were often the cause of major domestic disturbances. As royal officials lessened their penalties, the burden of upholding the code of honor fell increasingly to the Catholic Church.[11]

Ecclesiastical officials reasoned that making a less drastic alternative available would ensure that promises were fulfilled, but that men who were not truly interested in marriage would not be so ineluctably forced into it.[12] Church officials turned to a traditional ecclesiastical alternative and presented the man with a choice: either carry out his original promise to marry, or compensate the woman financially. Called a dowry, this money was intended to remedy the woman's loss of virginity by making her economically attractive and by compensating her for the expense of birth and child rearing. This less drastic alternative to marriage became increasingly common in the succeeding decades, and it had a lasting effect on the code of honor.

Once a fine—a mere financial consideration—began to replace the severity of marriage, exile, or imprisonment as the most common penalty in cases of broken promises, the degree to which men were held personally responsible for female virtue waned. The consequences of depriving a woman of her virginity no longer had to be endured mainly by the man in question himself; he could now call upon his family or friends to help him by giving financial assistance. In short, promises that had formerly been disregarded only at considerable personal cost could now be treated cavalierly, even cynically.

The promise to marry was also central to the church's rationale for intervention: historically such a promise (known as *sponsalia per verba de futura*) had been specially privileged in canon law, regarded as a sacred commitment that could be broken only under special circumstances. In enforcing marriage promises, church officials had relied upon both popular cultural attitudes about honor and the canonical tradition upholding the sanctity of such promises. As uncertainty grew about the trustworthiness of promises, more evidence was needed to prove the existence of a marital commitment. Consequently church officials first began to respond with greater caution to requests for assistance in protecting a woman's sexual honor.

Pressure on the church to conform to the increasing uncertainty regarding the existence of a promise eventually made itself felt. Then, in the late 1720's, church officials adopted the position that questions of honor should be settled between the parties rather than by the church. In the language of canon law this meant the church assumed such cases to be *de parte* or private suits, not *de oficio*, or actionable by the church in its official capacity.[13] This decision in itself had still further repercussions for attitudes toward keeping marriage promises.

On May 25, 1729, in the cold, dry region between two river basins just west of Mexico City, María González entered the ecclesiastical court in the town of Xalatlaco. María, the daughter of a poor but honorable man, was in love with the son of one of the town's wealthiest citizens, but José Antonio Bobadilla's father had spirited his son away to a mill in Malinalco, many miles to the south. From the mill José Antonio wrote María with desperate longing. "I am in prison because of you my dear. . . . I have a thousand desires to see you, and if you cannot come, write me to let me know how you are. . . . When I leave here I will marry you immediately and therefore let me know that you are my love." With his letter in hand, María entered the church court and asked that José Antonio fulfill his promise to marry her.

Young José Antonio was asked to appear before the priest of Malinalco and state his side of the story. Nearly a month passed before he made his appearance, and in the meantime his position had changed. Although he had sworn to María in writing that he would marry her even if his father locked him up for three years, before he appeared a second time he wrote her quite a different letter. The letter began somewhat more formally. "I hope that upon receiving this you are in good health. My lady, the promise [of marriage] I gave you was conditional upon my father's liking and if not [there will be no marriage]. You should obey the will of your parents as well.

. . . In these things the trust must reside with my father." He then warned her not to pursue the matter.

María proceeded nevertheless, convinced that he did love her and hopeful that the church court would help her overcome the father's opposition. When José Antonio finally appeared in church court in Malinalco, his statements were contradictory. At first he said he had never promised to marry María but had only had sex with her for three months. Then he said he had promised to marry her if she were a virgin, but added that she had not been a virgin when he met her. He produced three witnesses to swear that there had been no promise to marry. Another month passed, and two of the three witnesses began to have qualms of conscience. So they went together to the chief ecclesiastical judge in Mexico City and admitted they had lied. Two weeks later the third witness also recanted. Scenting victory, María's father asked the ecclesiastical judge in Mexico City to take charge of the case. The judge was willing, but María fell ill a fortnight later; the father realized that his interests would not be served by taking his sick daughter to the city. Fearing also that his simple country witnesses would be frightened by the city, the father asked that the case continue to be heard locally.[14]

The outcome of this case is unknown, but its prognosis was poor. Had it taken place in the seventeenth century, María could have entered a simple plea before the church court before her fiancé was spirited away: the court would almost certainly have called out the royal police, who might have been able to force the father to bring José Antonio to court earlier. Thus the boy's removal from the town, and the incarceration that changed his mind and his intention to marry, might have been prevented. But in the eighteenth century the father could not be stopped, so the burden fell on the injured party to remedy the effects of the removal. Once done, the damage proved exceedingly difficult to undo.

Because church officials no longer took the position that a marriage promise was a cause for official action, the initiative in this case came to reside with the woman to prove that a valid engagement had existed. Henceforth the aggrieved party bore the burden of having to prosecute the case against her despoiler. Furthermore, the woman or her father had to bear the cost of undertaking a suit in order to force the man to marry. Any economic disparity between the two families thus lowered her chance of success; not only was the promise to marry not fulfilled, but women of lesser economic means were effectively prevented from obtaining a remedy for their lost honor. As an indirect result of the church's adopting the position that suits over marriage promises were private, it became vastly easier for wealthy parents to prevent their sons or daughters from marrying because the party trying to marry had fewer economic resources.

In 1727, Matías Santa Cruz, nephew of the Augustinian curate of the town of Atotonilco el Grande, promised to marry María Patricia, the daughter of the local convent washerwoman. He then seduced her. Matías's mother, who lived in Meztitlán, wrote her brother-in-law, vehemently protesting the marriage and asking him to prevent it. The friar conveyed the message to María Patricia's mother, trying to bully her into dropping charges. María Patricia's mother refused to be intimidated. She took her case to the church judge in a neighboring town, but that priest told her he lacked jurisdiction in the case and suggested she write to the chief judge of the ecclesiastical court in Mexico City. When the vicar general of the archdiocese responded by asking her to bring her daughter to Mexico City, the mother replied sadly that she could not afford to do that. If that were the case, the vicar general replied, she would have to come to a private agreement with the boy's uncle. In other words, simply because she lacked the funds to pursue a case, a woman whose honor had been damaged was helpless. The church officials, who in former days would have ordered the matter heard locally by an impartial judge from a neighboring community, now ordered the girl to Mexico City and revealed their unwillingness to defend the cause of honor by insisting that the issue was a private matter.[15]

Wealthy parents gained a double advantage by the church's adoption of a passive role in the 1720's. Taking the initiative in requesting ecclesiastical intervention required a sophisticated knowledge of court procedure and requirements, knowledge that of course was rare among the poorer and less well educated. Consequently, the less privileged either did not bring suits, or entered them improperly, and thus saw them dismissed on procedural grounds. Even if the poorer person, like María Patricia's mother, learned what was needed to initiate a suit, it was likely that she would later have to drop it for lack of money. Wealthier families knew the appropriate procedures or could afford to hire experts, while the poor were left to fend for themselves.[16]

Families trying to force a man to accept responsibility for a promise to marry found that the church's passive role made their efforts vastly more difficult. Church law historically made it necessary to prove that there was significant reason why a man no longer wished to marry a certain woman, especially after the initiation of sexual relations. When church officials adopted the attitude that such matters were private affairs between the two parties, canonical requirements became less compelling and women and their families saw their ability to enforce the other side of the bargain diminish.[17]

When families backed by the power of church and state could force men into marrying women with whom they had had sexual relations, there was a certain fairness about the double standard. If a woman promised to marry and then lost her virginity, her breach of the code was founded on the reasonable expectation that she would marry. Reducing the use of threats of exile or imprisonment by the state left women far more vulnerable. The church's eventual abandonment of enforcing marriage promises *de oficio* left the woman who had broken the code essentially without ultimate recourse, and it deprived the man-woman relationship of a symmetry that had long characterized it. Transgressing the bounds of honor had been a grave matter for both sexes, but by the eighteenth century only the woman was likely to suffer.

Thus this second change, like the dropping of dispensation of banns in 1690, worked to the women's disadvantage. Eliminating secret marriages had exposed women to a greater likelihood of disgrace for premarital sexual activity, since the forthcoming marriage of an obviously pregnant woman would be announced from the pulpit of her church; turning the question of engagement into a purely private matter left women more responsible for sexual activity. Perhaps the most significant consequence, however, concerned the capacity of couples to use the code of honor to force their parents into accepting marriage partners they objected to. In the seventeenth century, ecclesiastical support for the protection of a woman's sexual honor had been an effective weapon in defeating the aims of parental authority. When church officials ceased to protect women from public disclosure of their premarital sexual activity, and when they ceased to enforce promises to marry *de oficio*, couples who wished to wed lost one of their most powerful weapons in combating opposition to their marriages.

Although the church's new attitude toward protecting sexual honor and enforcing marriage promises reflected the dominant trend in colonial society, the change in beliefs was far from universal. After 1730, young people who wished to marry despite parental objections continued to argue in ecclesiastical court that their obligations, contracted on the basis of lost virginity, should outweigh the demands of parents. Establishing the priority of protecting sexual honor, one lawyer argued in the classic tradition of seventeenth-century Mexican church law that if a man took a woman's honor under promise of marriage his Christian duty was to repair the damage he had done by marrying her: "It would be in the service of God and the noble Christian obligations Don Joaquín owes Doña Antonia to repair her honor." The church's principal work was not the maintenance of the social order but the "service of God and the eternal health of souls."[18] The only thing the church required for a valid marriage, this lawyer argued, was the will of the parties, for the essence of church doctrine on marriage was that "the church does not marry ranks, but unites wills." This same phrase recurred in the demands of other young women.[19] Another young man argued that the failure to marry after violating a woman's virginity under promise of marriage was a mortal sin, although his father considered the engagement null and void because it lacked parental consent.[20]

Many couples continued to argue that seduction of a woman and her loss of virginity were valid reasons for marriage despite family opposition, but the disappearance of the church's automatic support for their position had significant consequences. Increasingly the desires of parents to prevent a marriage took precedence over the protection of a woman's reputation for virtue and her family's honor. In this respect, the changing attitudes toward protecting sexual honor and toward enforcing marriage promises together constitute one of the major social transitions of the colonial period. In the sixteenth and seventeenth centuries the Catholic Church allowed men to carry out the pledges they had made to marry against the wishes of their parents. Attempts to impede the marriage, such as locking a son away, made parents subject to the full weight of both ecclesiastical sanctions and popular opposition. But there was no public outcry in 1729 when the father of José Antonio Bobadilla kidnapped his son and kept him away from the church courts because the boy had promised to marry a poor Spanish girl. The young men who lied to the court about their promises to marry may have been stricken with attacks of conscience, but there were no complaints about the immorality of the father's action. The right of José Antonio's father to deprive José of the opportunity to fulfill his obligation to redeem the girl's honor was never challenged and the young woman who was seduced and abandoned had to petition the church for fulfillment of the promise to marry, but with little hope of achieving her goal. If men could claim a higher aim than that of restoring a woman's reputation for honor—including the demands of parents, class, and status—then the priority of both protecting sexual honor and carrying out marriage promises had diminished considerably.

Some historians have argued that this change in attitudes toward keeping marriage promises, which occurred not only in Mexico but throughout Western Europe, can be attributed to the progressive impoverishment of large segments of the population: the ability of young men to carry through on their marital promises deteriorated because of a lack of means.[21] This argument may be sound for some countries, but there is no evidence to support it in colonial Mexico. The period between 1670 and 1730, when the dramatic shifts occurred in social attitudes and the church's responses to the loss of sexual honor, was one of steady improvement in the general economic status of the Mexican population who feature in the prenuptial conflict cases. The young men in these cases were the sons of well-to-do provincial merchants, miners, and landowners, a group whose general level of prosperity was rising throughout this period. The increasing uncertainty about the trustworthiness of marriage promises in colonial Mexico thus cannot be linked to increasing impecunity.[22]

Very clearly, this period between 1670 and 1730, when much of the traditional support for enforcing promises to marry and protecting women's sexual honor began to erode and couples seeking to force their parents to accept marriages lost one of their most powerful supports, also marked the beginning of a de facto increase in parents' control over marriages. But this early change occurred *without* the emergence of any explicit ideology of patriarchy or other formal articulation of a belief in the superiority of parents' rights. The first step toward a doctrine of normative patriarchy was thus simply the loss of the social consensus that provided crucial support for the position that the rights of couples took priority. The appearance of an explicit ideology of parental rights to control marriage choices of children was the outcome of another, related set of changes in long-standing cultural values.

CHAPTER 7

Changing Attitudes Toward Love and Will

Although the changing attitudes toward the enforcement of promises and protection of feminine sexual honor that oc-curred in the last third of the seventeenth century deprived couples of a powerful weapon in opposing parental interference, they did not immediately have the effect of providing normative support, popular or institutional, for parental control of marriage choices. Until the early years of the eighteenth century, a belief in the necessity of exercising individual will in marriage, the positive regard for love as an expression of the rational will, and antipathy to marriages motivated by gain still supported the conviction that parental interference in marriages was often malicious and unjust.

Between approximately 1700 and 1750, however, cultural atti-tudes toward will and love were altered by the same pressures that had curtailed protection of women's sexual honor. The increasing reluctance of men and later of women to honor their promises to marry led not only to doubts about the wisdom of ecclesiastical in-tervention but also to a questioning of the firmness of individual will behind the promises. As couples increasingly came to vacillate, recant their original promises, and shift responsibility or blame for marital choices to third parties, skepticism about the steadfastness of will grew. Attitudes toward love were affected, since love had been understood as the cultural expression of a settled will. As a result, parents began to argue that love and will were unstable emotions, unreliable guides for the choice of a spouse. Like the increasingly punitive attitudes toward women's transgressions of sexual honor, challenges to cultural assumptions about love and will further undermined the position of couples. Even more, the growing mistrust of love and will provided the impetus for an explicit and normative discourse about parental authority that indeed began to appear in prenuptial conflict records around the middle of the eighteenth century.

Until then, respect for individual will had been one of the basic reasons why social institutions had favored couples in conflict with their families over the choice of a marriage partner. Seeking to counterbalance the Protestant emphasis on predestination, Catholic theologians had stressed the centrality of free will, including free will to marry, at the Council of Trent. Popular religious literature established that one's likes and preferences regarding a marriage partner were an indication of God's intentions, and that family members, especially parents, lacked the authority to counter God's will. The increasing dominance of Thomistic teaching at Spanish universities in the late sixteenth century reinforced the importance of this interpretation of will in Hispanic religious teaching.

The erosion of the cultural importance of individual will in marriage choice did not take place quickly or all at once in any sort of direct attack on religious doctrine or in any formal challenge to ecclesiastical teachings. The process was slow and circuitous, moving from certain misgivings about the steadfastness of marital intentions to a point where many in Spanish society began to doubt the ability of couples to make marriage choices based on their own intentions.

The source of this skepticism was the growing suspicion about the sincerity and stability of the intentions that had prompted marriage promises in the first place. These changes can be seen in the responses of men who changed their minds after pledging to marry. In the late sixteenth and early seventeenth centuries, when men wished to refuse to carry out their promises to marry, they were more readily prevailed upon to fulfill the obligations of their conscience. In the period between 1670 and 1700, when men began to feel themselves less bound than formerly by promises to marry, although they still acknowledged their original pledges, they followed the tortuous reasoning of canon law to justify breaking their word. As the gravity of the consequences for violating promises declined, a new and radically different set of attitudes toward the marriage promise began to emerge. In the first years of the eighteenth century, young men began to invent what ecclesiastical officials of the period would refer to as "clear injustice and vain pretexts . . . for violating a woman's honor and leaving her ridiculed." These "vain pretexts" were invoked with increasing regularity as the century progressed, until eventually they undermined both the religious and the cultural underpinnings of promise keeping.[1]

The growing tendency to treat marriage promises lightly intensified the propensity of young men (and later young women) to invent trivial excuses to avoid fulfilling their obligations. One of the first such "vain pretexts" to be invoked was the argument of immaturity. An early instance of this occurred in 1702, when an eighteen-year-old Spaniard became involved with a woman six years older than he and then attempted to dissolve the relationship between them on the grounds that he "was of such young years that he did not know what he was doing" when he promised to marry her.[2]

An even more frequently used excuse was that a disturbed mental state prevented knowledge of what one was doing. In 1704, Juana Josefa Artiaga Velasco, a seventeen-year-old orphaned Spanish girl in Mexico City, fell in love with and became engaged to Francisco Núñez Merio. Juana Josefa's uncle, perhaps hoping to hold on to the inheritance which he controlled as her guardian, opposed the marriage. Francisco took the matter to the church court judge, who ordered Juana Josefa to appear before him and let her wishes be known. Intimidated into renouncing her intent to marry, Juana Josefa attempted to deny her responsibility for the written promise of marriage she had given Francisco. She told the church court judge that she had written the promise to marry in a fit of anger at her relatives and had not known what she was doing when she said she wanted to marry Francisco. Behind her disavowal probably lay pressure from her uncle, who may have suggested that she make a statement alleging that her anger had resulted from a disturbed mental state. In this case, Juana Josefa, freed from the uncle's vigilance during two weeks in temporary custody, acknowledged the promise she had made Francisco, and the pair were married.[3]

Another young woman, this one genuinely wishing to deny the responsibility for having signed the promise to marry, told the church court that she had only agreed to marry in order to get rid of her fiancé and that he had forced her into it. Outraged by her remarks, the man wrote, "Never have I importuned a woman with force, since I would only live with loathing with her." Her lack of consideration for his honor left him unwilling to continue his efforts to marry her, and the engagement was dissolved.[4]

These attempts to downplay the import of promises to marry involved a fundamental challenge to church law. In the sixteenth and seventeenth centuries, the strict canon law guidelines for breaking an engagement had reinforced the solemnity of the marriage promises. Canon law permitted unilateral termination of an engagement under certain grave circumstances—if the existence of a diriment impediment could be proved, for example, or if a profound change had taken place in the person one had promised to marry, whether from leprosy, loss of a limb, a drastic reversal in economic standing, or similar causes. Allegations of immaturity or anger trivialized the original ecclesiastical concept. When they were invoked, the gravity of the promise was compromised, as was the ecclesiastical commitment to protect and enforce such promises in the face of parental opposition.

The increasing fickleness of young people promising to marry thus greatly undermined their position in prenuptial conflicts. The causes of this appear to be a declining sense of obligation associated with marriage promises, which had been firmly linked to traditional ideas about honor. The bonds of moral obligation created by promises appeared to be less strongly felt, and consequently couples became increasingly more willing to rescind promises under pressure. At the same time, the increase in instability of marital intentions was grist for parents seeking to legitimize their intervention in conflicts over the choice of a spouse.

All the pretexts invoked by young people to escape their marriage promises—disturbed mental state, youth, ignorance—undermined the idea that one was responsible for one's own behavior.[5] These pretexts provided the opportunity for parents, relatives, or employers to argue directly that children wishing to marry were indeed not responsible for their own actions. This provided a basis for the challenge to young people's autonomy that parents were to mount. Seizing the initiative, parents began to invoke their own derogatory pretexts of "imbecility" and "immaturity," thus laying the groundwork for subsequent claims that they were justified in disregarding the independent wishes and desires of their offspring and wards.

In some instances the reasoning became exceedingly tortured, as parents argued that they had better understanding of the interior mental states of their offspring than the offspring had themselves. The goddaughter of the Marquis of Prado Alegre, herself from a humble family but one that was an important client of the Marquis, became engaged to a military cadet. His wealthy father was firmly opposed to the match and argued that the son's written promise to marry was only an external indicator that gave no insight into the boy's state of mind at the time it was made. He even introduced a tender love note in which the young cadet expressed his desire to be alone with his beloved as evidence that the boy wanted to see her in order to rescind his promise to marry. The note, however, showed great enthusiasm for carrying out the intent to marry, and bore the solemnity of a sworn statement. In rebuttal, the Marquis pointed out that if the argument for mental reservations was upheld then no promise was worth anything, since one could always argue post hoc that one had had a mental reservation. Eventually the young cadet's father was forced to pay the princely sum of 700 pesos to the Marquis for breaking the promise.[6] But arguments like the wealthy father's would not have been made a hundred years before. Underlying them was the conviction that one was no longer wholly responsible for one's own actions, a conviction that justified the assumption of responsibility by parents.

First evident early in the eighteenth century, this trend to parental claims of irresponsibility in the will of their child became stronger during the latter half of the century, and the range of arguments for intervention became greater.[7] Elaborate excuses that would sound familiar to modern ears appeared, such as the argument that a child would not have acted in a certain way on his or her own accord, but rather was following the wishes of the fiancé(e). The father of a twenty-six-year-old woman in Pachuca asserted that his daughter could not have written and signed the promise of marriage that had been produced in ecclesiastical court with her signature affixed. "It is so well written, so well put, so well detailed that she has me persuaded and believing that it is not of her own ability or her skills. She is a girl raised without worldly concerns, and with the education, candor, and Christian and civil breeding that this flagrant effort lacks. She is not versed in these matters and knows neither the formula, style, nor response that grace the promise to marry. Therefore she could only have written it in such language if she were seduced by a person or fellow of sufficient instruction who being interested in the marriage ordered it written so that she might copy it."[8]

A variation of this argument was used by wealthy families when parents shifted the blame to servants who acted as their mistresses' willing accomplices in arranging meetings with young men. Blaming the go-betweens was an established practice in Spain exemplified by the destructive machinations of that interfering old woman, *la Celestina*.[9] Similar stereotyping of go-betweens emerged in the prenuptial conflicts of eighteenth-century Mexico. In 1728 the father of Doña María Castillo Altamirano said that his daughter, "persuaded by two black women, my slaves, gave a promise to marry Nicolas Sánchez. With this frivolous pretext [Sánchez] has transgressed and offended the decorum owed to my house and credit. It is not my daughter's wish to marry, nor does she have such intent nor could she even have imagined it. [She] could only have written those papers [the romantic correspondence that passed between them] influenced by the aforementioned blacks, my slaves." The father assumed that he had greater knowledge of his daughter's intentions than she did, saying that it was neither her wish to marry "nor could she even have imagined it."[10] His language was typical of the period: he assumed the authority to speak for his child, but did not insist that his own will was superior to hers—a step parents would take later in the century. The young woman had in fact written the letters voluntarily; only when confronted with her father's hostility did she offer the hapless servants as scapegoats. The ease with which the servants, who after all had only served their mistress loyally in this instance, were abandoned and prosecuted demonstrates the callous disregard of the wealthy for their servants; and her family's willingness to sacrifice those most readily available was quite typical.[11] The practice of blaming third parties lessened the sense of individual responsibility and supported the parent's argument that a child's declaration of individual will was no longer a reliable factor in choosing a spouse.

While the increasing vacillation of couples promising to marry greatly undermined the general position of couples in prenuptial conflicts, parental challenges to the stability of marital intentions were not always a result of fickleness, insincerity, or third-party machinations. An example is the case of seventeen-year-old Manuela Gómez del Pinal, the daughter of a wealthy Mexico City merchant who owned a string of small shops. Manuela's boyfriend, Augustín Gómez, was a twenty-six-year-old apprentice merchant, as yet without capital or shops. Manuela's parents opposed the marriage because he was not already established, and they, of course, were not about to help out. When the pair decided to marry despite her parents' continued opposition, Manuela ratified her intentions before church officials and was placed in temporary custody. Because she continued to affirm her intent to marry, her father charged that her will had been unduly influenced and that she lacked sufficient freedom to state her true intentions. He therefore demanded that she be moved to another house. Unable to convince the church court to remove her, he set about depriving his daughter of emotional support. First, he alleged that a servant who had been with her since she lived at home was also exercising undue influence over her, and he managed to persuade the church to force her to dismiss the servant. The couple with whom Manuela was staying were sympathetic to her marriage, and this greatly annoyed her father. He complained again to church authorities that her custodians were exercising undue influence; anyone who did not agree with him clearly exercised "undue" influence. After two months had passed, Manuela made the mistake of having Augustín come visit her for a half-hour one evening. Her father was having the house watched, hoping for exactly such a violation of the custody arrangement. He was finally able to have Manuela transferred to a thoroughly unsympathetic custodian. Prevented from any contact with Augustín by her new custodians and succumbing to her mother's blandishments, where she had always resisted her father's, after another four months with the custodian Manuela changed her mind and said she no longer wished to marry.

Naturally at this point her father declared that at last she was indeed in a place in which her will was sufficiently free and he demanded an end to the case. Now Augustín began to complain of exactly what the father had complained of earlier—that she lacked liberty and was subject to undue influence. Her father, it seemed, had been able to get messages in and out of the house where she was staying (in violation of custody requirements) and had even managed to have smuggled in a list of the responses she was to give church authorities when they questioned her about the engagement. After another three months, Manuela was transferred to yet a third custodian, in whose residence she repeated her refusal to marry.

The story might have been interminable, except for the sudden serious illness of Manuela's mother. With the death of the parent who had spent the last months of her life trying to persuade Manuela not to marry, the prospects for marriage to Augustín were nil. After two months of mourning, Manuela was placed back in custody, only to reiterate her wish not to marry Augustín. It was undoubtedly hard for Augustín, who had truly loved Manuela and who had seen abundant evidence of her love for him, to accept the evidence that she had been persuaded not to marry. He held out as long as he could but finally accepted his defeat and the year-long suit came to an end.[12] Accusations of unstable intentions thus became self-fulfilling prophecies. Once having achieved the desired change of mind, parents had the necessary proof that will or intention was unstable. This in turn allowed them to question the basis in religious doctrine upon which the church support of children's choices rested.

At the core of this was a debate over the firmness of will as charges by both sides mounted that the other was subjecting the parties to undue influence. In many instances, parents argued that their offspring's will was manipulated by the intended spouse, or by third parties.[13] This was a charge that the couples readily threw back at parents, other relatives, and guardians, for they could always allege that they had seduced (led astray) or exercised undue influence over the will of their intended.[14] The attorney in one lawsuit accused a young woman of "imbecility, ignorance, or an inability to determine what her will was" when she refused to change her mind to suit her father.[15] Both sides were cognizant of the growing susceptibility to influence of individual intentions. This contributed to the perception that such motives were becoming an increasingly uncertain means of anticipating human behavior. The reliability of stable intentions or will to marry, upon which the code of honor depended, was weakening.

The different rationales parents used to assume responsibility for marriage choices—blaming third parties, arguing that young people were unable to know their own minds—were often efforts to counter freely assumed and steadfastly maintained commitments.

The consequence of this would be an increasingly difficult position for couples, since parental demands for control sometimes were placed squarely at odds with the requirements of individual conscience.

One of the tenets of the argument for personal choice of a marriage partner was the idea that one was ultimately responsible for one's own salvation. Therefore one was accountable for all one's actions, including the choice of a mate. Even though the fundamental ethic of individual responsibility for salvation persisted, the changes that took place early in the eighteenth century allowed parents to challenge the idea that the demands of individual conscience on the part of dependent children had a priority over the family's (the parents') social, economic, or political ambitions.

Young people who were serious about their obligations thus found themselves in a difficult situation. Should they heed the moral promptings of their own conscience or the social importunings of their parents? When one young man told his confessor that his father had threatened to prevent his marriage by sending him off to prison, the confessor couched his response in terms of the traditional Catholic ethic: How, he asked the young man, was his father going to get him out of hell, which was where he was going if he failed to marry the young woman?[16] The old morality persisted, but it was increasingly countered by parents arguing that their offspring suffered from some form of unstable will.

Belief in the soundness of will had been critical to the positive valuation of love in seventeenth-century Mexican society. Ecclesiastical and secular authors saw the act of loving someone able to marry as an exercise of individual choice. As faith in the stability of will was challenged, so also were attitudes about the soundness of love undermined, for the two were profoundly linked. The fickleness of will in the context of youthful passion in courtship and marriage tainted the respect that adults and social institutions like the church had formerly granted will's emotional expression as love. This shift was registered in emerging usages of language that associated youthful marital intentions with unstable emotional states arising from sexual desire.[17]

The shift in emphasis began roughly in the middle of the eighteenth century. Instead of a profoundly enriching emotion that reflected a stable will, love was now described in the complaints of parents who opposed their children's marriages as an overmastering feeling that needed to be controlled, disciplined, and subjected to other more rational forces. In turn, marriage for love was less often celebrated for its stability—as Lope de Vega expressed it, "The greatest good that comes to be / . . . in being always in love / a man of his wife"—than criticized for its capriciousness.

The attack on the capriciousness of love, founded on the growing skepticism about the firmness of will, focused on the need to restrain love. In one instance the notary recorded the language he had used to warn a young woman of the consequences of her action. Urging her to reconsider, he said, "It is not bad to think over the decision with more time and prudence . . . the states [of marriage and celibacy] have as their goal not losing sight of God. With [your] eyes, which are presently closed by willfulness, immaturity, and inexperience, open to reason, such inequality tomorrow or some other day could [lead you to] repent [of the marriage] and . . . commit absurd actions that result in offenses to God and the loss of your soul." The emotions prompting her to marry were thus portrayed as the outcome not of legitimate will, but of "willfulness." The potential for inconsistency and capriciousness is denoted by "immaturity" and "inexperience," as well as by the suggestion that she will later repent of her action: emotions, therefore, are an unreliable basis for marriage and the decision to marry should be subjected to the operations of "prudence" and "reason." In this instance the young woman firmly replied that she knew what she was doing, and that she wanted to marry the young man.[18] Love, which Aquinas had defined as compatible with reason, was now wholly opposed to it.

One father used classic late eighteenth century terms to establish the unreliability of his daughter's thinking: she was guided in her desire to marry by "a passion that was not influenced by the rational liberty of human understanding."[19] The emotional attachment of love was a passion to which one was subjected and to which one lost control. These remarks suggested that the influence of "rational liberty" would produce a different outcome, and implied that love, at least in this parent's opinion, was an unreliable guide to conduct.

The courage to persist in a love relationship was similarly denounced. A relative in one case noted that despite efforts at persuasion by persons of "character, distinction, and Christian virtues, nothing had sufficed to undo the idea formed between these two young people who are possessed by the evil passion of love."[20] In the sixteenth and seventeenth centuries love that sought legitimate marriage was rarely characterized as an evil passion. In the earlier period, the persistence of this couple in their efforts to marry would have been evidence of the stability of their will and the legitimacy of their claim to be married. But in this case (in 1788), because their wills were constant, the attack on their intentions had to focus on the emotion of love, now characterized as "an evil passion."

The second dimension of the attack on the instability of love associated the intention to marry with an emotional drive long criticized in Hispanic society, that of sexual desire. The use of the phrase "attachment and will" or "liking" rather than the word *amor* to describe a couple's feelings for each other, typical throughout the sixteenth and seventeenth centuries, had clearly established the presence of both an emotional bond and a voluntary choice, and it had reflected the reluctance to use any term that at all implied sex as a motive for marriage. The plural form of *amor*—*amores*—means sexual lust. Up until the early eighteenth century, the language of couples still reflected the conviction that the worthy motives for marrying were "attachment" and "will."[21]

The advent of the word *amor* in prenuptial conflict cases replaced the semantic void left by the eroding notion that love primarily expressed will. Sexual passion is not the result of an act of will, and often does not respond readily to efforts at control; it arises from deep and poorly understood wellsprings of emotion. As couples increasingly used *amor* to describe what had been called attachment or will, the connotations of uncontrollable sexual passion were brought to bear on the concept of love.[22] As this semantic drift continued, "love" was increasingly characterized not as evidence of a rational choice but as the embodiment of emotional capriciousness.[23]

Hispanic authors, religious and secular, had always insisted that marital love involved more than strictly sexual passion. With the increasing emphasis on the sexual dimension of love, one aspect of love came to signify the whole. The understanding of love as primarily desire, if not lust, became more and more apparent in the prenuptial conflicts: one parent maintained that "a bond as close as matrimony [should not be] held to in misery because of an incautious proceeding or for the lack of caution or the effect of a lascivious juvenile appetite."[24] Another father who did not wish to see his daughter marry declared that "it was not a just inclination but a violent passion that dominated." The violent passion he referred to was evidence that the couple had engaged in sexual relations.[25]

Several historians have suggested that the growing use of the word *amor* in the late eighteenth century indicates a development of marriage for love, but the evidence actually points to the contrary.[26] *Amor* still had connotations of lust, and its increasing usage to refer to the emotional attachment between members of the opposite sex in fact indicated the decreasing value and respect in which such attachments were held. Through the first two hundred years of colonial Mexican history, couples, neighbors, and family members had sought the support of church courts to protect marriages for love. When the emphasis in concept shifted from love as an expression of individual will to love as an emotion that precluded rational choice, this support diminished and eventually all but disappeared.

Thus parents could allege that children were incapable of making decisions on their own because they were in the grip of an inherently unstable emotion.[27] A mother argued against marrying couples in love by saying, "It was necessary to guard against the imbecility of children's judgment that precipitates them into striking bonds that have an unhappy end, will bring an unfortunate life, full of bitterness that will perhaps end in eternal perdition."[28] Her son's judgment emanated not from will but from a condition of "imbecility." The transience of his marital intentions was stressed by repeated references to future possibilities rather than present realities—"unhappy end," "unfortunate life," and, worst of all, "eternal perdition." A mother argued in the same vein that fatal consequences could be expected if children made their own marriage choices.[29] By focusing on potential future actions or changes in intention, parents thus laid the groundwork for asserting that their wishes—which they implicitly but no less arbitrarily linked to eventual positive outcomes—should prevail over individual will as expressed in children's present emotional states.

One father even openly argued that his authority was more important than his son's freedom to make choices. He wrote, "The [canon law] literature . . . [states] that children should neither aggrieve nor offend the decorum of parents and this obligation comes from natural law and is preferable to that which the child might have for his or her liberty."[30] In other words, according to this father, individual liberty (a necessary condition for the exercise of free will) was no longer the paramount consideration in marriage choice; the obligation "to neither aggrieve nor offend" parents had replaced it.

Asserting the superiority of the obligation not to offend parents made it possible to ignore the fact that parents and children did not necessarily have the same preferences and desires. The seventeenth century had implicitly recognized that the desire of a son—redeeming a woman's honor—was not identical with that of a parent or guardian, who might only want to hold on to an inheritance. The very existence of prenuptial conflicts gave the lie to the idea that the wills of parents and children were identical. When in the eighteenth century parents began to argue that they had a right to speak for their children, they were asserting an identity of aims between parent and child that the children vociferously contested. This argument denied the validity of children's separate aims and individual wills in marriage choices, a notion that had been fundamental to marriage in Spanish colonial society during the sixteenth and seventeenth centuries.

Young people continued to assert that reasoned will was the significant factor in their marriage choices. When the orphaned daughter of a constable tried to marry a military officer, she was kidnapped and locked away. She nevertheless persisted in her desire to marry, insisting, "Will is the only thing that marriage requires."[31] Another young Spanish woman, facing opposition to her marriage, answered the judge in the traditional words of the church: "The Church does not marry statuses but unites wills."[32]

In order to justify their authority over marriage choices, parents and guardians needed to assert that their own convictions and ambitions were superior. The pretexts young people used to escape from engagements—that anger or immaturity temporarily prevented them from knowing what they were doing—not only gave parents a justification for intervening and exercising their authority, but took the argument for parental authority a step further: they contributed to the perception that individual free will manifested in love was becoming an increasingly unreliable means of ordering human behavior, specifically marriage choices.

The reevaluation of marriage for love in the eighteenth century originated with a decline in the sense of obligation to keep promises to marry that appeared in the final decades of the seventeenth century as first young men and then young women increasingly began to use "vain pretexts" in order to break their engagements. Their arguments were extensions of the canon law tradition that allowed nullification of promises made under threats to life and honor, but they trivialized the church's intention. Individual responsibility for the promise to marry, and indeed to love, was further evaded by placing the blame on third parties, particularly servants and intermediaries.

The earlier stability of couples' marital intentions had been reinforced by the code of honor and Catholic doctrine on the gravity of marriage promises. The declining sense of obligation regarding marriage promises shook the foundation of honor upon which rested the defense of couples by church and community. As marital commitments were more frequently altered, eroding their reliability, parents began to look for a more stable motive for marriage. They used such words as "prudence," "calculation," and even the traditional controller of passions, "reason." Cognizant of the growing susceptibility to influence of individual intentions, parents turned to a motive that historically had been spurned by Hispanic society but was gaining legitimacy in the eighteenth century: interest.

CHAPTER 8

Interest and Patriarchy

From the seventeenth to the eighteenth centuries attitudes toward two basic human appetites were challenged in colonial Mexico. Whereas in the seventeenth century marrying for love, as an expression of personal will, was widely esteemed, in the eighteenth century parents began to argue successfully against the legitimacy of such a motive for marriage. And whereas in the seventeenth century the calculated pursuit of money and status—interest—was generally frowned upon as a reason for preventing marriage, in the eighteenth century some parents began to question the idea that interest was a malicious or unjust consideration. What was occurring was a shift in cultural attitudes toward the motives involved in the decision to marry. In seventeenth-century prenuptial conflicts parents were seen as prisoners in the grip of uncontrollable greed; in the eighteenth, parents began to argue that children were victims of passion, of lust masquerading as love. Behind this shift lay not only an increasing skepticism about love as an elevated sentiment, but also a greater respect for the motive of self-interest in the form of self-aggrandizement and gain. Increasingly, "interest" was regarded not as a demeaning passion but as a sensible motivation for everyone. The change was directly related to the increasing involvement of New Spain's merchants, miners, and bureaucrats in a world market, which aroused in them attitudes toward money and interest that were new to Hispanic culture.

As a result of these parallel shifts in the cultural evaluation of love and interest, two changes occurred in the prenuptial conflicts. In the past, parents had often tried to prevent marriages for their own interests, but widely accepted cultural values and the institutions of social control had thwarted them. Now, public opinion and social institutions sometimes furthered their aims. Second, because seeking economic advantage had gained a degree of cultural legitimacy, parents—especially fathers, who were more closely concerned with economic matters in the family—developed a new line of explicit justification for greater control over the marriages of their children.

In *The Prince* (1532) Machiavelli recommended rationality and calculated interest as proper conduct for rulers of states. The word interest soon came to apply to any rational calculations generally manifested in human affairs and a disciplined seeking after power or economic gain. When the concept came into general use in Western Europe in the late sixteenth century it implied an element of calculation in the pursuit of human goals. In the seventeenth century, the concept became constricted to mean specifically the calculated pursuit of only economic ends or material benefit. Both connotations—the element of calculation and the idea of financial gain—persisted in Spanish culture well into the late eighteenth century.[1]

Traditional Catholic morality had, of course, always condemned self-seeking, particularly for economic ends, as an offense against religious law, associated with the deadly sin of covetousness. Even when the riches of New Spain made possible a degree of social mobility unthinkable in Old Spain, the traditional Spanish cultural values condemning greed and the pursuit of gain or status continued to prevail. In both societies, motives of gain were rarely acknowledged, and the moral superiority of the critiques of interest gave legitimacy to a wide range of cultural critics, from Bartolomé de las Casas's attack on treatment of New World Indians to Miguel de Cervantes's commentary on Old World Spanish conduct. Las Casas attributed the high mortality rates among New World Indians to exploitation by greedy Spaniards. Decrying the prevalence of interest among his contemporaries, Cervantes in *Don Quixote* painted a portrait of a glorious past in which gold was not so much admired as it was in his own day and in which nature offered anyone a fertile harvest without any "interest" whatsoever.[2] In sixteenth- and seventeenth-century Hispanic thought, the pursuit of economic goals was regarded as a passion devoid of redeeming merit.

Elsewhere in Europe in this period, interest was regarded far more favorably. From the time of the Greeks, human aspirations for economic gain had been looked upon as passions that needed to be constrained by reason,[3] but in the seventeenth century, as merchant capitalism began to develop in Western Europe, this notion was profoundly changed by new philosophical inquiries. Both Francis Bacon (1561–1626) and Spinoza (1632–1677), reanalyzing the concept of gain, proposed that the pursuit of gain—that is, interest—based on calculation could be a means of controlling the passions. As a result of their thinking, the pursuit of economic goals was transformed into a positive way of dealing with human emotions. Calculation became a desirable human characteristic, and acquisitiveness a means to achieve order, peace, and predictability in human society. These ideas were fundamental to the concept of *Homo economicus*, the rational economic man, who in submitting himself to the new market environment based all his decisions on a careful weighing of how much he stood to gain or lose financially. The philosophical assumption that decisions should be so made underlay the economic models of the so-called "free" market. The reinterpretation of philosophical tradition along with the emergence of a new economic order in Western Europe in the seventeenth and eighteenth centuries resulted in a concept of interest as confidence in the free play of private interest which would result in predictability in human behavior and public good.[4]

This new Western European regard for self-interest and gain did not find a positive reception in Spain until that country began its own period of mercantile capitalism in the eighteenth century. New industries sprouted—silk manufacturing in Valencia, ironworking in the Basque province, cotton and muslin cloth production in Barcelona—and restrictions on their development were removed by the state in an effort to enhance Spain's position in the economic competition among states.[5] In eighteenth-century Spain, as elsewhere in Western Europe, entrepreneurship was furthered by the state's adoption of mercantilist policies.

The purpose of mercantilism was to unify a nation's economy in order to provide the state with greater resources vis-à-vis other states. It put great emphasis on the expansion of exports and on the creation of a surplus of exports over imports. In Spain, in keeping with the tradition that wealth consisted in holding precious metals, mercantilism had to be accompanied by a steady inflow of bullion from abroad, since performance in trade and the supply of bullion were regarded as the key indexes of economic strength.[6] Spain's economic relationship to her colonies had always been marked to some extent by mercantilist practices, but until the eighteenth century and the renaissance of mercantilism, the effect had been relatively insignificant.[7] The revitalized mercantilist assumptions reshaped the eighteenth-century relationship between Spain and New Spain, which was one of the mother country's two principal sources of silver bullion. Government incentives for mining were increased; mining production itself grew rapidly in New Spain in the eighteenth century. On the export side, Spanish manufacturers began to look to the potentially lucrative New World markets as buyers for Spanish goods.

The renascent mercantilism and the development of business organization and practices associated with it brought attitudes toward money and interest that were new to Hispanic culture.[8] These ideas were widely influential among the Spanish political and intellectual elite; royal ministers, such as the Count of Campomanes, identified the common good with economic prosperity, and argued for the encouragement of economic endeavors and the entrepreneurial spirit.[9] Spanish writers of the eighteenth century increasingly questioned the traditional prejudice against commerce. The new mercantilist and merchant capitalist thinking challenged traditional religious and moral attitudes toward gain and the social prestige of entrepreneurship.

The ideal of nobility, emphasizing honor as the pinnacle of virtue, and church doctrine had been the major bastions discouraging commercial pursuits in Spain. Both changed with the renaissance of mercantilism, the former dramatically, the latter much more subtly and reluctantly. The idea of honor as virtue had held commercial enterprise to be incompatible with noble status. Conservative theorists in the past had conceded that a nobleman could engage in wholesale commerce, but they presumed that such activities would be exceptional. In the eighteenth century, however, the considerable intellectual support for commercial activity that developed among the nobility was validated by royal legislation which affirmed the right of noblemen who became entrepreneurs or who invested in commercial enterprises to retain their customary privileges. The crown also granted both honorific positions and occasionally even titles to manufacturers, since such activities were seen as contributions to the economic progress of the kingdom.[10]

By the middle of the eighteenth century, a large body of Spanish literature had appeared that depicted economic activity as worthy. After 1750, several secular writers argued that men might seek to make life happy and agreeable through money, and were more inclined to admit the benefits of material possessions. Some even advocated luxury, arguing that the spending it occasioned supported artisans.[11]

These novel ideas attracted their share of opposition, particularly from the clergy, who historically had been the most vocal in denigrating motives of gain. Most clerics defended traditional morality and argued that the search for wealth was a selfish and therefore sinful pursuit of pleasure. Clerical resentment grew toward ideas that "seemed to exalt the role of the state in economic matters above theological and moral considerations."[12]

Commerce, self-interest, greed, avarice, covetousness—all these were related moral offenses. The popular preacher Pedro de Calatayud, denouncing avarice, published an attack on usurial practices that underwent five printings between 1737 and 1800. But such attitudes were by no means universal, since some authors of spiritual guides tolerated a discreet search for material satisfaction. The clergy thus found itself divided between a majority who condemned acquisitiveness as one of the seven deadly sins, and a few who were willing to tolerate less rigid standards.[13]

Spanish mercantilist practices reshaped New Spain's economic structure in the eighteenth century. By 1789, the value and volume of colonial trade with Spain had risen noticeably. Spanish exports to the New World had increased significantly, and Mexico, the source of 66 percent of the world's silver, was supplying Spain with large quantities of bullion.[14] With the revitalized commerce came increasing numbers of Spanish merchants, many of whom openly advocated mercantilist ideals. By the late eighteenth century, large numbers of members of a Basque economic society known as "Friends of the Country," devoted to promoting the ideals of merchant capitalism, had settled in Mexico City. By 1773, the city was home to the largest overseas concentration of these advocates.[15]

While reinvigorated mercantilist ideas and practices of merchant capitalism redefined the relationship between Spain and her colo-

nies, many in New Spain had direct experience of a new economic
reality, the world market. From the early years of the eighteenth
century, British exporters based in Florida, Louisiana, and the Ca-
ribbean sold goods regularly to Spanish merchants through an elaborate but stable contraband network. Later in the century, Anglo-
Americans established significant commercial ties with local merchants and manufacturers. A sizable group of New World Hispanic
merchants thus learned the ways, and advantages, of an economic
system in which people could be relied upon to act according to
their interests—a system enjoying the predictability of "free"
trade.[16] Spanish mercantilists and free traders may have been at odds
during the second half of the eighteenth century, but they shared a
common belief in the utility of economic gain for private benefit
and public good.[17] Thus revitalized mercantilism and the direct experience of a "free" world market exerted a forcible pressure on the
traditional antipathy to "interest" in New World Hispanic society.

The same conditions, the mercantilist renaissance and growing
association with the world market system, molded the internal organization and values of families in the New World.[18] Distinct status
hierarchies openly based on wealth appeared, and as they took
shape, the practices of the most successful Hispanic families in Mexico served as models and set the fashion for others. And not surprisingly, the new legitimacy of the appetite for gain and the importance of calculation also affected ideas about the proper aims of
marriage and the role of parents in marriage choices.

Those economic and cultural changes in colonial society were
strikingly registered in the altered language of the participants in the
prenuptial conflict cases. Three features stand out: a new toleration
by church courts of parents' use of economic sanctions in opposing
their children's marriage choices; an increasingly general acknowledgment by some church officials, parents, and their allies that considerations of social status and economic self-interest should take
priority over love and attraction in choosing marriage partners; and
a novel legitimation of the role of parental authority in children's
marriages. The newly recognized parental authority was specifically
patriarchal authority. Fathers, who were responsible for the family's
financial well-being, saw their position in the changing economic
order reinforced in the matter of marriage, because authority over
purse strings became a legitimate reason for control.

The first of the major changes in social discourse accompanying the legitimation of interest was the church's toleration of economic sanctions. In the seventeenth century, couples as well as the members of the community who testified on their behalf condemned the use of economic sanctions as evidence of malicious interference in the choice of a marriage partner. Threats to disinherit were made and challenged as malicious in over 10 percent of the conflict cases between 1574 and 1689, and church officials uniformly granted those couples secret marriages to prevent such parental interference. In the eighteenth century, young men cynically seeking to rid themselves of matrimonial responsibilities argued that their parents' threats to impose monetary penalties were legitimate cause for terminating an engagement without fear of contradiction from church authorities or public opinion.

José Luis Ríos, the son of the wealthy constable of Querétaro, became engaged to a young Spanish woman of some social standing but no great wealth. After giving his solemn promise to marry her, he was allowed in her home, and even took up residence. His widowed mother, who was adamantly opposed to the match, called the young woman's mother a procuress because she had allowed her daughter to engage in carnal relations with the boy. To win José Luis over to her side, his mother threatened to withdraw the financial support he was receiving and to cut him out of the additional inheritance she had promised him. In sending his regrets to the young woman, José Luis cited this threat as a "serious and just" reason for breaking off the engagement. The young woman vigorously protested his argument, saying that such threats were not a valid reason for ending an engagement. Ultimately she was unable to compel him to marry her, and gave up her case.[19] Because of the change in attitudes toward the importance of money, church courts were willing to entertain the argument that such financial sanctions could affect a marriage.

The second changed feature of marriage conflict cases was the increasing acknowledgment of the priority of interest over love, which legitimated parental authority over the marriage of children. Under church law and Hispanic custom, the formal authority of parents in the sixteenth and seventeenth centuries had been limited to giving advice and counsel. In the words of one of the moral authorities of the period, parents might inform children of their own likes and dislikes, but they must not veto, threaten, or use coercion to prevent a marriage.

Choosing a marriage partner itself had been a matter in which young people were to be guided by their own inclinations and liking because it was believed that personal preferences were a direct sign from God of His plans for the person. Parents and guardians had neither the moral nor the personal authority to circumvent God's wishes. Yet because of the increased respectability of "interest" or calculated self-seeking, around the middle of the eighteenth century parents for the first time in New Spain's history began to insist that they had a right to interfere in what had been seen as the manifestation of God's will. They began to insist that they were the final arbiters of their offspring's choice of a marriage partner and to demand a veto over marriages.

The new respectability of interest made it easy for parents to argue that they should have the power to decide, or at least veto, the choice of a marriage partner because they were both more responsible and more able to define a family member's long-range interests, whereas the children themselves in matters of marriage were likely to be controlled by less responsible, less stable emotions. Now that calculated self-seeking was being recognized as an appropriate motive for human conduct, parents could argue that they were not blinded by unstable emotions and could therefore make the calculations necessary for marriage decisions. The parent who argued against personal choice, citing "the imbecility of children's judgment," and warned that parents should "reflect on the engagement or marriage" and "think prudently" brought a novel emphasis to the subject.[20] The former language of marriage choice, "will," had emphasized the desires of the children; the new language, "judgment" and "prudence," implied maturity, that is, the judgment of parents. Will now came to imply instability, as love implied passion; and interest was now looked upon as a valuable goal for human conduct. Interest was, to be sure, no less a passion than love, but it had a new respectability.

Of course, the parents' contention that children were incapable of making decisions on their own because they were controlled by emotion or were unable to judge or think prudently often meant that the couple failed to think along the lines the parents may have desired.[21] In an earlier era parents had been silent; the discourse about motives for marriage—will, attachment, affection—had all favored couples. The emerging socially sanctioned language of interest turned the discourse in the parents' favor.

By the middle of the eighteenth century, parents began openly to advocate their authority to veto their children's choice of a marriage partner. Some argued that "the father may justly impede his daughter (more than counsel) to become engaged. . . . Many important [church] authors have conceded fathers the right to consent or veto matters of this nature."[22] Other parents made similar statements: "It is legal . . . for the mother to impede said marriage (against her wishes) and even more so when . . . total ruin and perdition [will result]."[23] Yet another parent argued that "solid [ecclesiastical] doctrine stated that it was a mortal sin to contract an engagement without parental will and consent."[24] Others went even further, stating that the law rendered null a marriage made without parental consent.[25] To justify their authority, these parents frequently stressed the long-term consequences of marriage decisions rather than the present will of the parties, thereby emphasizing the stability of their judgment over the alleged fickleness of children's desires.

This position did not lack for critics. Some parents and young people pointed out the clear assertions of Council of Trent and canon law that parental consent was not a requirement for contracting an engagement, and held that the religious canons overrode the older civil laws requiring such consent.[26] Others pointed out that parents and relatives who threatened most vocally to disrupt a marriage were often the first to be reconciled once it had taken place, suggesting that parental oppositions were often undertaken in the heat of passion and readily forgotten afterward.[27] Nonetheless, despite the numbers of families who continued to argue against the legitimacy of parental vetoes, the rhetoric of parents demanding authority over their children's marriages was a significant new development.[28]

A final and even more profound change took place in the role that parents, and especially the father, played in marriage choices. In the seventeenth century there had been little recognition of parents' rights to intervene, nor had there been discussion about the rights of one parent over the other. Mothers as well as fathers had opposed marriages. In the eighteenth century, although many widowed mothers continued to oppose their children's marriages, legitimacy began to be claimed for the rights of one parent only—the father.[29] For the first time it was argued in conflict cases that patriarchy, or the rule of fathers, was desirable.

These new claims went further than even medieval Castilian civil law and tradition in asserting parental authority over marriages. Unlike the old Castilian law, which restricted parental control to daughters' marriage choices, eighteenth-century proponents of normative patriarchy demanded such authority over the marriage choices of both sons and daughters.[30] Similarly, the Castilian law extended authority over marriage choices to mothers as well as fathers, but the eighteenth-century advocates of normative patriarchy argued that fathers, not mothers, should exercise authority over marriage choices.[31] Such claims emphasized the belief that marriage decisions were strategic rather than personal, and that the role of the father in such decisions was critical.

How families in colonial Mexico made these connections is illustrated in a case involving José Pérez Marañón, a leading merchant-lender of Guanajuato. Pérez Marañón's son Fernando, who had been studying for the priesthood, decided instead to marry, thereby arousing his father's ire. José Pérez Marañón's opposition to the son's marriage may have grown out of his interest in preserving his capital and preventing it from being further divided among his seven children, but the son's choice was less than ideal. The woman was thirteen years older than Fernando, and although peninsular born and the daughter of a former corregidor of the province of Cuernavaca, without fortune. Pérez Marañón threatened to withdraw the financial assistance his son had been receiving and remonstrated with him for choosing a woman thirteen years his senior, and then he hired a lawyer to oppose the marriage in the church courts. Five months later the lawyer succeeded in getting young Pérez Marañón out of Mexico City, where he had been studying for the priesthood, and back home to Guanajuato.[32]

Statements by both sides depict the underlying tension in the eighteenth century between two antagonistic concepts of marriage: the long-standing belief in personal choice and the newer argument that economic power should translate into political authority within the family. The argument used by José Pérez Marañón to oppose the match was that "solid doctrine" held it to be a mortal sin to become engaged without parental consent. The father's authority over the choice of a marriage partner came from his role as economic provider for the family: "On him depends nothing less than the subsistence of this life." But the father added a phrase that made grander claims for the father's economic role. Not only the subsistence of this life depended on the father, he continued: so did "the happiness of eternal life." This challenged the classic seventeenth-century vision of the operation of God's will in marriage choices. Under earlier Catholic doctrine, individual preferences were the indication of the Almighty's plans. In the eighteenth century, the father's functions were raised to the level of the operations of the Deity.

The response of Doña María Ana Jiménez de Cisneros to the allegations made by Marañón senior was sarcastic: "It has not come to our notice that there is any great or lesser author who asserts that a son commits a mortal sin in disobeying parental precepts that are disgraceful, unjust, or imprudent." Believing that the senior Pérez Marañón opposed the marriage because of her lack of money and for other reasons irrelevant to the choice of a spouse, she argued that obedience to parents was not an absolute obligation but was conditional upon the morality of the parents' orders. Parents therefore could not demand what God required of man. Rather, parental orders could be judged by a higher standard of morality "because it is written that we are more obliged to obey God than man." Her statement denied the legitimacy of the connection that Pérez Marañon was making between the parental role and the divine one.[33]

Monarchs in the classic era of Divine Right similarly ascribed the political process by which they achieved power to an act of heavenly selection. The analogy between divine right and patriarchy has been remarked by historians. Lawrence Stone points out that "authoritarian monarchy and domestic patriarchy form a congruent and mutually supportive complex of ideas and systems"; patriarchy was politically helpful in that it socialized family members into obedience toward a male authority figure.[34] The idea that families imitated the relationship between monarch and subject is, however, inappropriate for Hispanic society. The Hapsburg kings had functioned as authoritarian monarchs since the sixteenth century, and yet no imitative discourse of patriarchy in the family emerged until the early eighteenth century.[35] José Pérez Marañón's statements indicate the genesis of the change: they suggest that a father's economic role legitimized his authority over the family in a new and original fashion. Where parental authority had previously been justified by biblical precedent and the traditions of Roman law, the enhanced esteem for wealth and the admiration for the power money brings were ultimately responsible for a new and different legitimation of the role of parents, and more particularly the father, in matrimonial choice. Later in the eighteenth century, when royal decrees granted parents a veto over their offspring's choice of a spouse, this legislation specifically supported fathers. Mothers were admonished that their only role was to support the father's wishes.[36]

Thus in Mexico, as in all Western Europe in the seventeenth and eighteenth centuries, a reevaluation of attitudes toward the process of accumulating wealth transformed acquisitiveness, the driving motive behind capitalism, from a passion that deformed and distorted human behavior into an attribute superior to all other emotions and rightfully capable of controlling them. Emotions such as love, which no longer expressed the steadfastness of will, became unreliable motives for marriage. Marriage for love, formerly an exalted motive, was now seen as impulsive emotional behavior and was replaced by a new emphasis on predictability by prudence and calculation in making marriage choices. This new way of thinking altered the relationship between parents and offspring. Where previously the desires of children enjoyed a certain cultural legitimacy, now parents began to gain ascendancy. Patriarchal authority was now paramount, since young people were apt to be moved by affection, liking, sex, and love rather than by the weightier considerations of money and other material or status benefits. These new attitudes upset a system of values that not only had buttressed the notion of marriage for love but also had placed self-interest and overweening financial ambition in the category of ignoble passions.

The shifting emphasis of attitudes toward love and interest in marriage created a critical basis for normative patriarchy in marriage choices. When acquisitiveness became a culturally approved motive for action, it became possible for parents to make an unprecedented argument for the superiority of their wishes over those of their children. And as control of the purse strings was elevated from part of a father's relationship with his offspring to a central function, the father's authority over marriage choices was newly legitimized.

Not everyone supported the new doctrine of patriarchal control over marriage, but for the first time, significant numbers of primarily well-to-do Mexican families began to argue that such rights should legitimately be considered theirs. The new acceptability of acquisitiveness lent greater weight to paternal authority within the family. Other factors, especially the changing social and demographic patterns of intermarriage, further strengthened the argument that fathers should exercise control over marriage choices.

Although these new attitudes did not prevail throughout colonial Mexican society, they did attract a significant following in the new class of very wealthy aristocratic families whose claim to traditional social status was shaky. Many of the families who became rich during the economic expansion of the eighteenth century were those who most vigorously favored the supremacy of the economic role of parents. These families were not bourgeois in the modern sense of the word; they had made their money principally in commerce, and to a lesser extent in mining and agriculture, much as families had always made their fortunes in colonial New Spain. They lacked class consciousness. They did, however, have a different perception of the world and a new view of the importance and function of economic power in society. Their increasingly direct involvement in Spanish mercantilism or the world capitalist market had a great deal to do with their assumption that economic power in the larger world also implied authority over the family, especially over marriage. They defended this position vigorously, and to support their position in society they created new claims about social status and began to challenge the historically dominant ideas about social stratification in colonial society.

CHAPTER 9

Honor as Status

During the first period of this study (1574–1689), the rhetoric and the behavior of wealthy and powerful colonial families in prenuptial conflicts were indistinguishable from those of the less well-to-do. Powerful and poor-but-honorable families tried the same strategies—persuasion, threats of force, coercion—to keep their offspring from marrying. Both confronted the same set of cultural norms that viewed parental interference as malicious. Neither the wealth nor the influence of prominent families gave them a special opportunity to protest to church officials against the dominant beliefs regarding parental roles in marriage choices.

Nor were the outcomes of prenuptial conflicts any more likely to be successful among the prosperous. Wealthy and modest families alike were forced to accept in-laws they objected to; church officials intervened evenhandedly to counter malicious interference. If any stricter enforcement of the rules against unjust parental interference took place, it was the wealthier families who were more often compelled by church rules to accept marriage partners they did not like. In the first half of the eighteenth century, however, this lack of differentiation ended as the upper level of Spanish society began to dissociate itself from the layers beneath it. Affluent families evolved a distinctive rhetoric to prevent marriages which they expounded at great length to church officials. These aristocratic voices became the loudest and most outspoken of the parental protestors.

As they always had done, such families sought to prevent marriages of their sons and daughters with less wealthy and less important Spanish families. But because the underlying social rationale for protesting undesirable matches was changing, aristocratic parents began to speak openly against such marriages, basing their arguments on an aspect of honor that had previously not been mentioned in these disputes—that of honor as status—in which honor is related directly to wealth and position. Their new key word became *desigualidad,* "inequality," by which they meant not the equality of honor (virtue) mentioned by seventeenth-century theologians and writers but precisely those differences of income or position that sixteenth- and seventeenth-century Hispanic society had condemned as unworthy considerations for interfering in a marriage. With this step, the social discourse about marriage underwent a major change.

These families from the upper reaches of colonial society, referred to here as "aristocratic families," came from one of two groups. In the first group were mainly wealthy merchants who had made their fortunes in the spectacular economic boom of the eighteenth century. Members of the titled nobility and royal bureaucrats were also heavily represented in this group. In the second were those who had enjoyed superior social status at the start of the century, but whose economic and social position was deteriorating. The preoccupation of these rising and declining elements of the aristocracy with "inequality" stemmed from a growing concern with social differentiation common to both. Whereas the one group was eager to establish its new preeminence, the other was preoccupied with preserving its status. Hence both were highly sensitive to indicators and boundaries of status, especially those that were emphasized in marriage alliances. Two forms of status differentiation were of particular interest to the aristocracy: distinctions made among Spaniards, and distinctions made on the basis of race. Although the aristocratic concern with "inequality" figured in only a third of the prenuptial conflicts, it would prove to be a highly influential third, because this aristocratic preoccupation would eventually shape a new colonial law on the role of parents in marriage choices.

Scattered and occasional references to the lack of equality between marriage partners appeared in prenuptial conflicts throughout the colonial period.[1] Rarely, however, were the earlier allegations of inequality—whether social, economic, or racial—proposed as reasonable causes for preventing a marriage. In fact, opposing a marriage because of economic inequality in particular had been one of the principal examples of "malicious interference." Yet by the middle of the eighteenth century, a new chorus of voices appeared in prenuptial conflicts. Parents, guardians, and relatives from aristocratic families began to make open demands for a veto over their offsprings' marriages explicitly to prevent socially or economically "unequal" alliances.[2] The lack of equality of wealth or position constituted a novel argument for a parental veto over marriage choices.

One of the first definitive demands for social equality of marriage partners was made in 1749 by the financial guardian of a distant relative of the Marquis of Torrecampo, the son of a member of one of the honorific military orders. Much to the disgust of his guardian, the young man, Joaquín Fuente Rosillo, had fallen in love with a young Spanish woman, Antonia, whose family though well connected—she was a distant relative of a high court judge and a prominent Spanish churchman—was neither distinguished in Mexico City nor rich. The guardian's reaction to the social disparity was violent. Although Antonia was Spanish, he alleged that she was the daughter of a barber (a "vile, manual occupation")—a lazy, dissolute vagabond who had failed to educate his children properly. Spaniards or no, the guardian argued, the two families were unequal—indeed, he added, no greater inequality between families could be imagined than that between the Fuente Rosillos and the undistinguished Ladrón de Guevaras.[3]

This claim that enormous social inequality existed between Spaniards was quite novel. A major social difference had always separated Spaniards from the rest of society—the difference of race. To assert that the ultimate inequality existed between Spaniards was a considerable exaggeration.

The guardian's trenchant opposition to Antonia also focused on her behavior. Her birth was undistinguished, therefore it followed that her conduct would be ignoble. As further evidence of her inferior social status, he contended that she did not observe the proprieties that honor demanded of a young, upper class Spanish woman. She was allowed to spend time in the company of women who had illegitimate children. She had been permitted to walk publicly in the neighborhood. Joaquín had taken her virginity. She was, therefore, a woman of "such inferior quality and such disordered conduct" that grave damage would be done to the family because of the conflict her behavior would evoke between the pair. "Parents, guardians, and kin may justly impede a marriage when the inequality between the parties is notable and there is firm basis to fear the pernicious consequences, damage, scandal, and dishonor that would result to the illustrious family."[4]

The traditional Hispanic and Catholic belief in a young man's responsibility to the woman he had seduced is notably absent here. Missing too is the concern to protect her reputation and that of her family. No longer was sexual involvement a valid reason for the couple to marry; the guardian contended that Antonia's loss of virginity was a reason why they should *not* marry. The time-honored practice of remedying the young woman's loss of honor by marriage was in his opinion misguided; in the new mode of placing sexual responsibility on the woman, he introduced the idea that she should be blamed for her conduct. Sexual involvement, formerly considered an urgent reason for secrecy and immediate marriage, now offered an opportunity to embarrass the woman and prevent the marriage.

The guardian's assertions did not go unanswered. Antonia's lawyer argued from the traditional beliefs of church law and Hispanic culture: her loss of virginity to Joaquín did not constitute an impediment to marriage, for ecclesiastical teachings established matrimony as a remedy for concupiscence. Furthermore, it was even less an obstacle to marriage when the breach of chastity occurred with the man the woman intended to marry. Joaquín was obliged by natural, divine, and positive law to redeem her honor and fulfill the promise to marry.[5] He defended her association with women who had illegitimate children as having been limited to a brief period in which certain skilled needlewomen had taught Antonia to sew and knit in their homes.

In his response to the guardian's more fundamental objections of differences in social status, Antonia's lawyer relied on the classical arguments of church law. "Among the [impediments] sketched by the sacred canons and the holy Council of Trent . . . one does not encounter any such impediment. It is . . . the vain policy of this century to introduce the new [impediment] of disparity in lineage and fortunes. Never has the Church, common mother to all the faithful, shut her doors to those who want solemn marriage, even when there is great distance and glaring difference of condition or rank. [The Church] has always been constant and firm in acting against the secular powers and contradicting the powerful in order to marry nobles and plebeians, slaves and freedmen, rich and poor, lords and serfs in matters of conscience."[6] With considerable shrewdness, the lawyer argued the other side of the case as well: the judge would be justified in using his powers of persuasion to prevent the marriage if one of the families stood to lose respect by such a marriage, but the young man had neither a title nor an entail that would be vigorously contested. The majority of his family resided in Manila, and the few relatives he had in the capital of New Spain were distant ones. Finally, he added that "even parents and children frequently reconcile and resign themselves to great inequalities in their sons- and daughters-in-law."

This case, between a defense of the classic and ancient tradition of the church in New Spain and a new and untried argument for a veto voiced principally in terms of the social inequality between the parties, was more than just a challenge to the preeminence of traditional canon law. Status is a dimension of social reputation; it is the claim to esteem in the eyes of one's contemporaries. Since reputation and social esteem are the bases of social honor, Joaquín's guardian was arguing for nothing less than acceptance of a different understanding of the concept of honor.

Honor in Spanish society had two separate meanings: a person's integrity and the superiority of rank and birth. In the traditional Hispanic culture of New Spain, honor as moral integrity or virtue had been more important than honor based openly upon distinctions of status and birth. Protecting sexual honor, however, which was one of the primary components of the former, had been declining in importance since the final third of the seventeenth century, as was shown in Chapter 6. By the middle of the eighteenth century, preserving the appearance of moral virtue was no longer the compelling social priority it once had been. Joaquín's guardian completely dismissed the notion of shielding a woman's reputation for sexual honor; on the contrary, Antonia's loss of her virginity to Joaquín was evidence of her inferior status. In contending that "parents, guardians, and kin may justly impede a marriage when the inequality between the parties is notable" the guardian voiced a greater concern for defending social status than for protecting a reputation for sexual virtue. In other words, honor as social status was more important than moral honor. By the end of the century, social superiority was on its way to becoming the most important dimension of honor.

Joaquín's guardian was also arguing for the superiority of the claims of status over conscience. It was not Joaquín's personal moral responsibility to Antonia for having taken her virginity—his obligation in conscience, or even his love for her—that mattered, but the "consequences . . . for the illustrious family." The family's status was a worthier consideration in marriage than conscience.[7]

The case dragged on for months, until the guardian suddenly died. With his death all opposition to the match expired, and the pair were married. The lack of opposition by other members of Joaquín's family lends credence to Joaquín's contention that the guardian was only trying to hold on to the boy's inheritance, and indicates that the guardian's main objection was not his stated one, the extreme inequality of social status, but Antonia's lack of a large dowry and the fact that her family was not rich and powerful. The guardian's vehement insistence on the consequences of ignoring social disparity is striking. "Pernicious consequences, damage, scandal, and dishonor" would attend a marriage to a woman who, though Spanish, had no great distinction or wealth. Emphasizing social inequality was in part a covert attempt to introduce the notion that differences in economic position—what Antonia's lawyer called "the vain policy of this century"—were a valid reason for opposing and indeed preventing a marriage.

The rhetoric of this conflict marked the commencement of a struggle between two competing visions of marriage. For the first time, a guardian argued for a veto over a marriage choice on the grounds that the need to maintain a family's social prestige should override both the moral responsibilities of conscience and the need to protect a less important family's reputation for honor. In subsequent decades, dozens of other parents and guardians professed horror at the "scandal" or dishonor that would result from marriages to men or women of lower social standing, even going so far as to assert that considerations of social class were as important as canon law. For the most part these conflicts pitted a family preoccupied with achieving or maintaining social status against another that supported traditional concepts of honor and defended the traditional position that disparity of fortune or lineage had never been a valid reason for opposing a marriage.[8]

In 1773, the niece of the priest of the town of Atzcapazalco became enamored of Lorenzo Hidalgo, a convicted jewel thief who had spent eight years in prison—four for the theft, four for attempting to escape. Her brothers, who like the priest hoped to halt the marriage, argued that such a marriage would "leave her family exposed to a public dishonor" and would "probably result, contrary to the holy ends of that institution, in grave prejudice to the Girl and all her Lineage" because Lorenzo was a man "lost without either honor or shame." The young woman, however, had given Lorenzo her virginity, and she told her brothers that she felt that remedying *her* loss of honor was a greater priority than upholding *their* social honor or reputation.[9] In the seventeenth century, her claim would have been validated by the church; the brothers' rhetoric was purely eighteenth century.

As the century progressed, protestations of extreme social inequality between Spaniards were voiced repeatedly. For Blas Santo, the son of a captain of the cavalry, the occupation of the father of his Spanish girlfriend became a reason to break off the relationship: "I have heard that she is inferior in rank to me because she is the daughter of a tailor." The chief constable and councilman of Mexico City in 1777 hurled accusations of "considerable inequality" at the goddaughter of a marquis "for being of a family of artisans and servants." A wealthy merchant of Amilpa, Don Antonio Villalobos, accused his former clerk of trying to marry his daughter, of having "a mechanical trade of tailor," and of being "of such irregular licentious behavior that he does not even work in his trade." In all cases, the young men and women were of Spanish origin, and the objection to their marriages lay in the inferiority of their heritage, albeit Spanish, to that of families with considerably more wealth and power.[10]

A number of young people pointed out that although their parents spoke of inequalities of social position, they really meant inequalities of wealth. Doña Ana Cámara Enciso argued, "The lineage of [my son] is well known in this city because his relatives are of notable and manifest luster, and his rights and privileges of nobility are well published . . . and by this same token, the woman he intends to marry is of ordinary rank not corresponding to that of the Guerreros. From this inequality not only will considerable dishonor result but . . . serious dislike among his relatives." In reply, Doña Gertrudis Miranda's lawyer pinpointed the family's real objection: "Even supposing that . . . his privilege of nobility came from the Goths and that Doña Gertrudis came from the most despicable sphere that has been attributed to her (*for being poor*) . . . to marry, equality of blood or fortune is not necessary, only precisely the free and spontaneous will to do so."[11]

Marriages between estate owners' sons and servants, between tailors' daughters and sons of marquises and captains, or between impoverished branches of distinguished families and the very wealthy—all were opposed on grounds of disparity of social status. Indeed, there often was significant social disparity; but in many of these cases differences of wealth or income existed as well. Rarely identified as such, economic disparities were most frequently described in terms of social status, but the vocabulary used to refer to them is telling. One young man without much money was described as "extremely vulgar."[12] In another case, Doña María Gertrudis maintained that the only reason her fiancé's mother described her condition as "common" was that she was poor. Licenciado Joaquin Velásquez de León fell in love with the daughter of an illustrious and distinguished family of New Spain who opposed the marriage because, compared with her, he was "ordinary." Even though Velásquez was studying for the priesthood at the time, and the priesthood was a traditional indicator of Spanish status, he had only a modest income; hence the epithet "ordinary."[13]

The use of characterizations such as "ordinary" or "common" to downgrade the social standing of other Spaniards introduced a direct link between great wealth and social position. In traditional Hispanic culture, nobility and poverty had been considered compatible. The poor nobleman or noblewoman in reduced circumstances was a popular feature of fiction and drama, a favorite object of charity.

In the eighteenth century, with the advent of new ideas about interest and the new respectability of acquisitiveness, several of Spain's leading writers, including Feijoo, Gaspar de Jovellanos, and Juan Francisco de Castro, contended that high social status and great wealth should be associated. Medieval Spanish law, Jovellanos asserted, demanded "a rich nobility"; Francisco de Castro declared that "nobility and riches are inseparable." Their prescriptions were eventually fulfilled in Spain when the ideal of nobility founded on virtue collapsed, leaving behind what one commentator has termed "a relatively small aristocracy and a mass of noblemen distinguished from commoners only by their obsessive genealogical preoccupations."[14] A similar push to acknowledge and even encourage the association between high social status and wealth also occurred in New Spain.

In the middle of the eighteenth century, some members of the Hispanic aristocracy of New Spain endeavored to change the traditional definitions of social status—a quality related to acts of valor by one's ancestors, or one's place of birth—and to redefine it as the possession of great wealth. Yet because the antipathy to openly valuing riches still ran deep in the culture, disparities of wealth were rarely alluded to as such.[15] Economic differences were often characterized as a lack of means to maintain a spouse. Sixteen-year-old Doña María Estrada declared, "The small fortune of Malpica is not sufficient for him or for me, nor can it bear the burdens of marriage," words that were echoed by other young women.[16]

It is perhaps ironic that the greatest demands for "equality" of marriage partners originated within the ranks of the well-to-do. The marriage between Joaquín Fuente Rosillo and Antonia Ladrón de Guevara set two families against each other. If one could proudly cite a relationship to the political elite of the Philippines, the other could point to its own connection with the political elite of Guatemala; both could claim a certain social position. Yet Joaquín's guardian opposed the match on the grounds that "*unparalleled* social inequality" existed because Antonia's family lacked great wealth or distinction. In 1764, in the town of San Juan Teotihuacán, Don Diego Manuel Fernández became engaged to marry Doña Teresa Bravo, a young Spaniard who was capable of signing her own name to the marriage petition. After the banns had been read twice, Don Diego called the marriage off, saying that Doña Teresa Bravo was "notably unequal, of the most inferior status." Both were Spanish, both were addressed by the honorific "don," both were able to write. The hyperbole behind the fiancé's—or, more accurately his guardian's—claims of "notable" and "extreme" social inequality between Spanish families suggests a certain anxiety about their relative positions.[17]

There was good reason for this insecurity. These Spanish families were attempting to establish differences of position and power within a community that had previously underplayed its internal status distinctions so as to close ranks more effectively against the other racial segments of colonial society which were viewed as decidedly inferior. All the Spaniards who now faced exclusion could be expected to contest the new order. The wealthy and aristocratic within the Spanish community were the ones who felt most threatened by socially unequal unions. In this situation of struggle for position, not only by the undistinguished among the Spanish but also by the newly rich among the mixed and other races, only the wealthy Spanish aristocrats had something to lose.

In 1768, in the town of Zultepec, Doña Manuela Ortíz, daughter of the town's wealthiest merchant, became engaged to Don Luis Navarro, a middleman in the mining business who bought silver from miners and sold it to smelting plants. Doña Manuela's father described Don Luis as "a lazy vagabond, without a profession . . . [and of] inferior rank," a "plebeian." Doña Manuela replied with considerable dignity that she did not wish to marry a wealthy man, only a good one, adding that she believed goodness was what her parents had always instructed her to look for in a husband. Her father, however, was more concerned with the potential benefits to him of a son-in-law of wealth and position. "It is not easy," he stated, "to find [in this town] someone equal in status," meaning someone with wealth or influence. According to the priest sent from Mexico City to hear the case, Doña Manuela's father was the richest man in town, not to mention the most captious and fault-finding. His principal aim in trying to prevent his daughter's marriage was that he wanted to have the town's notary as his son-in-law so that, in the words of the priest, "between the two of them they would have the town sewed up."[18]

The increasing openness with which wealth and power were acknowledged in establishing social status could have taken place anywhere in Western Europe. Similar prenuptial conflicts occurred in seventeenth-century France between the *noblesse d'epée* and the *noblesse de la robe,* and in England between what one historian has called the rising and falling gentry.[19] Prenuptial conflicts became significant in early modern Europe as boundaries of status came into question. The disputes over status boundaries in New Spain had an unusual dimension, however. A fraction of the newly emergent wealthy were descendants of slaves and Indians, and intermarriages of these racially mixed young men and women with families of Spanish birth provoked considerable protest. Besides threatening the claim to social preeminence that derived from the mere fact of being Spanish, interracial marriages challenged Spanish males' exclusive access to Spanish women.

Throughout the sixteenth and seventeenth centuries, interracial sexual contact took place primarily outside marriage. The predominant form of miscegenation occurred between Spanish men and Indian or black women who were their long-term concubines or short-term sexual partners. The offspring of these unions were illegitimate, and thus the words "mulatto" and "mestizo" were synonymous through the seventeenth century with illegitimate birth.

Following on the heels of the economic expansion, in the second decade of the eighteenth century a dramatic increase occurred in interracial marriage. The index of overall interracial marriage in Mexico City took a sharp upward swing in 1720 and continued to climb steadily for the next fifty years. Historians who have noted this increase have in general believed that the increase in intermarriage failed to erode the boundaries between racial groups, in particular the critical distinction between the Spaniards and the castas, or persons of mixed racial origin.[20] A careful examination of the patterns of interracial marriage and change in prenuptial disputes suggests that this was not the case. In the Sagrario, Mexico City's main parish, the greatest increase in levels of interracial marriage after 1720 involved Spaniards, of both sexes.[21] The increasing occurrence of this sort of marriage—Spaniards, both male and female, marrying mulattoes, mestizos, or castas—presented potentially catastrophic consequences for a social structure primarily organized on the basis of racial distinctions.

Hand in hand with the statistical change through the middle years of the eighteenth century a full-scale attack on racially mixed marriages was conducted by a large number of families. Fully 22 percent of the marriages opposed after 1715 involved a Spaniard and a non-Spanish partner. This contrasts sharply with the nearly invisible 6 percent of the conflicts that such marriages represented between 1580 and 1690. The preceding two hundred years of interracial activity in New Spain had failed to provoke a similar reaction because the unions had been, for the most part, nonmarital, and therefore not a challenge to the fundamental social distinctions of race. When Spanish men in substantial numbers began to marry women who had once been considered acceptable only as concubines, the practice of making social distinctions by race was jeopardized. The percentage of interracial marriages by Spanish men nearly doubled from the earlier period, threatening the presumed integrity of Spanish status as a prestige category. The hostility within the threatened elite Spanish community against such matches became intense and was reflected in the rhetoric of the conflicts.

In 1744, Don Jacinto Rodríguez de Zuaznavar, a Querétaro councilman, tried to marry his mulatta concubine of many years, Ana Ocio de Taloya. His brothers, however, were intensely hostile to Ana, whom they characterized as "arrogant, boisterous, and rash"; she had the temerity, they said, not to comport herself with the accustomed humility of a concubine, and to take over the management of Rodríguez's household and servants. They further characterized her as a woman of "dreadful character, made worse by her rebellious and arrogant behavior. To sum it up [she is] a woman who has not known shame."[22] Furthermore, she was "inferior in worldly goods and rank." Their objections to this marriage were that Rodríguez's family's social status and prestige—more specifically, *their* prestige—would be damaged by "tarnishing his illustrious blood with such a hideous stigma, [leading to] ignominy for his house and a fall from honor." They alleged that death, discord, and affliction (undoubtedly of their own causing) would result from such a union.[23] Don Jacinto replied that the "scandals . . . and all the rest [they alleged] exist only in the heads of men with law degrees and are imagined without any proof."[24] Intense antagonism and vicious resistance to interracial marriages characterized oppositions to interracial marriages for the duration of the century.

The dramatic change in the gender of Spanish interracial marriages was the second powerful reason for the chorus of opposition to interracial unions. For the first time in colonial history, significant numbers of Spanish women were beginning to marry men of non-Spanish origin, men who had established themselves in an economic sense. In 1758 in Otumba, a small town northeast of Mexico City, María Rosalia Roldán, the daughter of the notary to the town's Inquisition, became engaged to the owner of a small local estate. Her family enjoyed considerable social prestige, while he was the upwardly mobile son of a pulque-growing and marketing family from the region. His father, however, had been publicly disgraced by the Inquisition for blasphemy. In addition, Francisco Bautista's features and kinky hair led some people to label him mulatto. Her brothers tried to prevent the marriage because of Bautista's suspect ancestry, as well as his family's disgrace because of punishment by the Inquisition. María replied that even if he were not simply mulatto but black, she would still marry him. But though she was undeterred by the disparity in racial origin, she was at last persuaded to change her mind when the evidence that Bautista's father had been convicted of murder was placed before her.[25]

Marriages between Spanish women and men of African and Indian ancestry were fewer than marriages between Spanish men and women of African or Indian heritage, but they were opposed twice as often as those of Spanish men outside their race.[26] Such marriages provoked resistance even more than interracial marriages by Spanish men.

The difference in attitudes toward racially mixed marriages by men and those by women was apparent even in the conduct of clergymen, who historically had been most favorable to marriages across social boundaries. The church had furthered interracial marriage by men, forcing them to marry their long-term concubines despite racial differences. Such marriages were perhaps not socially desirable, but the church considered them superior to concubinage, which endangered the men's immortal souls. As the eighteenth century progressed and such marriages became more frequent, the church's support of them became more problematic. Nonetheless, the church formally retained its commitment to unite wills rather than marry ranks—if the union was between a Spanish male and a woman of another race. In 1744, a Spaniard named Ignacio Abreu wanted to marry a young castiza named Margarita Salazar; Catholic officials raised no questions about his marrying a woman of inferior race.[27] Nor did they object to a marriage between a Zultepec hacienda owner's son and the daughter of a mestizo servant on the family estate in 1768.

But when Spanish women married men from lower racial ranks, church officials carefully questioned them about their intentions. In 1694, Lugarda Jirón, an orphaned Spanish girl, was brought before the Mexico City ecclesiastical magistrate because her relatives opposed her marriage to Juan Aranda. She stated that she wished to marry Juan "in spite of his being castizo," suggesting she had been questioned about the difference in races.[28] In 1731, in virtually the same circumstances, a Spanish woman who expressed her desire to marry a castizo male was asked if she had full knowledge of his social status.

When a Spanish woman wished to marry a man of slave ancestry, church officials went even further. In 1715, for example, a well-to-do man of mixed Spanish and mulatto heritage wanted to marry a Spanish woman. Her father opposed the match. Dispatched to take her marriage declaration, the church notary asked young Antonia Díaz Mayorga if she was aware of her intended's race and still wished to marry him in spite of it. She answered yes to both questions and was removed from her parents' custody. Five days later she reiterated her intent to marry despite the defect in his status. Still not satisfied, church officials interviewed her mother, who revealed that the daughter was adopted. Since the mother did not object to her adopted daughter's matrimonial intentions, the next day the judge ordered the marriage preparations to continue. Church officials were noticeably reluctant to allow the interracial marriage, but they had no valid excuse to prevent it.[29]

Sometimes church officials also pointed out to the young women the disadvantages of an interracial match, explaining that any children would be ineligible for honorific posts in the church or in government. In at least one case the church notary discussed the likelihood that the young woman would repent of such a match, and insisted on outlining at great length all the possible dangers to her soul of her subsequent behavior, but she stated firmly that she knew what she was doing and insisted on marrying.[30] The fact that the church made such queries and discussed such consequences reflected a concern about women's interracial marriages that had not been apparent in earlier decades, or centuries, when men married across racial lines. Clergymen were as disturbed by such marriages as were their secular male counterparts.[31]

These unions not only threatened the racial basis of social dis-

tinctions, as did interracial unions by Hispanic males, but also posed
a challenge to Spanish tradition. One of the fundamental principles
of the honor system was the protection by Spanish males of their
women from African or Indian men. Controlling the sexual conduct
of their sisters and other female relatives had been central to this system. This control created a basic social and sexual privilege for
Spanish men by simultaneously granting them access to women of
other racial groups and reserving exclusive access to women of their
own group for themselves. When Spanish women began marrying
non-Spaniards, the loss of exclusive sexual access to the women of
their own group caused changes in behavior that suggest they found
the loss threatening.[32] For the first time Spanish men were forced to
compete with men from other social groups for sexual access to
Spanish women; they lost the superior status they had once enjoyed.
This sexual-status insecurity of Spanish males was a powerful
undercurrent in the eighteenth century and undoubtedly contributed to the extreme vehemence with which such marriages were
opposed.

But the anxiety about sexual dominance was only one aspect of
the general crisis of status insecurity among the colonial aristocracy
that had resulted from New Spain's economic transformation during the eighteenth century. While the doctrine of parental authority
was emerging, Mexico's economy was undergoing a dramatic expansion, growing most rapidly in the first half of the eighteenth
century. A subsequent brief burst in colonial mining production between the late 1750's and 1779 was followed by a period of decline
that lasted until the end of the colonial period, but from 1695 until
the middle of the eighteenth century the colony enjoyed an unprecedented series of economic booms. The result was a massive transformation of the social order.

Economic expansion allowed a number of families from lower
social groups, descendants of Indians and slaves, to improve their
financial lot dramatically. To complement their new wealth, these
groups sought and gradually acquired the accoutrements of superior
Spanish status—privileges to bear arms, to ride horses, to sit on the
town council, to enter the priesthood, or to study at the university.
Historically, the trappings of status had been available to those who
ameliorated their economic standing, and once purchased, they
made it easy for assimilation to take place.[33] However, New Spain

had not faced such a rapid, long-lasting economic expansion or such massive upward movement through the social hierarchy since the time of the Conquest.

Many of the families that became socially mobile during the eighteenth century were of mixed race, some descended from Indians, others from slaves. As the offspring of these unions sought to intermarry with the established Spanish elite in subsequent generations, they reached the levels of the very wealthy; social tensions began to acquire racial overtones.

About 1740, in a predominantly Indian town in what is now the Costa Chica of the state of Guerrero, the second most powerful political official of the area married a dark-skinned woman from his district. Some people said she was the daughter of an Indian chief, others simply said she was dark. By all accounts, however, her family was fairly wealthy. In 1770, a well-to-do Spanish merchant objected to his daughter's marrying the twenty-six-year-old son of this couple on the grounds of his racially mixed heritage. The young man's birth certificate listed his race as Spanish, a description that was consistent with his family's influence and with the testimony of witnesses, who declared that his family enjoyed considerable social prestige in the community. His mother's race had not been a stumbling block for her husband's family. But it became one when her son tried to move farther up the social ladder into the wealthy elite of New Spain.[34]

The continued acquisition of the trappings of superior social status and the uninterrupted intermarriage with established families by large numbers of families of different race or lower social origins gradually eroded and rendered increasingly meaningless many of the traditional distinctions of Spanish social status. Not only was the social complexion of colonial Mexico irrevocably altered, but the traditional accoutrements of Spanish social prestige suffered wholesale devaluation. The purpose of distinctions of status is to maintain exclusiveness: when status symbols are very widely held, they become meaningless. Simply to be Spanish was no longer the guarantor of superior social standing that it had been in the seventeenth century. The result was greater insecurity about status.

A final noteworthy dimension of the conflicts over interracial marriages after the middle of the eighteenth century was that many of the objections were directed at one racial group, the descendants of slaves. Historically the most discriminated against by law, descendants of blacks benefited along with other groups from the economic boom in the early eighteenth century. Initially they, like the Indians and their descendants, intermarried with Spaniards with relatively little opposition.

Opposition to marriages between Spaniards and descendants of slaves certainly existed early in the eighteenth century, but it was no more frequent than opposition to marriages between Spaniards and descendants of Indians. Catholic Church officials enforced marriages between Spanish men and mulatta women as often as they enforced those between Spanish men and mestiza or castiza women. In 1715, for example, the parents of José Guerrero, a twenty-year-old Spaniard, opposed his marriage to a young free morisca—daughter of a Spaniard and a mulatta—named María González, because of the racial disparity between the two. José argued that because he had promised to marry María and had taken her virginity, he had an obligation to her that surpassed his responsibility for marriage to someone within his racial group. The judge of the ecclesiastical court agreed: "[These reasons] are sufficient to resolve for repairing the woman's lost [honor] and the marriage should not be unjustly impeded." He promptly ordered the marriage to take place.[35] As late as the early eighteenth century, then, racial difference was not as important a consideration as the loss of a reputation for sexual virtue, even when the young woman was the descendant of slaves.

Allegations of racial inferiority based on a slave heritage were still regarded as unreasonable opposition as late as the 1730's,[36] but as increasing numbers of families of slave ancestry improved their economic positions, these attitudes changed. The Spanish elites responded defensively to the efforts of increasingly well-to-do mulattoes to intermarry with their ranks. In 1753 in Texupilco, a wealthy man whose family on both sides was mulatto attempted to marry the daughter of an important local Spanish family. When her parents pressured her not to marry him and she then denied that a promise to marry existed, he took the matter to the local church court. The judge was singularly unsympathetic to the man, partly because of his social pretensions. "The groom, being of inferior quality, a vulgar mulatto . . . tries to deceive the superior judges . . . passing himself off as Spanish . . . because he has money."[37]

Prejudice against successful descendants of Africans showed itself on other occasions. Slaves had been imported into the sugar-growing region around Cuernavaca in the sixteenth century, and some of their descendants became themselves successful landowners. One such landowner was Juan Cristóbal's father in Yautepec. In 1761 Juan Cristóbal wanted to marry a very light colored widow, described as both a castiza and a morisca. His father opposed the marriage on the grounds of a difference of status (because she was poor), but church officials could see nothing wrong with the marriage. Ecclesiastical officials condemned the father's opposition as typical of that of "the despicable people who become presumptuous with the few faculties that they enjoy in that area." That is, the conceits of status and attempts to establish social inequality in economic terms were legitimate enough for Spaniards, but *not* for descendants of slaves.[38]

Similar antagonism was not in evidence when Indians marrying Spaniards attempted to pass themselves off as Spanish. In 1768 a young couple from outside Mexico City appeared before the chief church court judge and asked to be married. Both stated their racial status to be Spanish, and clearly they were able to pass as such in Mexico City. When the request to verify the young woman's single status was sent to the priest of her hometown, the priest complained that there she was known as Indian, not Spanish. His informants were the principal Indians of the town, who considered her Indian. Unperturbed, the ecclesiastical judge termed her misrepresentation of her racial status "a falsehood that is in no way prejudicial," and ordered the marriage to take place.[39] For an Indian to pass herself off as Spanish was "in no way prejudicial" whereas the would-be groom in Texupilco was termed a "vulgar mulatto" and condemned for "passing himself off as Spanish . . . because he has money." Black ancestry was clearly far more a problem than Indian ancestry.[40]

Further into the century, the accusations of distant descent from blacks increased in conflicts. One reason for this was historical. The crisis of status occurred just as the population of African origin was becoming increasingly amalgamated into the racial mix of colonial society. In other words, distant descendants of blacks were increasingly intermarrying with Spaniards of ever higher social standing, so the social distinctions between those of pure Spanish ancestry and those with some black ancestry became more and more unrecognizable. In 1778, the peninsular son of a physician in Pachuca wanted to marry Doña María Antonia Encarnación Zapata, a twenty-five-year-old creole woman from a prominent local family. Her mother was descended from upwardly mobile stock; her maternal great-great-grandfather, who had dealt in cattle in the small town of Monte Alto, was by some accounts mulatto. His descendants had successively intermarried with Spaniards, but the connection to a mulatto four generations removed persuaded the physician's son not to marry because of the disparity of racial origin.[41]

Often, however, parents who objected to a match with a social inferior used the designation "mulatto" with no evidence whatsoever, as a way of attacking the person they disliked.[42] The administrator of the estate of San Ignacio in the town of Xilotepec was appalled when his younger brother decided to marry the poor mestiza orphan girl who had been raised with them. He flung every epithet he could think of at her: "libertine," "dishonest," "provocative," "daughter of a criminal." Significantly, he also lowered her racial rank to "wolf," that is, a mestiza with an admixture of black ancestry.[43] In 1759, Don Martín de la Borda, the son of peninsular parents, wanted to marry a servant girl of racially mixed origin. His widowed mother objected to the match on grounds that the young woman's mother was a mulatta; Don Martín countered that while it was true she was of lower social status, she was not a mulatta.[44] In another instance, Don Joaquín Cevallos said, "All the basis of my father's opposition can be reduced to saying that the marriage cannot be celebrated because the parties are very unequal . . . which he promises to prove by information on María Gertrudis's status . . . and what can be shown from the witnesses is that the mother of María Gertrudis was in the house of Licenciado Martín de Aranjuez as a wet nurse, . . . and the face of her mother did not appear Spanish."[45]

In 1770, a literate apprentice merchant from Tenango, described in all the records as Spanish, was accused by the father of the girl he wanted to marry of being the distant descendant of mulattoes. Augustín Gómez was the son of the chief constable of the Coatepec region, one of the important local political posts and a position gained only through considerable regional influence. His fiancée's father, however, declared that Augustín's maternal grandfather, Bernardo

Chimalpoca, was black. A series of witnesses was clearly put in a quandary when asked to specify Bernardo Chimalpoca's race. Some said he was "inferior" or "low," others "suspicious." One witness summed up the indecision of the rest by saying "his color was not Spanish, but I do not know whether it was black, mulatto, or Indian." The boundaries between Indian and black had never been maintained with great diligence by the Spanish, who were preoccupied mainly with differences between Spaniards and non-Spaniards. Consequently it was very difficult to determine the racial origin of any person of mixed ancestry. The term "mulatto" or "of mulatto descent" was not a literal definition of ancestry but a popular symbol of social inequality.[46]

The use of the epithets "mulatto" and "black" to tarnish a person's reputation clearly showed the relative position of the two non-Spanish groups in the hierarchy of status honor. One young woman described the status order thus: "A black is the lowest that could be." Descendants of blacks were the heirs of slaves, a social origin of greater ignominy than that of Indians. Indians had historically been granted preferential access over blacks to both economic opportunities and the trappings of status. Indians were allowed a separate political organization to run their society, theoretically the equal of Spanish society. Blacks were denied the right even to gather together in groups of three or more, much less to govern themselves separately. Also, although regulations forbade members of either group to become master artisans, especially in trades that were financially rewarding, blacks and mulattoes were denied entrance into many more crafts than were Indians. Therefore to accuse someone of being descended from blacks was to allege the greatest possible social disparity.[47]

The preoccupation with interracial marriages, however, like the preoccupation with marriages to persons of lower social status, was primarily a concern of the aristocrats of colonial New Spain, who saw their customary privileges on the basis of racial status being eroded by intermarriage with persons of African or Indian origin. Don Pedro León y Heredia was the second-ranking royal political officer of Xochimilco. In 1768 his stepdaughter eloped with Mateo Ruíz, the son of two respectable citizens of the town of Tepotzotlán, but of some racially mixed ancestry. Mateo was dark in appearance, so the stepfather taunted him with being not Spanish but a coyote, which, like wolf, was a familiar derogatory term for a person of black-Indian ancestry.[48]

Families of mixed race frequently welcomed intermarriage with wealthy, albeit darker, members of their own group.[49] Poor Spaniards were also seldom bothered by marriages to better-off castas. Even when the rare poor Spanish parent objected to a marriage on grounds of racial inequality, the lack of a significant financial or social incentive to prosecute the suit was apparent.[50] The concern about interracial marriage was simply part of a more general crisis of status among the aristocracy in the eighteenth century.

The demands for equality of marriage partners that began to be made in the 1740's had two fundamental roots. The reevaluation of wealth, "interest," and economic calculation led to the increasing importance of economic considerations in marriage. Wealth and privilege, traditionally regarded as a usual though not necessary component of superior status, became for the elite an ever more significant component of their own definition of elevated position. Their efforts to denigrate the social standing of persons of modest but completely Spanish heritage were attempts to downgrade the status of honor as sexual virtue. The Spanish aristocracy of New Spain sought to redefine the criteria for marriage partners in terms of these new values by demanding "equality" of marriage partners, that is, similar backgrounds and prospects.

The second root of this demand for "equality" was the improvement in social status of a large part of the population, which created problems for the elite of New Spain. The traditional markers distinguishing them from the rest of their society lost the cachet of exclusiveness they had once enjoyed, as more and more non-Spanish were able to buy the perquisites of "Spanish" status that formerly could only be acquired by the wealthy few. The result was both a pervasive sense of insecurity among the wealthy Spanish aristocracy and a preoccupation with reestablishing an effective barrier to intermarriage between themselves and those of lower social as well as racial origins. The aristocrats' anxiety was heightened when the sexual privileges Spanish men had traditionally enjoyed were threatened by the increase in intermarriage of Spanish women and non-Spanish men. It became increasingly clear to the elite that one way to prevent further devaluation of the traditional superiority of Spanish status was to halt marriages between men and women of different racial ancestry.

With these changes, aristocratic families mounted a major challenge to the traditional social significance of honor. Honor, which had always been valued as an indicator of moral worth and integrity, was no longer enough, and the old satisfaction with the idea of equality with the poor but honorable began to fade. Under pressure from threats to social status, the increasing frequency of interracial marriage, and the increasing importance of wealth in defining social status, aristocratic families began to associate honor with superiority of birth and social standing, which was ultimately founded on financial superiority. Their convictions thus challenged traditional social priorities. For these aristocrats, concern for the social position of a family group outweighed concern for the sexual virtue and honorable conduct of its less influential members. In their minds, social status supplanted a reputation for honorable behavior as the basis of social repute. Although these corruptions of materialism were by no means universal, they were extremely important trends in colonial society because they originated with the wealthy and influential. The new attitudes concerning racial status were communicated to the peninsular Spanish rulers of the colony, and eventually, in 1779, were formally incorporated into royal legislation governing marriage conflicts. Before such legislation could be implemented, however, the changes had to be dealt with by the institutions that had intervened in marriage disputes: the church and the state, whose relative position and mutual relations had also been changing during this period of social transformation.

PART THREE

The Transformation of Church and Crown

CHAPTER 10

Changing Positions of Church and Crown

In the final decades of the seventeenth century a subtle shift began to take place in Mexican church-state relations, a shift that originated not in high-level political debates about the relationship of the two but rather on a more practical, day-to-day level. Despite its subtlety, it nonetheless had significant consequences for the resolution of disputes over marriage choices.

Before the second half of the seventeenth century, church and royal officials in colonial Mexico had been relatively equal in authority, but after 1650, continual competition between the two hierarchies began to result in greater influence for the royal bureaucrats at the expense of church officials. The issues may not have been major ones, but they accumulated. For example, one battle was fought over the issue of precedence in processions at major religious ceremonies. It had been the custom for some time for the pages of the archbishop to precede those of the viceroy in processions. At mid-century, however, Viceroy Antonio Toledo, Marquis of Mancera, insisted that his pages should take precedence, and he and Archbishop Mateo Sagade Buqueiro quarreled bitterly over the order in processions attended by both. The obvious solution, and the one that Sagade Buquiero insisted on, was for the two sets of pages to walk side by side as equals. But Viceroy Mancera was determined that his retinue should have priority, and he succeeded in winning the crown to his side in 1660. After 1665, all archbishops acquiesced in the king's order. In a society highly sensitive to questions of precedence, the viceroy's victory signaled that the scales of influence and power were starting to tip to the secular side.[1]

The archbishop's loss of prestige to the viceroy in this seemingly trivial matter began a process of slow but definite erosion of the position of the Catholic Church relative to the royal secular hierarchy. The decline affected church–state relations in numerous ways but had a particular impact on prenuptial conflict cases. One of the most important assets of church officials in enforcing decrees regarding marriage was the ability to call out the royal police. Although this was rarely done, the police were nonetheless vital because they represented royal power in New Spain; even the threat of their use often compelled rebellious or recalcitrant guardians and relatives to surrender their wards and offspring to church officials despite deep hostility to proposed marriages. When the threat of enforcement was not sufficient, the royal police actively intervened. The potential for disobedience of church orders was rapidly and effectively circumscribed.

The right of the church to use the royal police was a well-established custom, dating from the sixteenth century when the crown granted New World church officials authority to request royal assistance in enforcing ecclesiastical orders, leaving considerable leeway in details about procedures to be followed and precisely which royal officials could be called upon for assistance. From the high court to local royal representatives (*corregidores*) and their lieutenants to the local royal constables, church officials called upon the secular arm as they saw fit. Royal officials bearing the long, black standard of justice stood before dozens of homes in the sixteenth and seventeenth centuries and ordered the residents to allow young men and women to be released into the custody of the church so that they might state their desire to marry. A royal constable stood beside the church notary in 1591 when Gerónimo Valverde's father refused to surrender the key to the room in which he had locked Gerónimo to prevent the boy's marriage to Juana Herrera. The presence of the royal standard bearer was essential in persuading the Mexican Romeo's father to turn over the key that unlocked his son's room and released him from his irons.[2]

In the second half of the seventeenth century, royal high court officials throughout Spanish America became increasingly exasperated by the freedom of church officials to request police assistance from anyone they liked. In Mexico the conflict began in 1658, when the archbishop attempted to arrest a servant of the viceroy's by using the police power granted to him by another royal official. The viceroy responded by ordering the archbishop in the future to request police assistance only from the high court. When the king, refusing to support the viceroy, reaffirmed the right of church officials to seek police assistance from whoever could grant it, the high court began a policy of resistance: church officials were harassed with lengthy inquiries when royal assistance was requested, and pleas for royal police help were met with foot dragging.[3] By contrast, in the early years of the seventeenth century, church officials received royal police help on the same day they requested it. It was only a matter of hours between the time a young man appeared in church court to say his fiancée was being held against her will and the time the church notary, accompanied by the royal police, arrived at her doorstep to rescue her. By the 1670's, a similar request took at least a day, more often three to four days and sometimes longer, to execute. In 1670, a judge of the royal criminal court took five days to amass what he considered sufficient information to order the royal police to assist the church notary; still another day passed before the order was actually carried out. Because such delays sometimes made a crucial difference in the outcome of a case by allowing parents to evade ecclesiastical jurisdiction, the procrastination of the secular arm reduced the church's ability to protect young people from what was customarily seen as unjust interference in their choice of a marriage partner.[4]

Attempts to limit the church's access to the royal police were not initially aided by the crown, which had always fostered competition between the two. To the contrary, the king tried to cripple the high court's efforts to obstruct the church's use of the police. In 1678, Charles II reiterated the 1658 ruling that bishops should not be confined in their requests for police help to the high court but rather should be able to ask for assistance from any royal official. By 1690, however, high courts throughout Spanish America had been successful in forcing bishops to request police assistance only from them. The consequence was that officials of the diocesan court were no longer able to use the royal police at all when guardians or relatives threatened to unjustly impede a marriage: in the first place, the extremely high fees for police assistance from the highest royal court made such assistance beyond the reach of most of the petitioners to religious authorities. Second, the high court had so restricted access to the royal police that church officials, in the interest of conserving the goodwill of their royal counterparts, began to limit their requests to those in which the church had a specifically religious interest—such as ridding a diocese of a scandal-giving priest who ignored the church's order to stop celebrating Mass. Neither petitioners nor church enjoyed free and ready access to the royal police after this period. The consequences for religious authority over marriage oppositions were considerable.[5]

Without the royal police to insist that recalcitrant parents surrender their offspring to religious jurisdiction, ecclesiastical requests for parents to produce their children were backed up by the threat of excommunication alone. This practice had begun in the 1670's and 1680's, when royal police assistance first became more difficult to obtain. The threat of excommunication was used, largely successfully, to secure the release of young men and women who were involuntarily incarcerated by relatives, masters, or even the authorities. The request to release a person accompanied only by the threat of excommunication was relatively rare between 1670 and 1689, but after 1690 the threat alone became the principal means of securing a person's release to church custody.[6]

Loss of access to the royal police in 1690 quickly produced serious problems for church officials trying to enforce decrees. José Barrios was a young mulatto journeyman tailor in Mexico City He fell in love with a young woman named María de Córdoba and, because of his parents' opposition to the union, eloped with her on the evening of Easter Monday, 1710. When the couple came to church court to ask permission to be married, the court placed María in temporary custody, as was required for women who eloped; however, it was not María who needed protection from interfering relatives, but José. While María was in custody, José's parents, in league with the master tailor for whom José worked, managed to have him shipped to a distant town, supposedly for work-related reasons. In early June the church constable and notary paid a visit to the master tailor and asked him to produce José "in the service of God" and under pain of excommunication. The tailor ignored their threats. After several days, the constable and notary approached José's parents and his employer as well, threatening excommunication more emphatically than before. José's parents were polite but not overawed by the church officials. They said they would comply but that it would take time. Another six weeks passed before José Barrios appeared in church court. By this time it was clear that the reason for his parents' procrastination was their need for additional time to pressure José into forsaking María de Córdoba. It was also apparent that they brought José to court not because of the threat of excommunication but because their efforts had been successful: in August 1710, José declared to the church judge that he no longer wished to marry the woman he had eloped with at Easter time.

José's parents' interest in this affair was more than simple dislike of María. José supplied them with a good and steady income from his wages as a journeyman tailor, and if he were to marry, that economic support would be diverted from them to his wife. A desire to hold on to the services or wages of a child had been denounced by moralists for generations but José's parents were successful in preventing his marriage because they could easily ignore the church's threats of excommunication. They were not openly scornful or contemptuous, but they clearly had little respect for the church's orders when lacking royal sanctions.[7]

Eventually the crown dropped its opposition to the local high courts' restrictions on ecclesiastical use of the royal police. In 1712 the king capitulated to the high court's bureaucratic ambitions, but he attempted to temper the court's ascendancy by insisting that their control of such requests be limited to the territory the court governed directly. In Mexico this territory included the city of Mexico and its environs. This meant that in rural areas in the archdiocese, church courts could continue to request assistance from local constables. The response by the latter officials, however, was usually half-hearted and frequently self-defeating. Near the middle of the eighteenth century, in the rich agricultural area of Chalco, a young Spaniard named José Díaz eloped with the daughter of a muleteer; they went from one town to another, hotly pursued by José's father, who adamantly opposed the marriage. Near the edge of Mexico City the father caught up with them, took José away, and locked him up in the house of a relative. The girl went to the church for assistance, and the church sent for the royal police. The local royal constable removed José from the relative's house, but instead of placing him under guard he merely left him unsupervised in the constable's own house. When the church court finally reached the decision that José was responsible for restoring the young girl's honor by marrying her over his father's continued objections, it was discovered that José had fled on his own or had been taken from the constable's house. He was not heard from again. Ineffectual and half-hearted cooperation from the royal police could be as devastating as a complete lack of cooperation.[8]

In the past, the mere presence of the royal police had been a powerful deterrent not only to open defiance but also to attempts to ignore or push aside religious directives.[9] As ecclesiastical orders were increasingly disparaged in the first third of the eighteenth century, it became clear that the church's authority was suffering a severe loss of respect. The inability to enforce decrees because of the withdrawal of the royal police was not the only reason for this loss of respect, but it was a major contributing factor.

The ebbing of the independence of the Catholic Church in the New World that commenced around 1650 continued in a slow, subtle fashion until the end of the next century. Local viceroys and high courts were not the only agents of the church's gradual decline, since at about the same time the Council of the Indies, the Spanish governing body of the American colonies, instigated its own efforts to bring the ecclesiastical hierarchy under bureaucratic control. It did this, however, not by restricting the role of the police or the jurisdiction of church courts but by transforming the system of clerical appointments to American sees.

A mid-seventeenth-century decree by the Hapsburg king Philip IV forbade promotions and lateral movement within the American episcopal hierarchy. The decree was ineffective in wiping out movement between posts, but it did establish an official policy of non-promotion, and in 1689 the Council of the Indies indirectly challenged this policy by asking for exceptions. King Charles II agreed, and in the following decade the council made a few cautious promotions within the episcopate. In 1701 and again in 1722, however, the crown demonstrated its continuing opposition to the establishment of a general policy of promotion, in the latter year requiring royal approval in advance of any recommendation of a promotion.[10] The crown's noticeable reluctance to allow promotions probably stemmed from wariness of the council's increasingly secure position in naming new bishops. If a system of promotions were instituted, the process would become regularized, indeed bureaucratized, and the power of the council to name bishops would be expanded at the expense of the crown.

In fact the council's influence over the appointment of bishops increased despite the crown's efforts to curtail it, and by the first decades of the eighteenth century the council had come to control all appointments and promotions within the American episcopate.[11] One consequence of this shift was an increase in the number of Spanish-born prelates occupying American sees. In the eighteenth century, creole clerics were excluded from the posts in New Spain to such an extent that between 1713 and 1800 only one American—a Cuban, not a Mexican—was named to any of the three wealthiest dioceses of New Spain; the few New World natives who were appointed were named to the vastly poorer dioceses. Overall, the total number of American-born bishops was half what it had been in the previous century.[12] Because the members of the council were more familiar with their countrymen, and because Spanish-born prelates retained their European connections, the names of Spaniards were certain to be proposed for American vacancies over those of their creole contemporaries.

A more important aspect of the new system, however, was that for the first time a single body, the Council of the Indies, controlled both promotions and appointments for both ecclesiastical and royal officials. This change in the appointment system made expedient a change in the manner in which ecclesiastical officials dealt with their counterparts in the royal bureaucracy. With promotions being judged by the same body that reviewed royal bureaucrats, it behooved the ambitious prelate to maintain good relations with his secular colleagues. Many churchmen realized that espousing ecclesiastical causes that did not coincide with the interests of the royal bureaucracy could damage their own careers. As a result, not only did the eighteenth-century church become less combative, but church officials became increasingly solicitous of the opinion and goodwill of the royal bureaucracy, seeking bureaucrats' opinions in instances in which formerly—in the seventeenth century—they would have acted independently and without regard for the opinion even of high court judges.

These changes, in procedure as well as in church combativeness, inevitably affected the church's sway over marriage practices and

customs. In the early seventeenth century, church officials had managed to marry relatives of high court judges against the judges'
wishes and to unite courtiers of the viceroy against his will. The inability to request royal police assistance from any but the highest
court sharply curtailed the church's ability to intervene in such circumstances. And since church officials now relied on the high court
to enforce church orders and were being evaluated by the same officials who evaluated these royal bureaucrats, they could ill afford to
be on bad terms with high court judges. The result was that marriages opposed by members of the high court were rarely protected
by the church after the beginning of the eighteenth century. One of
the few stunning exceptions to this policy was the marriage in 1744
of a female relative of the man destined to become one of New
Spain's most eminent jurists, Baltasar Ladrón de Guevara. Antonia
was involved in a long-term sexual relationship with the son of Don
Felipe Tineo, a supernumerary judge of New Spain's criminal
court. But his father, a peninsular, adamantly opposed the marriage.
When Antonia became pregnant, church officials secretly married
her to the judge's son. Such was the secrecy surrounding this marriage that it was never recorded, even by church officials, until after
Don Felipe's death.[13]

Instead of countering the unjust interference of royal officials in
the marriages of their kin, church officials in New Spain for the first
time began openly to foster such marriages and to protect the interests of royal judges. In the sixteenth century, the crown had prohibited its officials from marrying women who were residents of
the district they governed; such marriages could take place only
with a special royal exemption. The law was irregularly and often
feebly enforced in the seventeenth century, but in the eighteenth
century several serious efforts were made to curtail these marriages
altogether by refusing to grant exemptions. In 1728, during a period
of strict enforcement, church officials allowed Don Juan Picado Pacheco, a judge of the high court, to secretly marry Doña Josefa Ignacia Carranza Bocanegra, the daughter of a wealthy cattle rancher
in the viceroyalty of New Spain. The reasons for secrecy were
stated to be not only the judge's position but Josefa's "honesty," undoubtedly a reference to their sexual involvement and her likely loss
of virginity. In later years, when the crown increasingly refused to
allow such marriages, Mexican church officials started a whole new

policy of making secret weddings available and recording the illicit marriages in a separate book that was kept out of the hands of suspicious crown officials. Instead of being in conflict with secular officials, church officials, with an eye to their own best interests, actually sought complicity with them.[14]

Conventional interpretations of the changing relationship between church and state have attributed the decline of the church's authority in the New World to the policies of the new ruling house at Spain's helm after 1713. Yet the Bourbons arrived on the throne fully four decades after the erosion of ecclesiastical independence began in Mexico. The bureaucratic competition fostered by the Hapsburgs provided the conditions under which the royal bureaucracies were the first able to clip the wings of religious authority. Furthermore, it was the Council of the Indies, not the crown, that was fundamentally responsible for restructuring appointments to American bishoprics. Having the same bureaucracy in charge of appointments to both the royal and the religious hierarchies ensured that the "two swords" would find it mutually beneficial to cooperate. This action did more to end the repeated conflicts between the religious and secular bureaucracies than all the royal decrees together urging peace and harmony, but tranquility was created at the expense of the ascendancy and independence of the church.

Not until the middle of the eighteenth century did the new ruling monarchs of Spain openly support the high court's requirement that bishops seek the assistance of the secular arm only from the court, a move that coincided with a major assault on ecclesiastical privilege initiated by King Charles III (1759–88). By the end of the century, the state had consolidated its position: royal officials were even able to demand that ecclesiastical judges provide the evidence (or at least a summary) on which the request for police assistance was based. Thus the high court judges not only were apprised of what the church was doing, but also had obtained an informal means of checking up on the church courts and making certain that they would not be supporting any action that royal court judges themselves would not have ordered.[15]

The changing balance of power between ecclesiastical and royal officials that began in 1650 had wide-ranging effects on a variety of matters,[16] including, to a significant degree, prenuptial conflicts, simply because Spanish families were for the first time able to enlist

the aid of royal officials in seeking solutions to conflicts over marriage choices. When the balance between religious and royal authority began to shift, wealthy families began to use the royal courts
to prevent marriages that they viewed as socially undesirable. In
1688, the sixteen-year-old son of a bakery owner became sexually
involved with a mestiza servant girl named Juana de San Antonio.
He promised to marry her, but had no intention of doing so because
he was studying for the priesthood. About three months after the
relationship began, Juana began to insist that the young man marry
her. He refused, alleging that she had not been a virgin for him, having had sex with a number of her male friends.

What was unusual in this instance was that the boy's father had
his servant Juana arrested by the royal criminal court for "bother-
ing" his son. At the same time, Juana's mother, who knew of her
daughter's involvement with the baker's son, went to the church
courts and asked that Francisco de Amaya be forced to produce his
son so that the two young people could give a declaration of intent
to marry. The son appeared but denied any intention to marry.
Juana (who unbeknownst to her mother was in a royal jail) never appeared, nor did the father mention Juana's arrest to either her mother
or the religious officials. Four months later, Juana's mother reappeared in church court to ask Francisco to produce her daughter. By
this time the royal court had already decided in favor of the baker
and had sentenced Juana to a women's jail, euphemistically called a
place of retreat, in the city of Puebla. The royal court's decision became the defense of both father and son when church court officials
demanded that they appear to answer Juana's mother's demand for
fulfillment of the promise to marry.[17] The church officials insisted
that the son had an obligation to the young woman, the royal court
notwithstanding, but they were unable to enforce this position. The
case ended when Juana married a man she met in Puebla. Royal
courts, for reasons to be explored in the next chapter, were more
willing to prevent marriages than was the church.

As the power of the royal bureaucracy continued to grow in the
first third of the eighteenth century, the use of its authority to prevent marriages became increasingly common. The mother of Bernardo Ursana y García harbored a strong dislike for Ana María Machuca, her son's longtime concubine and mother of his infant son
(her grandson). When it appeared that Bernardo was about to marry

Ana María in order to legitimate his son, Bernardo's mother turned her son over to the colonel of a local regiment and sought a viceregal decree to banish him from the colony. Exiling him would prevent him from marrying. It may be recalled that the threat of such exile was considered unjust interference in the seventeenth century and was one of the major reasons for ecclesiastical intervention; but 1738 was not 1638. The mother's appeal to the viceroy alleged only that Bernardo was a layabout who only wasted his time; it said nothing about his matrimonial intentions. Meanwhile, Ana María appealed to the church court for help in stopping Bernardo's mother. Although the church magistrate sent a note to the viceroy asking to be allowed to interview the incarcerated Bernardo about his relationship with Ana María, the viceroy ignored the request, and Bernardo was sentenced to four years' hard labor in the Havana garrison.[18] Ecclesiastical authorities were unable to do anything to help Ana María because they lacked the power to enforce their ruling and were dependent on royal officials for such assistance.

Parents had become able to exile their offspring in this manner in the third decade of the eighteenth century. The son or daughter wishing to marry was accused of being "disobedient" or "lazy" and was not permitted to respond to the charges made against him or her. Sons were jailed, deported, or drafted by viceregal decrees; daughters were locked in reformatories. Religious officials were helpless in the face of such opposition. The use of these arbitrary methods parallels the development in France of the *lettres de cachet*, which were often used to detain, often for years on end, young men and women who had committed no offense. Although these abuses of parental authority would eventually provoke sharp criticism from a later colonial viceroy, they continued to afford parents a means of exercising arbitrary authority.[19] A significant number of the instances of exile or imprisonment of young people in colonial Mexico involved the efforts of relatives to prevent marriages that they thought were undesirable.[20]

Only rarely were young people able to overcome arbitrary arrest and exile by viceregal decree. One of the few was Don Joaquín Martínez Chavarelo, son of a prominent resident of Mexico City. In May 1743 Don Joaquín promised to marry Doña Manuela Rivadeneira y México, a young Spanish woman who apparently had some social standing, for the ecclesiastical officials invariably used the appellation "Doña" in referring to her. Don Joaquín's father was intensely hostile to the union. Evidence of his antagonism appeared the month following the engagement, when he secured a viceregal decree exiling his son to the penal colony on San Juan de Ulúa, an island just offshore from the gulf port of Veracruz, solely to prevent the marriage to Manuela. The extent of the father's opposition to the match can be gauged from the fact that the climate of Veracruz was known to be unhealthy and the death rate from yellow fever high. Don Joaquín, however, made a striking response to his father's gambit. While imprisoned on the fortress of San Juan de Ulúa, he wrote out a power of attorney, including a power to contract proxy marriage, to a close friend who was an official of the Royal Treasury in Mexico City. This was remarkable in itself, for Don Joaquín not only had to have money and influence to ensure that his message reached Mexico City, he also had to be sufficiently cognizant of ecclesiastical procedures to send the proper forms needed to contract a marriage by proxy. In other words, he had to be well educated and well versed in ecclesiastical procedure, in an age in which only a small fraction of the total population was even able to sign their own names.

Even when presented with this imaginative response, church officials did not leap at the opportunity to help a young man who had been unjustly imprisoned for desiring to marry, as they would have done in the seventeenth century. Only after the power of attorney had been presented and carefully examined was the church willing to undertake what Don Joaquín had requested. Furthermore, the church was so reluctant to incur the wrath of the viceroy that it interviewed a number of witnesses to make certain that Don Joaquín had been condemned to Ulúa solely for wanting to marry. Only after all of these procedures had been completed and a formal declaration of intent obtained from Doña Manuela did the ecclesiastical judge of Mexico City proceed to order the proxy marriage. This case fully illustrates the difficulties an eighteenth-century couple faced when threatened with exile if they failed to marry in accord with family wishes or wanted to marry someone the elders did not care for. Access to the viceroy strengthened the authority of wealthy and politically influential parents over their offspring's marriage partners.[21]

This case also contrasts sharply with the numerous seventeenth-century instances in which parents threatened to send their offspring to the Philippines rather than see them marry. Such actions were usually condemned as "unjust interferences," but both cultural values and institutional responses had changed in the intervening years. In the seventeenth century, parents were often unable to achieve their ends because church officials interposed themselves between the couple and the criminal courts by allowing secret marriages, often nullifying royal criminal court orders for arrest. One hundred years later, church officials, hampered by the political pressures on their leadership, were no longer willing to contradict royal authority. In the eighteenth century it was up to the couple to rescue themselves—if they could.

The slightly less well connected found that the royal criminal court provided another means of preventing marriages, based on essentially the same kinds of legal judgments as those issued by the viceroy. Parents lodged complaints of sexual misconduct (concubinage), disobedience, laziness, and vagrancy against their offspring before the judges of the highest royal criminal court. Ignacio de Rosas was condemned to involuntary military service in the Philippines for "vagrancy" when it appeared that his principal offense consisted in wanting to marry Luisa de la Paz. Vicente Hernández was jailed on the basis of his mother's denunciation of him for "laziness" when in fact the real issue was his desire to marry María González. Occasionally parents went further afield. One father resurrected a long-outstanding warrant resulting from a feud between his son and a cousin. The dispute had been resolved years before, but the warrant had never been officially canceled. When the son tried to marry, the father turned the warrant over to the royal police. His son was promptly arrested and the marriage preparations came to a halt.[22]

Parents also used municipal courts to prevent marriages. Don Rodrigo Peláez opposed his son's marrying María Manuela Espindola and denounced the pair to the municipal authorities for concubinage. City police arrested the couple and threw both of them in jail. Although Don Rodrigo's son was released on bond after four months, because of his father's opposition he did not marry María Manuela; he continued to live with her at irregular intervals, however, much to the annoyance of María's mother and the exasperation of María herself.[23]

Frequent recourse to institutional authority to stop marriages is a novel characteristic of this period. In the seventeenth century, direct personal actions by parents and relatives—threats, beatings, intimidation—were the chief means of attempting to halt marriages. In the eighteenth century personal actions continued but took place less frequently, as those opposing matches increasingly began to appeal to both royal and ecclesiastical officials. As a result, institutions came to play an increasingly important role in suppressing marriages. In a sense, colonial society was becoming tamed: people relied increasingly on bureaucratic institutions and rules rather than on extralegal, personal methods to achieve their ends.

From the viceroy to the royal courts to the humble municipal courts, a whole new range of possibilities opened up to relatives and guardians seeking to prevent marriages. Why these courts should have been more willing than the ecclesiastical courts to adapt to social change is an interesting question; the answer lies in the greater flexibility and expediency of the royal courts. The Mexican church was encumbered by a vast body of doctrine, hallowed by centuries of tradition that gave it the aura of the sacred and unalterable; but the viceroy, the royal courts, and the municipal courts were not so circumscribed. At the same time, the traditional Hispanic values that exalted honor and condemned the use of imprisonment, the Catholic extolling of virginity and belief that the choice of a state in life was God's election—all these were disparaged in an increasingly secular world. To control, by force if necessary, one's offspring's choice of a marriage partner was no longer contemptible but expedient. Less encumbered by tradition, royal courts and officials could simply mirror the prevailing changes of society.

Only rarely did church officials successfully counter the state's imprisonment orders. They were occasionally able to secure the release of a young man sent to exile and permit him to fulfill his promise to wed, but only if the royal authorities were inclined to cooperate. Augustín Pérez Torres, a widower from Mexico City's Indian elite, began living with a mestiza named Juana Barragán after his wife's death. He intended to marry her, but his mother opposed the idea violently. Realizing the seriousness of her son's intentions, the mother, herself a leading member of the Indian community, made use of her political connections. She contacted one of the senior judges on the high court, Diego de la Madrid, and asked him to imprison Augustín and Juana for sexual misconduct. Augustín was furious with his mother for treating him, a grown man and a widower, like a wayward child, and even more furious about the jailing of Juana. He told church officials that she had committed no greater crime than wanting to marry him and did not deserve to be jailed. Fearing also that prison might cause her to change her mind about their marriage, Augustín asked that she be removed to temporary custody until the nuptial arrangements were complete. Before granting his request, however, the church officials sent a note to Judge de la Madrid asking him to verify the story. De la Madrid replied that he had no information to contradict Augustín's allegations and would not object to Juana's removal to church custody. That step was promptly carried out, and shortly thereafter Augustín and Juana were married.[24]

The church's deference, even submissiveness, in this case contrasts sharply with the usual response of ecclesiastical officials in the seventeenth century, who never consulted royal officials before acting. In the earlier period, church officials had arranged secret marriages in the jail itself and had in effect nullified royal orders for arrest and punishment on grounds of concubinage, precisely the charges made in this case. The forceful and independent seventeenth-century church was a very different institution from the church of the eighteenth century, so respectful and deferential to royal authority.[25]

It might be tempting to attribute the increasing success of royal courts and viceregal decrees in preventing marriages to the rise of a class with a greater interest in defending or preventing certain kinds of marriages, but this explanation does not adequately describe the situation of colonial Mexico. The increased and successful use of jailing and exile was not restricted to a single class or ethnic group. Parents who halted weddings in this manner ranged from those at the very summit of the colonial elite, such as Don Francisco Martínez Chavarelo, who sent his son to Ulúa; to the middle sectors of society, represented by Joaquin Peláez, who had the municipal police arrest his son for concubinage; and even to the Indians, such as the mother of Augustín Pérez Torres, who used the criminal court to put her son and his intended behind bars. Nor did any single motive prevail: imprisonment was sought by parents who opposed marriages for reasons of economic inequality, disparity in social status, or difference of race. Neither class nor motive can explain why eighteenth-century parents so often used criminal charges against their offspring. The greater availability and responsiveness of royal courts, however, did play a significant role.

Faced with a decline in their authority to enforce its traditional marriage practices, officials of the Catholic Church in Mexico gradually began to modify the ways they intervened in marriage conflict cases. These changes, first in church practices and ultimately in church doctrine, are the subject of Chapter 11.

CHAPTER II

The Church's Retreat on
Aggressive Intervention

Deprived of the royal police and increasingly out of step with the changing social values of the Hispanic world, the Catholic Church nonetheless continued to protect young couples from parental opposition, albeit with declining enthusiasm, until 1779, when Charles III enjoined it from doing so. In the interim, however, church officials, caught between adherence to the traditional values regarding unjust interference and the changing attitudes of Hispanic society toward parental authority, entered into an apparent crisis of confidence in their policies. Their response was to make a number of changes in church bureaucratic procedure, always avoiding any direct conflict with inherited interpretations of religious doctrine. When church officials eventually came round to making a fundamental change in interpreting religious doctrine in 1770, their pronouncements had little or no effect on the outcome of disputes over marriages. Rather it was the incremental administrative modifications made before 1770 that had the greatest impact on the resolution of prenuptial conflicts in church courts.

As a result of the modifications in ecclesiastical policy, the church's traditional responses to unjust interference were less effective and made with greater caution than in the past, and it became nearly impossible to get the church to render an opinion on any matter relating to such disputes. Since ecclesiastical protection was more limited than before, it could be more easily overcome by a determined parent. The result was a significant increase in the number of parents who were able to prevent marriages. From a low of 7 percent between 1574 and 1689, parents' success rate rose first to 24 percent by 1715 and then to 36 percent by 1779.[1]

When in 1690 the church ceased to protect the honor of Spanish women by permitting de facto secret marriages, it eliminated one of its most powerful means for combating unjust interference in prenuptial conflicts. Dropping the dispensation of banns failed to provoke significant debate within the church over a replacement method. Instead, another way of countering unjust interference— temporary custody—emerged by default as the chief means of intervention. Until 1779, temporary custody was the primary response of church officials to conflicts over potential marriage partners.

Temporary custody had been used principally to allow a woman who had eloped time for deliberation, and occasionally to provide needed protection if a woman's life appeared to be endangered. These traditional uses continued throughout the eighteenth century, but when secret marriages were ended in 1690, custody began being pressed into service in a variety of other circumstances for which it had not been intended. Designed to protect a woman's honor, custody was, for instance, applied to men for the first time.[2] More important, it began to be resorted to in exactly the same kinds of situations in which secret marriages had been ordered before, principally instances in which there was evidence that force was being used. Threats on the life of a young couple, which formerly would have led to an immediate secret marriage, in the eighteenth century led only to temporary custody while the banns of marriage were announced.[3]

Although clearly a lesser measure than secret marriage, for about twenty-five years, from 1690 until 1715, temporary custody was a fairly effective means of protecting couples against the malicious interference of relatives or guardians, for it provided temporary protection when violence or excessive persuasion threatened to prevent the marriage. Sometimes, however, relatives and guardians gained access, against church orders, to their children and managed to prevent marriages; these incidents were in part responsible for the initial increase in marriages prevented after 1690.

The removal of a young woman from her parents' or guardian's home to temporary custody elsewhere was a delicate matter and one that followed strict protocol. The church notary and the ecclesiastical constable arrived at the woman's home and informed her parents or guardians that they wished to see her, "so they might do with her a certain business in the service of God Our Lord." They then accompanied her to the local church court, where the judge asked her if she wished to marry. Regardless of her response, church officials ordered her placed in temporary custody after her statement. If she responded affirmatively, she only waited out the days until her marriage could take place. If she said she had changed her mind or denied she had promised to marry, she was given a three-day period in which to reflect on her statement. Often this time away from intimidating relatives or guardians allowed her to reassert her own desires, and when she was brought back to court at the end of the three days for a second declaration the negative response was transformed into a positive one.[4]

The main drawback to temporary custody, which made it less effective than secret marriages, was the shortness of the time. The customary three days established by canon law were in most cases too brief an interval to allow a young woman to overcome her fear of her family and assert herself. One young woman kept in *deposito* for only three days later acknowledged that her parents had frightened her into denying that she wished to marry. In other cases, this acknowledgment came too late, after the marriage had been called off and the young man, thinking quite understandably that the woman no longer wished to marry him, had arranged to marry someone else.[5] A longer period, of at least nine to thirty days, in which the young women were away from their families often gave them a better chance to regain confidence in their own intentions.

Temporary custody was in some instances not even possible, for without the royal police, the church constable and notary had no more powerful weapon in their arsenal than the threat of excommunication. When in the early part of the eighteenth century parents became less and less troubled by the prospect of excommunication, it became increasingly difficult to compel parents to surrender their offspring voluntarily to make a declaration of intent.[6] As a result, church officials, rather than giving up on the declaration, fell back on the lesser of two evils, and in 1715 began to ask young men and women if they wished to marry before removing them to protective custody. This declaration of intent, which had previously always been made in the church court before the ecclesiastical magistrate, was now made in the house of the guardian or family.

Nothing else about the declaration of intent changed. The church constable and notary still informed the family that they were there for "a certain business in the service of God Our Lord." Young people were still frequently removed to temporary custody. But the simple fact of changing the place in which the declaration was taken—from church court to the home—was a sign of the church's eroding confidence. Barring unusual circumstances, church officials would not remove a woman from her home unless she acknowledged both the promise to marry and her continuing desire to fulfill that commitment. Obviously, this was more difficult when the woman had to speak within earshot of the very people who were threatening to stop her marriage.[7]

Declarations at home were still a moderately successful means of overcoming unreasonable interference in the choice of a marriage partner, but they were by no means as effective as secret marriages had been. The presence of menacing relatives was sometimes sufficient to cause the fainthearted as well as the terrified to deny the existence of a promise to marry or even an acquaintanceship with the intended. Since protective custody was rarely granted in instances of denial, more marriages were thus prevented after 1715 than had been earlier.

Late in the 1720's a third and more significant change came about. Because of the declining sense of obligation and increasing uncertainty about promise keeping, around 1730 church officials withdrew from their historically active role in forcing young men to marry women seduced under promise of marriage and instead waited for the parties to come to an agreement. This shift, discussed in Chapter 6, to treating disputes over broken engagements as private disputes had an additional unintended consequence for prenuptial conflicts.

Before 1730, relatives and guardians attempting to halt weddings had their hands tied by church courts. Because the church was committed to the principle of individual will in the choice of a marriage partner, the procedures it followed, such as dispensation of the banns, were not designed to allow time for a response, much less time to mount a formal lawsuit. Further, the only grounds permitted by church law to permanently prohibit a marriage were the diriment impediments. As explained earlier, these impediments related primarily to the presence of blood or spiritual kinship between the pair, being under age, the existence of a vow of chastity, or impotence. It was extremely difficult, if not impossible, for parents to invent such conditions. In other words, not only was the church court unsympathetic, but parents had few valid legal grounds upon which to sue.

The shift to treating engagements as private matters, which effectively loosened the bonds that had tied the hands of relatives and guardians in church courts, was linked to an obscure area of canon law known as the prohibitive impediments.[8] Unlike the diriment impediments, which were powerful enough to nullify a marriage after the ceremony had been performed, despite the existence of a sexual relationship and regardless of the existence of children, prohibitive impediments were only intended to delay a marriage that had not yet taken place. Although both diriment and prohibitive impediments could be dispensed, the consequence of contravening a prohibitive impediment was only a wrist-slapping penalty.[9]

The range of the prohibitive impediments was broad; many eighteenth-century canon lawyers proscribed marriage to not-yet-baptized converts or to someone having taken a simple vow of chastity, as well as marriages during Advent or Lent or if the church issued an order forbidding it for any reason. In the late sixteenth century, however, a new impediment had been introduced by the great Spanish jurist Diego Covarrubias y Leyva. He interdicted marriage when one of the parties had a prior undissolved commitment to marry a third party—in other words, was engaged to someone else. Covarrubias's wording, indicating that a preexisting commitment had to be uncovered before the marriage took place, was consistent with the general doctrine that prohibitive impediments had an impact only if introduced before a marriage was formalized.[10] A prior engagement was a great deal easier to invent than a bond of consanguinity or a vow to become a priest. Coupled with the church's new position on marriage after seduction, it provided exactly the pretext parents needed.[11]

At seventeen Doña Juana Monriquit became engaged to a respectable twenty-two-year-old Spanish merchant with good economic prospects named Don Augustín Nieto. Juana's stepmother was not pleased. She wanted to keep her hands on the inheritance to which Juana was entitled. To prevent Juana from marrying Don Augustín, she retained the services of an impoverished young man who probably fancied Juana himself. Handing him a rosary that belonged to her stepdaughter, Doña Antonia Letón directed the young man to present himself in ecclesiastical court and declare that Juana could not marry Augustín because she had promised to marry him. Juana was furious when the interloper made his claim. Characterizing him as a "ragged, lazy cigar maker," she added that he was neither intellectually nor financially capable of fabricating such a claim on his own. The disreputable hireling, undoubtedly responding to the stepmother's financial blandishments, refused to budge; he insisted that Juana had given him the rosary as proof of their engagement and testified that the engagement had been contracted two years before—the first and only time the two had ever met face to face. Juana replied that to allege an engagement based on a single encounter two years before was ridiculous, as indeed it was.

The ease with which Antonia Letón was able to invent a promise to marry between Juana and the cigar maker illustrates one of the novel characteristics of these conflicts. A prior commitment to marry someone else differed from other types of impediments to a marriage in that it did not depend on the existence of a fact that could be verified independently of the testimony of the parties, such as blood kinship or the time of year. An argument that a promise had been made, without witnesses, depended largely for its success upon the determination of the parties to stick to their stories. Claims of this sort were, of course, very hard to disprove if the party making the claim was tenacious. Evidence of a prior engagement, so easily fabricated, thus provided an excellent weapon in the arsenal of relatives and guardians trying to prevent a match.

Even more critical for the outcome of cases like this was the church's decision to treat disputes over engagements as matters to be settled between the parties. The church and its officials stubbornly refused to judge the truth of the appeal. Even the patent absurdity of the cigar maker's petition failed to jar officials from their newly assumed passivity. The church judge restricted himself to ordering the sides to respond to each other, and so the stepmother and cigar maker continued to make endless inane requests and the case dragged on for months. After five months of this affirmation and counteraffirmation, the cigar maker declared that he was short of funds to pay the church fees for the testimony of witnesses (what was probably lacking was witnesses who could be paid a sufficient sum to perjure themselves in ecclesiastical court). He then disappeared. Still the church held up the marriage for another two months, dutifully waiting for the cigar maker to produce the money for the witness fees. After finally convincing the church officials that the cigar maker was not going to appear, Juana eventually received permission to marry Augustín Nieto, just as she wanted—fully seven months after the lawsuit had begun.[12]

Had it not been for the financial collapse of the cigar maker, the debate could have continued unabated. Alleging a prior engagement could hold a marriage up indefinitely, since it was impossible for the couple to marry unless that condition was eliminated. Because church officials refused to intervene in matters concerning an engagement, a mere prohibitive impediment had virtually the same effect as a permanent or diriment prohibition against wedding.

Juana Monriquit's victory in the case was due to her persistence and determination. During the long months of separation from her fiancé in temporary custody, her commitment to marriage remained firm. Both she and Augustín endured considerable financial hardship. They had to sell nearly all they had in order to bear the costs of the lawsuit—Augustín even had to sell his own clothes. Their case shows how necessary it was in these circumstances, when the church chose to act only as a mouthpiece for the one who petitioned the court, to have persistence and the financial capacity to support a lawsuit, even against the most patently outrageous claims. Procrastination and time were on the side of the opposers; only powerful determination could counter them.

In this case, not only did the fight drag on beyond all reasonable expectations, but the stepmother's apparent financial interest in opposing the marriage was not taken as a reason to discredit her suit. With the church acting only as a neutral forum and not as a decision maker, and in the absence of a social consensus about the value of Doña Antonia Letón's motives, what seventeenth-century Spanish society had considered a malicious motive—the greed and personal ambition of Juana's stepmother—came very close to preventing the marriage. Other couples were not so lucky.[13]

Lawsuits like Juana Monriquit's over the existence of a prior engagement were significantly different from those created over earlier promises to marry in Mexican history. The questions at issue were not those of honor or revenge or financial restitution or child support such as had spurred litigation in earlier years.[14] Disputes over engagement as a prohibitive impediment were notable for their length, their expense, and above all the unwillingness of the parents opposing the marriage to reach a negotiated resolution. In cases where revenge, honor, or financial restitution was at stake, both sides were interested in eventual settlement, although the extent to which a party was willing to accommodate of course varied. In cases in which a prior engagement was being alleged by relatives in order to prevent a marriage, every possible opportunity was taken to try to prevent a resolution from being reached. In one instance, a requested three-day postponement of a court appearance was stretched into seventy-two days because the church courts refused to or could not enforce the deadlines they had established for response to the accusations.[15] Procrastination became the key to success in many of these suits; delays, often absurdly prolonged, were characteristic.

Historians have sometimes remarked on the slowness of church courts and their inefficiency as a means of solving disputes, arguing that these factors account for the emergence of secular courts as primary decision makers.[16] But the causes for this profound change in attitudes toward prenuptial disputes run deeper than the superficial criterion of efficiency. When the norms that the church enforced enjoyed the widespread support of the Hispanic community, the church could act swiftly and decisively. There was no question of waiting indefinitely for evidence, nor was there any question of waiting for the parties to come to an agreement, or of tolerating the endless delays that characterized these cases in the eighteenth century.[17] When the church realized that the fundamental values of society were no longer the traditional values the church supported, it retreated to the position that prenuptial conflicts were private affairs. The slowness of the ecclesiastical judicial apparatus was a reaction to the growing tension between the church's traditional policies and the eroding public confidence in the norms it represented.

The existence of a prior engagement served as a pretext for a succession of parental lawsuits to prevent marriages after 1730. The lawsuits were used in a variety of circumstances, from attempts to hold on to inheritances to efforts to prevent economically or socially unequal marriages.[18] Although they were not the chief means of opposition, they were important because of the volume of documentation they produced, the amount of time ecclesiastical officials spent on them, and the wealth and power of the families involved. Only the well-to-do could afford to pay lawyers' fees, or to buy witnesses to stand in for them in the dispute. These cases were further significant because they offered the wealthy a forum for articulating their interests and their dissatisfaction with ecclesiastical procedures and doctrine.

Because the courts had to be specifically requested to intervene, knowledge of the church's procedures was needed to launch a lawsuit; wealth was necessary to sustain one. Without funds, and ignorant of the technicalities of canonical procedure, humbler artisans and craftsmen hoping to marry lost the once-powerful assistance of ecclesiastical authorities. Young people seeking to marry were also deprived of a potentially great advantage, for they usually lacked the financial stamina and sometimes also the emotional determination to sustain a lawsuit.[19] The unintended consequences of the church's withdrawal to the position that conflicts over marriage arrangements were private strengthened the hand of opposers in general and the wealthy in particular, because it restored to them the advantage that had been partially equalized by active ecclesiastical intervention and normative values regarding unjust interference in the seventeenth century. Only rarely did someone of modest means attempt to pursue a case, and when an attempt was made, financial strictures invariably caused the case to be abandoned with as much speed as it had been launched.[20]

On the other hand—although it was nearly always very rich families who instituted these suits, and nearly always the rich who were successful—great wealth did not necessarily assure a successful outcome for the ones who instituted a suit. As the case of Doña Juana Monriquit shows, sheer determination was sometimes sufficient to prevent a lawsuit from interfering with a marriage. Sometimes, too, it was plain, ordinary luck that brought success. A wealthy hacienda owner from Zultepec who wanted to prevent his son's marriage to a mestiza alleged that the son had previously been engaged to a slave on the estate. The slave's sudden death in an epidemic, however, swept away the basis for his suit, and on the son's petition, the church courts ordered the planned marriage to take place immediately.[21]

The response of church officials in granting the petition to marry illustrates another dimension of ecclesiastical attitudes. In the case just mentioned, the church was not concerned with considerations of social inequality or with the merits of the father's objections, but only with the presence or absence of a prohibitive impediment. On the infrequent occasions when the church actually intervened, its actions were based solely on the abstract requirements of canon law, or, in other words, on the existence of a diriment or prohibitive impediment.[22] The case of the Zultepec hacienda owner also illustrates that church officials had not fully adapted themselves to the changing values around them; its decision did not rest on what eighteenth-century Hispanic elites were increasingly critical of, namely, marriage between Spaniards and castas.

Beginning in the 1740's, church officials showed signs of being caught in a crisis of confidence in their traditional position of combating unjust interference. Unwilling to countenance any alteration in the formal church doctrine opposing unjust interference, but aware of the changing attitudes toward status, "interest," and patriarchal authority, they appeared to doubt more and more the wisdom of the policies under which they operated, and reacted by beginning to treat not only disputes over broken engagements but all prenuptial conflicts primarily as private disputes between two parties.[23] Church officials no longer openly interfered with the decisions of families regarding choices of marriage partners, and they refrained even further from intervention in prenuptial conflicts after the 1740's. Temporary custody, if requested, was still granted, but if the parents protested, church officials withdrew to their passive position. The result was a sharp upswing in the number of marriages prevented by means that were previously regarded as unjust and malicious.[24]

The refusal to intervene was most noticeable when couples met all the traditional requirements of church law. One young woman, placed promptly in temporary custody, declared her willingness to marry. But the church officials, taking the position that such conflicts were private disputes, refused to perform the ceremony and allowed her father to harass her for nearly a year before she finally capitulated to his pressure and renounced her intention to marry.[25]

The shift to treating prenuptial conflicts as private affairs extended to all cases in which parents' actions—attempts to hold on to an inheritance, and the use of coercion and incarceration—were of the type that in the seventeenth century would have been treated as unjust interference. The responses of church officials in such cases contrast strikingly with the church's responses in previous eras. José Mariano Ibáñez, the younger son of a wealthy and prominent Oaxaca merchant, was sent off to study for the priesthood, as was often the case with younger sons. However, he discovered that he cared for a young woman more than he welcomed the prospect of taking orders, so he resigned from his studies and set about trying to marry Ana Josefa Téllez Malpica. He presented witnesses to the church court and asked for the required prenuptial publicity. Only one week remained when his older brother, accompanied by the guardian of his deceased father's estate, swooped down on him, locked him up in a room, and sent a lawyer to state falsely in church court that he no longer wished to marry. The older brother and the guardian wanted to keep the entire estate for themselves and had no intention of sharing any of the benefits with the younger son, whom they had hoped to keep buried in the priesthood.

Locked in a room and without the freedom to move about, young José Mariano Ibáñez did what Gerónimo Valverde had done in 1591, when Herrera's father locked him up for attempting to marry Juana Herrera: he wrote a note and smuggled it out. His fiancée took the message to the ecclesiastical court, just as Gerónimo's uncle had done for the sixteenth-century Romeo. But in 1769 the Catholic Church was no longer an active intervenor, and restriction of matrimonial freedom no longer pricked the church's conscience. The report went unnoticed until the young man's brother heard of it. Realizing that Ana Josefa and José Mariano were not easily intimidated, the brother and guardian took yet another step. They sent a lawyer in Ana Josefa's name, without her knowledge, to state that she no longer wished to marry José Mariano. This might have ended the case, except that church procedure required that any withdrawal be ratified by the participant after a cooling-off period. Ten days later, the church notary appeared at Ana Josefa's door and asked her to verify her withdrawal from the marriage. Furious, Ana Josefa informed him that she had never authorized such a withdrawal and had no intention of withdrawing in the future. The notary left in some confusion. Two days later, however, the mendacious lawyer reappeared in church court to state that Ana Josefa's emphatic declaration had been a misunderstanding, for she had never intended to marry. At this point the documentation ends prematurely, and we are left in suspense.[26]

The great contrast between the church's immediate defense of matrimonial liberty in 1591 and its reluctance to help in 1769 indicates just how much not only outcomes but attitudes had changed. Depriving a child of the liberty required by marriage was no longer treated by church courts as unreasonable conduct, and as a result force played a greater role in determining the outcomes of conflicts over marriage. Furthermore, the intent of José Mariano's relatives to hold on to his inheritance was no longer a matter to elicit social opprobrium, nor was the use of excessive force regarded as malicious interference in a marriage.[27] Such behavior was met with indifference, if not approval.

In the seventeenth century, the testimony of friends and neighbors on the suitability of a match and the reasonableness of the parents' objections had been critical, for it established a social consensus about the injustice of parental behavior. The actions of the church simply reinforced the normative values of the society regarding prenuptial conflicts. The changing normative values of Hispanic society no longer condemned marriage for gain or preferred the protection of feminine honor to the preservation of distinctions of status; and thus the basis for intervention was undermined. There was, however, another significant lesson in these conflicts. The church's shift to treating first engagements and then prenuptial disputes as *de parte*, or conflicts between two parties, lent strength to the growing belief that disputes over marriage choices were no longer matters of public concern in which neighbors and community members should intervene, but rather were "private" matters between the individual and his or her family.

When an advisory body was convened by the crown to consider church jurisdiction over prenuptial conflicts in 1775, it alleged that the church was culpable for promoting individual free will in marriage. The opening paragraph of the advisory panel's report began:

"The excessive support that church officials provide the poorly understood [concept that] freedom to marry is absolute and unlimited, fails to distinguish among persons, and at times goes against the just resistance of parents and relatives. . . . [This support for freedom to marry] is the principal origin of the . . . prejudicial effects . . . of unequal marriages."[28] In other words, from the crown's perspective, all the modifications made by ecclesiastical officials in procedures were inadequate because they continued to protect children's rights rather than parents' and did too little to prevent socially unequal marriages. The primary reason for the church's loss of authority over prenuptial conflicts was its continuing commitment to the traditional ecclesiastical norm of impeding unjust interference, however feebly that commitment was enforced.

But if church practices had changed slowly to conform to the changing relationship between church and state and the shifting cultural priorities of colonial society, church doctrine was even slower to shift. In 1770, just nine years before the state was to take away management of prenuptial conflicts from the church, ecclesiastical officials launched an effort to modify existing interpretations of church doctrine on parental authority over marriage. The effort was only partly successful, but it marked the extent of the change in clerical attitudes toward the position that the church had long sustained.

CHAPTER 12

The Church's Retreat on Doctrine

Long after aristocratic families had launched their attack against traditional cultural values concerning marriage, the Catholic Church in colonial Mexico clung to its old positions. It continued to promote freedom of marriage, to urge the enforcement of the code of sexual honor, and, above all, to oppose parental vetoes of marriage partners. Ecclesiastical policy changed, but only as a result of the church's withdrawal from its customarily energetic defense of traditional values, and not as a result of its active affirmation of another position. Between the 1730's, when it began to treat prenuptial conflicts as private, and 1770, the church was trapped in a state of suspended animation: it was unwilling to carry out its traditional defense of matrimonial liberty and yet also unable deliberately and self-consciously to alter its intellectual position. The reason for this was twofold. First, doctrine was believed to be divinely rather than humanly inspired, therefore churchmen could only consciously alter traditional interpretations in response to new social conditions by circuitous and awkward means in conformity with divine inspiration.[1] Second, the changes in social values took place slowly and were often vigorously contested even within aristocratic families. Consequently ecclesiastical attitudes were altered gradually and with great ambiguity, like the shifts that were occurring in society as a whole.

Well into the second decade of the eighteenth century, church officials remained skeptical about the role that parents' motives, ambitions, and interests should play in their offspring's marital arrangements. In 1715, the chief adviser to the judge of the Mexico City church court expressed reservations when a father appeared to ask for a permit for his son's marriage: representation of a child by a parent in a matrimonial matter excited suspicion, he wrote, "because of parents' regular practice of introducing themselves into their children's marriages to the detriment of their [children's] liberty." He insisted on a secret investigation. Only when the investigation showed that the father was not interfering but merely carrying out his son's wishes was a license for the marriage issued.[2]

As late as the third decade of the eighteenth century, church officials were still outspokenly opposed to claims of parental rights to veto marriage partners. In 1720, a wealthy resident of the northern mining town of Parral wished to escape from a marriage he had contracted only the previous year, but in which he was very unhappy. In order to be free of his wife, he had to allege that a condition existed that would nullify his marriage. No such condition existed, so he told the church court that he lacked the consent and will of his father to marry. The chief ecclesiastical judge for his territory, residing in Durango, stated unequivocally that such a marriage nevertheless was valid.[3]

By the latter part of the 1720's, however, a few isolated church officials had begun to express reservations about the traditional ecclesiastical position denying parental vetoes. Their early, tentative statements appeared in discussions of the long-standing ecclesiastical doctrine of "reverential fear." In classic canon law, reverential fear results from the exercise of moral compulsion by a parent or guardian over a child. The legitimate type of moral compulsion regarding marriage choice was restricted to persuasion, and excluded the use of force. Among Hispanic canon lawyers there were two opposing views of the role of moral compulsion. On the one hand, some theologians held that such compulsion could deprive a child of the real freedom to marry, and that a marriage contracted under these conditions was invalid. Others believed that the moral pressures exercised by parents were insufficient to cause enough fear to prevent a marriage, and argued that apprehension of a graver ill was needed in order to invalidate a marriage.[4] The standard that came to prevail in the Mexican church was the former; compulsion by parents meant a deprivation of the liberty required in marriage.

Although seventeenth-century Mexican clerics uniformly considered the use of reverential fear to be evidence of unjust interference, this consensus disappeared in the early years of the eighteenth century. In one dispute in the 1720's, the chief judge of Puebla decided that reverential fear did not invalidate an engagement, but his counterpart in Mexico City disagreed and declared that it nullified a promise to marry.[5] Accepting the legitimacy of reverential fear, however, was still several steps away from accepting parental vetoes as just. In the next thirty years opinion within the ecclesiastical community diverged sharply, and by mid-century some clergymen were openly advocating a parental veto for certain kinds of marriages.

The acceptance of such beliefs among clerics was furthered by a papal encyclical issued in 1741 by Pope Benedict XIV to reduce the incidence of secret marriages. "Far too many marriages have been performed and are celebrated so secretly that official notice of them . . . is erased and lies buried eternally in darkness," he wrote. The danger the Pope noted in these marriages was that a second marriage might be contracted while the first spouse was still living. As part of the procedures to be carried out before executing a secret marriage, therefore, the Pope urged bishops to inquire "whether they [the couple] are of that quality, rank, and condition which they rightly claim . . . [and] whether the marriage is hidden from a father who forbids it . . . [which would thus] provide an easy opportunity for a son to be disobedient." Although he did not openly order church judges to prevent marriages that were contrary to parental wishes, the Pope clearly favored making such matches more difficult to contract.[6]

Benedict's encyclical indicated the direction in which the Mexican church might move; the more immediate impetus inclining local church officials toward approving parental interference was the state. The church was steadily losing much of its traditional independence to the royal bureaucracy, and normative cultural support for personal choice in marriage was slowly evaporating. In 1752, one of the first articulated statements of the position of some churchmen supporting parental veto of marriage partners appeared. Responding to the query of an ecclesiastical judge who was befuddled by the conflicting claims of children desiring matrimonial liberty and parents seeking to prevent unequal marriages, Don José Tenebra, a clergyman from the diocese of Tlaxcala, argued that church judges should not allow unequal marriages to take place, even though he admitted that this would be "contrary to the current practice commonly observed by all judges and priests." The reasons he advanced for advocating such a change were the arguments for honor as status among the elite. Equal marriages were necessary "for the conservation and increase of noble and honest families so that they are neither harassed nor stained by undignified marriages." In other words, his principal motivation was the desire of the wealthy and powerful to avoid dishonor—loss of social prestige. To this end, he argued for the devaluation of sexual honor. "Even though violation of virginity has occurred under promise of marriage . . . the man does not have any obligation to marry an undeserving woman. . . . [A man] is not obligated by [such a] promise, nor by the damage, therefore by no cause."

Tenebra's purpose was to maintain racial boundaries, and specifically to preserve the distinction of being Spanish, which was rapidly being eroded by the increasing frequency of interracial marriage. If loss of sexual honor occurred between Spaniards who differed in wealth or prestige, he urged that the marriage be permitted. His intentions were thus what another age would label racist: "Such unequal marriages frequently lead to so many racially mixed persons that we [Mexicans] are dishonored before all other peoples, leading us to believe that there is not a drop of pure blood anywhere in this kingdom." He added that ecclesiastical magistrates were best suited to prevent such marriages.

Tenebra's suggestions were not taken up by the church judges of Mexico, who during the next twenty years continued the policy of abstention described in the preceding chapter, allowing conflicts over interracial marriage to be decided above all by the perseverance and determination of the parties involved.[7] But as interracial marriage increased and support for normative patriarchy grew among aristocratic families, more and more church officials came to favor preventing socially unequal marriages—those that were racially mixed as well as those between Spaniards of different status. By 1768, the legal adviser to the chief court judge of Mexico City argued that parents had the right to oppose a child's marriage if the intended spouse was of considerably lower social rank, and if scandal and serious quarrels would result from the marriage.[8] His position was more advanced than Tenebra's at mid-century. Whereas

Tenebra recognized only differences of race, the adviser considered differences of status to be a legitimate reason for parental opposition. In other words, he acknowledged the importance that aristocrats in colonial society were beginning to attach to the social status of the family. Very clearly, the kind of honor at issue was very different from the honor that had been at stake in the seventeenth century. Then it was not the precedence of the family that mattered to the church, but rather the protection of the sexual honor—virtue— of Spanish women and their families.

The eighteenth-century aristocracy's concern with social rank reflected a greater emphasis on the honor that proceeds from superior birth. The court adviser regarded damage to this kind of honor as sufficiently grave for the church to prevent the match. Furthermore, he supported the belief that parental authority was more appropriate in marital arrangements than the traditional ecclesiastical doctrine of individual will.[9] During the final third of the eighteenth century, some members of the ecclesiastical hierarchy like this adviser began to depart from the traditional defense of matrimonial liberty and to favor parental intervention when questions of the honor—status— of the family were at issue.

The tendency was by no means universal, for some judges held firmly to the doctrine of matrimonial liberty. Church officials routinely granted requests for temporary custody so that the woman could state her intent to marry, free of "reverential fear of her parents."[10] Furthermore, until 1778 church officials continued to ask young women making their declarations of matrimonial intent if they were free of such reverential fear.[11] Women who stated that reverential fear was depriving them of liberty were placed by the church in temporary custody. However, church officials did not intervene when young women willingly desisted from their marriage decision on grounds of reverential fear.[12]

The split in attitudes within the church on the question of parental opposition deepened gradually, and was only resolved in 1770, when the Mexican church convened what was to be the last of the colonial meetings of bishops to set church policy. The Fourth Mexican Provincial Council met under terms vastly different from those of the previous century and even of the mid-eighteenth century, particularly regarding its relationship with the crown. Initially the Catholic Church and the state had been viewed as equal partners in ruling the Spanish empire, but as discussed in Chapter 10, in the seventeenth century royal bureaucrats in the New World had slowly chipped away at the autonomy of the church, and the Council of the Indies gradually brought the new bishops it appointed into line. It remained only for the crown itself to attack the power of the episcopate. Beginning in 1759 with Charles III, curtailing the independence of the Catholic Church in the New World became a royal project.

Charles III, who reigned from 1759 to 1788, attacked the traditional economic and political privileges of the church by eliminating some of its tax exemptions and by removing the immunity from prosecution that clerics had enjoyed in ordinary civil and criminal suits.[13] Other royal actions, though less alarming to individual clerics than the attack on their privileged judicial status, were also of critical significance. For most of the colonial period, Spanish America had two overlapping judiciaries, that of the church and that of the crown. Boundaries between the two were often ill defined, and the choice of a court was often haphazard. Under Charles III and his successors the crown curtailed the church's independent judicial functions. Some matters that had traditionally been handled indiscriminately by both ecclesiastical and royal courts, such as inheritance, became the sole province of the crown.[14] Others that had been shared by ecclesiastical courts, the Inquisition, and royal courts, such as the prosecution of couples living together in concubinage, also became the sole preserve of the royal courts.

At the same time, despite their protests about growing royal control, ecclesiastical judges were becoming increasingly reluctant to press decisions that might antagonize powerful political or economic interests. It was at this time of ebbing ecclesiastical autonomy on several fronts that the Fourth Provincial Council convened and formally approved parental vetoes over marriage partners.

The Fourth Mexican Provincial Council (1770–71) was one of the most controversial in the history of the church in Mexico, not for the theological debates it provoked, which were few, but because of the extent to which royal officials meddled in the internal affairs of the council, setting its agenda and advising churchmen on church law.[15] The excessive enthusiasm shown by Mexican church officials for royal intervention in ecclesiastical matters, though perhaps not surprising, was another problem. The prelates who attended the

conference were the highest ranking in New Spain, exceedingly ambitious and most eager to curry royal favor, which was essential to
advance their careers in an era of increasing royal influence. Hence
their views were in many cases not those of Rome. Indeed, the
opening canons produced by the council referred to the King of
Spain as the head of the church and the chief guardian of canon law
in America. Such subservient expressions of loyalty to the Hispanic
crown were unlikely to be well received by the see of Rome, which
had once excommunicated an English king for such a statement. As
a result of both the extensive meddling by royal officials and the degree of concession offered to royal authority, even the Council of
the Indies deemed it unwise to submit the decrees of this provincial
council to Rome for the approval of the pontiff. Consequently, the
decrees of the council never became binding or authoritative guides
for church decision making. Nonetheless, the decrees marked a dramatic change in the traditional ecclesiastical approach to the questions of matrimonial liberty and parental authority.[16]

Changing the requirements for marriage was low on the council's
agenda, but it was of considerable significance for social and family
relations. Not all the canons were innovative: some confirmed the
church's historic teachings on the necessity for free consent to a marriage partner, and the need for consent to be free of force. But others
would have significantly altered church teachings on marriage.[17]
The protection afforded the matrimonial liberty of young people
would have had several new and restrictive conditions attached to it.
The use of temporary custody, which had been the church's principal means of shielding young people from unreasonable parents,
would have become more limited. Parish priests would not be able
to remove a young woman from her parents' custody until after the
bishop had been notified and had determined whether or not the
parents' position was reasonable. Temporary custody would thus be
rendered virtually ineffectual in protecting matrimonial liberty,
since forcing young people to remain at home meant that whatever violence or undue pressure was being used could continue
unchecked.

The change in temporary custody would have had another significant impact on prenuptial conflicts. By requiring bishops to investigate the reasonableness of parental objections, the council
would be guaranteeing parents the right to a hearing by church of-

ficials when children wished to marry against parental wishes. Never before had church policy allowed parents a formal role in the decision-making process over marital choices. Previously, parents could only intervene informally by counseling their offspring: the formal practice of church courts had been to protect the freedom of individual will. To introduce their claims in ecclesiastical court, parents had to argue for the existence of a diriment or prohibitive impediment. According to the decrees of this council, they would no longer have to resort to such pretexts, since an argument for parental authority could be made directly.

The council made two major innovations in Mexican ecclesiastical tradition regarding marriage. The first was to stipulate that marriage partners be "equals," seeking not the equality of "honorable" families that had characterized the seventeenth century, but that of wealth and position. To this end, couples alleging unjust opposition because of unequal social status would no longer be allowed to protest in church courts. In the case of an engagement between a man and a woman of unequal social status, the ecclesiastical judge was supposed to order them to desist from their intention to marry. This was at odds with classical interpretation of canon law, which held that the only thing marriage required was the free consent of the parties and affirmed that the church's only role was to act as witness to the mutual contract. In effect, church officials were urged to become active supporters of status considerations in marriage. The council also declared opposition to a marriage valid if infamy or scandal would result from the match—in other words, if the marriage would lower the prestige of a family. Bishops were ordered not to dispense with premarital publicity in such cases, although this was a practice they had in any event all but forsworn nearly eighty years before for different reasons.[18]

The second change the council intended to institute was contained in canon five, in which church officials affirmed that the authority of fathers in families (*patria potestad*) was derived from divine, natural, and positive law.[19] Respect for fathers had, of course, long been part of Hispanic tradition, but this assertion of multiple sources of legitimacy was intended to extend paternal authority over an area in which it had previously been subjected to stringent controls, namely marriage choices. The decree of the Council of Trent regarding clandestine marriage was reinterpreted so that it supported the legitimacy of parental vetoes.[20] Thus, although the church's changed position actually was a response to intensifying demands by aristocratic parents for greater control over their children's marriages, the church leaders rationalized the change not by reference to growing social pressures but rather by reinterpreting traditional ecclesiastical categories to suit the new social demands.

Clearly, if the new policies had been introduced, they would substantially have altered existing ecclesiastical practices. Not only would the church have altered its customary procedures by allowing parents a formal role in the decision-making process for selection of marriage partners, it also would have altered the traditional interpretation of canon law. To find support for a parental veto, church officials were forced to overlook a two-hundred-year tradition of canon law interpretation and turn to a single letter that was purportedly written by a second-century Roman pope to the bishops of Africa but was in fact a ninth-century fabrication—and also, ironically, had once been considered a Protestant heresy, since this spurious letter was one of the few canonical sources that Martin Luther cited when he argued in favor of making parental consent mandatory for marriage.[21] Most important, the council was bypassing the central body of established interpretation of canon law and presenting a new set of requirements based on status. The new criteria placed status considerations in the same category as the diriment impediments: that is, they could prohibit a marriage forever.

Even while the council was deliberating, couples were still appealing to ecclesiastical courts to allow them to marry on the grounds that parental opposition based on differences of social status neither was nor could be a diriment or prohibitive impediment.[22] The council simply ignored traditional Spanish interpretation of canon law, but as one might expect, its statements emphasized not the novelty but rather the presence of divine inspiration. If radical change is to be made in the interpretation of a stubbornly contrary theological tradition, the plea that the Almighty ordained it is still the strongest rationale possible.

At the same time that it supported parental authority, however, the leaders of the council also paid token respect to traditional interpretation of ecclesiastical doctrine, so that the decrees they produced were unsatisfactory from the start because they failed to resolve potential contradictions among different canons. On the one hand, parents were not supposed to force children to marry against their own wishes, but on the other hand, children were not to marry against the will of their parents when such marriages were unequal or would bring infamy or scandal. Although these statements do not on the surface appear to be in disagreement—children should only be prevented from marrying if the marriage would disturb the social order—there were potential situations in which the two statements might conflict. What if parents were to object to any and all marriage partners on the grounds of inequality, scandal, or infamy? Parents could use their right to veto for what might be their own selfish ends, then cloak their actions in the language of the council—as the guardian of Joaquín Fuente Rosillo in 1749, and dozens of other aristocratic parents and guardians after him, had done. It might be argued that parents were only being told that they could not force a child to marry a particular person, yet by vetoing all other suitors as "unequal," "infamous," or "scandalous," parents could, if they wished, force a child to marry a particular partner or compel the young person into an undesired state of celibacy. The support offered matrimonial liberty was, in fact, very limited.

Second, even the nominal defense of matrimonial freedom was not supported by concrete means of protection. Since 1690, temporary custody had been the principal means used by the Mexican church to shield young people from unjust interference. In endorsing the delaying of temporary custody until the validity of the parents' position had been verified by a high-ranking ecclesiastical official, the council implied that parents were more trustworthy than their offspring; the council's backing had clearly shifted from couples to parents. Temporary custody was no longer to be granted merely for violence or excessive coercion. This shift of sympathies meant that abusive parental behavior could continue unchecked. Under these circumstances, it is difficult to imagine how matrimonial free will could be protected.

The pronouncements of the Fourth Provincial Council, though never submitted to Rome, were an important indication of the extent to which opinion among the leaders of the Spanish church had already moved away from their traditional defense of matrimonial free will.[23] Among the lower ranks of the clergy, who, unlike the bishops and diocesan functionaries, were not appointed by the crown, traditional ideas continued to be strong. Local clerics in particular still insisted that considerations of honor as virtue had a higher priority than differences of social status.[24] Church courts even in the heavily peninsular archdiocese of Mexico continued to favor couples over parents until the end of the decade. As late as 1779, the chief magistrate of the church court in Mexico City took the unusual step of granting a secret marriage to a young couple whose parents opposed the match.[25] Not until forced to by the crown did church courts uniformly begin to urge acceptance of the superiority of parental wishes.

In 1776, the Spanish king promulgated a royal pragmatic on marriage that required parental consent to the selection of a marriage partner for all persons under the age of twenty-five. For those over twenty-five, formal notification of parents was necessary, although permission was not mandatory. Two years later this Pragmatic was extended to the American colonies. For the first time in the history of New Spain, parents could exercise a formal veto over their offspring's choice of a marriage partner.[26]

Not only was the doctrine of parental authority institutionalized by the Pragmatic, but the role of the Catholic Church, the traditional defender of matrimonial free will, was sharply curtailed. In the case of an irremediable difference between parents and offspring, the legislation ordered royal rather than church courts to decide between the two. Thus the Catholic Church lost its exclusive judicial control over prenuptial conflicts. A second restriction on the authority of the church was imposed when the Pragmatic was promulgated in New Spain. Bishops were ordered not to allow marriages of persons under twenty-five until they had produced evidence of parental consent to the marriage. Furthermore, ecclesiastical courts were forbidden to hear cases on the validity of an engagement until after the royal courts had made a judgment on the merits of the parental veto.[27] Thus not only was the church unable to marry an under-age person without parental consent, but ecclesiastical decisions could only be made subsequent to the royal court's judgment of the merits of the parental veto. In other words, there was no room left for the church courts to maneuver in favor of matrimonial free will at the expense of parental authority.

The causes behind the promulgation of this legislation are complex and have been treated at length by other historians. To summarize briefly, the Pragmatic was issued in part as a response to the marriage by the brother of the king of Spain to a woman of inferior social status. But it was more than simply a solution to a problem in the royal family. The Pragmatic formed part of the general legislative movement of ecclesiastical reforms begun by Charles III, a major thrust of which was the curtailment of the independence and scope of jurisdiction of the ecclesiastical courts. No longer in need of an independent ecclesiastical judiciary to control a contumacious bureaucracy, the Spanish crown constricted the jurisdiction of the church courts in order to expand the power of the royal courts. With the intrusion of the royal criminal courts into the conflicts over marriage partners earlier in the century, the royal judiciary had gained a small but official role in the resolution of conflicts over marriage partners. The church's loss of jurisdiction over matrimonial disputes was simply part of the larger process by which the crown was slowly stripping the ecclesiastical courts of their independence and legitimating a role for the royal judiciary.[28]

The attack on the jurisdiction of ecclesiastical courts was a delicate operation for the crown, which had to reduce the authority of the church without jeopardizing the support it enjoyed from the church and without exciting opposition from ecclesiastical leaders and the populace. Both Spain and New Spain were robustly Catholic in the eighteenth century, and among the lower clergy and the people, perception of an attack on the church could have produced serious political difficulties even if some ecclesiastical leaders favored the new policies. Consequently, the crown adopted a conciliatory attitude toward canon law and maintained a deferential attitude toward church officials. On some points, however, it was impossible to disguise the conflict between the new royal legislation and the traditional ecclesiastical position. Since the tenth century, Catholic theologians had maintained that ecclesiastical courts had exclusive jurisdiction over matrimonial cases; the interjection of royal courts was an open repudiation of this position. A second major conflict was also unconcealable. Since the Council of Trent, an axiom of Spanish Catholic orthodoxy had been the defense of freedom of matrimonial consent. Royal sanctioning of parental vetoes of a marriage partner directly challenged this tradition.

The crown's attempts to minimize its attack on ecclesiastical jurisdiction over marriage included soothing language: "[This legislation is] without the slightest contravention of sacred canons and ecclesiastical dispositions. . . . [It] leaves ecclesiastical officials and canonical dispositions free to operate with respect to the value, permanence, and spiritual effects [of marriage]." Such language was intended to reassure ecclesiastical officials that the crown intended no major assault on the church's prerogatives, although in fact one was taking place. In an advisory memorandum to the king, the Council of the Indies noted that church officials could be reassured that the elimination of exclusive jurisdiction over marriage had taken place elsewhere in Catholic Europe without destroying the faith. The royal legislation outside Spain, they indicated, was based on the purely secular aspects of marriage.[29]

The latter argument was founded on the distinction, first made by Thomas Aquinas, between the "spiritual and temporal" effects of marriage. Distinguishing between the marriage of non-Christians (a contract) and that of Christians (a sacrament), Aquinas argued that all aspects of marriage between Christians were religious, hence ecclesiastical jurisdiction. The framers of the Pragmatic, however, referred to a different and more recent concept, offered by the French jurist Fevret in his reinterpretation of Thomist thought (1657). Fevret redefined Thomas Aquinas's spiritual and temporal (Catholic and non-Catholic) aspects to emphasize that there was in Catholic marriages a distinction between the spiritual (sacrament) and the temporal (contract) aspects. His arguments were widely accepted in France in the second half of the seventeenth century as a justification for the intervention of the French royal courts in marriage cases, and it was to his useful distinction between a sacrament and a contract that the Council of the Indies referred.[30] It should be noted that when the French royal courts were first interjected into prenuptial conflicts, seventeenth-century Spanish politicians had accused the French Catholic leadership of heterodoxy.[31]

A second element of the crown's strategy to avoid an outcry from the ecclesiastical community was to deemphasize the radical nature of the change being sought by stressing its traditional content and its derivation from ecclesiastical precedents. This was uphill work, for during the preceding two hundred years church policy had supported the free will of couples rather than parental vetoes. Similarly, the bulk of church doctrine favored freedom of matrimonial consent over parental vetoes. What royal authorities were forced to look to, therefore, was not the great body of work of the major ecclesiastical thinkers, but rather the writings of the minor contemporary canonists who supported royal policy. In applying the Pragmatic to America, they used as a pretext the idea that parental authority had already been established by the Fourth Provincial Council, failing to mention that the council's decrees had never been approved by Rome.

They also looked to the distant past and to civil law. Before the Council of Trent, royal officials in Spain had legislated the right of parents and of relatives to prevent marriages of their offspring. The earliest such law appeared in the ninth century, the latest in the sixteenth century, just before the Council of Trent's reform of ecclesiastical law on marriage. The Pragmatic made no mention of the intervening two hundred years of vigorous ecclesiastical defense of matrimonial liberty, but rather cited the codes of Visigothic barbarians of the ninth century.[32]

There was, it is true, some justification for an appeal to the "traditional" in Spain, but for eighteenth-century Mexicans the concept of "traditional authority of parents" with respect to marriage choice was quite novel. In colonial Mexico, freedom of marital consent, not parental authority, had been the dominant doctrine. As Max Weber has pointed out, the selective use of arguments based on "history" or "tradition" can be an important component in presenting radical political change in a reassuring manner, and they are an important way in which authority is legitimated; but by the very act of selective reading of the past, these appeals can readily create new meanings by selecting only minor or subordinated perspectives rather than reflecting the dominant traditions of interpretation.[33]

Certainly the Pragmatic ignored traditional mainstream attitudes in New Spain toward the threat of disinheritance. While the original Spanish pragmatic of 1776 had allowed marriages between persons whose parents had vetoed the union provided the couple were disinherited (a provision that was originally inserted so that the king of Spain could disinherit his brother for marrying a woman of lower social status), the Council of the Indies soon denied couples even this possibility. Ruling in 1784 in a case that originated in Cuba, the council said that a royal judge could not decide that a parental veto was reasonable and then permit the couple to marry if they accepted the penalty of disinheritance. In a related case originating in Chile and resolved by the council in 1787, the council told a bishop who had asked to marry a couple for the "spiritual effects" of marriage, as set forth by the Pragmatic, that he could not do so "even though the couple submit themselves to the penalties proposed by the Pragmatic." Not only was the deceptive language of "spiritual effects" unmasked by this decision, but the option of marrying was foreclosed: even if they accepted disinheritance, the couple could not marry. The parental veto of a marriage partner was absolute.[34] Even medieval Castilian law had not foreclosed this option so forcefully.[35]

Perhaps the greatest irony of this position was the dramatic shift in moral judgments from the sixteenth century. Threats of financial penalties, such as disinheritance, had been at the heart of a substantial portion of the cases that were submitted to the ecclesiastical courts, and these threats in the sixteenth and seventeenth centuries had been regarded as morally reprehensible and as prima facie evidence of malicious interference regarding the selection of a marriage partner. The changing attitudes toward the enterprise of making money in the eighteenth century had so altered society's attitudes toward the threat of disinheritance that it now was judged to be not only legitimate but absolute and irrevocable.

The Pragmatic itself was thus a complex document, which reflected on the one hand a royal desire to reduce the independent authority of the Catholic Church and on the other the social transition to a positive valuation of the use of money as a way of controlling behavior. It marked the first validation of the desires of aristocratic families to increase control over their offspring, and over inheritances as well. From the standpoint of historical tradition, the Pragmatic signaled a turning away from the traditional ecclesiastical defense of freedom to marry and toward the open approval of parental vetoes over the choice of a marriage partner. And like all previous policies concerning marriage, the Pragmatic also had social content and consequences.

CHAPTER 13

The Royal Pragmatic and
Social Inequality

Several different historical trends converged when the royal Pragmatic was promulgated in New Spain in 1778: the shift of jurisdiction over prenuptial conflicts from church to crown, the changing economic conditions that rendered definitions of social difference increasingly unstable, the expansion of normative patriarchy, and the increasing preoccupation of aristocratic families with interracial marriages. The legislation thus marked a culmination of the social, cultural, and political changes that affected prenuptial conflicts during the eighteenth century.[1]

Some of these changes—the church's loss of jurisdiction and parental vetoes over marriage choices—were registered decisively by the Pragmatic. Clergymen protested the loss of jurisdiction, as might be expected, but their protests found no echo among nonclerics. The legitimacy of parental authority was of course challenged, particularly by young couples. But by far the most problematic aspect of the legislation, for both families and royal judges alike, was the question of racially unequal marriages.

According to the Pragmatic, parents could prevent the marriages of their offspring if there was substantial social inequality between the partners. Substantial social inequality was given a very strict definition, however: racial disparity, and racial disparity only.[2] Differences unrelated to race, such as status, wealth, or political power, did not constitute inequality under the terms of the Pragmatic. People of widely different levels of wealth or power were thus implicitly equal, provided they were of the same race. According to the legislation, the daughter of a white (Spanish) tailor was on a level with the son of the marquis, and a marriage between them united equals. Only interracial marriages were officially unequal.

The assumption of equality among Spaniards by the framers of the Pragmatic echoed long-dominant ideas within Hispanic New World society about the fundamental equality of all Spaniards.[3] As a tiny minority governing a large conquered population, it had behooved Spaniards to gloss over differences within their group. Furthermore, the prohibition against interracial unions applied only to marriages between Spaniards and blacks or Indians and blacks; in effect, according to the Pragmatic, Indian-Spanish marriages united racial peers. Taking the legislation at its face value, a poor Indian peasant boy was on a par with a Spanish count's daughter and fully entitled to wed her.

Why was black ancestry thus isolated as the fundamental determinant of social inequality? As was discussed in Chapters 1 and 9, in New Spain, social inequality had traditionally been expressed in terms of racial inequality, and the belief was ingrained in the culture's legal codes, language, and consciousness. The choice of black rather than simply non-Spanish ancestry perhaps stemmed from the relative position of the two non-Spanish groups in the hierarchy of social honor. Indian heritage, though perhaps undesirable, had never been viewed with the same kind of scorn that had been reserved for descent from slaves, who suffered the burdens of legal handicaps and vastly lower social prestige.[4]

The definition of social inequality in terms of descent from black (slave) ancestors was also supported by the language of aristocratic families, who since the middle of the eighteenth century had frequently used the epithet "mulatto" in marriage conflicts to refer derogatorily to a family of lower social status. The distinction made by the Pragmatic therefore corresponded to a usage that had been common among the well-to-do in colonial Mexican society since the middle of the century.

Under the procedures established by the Pragmatic, a family member who considered a marriage to be unequal could complain to the local royal official, the *corregidor*, who would then render a decision on whether racial inequality existed. Since the law also made parental consent mandatory for a marriage, young people whose parents were stalling could resort to the court as well to force their parents' hands. If the corregidor rendered a decision that was unsatisfactory, and if the person or family had the funds to continue the suit, the decision could be appealed to the high court, the Audiencia. Parents from many social classes used the Pragmatic, but only the well-to-do took their cases to the higher court. Forty-six of New Spain's most prominent families appealed to the Audiencia of Mexico between 1779 and 1817.[5] A few, disregarding a specific prohibition in the Pragmatic, further appealed decisions by the Audiencia to the Council of the Indies in Spain.

Despite the Pragmatic's strict definition of inequality, most parents failed to use the legislation as intended. Instead they advanced other reasons for opposing marriages, implying that these were as significant as differences in racial heritage. Oppositions unrelated to racial inferiority thus accounted for fully 72 percent of the cases appealed to the Audiencia. Many petitioners argued that disparity in morals was sufficient cause to prevent a marriage. Others argued economic disproportion. Distinctions of social status only distantly related to economic differences were raised by still others. A number of fathers in unhappy marriages used the occasion of a daughter's marriage to revenge themselves on their wives. A small group of parents, whose motives were ill defined, introduced such trivial objections as the intended spouse's smelly feet or lack of good looks. Only 28 percent of the families actually argued that racial inferiority was the reason for their objections to the marriage.[6] How was it that over 70 percent of the marriage conflict cases brought before the highest tribunal of Mexico were not racial questions, in flagrant violation of both the letter and the intent of the Pragmatic? Obviously, most aristocratic families were not objecting to interracial marriages. What were their principal objections? What language did they employ, and what lay beneath the language?

Although the Pragmatic sanctioned opposition arising from only one type of inequality, aristocratic parents used the legislation to oppose marriages because of differences in status, wealth, or position—the classic eighteenth-century indexes of social worth. Since mid-century, parents had searched for a way to express these differences, but no language was available that adequately conveyed these concerns. After the passage of the Pragmatic, their attempts to express these differences in arguments before the royal courts included use of a concept of honorable conduct that ultimately related to wealth, recourse to a sexual double standard, and an attempt to revive the medieval definitions of social status, access to the priesthood or the military. In other words, their efforts to develop a new language of social difference revolved around efforts to reinterpret older discourses about social inequality. Their efforts were ultimately aimed at describing social distinctions—the inequalities of class—for which neither the word (in its later meaning) nor the concept yet existed. Royal court judges were sympathetic to these pleas because the parents' arguments were rooted in familiar Hispanic cultural values as well as in the uncodified and informal late eighteenth century Spanish beliefs about social inequality.

The concept of honor as virtue in seventeenth-century colonial society was founded on the maintenance of a reputation for rectitude. Only one dimension of this long-standing conception was resurrected in the attempt to use honor to express inequalities of position, wealth, and power. Missing was any idea of honor as promise keeping or the need to protect feminine sexual reputations. Instead, parents sought to have marriages prevented because relatives of one of the partners had been accused of criminal activity. Making such accusations—even mentioning the criminal record of a potential spouse—had been rejected as unjust interference by ecclesiastical courts just six years before the Pragmatic.[7] After 1778, it was no longer rejected, and long-standing beliefs about the disgrace of prison terms were linked to differences in status, since criminal behavior was associated with lower-status groups in society. Raising the issue of honorable behavior was only an indirect way of talking about differences in status or prestige. In a larger sense, it was part of the ongoing effort to redefine honor as status.

In one particularly lengthy case, an Iberian-born merchant residing in Mexico City wanted to marry a girl who was the daughter of a musician and the granddaughter of a dancing master. Entertainers were not regarded as honorable people, but the objection voiced in this case was not so much to the father's occupation as to his conduct. At the time the case began, the father was serving a four-year prison term for adultery and embezzlement. His arrest and imprisonment created a loss of honor for his daughter. The judges of the Council of the Indies ultimately decided that this loss of honor indicated substantial social inequality; the marriage thus fell within the Pragmatic's definition of inequality and permission was denied.[8]

A similar case had a different resolution because the person accused of criminal conduct had managed to avoid serving a prison term. A young woman's grandfather, arrested for murder, escaped punishment for his crime by paying a substantial bribe to court officials. In colonial Mexico, one was rarely dishonored by such actions. The judge who rendered an opinion on the proposed marriage of the murderer's granddaughter made it clear that as long as there had been no prison term, there was no dishonor.[9]

In other words, face was everything; morality was irrelevant. Appearances were so overwhelmingly important that so long as there was no publicly known punishment, conduct that was immoral or illegal, or both, did not signify a loss of honor. It was not guilt or innocence that determined honor or infamy but punishment and its attendant publicity. Honor was neither a moral nor a private consideration but a public and social consideration mediated by wealth.[10]

A second dimension of honor that parents attempted to reinterpret in terms of disparities of status was the sexual honor of Spanish women. Since the final third of the seventeenth century, male responsibility for taking a woman's honor had ebbed, leaving the woman solely responsible for the consequences of sexual activity. This had led to an increasing tendency to blame women (but not men) for sexual activity prior to marriage. Beginning in the middle of the eighteenth century, aristocratic parents and guardians had often sought to embarrass the young woman, and to claim that her sexual activity with their son or guardian created inequality for her by making her—not him—inferior. This new concept of gender-related honor framed an elaborate double standard that allowed young men to take the honor of young women without damage to their reputations or matrimonial consequences, but at the same time condemned women for the identical action.

The new approach to sexual honor was the source of a series of objections by parents to potential marriage partners under the Pragmatic. Loss of sexual honor was used not as it had been in over half of the conflicts of the sixteenth and seventeenth centuries—a reason for the prompt marriage of the couple to protect the woman—but rather as an opportunity further to shame her. Again, it was not private, undetected violations that created infamy, but public ones. Pregnancy, of course, visibly announced the violation; so too did open sexual relations. Matches with young women who had openly flouted the standards of female chastity by having illegitimate children or by lengthy public concubinages with other men were opposed by the young men's parents.[11] In these instances, the courts declared that such conduct did indeed constitute substantial social inequality and ordered the marriages prevented.

In many cases, however, allegations about a woman's lack of sexual honor were merely the pretext for something else: hand in hand with the objections to social inequality because of loss of sexual honor went objections based on disparities of fortune, political power, or standing in the community.[12] The son of a prominent Mexico City councilman fell in love with the daughter of a prosperous silversmith. The pair began having sexual relations in the silversmith's stable; soon the young man rented the apartment next door so that they could meet for evening trysts. Yet the girl's father insisted to the court that he had had no idea of what was going on until his daughter became pregnant. The judge was incredulous; how could the silversmith not notice, if the father, wife, and daughter all slept in the same bed? How could he have failed to realize she was not there? He had to have known what was happening, but he had turned a blind eye to the situation. (Indeed, even today among traditional Mexican and Spanish families the father must pretend not to notice the courting of his daughter.)[13] When the daughter did become pregnant, the silversmith demanded that the young man marry her and preserve her honor. The town councilman, however, alleged that the girl's sexual activity with his son was evidence of her dishonor and thus rendered her unfit as a spouse. What the councilman really objected to was the discrepancy of social status between the two, since her family did not enjoy the great wealth and influence that his did. His allegation of improper conduct was a way of talking about a difference in social status.

In this instance, there was no possibility of using the argument of race. Silversmiths by law could only be Spanish, so the silversmith's daughter was indisputably Spanish, hence under the terms of the Pragmatic the equal of a councilman. But the town councilman insisted that his son enjoyed status superior to an artisan's daughter by virtue of his political position, and even though the girl was Spanish, the courts agreed. Using the double standard of honor, they also agreed that the girl's conduct had damaged her honor (but not the boy's) and contributed to rendering her an inferior spouse. The accusation of immoral conduct was thus a means of asserting superior social status.

Allegations of lost feminine sexual honor also were used to assert honor and status from the vantage of great wealth. The most voluminous opposition in the history of the legislation in New Spain pitted an enormously wealthy, Iberian-born merchant against an official of the Audiencia's criminal division. The bureaucrat had a modest salary but received additional income from a gambling house he ran with his widowed sister-in-law. Gambling was officially illegal, but his position at the royal criminal court meant that there was little danger of arrest, and the gaming, which was carried out in the sister-in-law's home, was frequented by many of the capital city's highest-ranking bureaucrats and clergymen. Because visiting this respectable gambling house did no harm to one's clerical career, some of the wealthiest seminary students also attended. On one fateful day, a new seminarian, Don Manuel Fernández Arcipreste, was brought to the house, and there met the widow's sixteen-year-old daughter. The two fell in love. Although their courtship was conducted in a gambling house, it was carried out in the most respectable Spanish tradition: the mother, fearful for her daughter's virtue, had for years employed a chaperone to attend her when the gamblers were present. Eventually, young Manuel decided to marry Doña Joaquina López Carrasco, daughter of the gambling operator, and received permission to abandon his studies for the priesthood.

Don Manuel's father was much opposed to the marriage and filed suit. Although he may well have been dismayed by his son's association with the daughter of a gambling parlor operator and the prospect of dishonor, he neglected in his suit to mention how his own position would be damaged by this marriage. He was a widower, and his deceased wife's vast fortune was the principal source of his working capital; if the son married, he would be obliged to turn this capital over to him. This potential loss may well have served as the incentive that drove the father to seek out reason after reason why this marriage should not take place. Because the young woman was the subject of several ill-founded rumors, he decided to accuse her of a lack of premarital chastity. He first presented evidence that the family had adopted a young baby. This baby, as the family was able to prove, had been adopted by the girl's mother from a poor woman who had given birth to twins and was unable to feed two new mouths. The father tried another gambit, saying that the girl had previously had sex with another cleric who had frequented the house for gambling. The cleric's story was discredited and a reluctant parade of the high-ranking clergymen who patronized the gambling house established the girl's virtue, testifying to the mother's vigilance and the daughter's notably modest demeanor and behavior in all circumstances. Although the case dragged on for years, the father's slander was eventually revealed and the couple was permitted to marry.[14]

In several cases, parents openly raised the issue of status distinctions, rather than veiling it in charges of sexual misconduct. Social status does not presume a basic equality of people within a community based upon their possession of honor as virtue, but rather predicates an equality defined as ranking or ordering in the community. It is honor as precedence,[15] a concern that had emerged among the aristocratic families of colonial Mexico in the middle of the eighteenth century. Aided by the shift in values that was making acquisitiveness more respectable, families who had enriched themselves in the economic boom of the eighteenth century sought ways to mark their superiority to those in the Spanish community who were less wealthy and prominent than they were. Their concerns about status differences, though real enough, never quite coalesced into a specific language for talking about the kinds of differences in wealth and status that they meant. Under the Pragmatic, they attempted to evolve such a language by returning to medieval traditions about social status.

These families' claims to greater deference or greater social status were based on having members of the family admitted to the priesthood, or appointed to high-ranking posts in the military, or possessing a seat on the town council. All three were invoked as the principal indicators of prestige in the Spanish community. All, however, stemmed from the attributes of status in bygone eras. The association of the military and the priesthood with superior standing are medieval concepts of status, founded in the two principal loci of power in the Middle Ages: the lord with his knights and the Church. The persistent power of these symbols of social status betrayed both the force of tradition in colonial Mexican society and the society's inability to create new terms to define its fundamental disparities. The third of the social symbols, position on the town council, originated in the reconquest of the Iberian peninsula and had been the means of transforming the principal military figures into the political rulers of the area; posts on the Mexican town councils had similarly been granted to the chief military leaders of the Conquest.[16]

The problem with these historical ideas about status was that they were inadequate. Under the new conditions, they no longer accurately defined aristocratic status, nor did they at all guarantee wealth and position. Many poor Spanish families had sons who had been accepted into the priesthood, and many impoverished conquerors' families had sold their positions to upwardly mobile families, so that possession of a council seat no longer indicated illustrious ancestry. Under the Pragmatic, many families maintained that the presence of priests in the family and positions on the town council gave them superior social status. Usually such information did establish their claims, but when it suited the ends of a particular parent the conclusion was challenged. One mother opposing a marriage because she wanted her son to be a priest protested that evidence that the girl's brother was a seminarian and her uncle an ecclesiastical judge did not prove superior social status.[17] The corregidor accepted the mother's argument, although the decision was reversed on appeal to the Audiencia. The old symbols were, in the eighteenth century, newly vulnerable.

Other families raised the issue of status by asking how long their opponents had enjoyed their position. It was difficult to discern a difference of status between two families who both held seats on the local town council or prominent posts in the local military. When allegations of social inequality were made, the objecting family often stated that although the other family was presently privileged, this status was only "accidental," "external," or "individual."[18] In one instance, both the young man and his intended's cousin held prominent positions in the local military in the town of San Miguel Allende. The girl's brother objected to the match on grounds that the young man had not begun his military career as a cadet, as did the young men of wealthy families, but rather had worked his way up. The fiancé's social status, the brother argued, was therefore only "personal," and was inferior to that of a family whose status was

inherited. In this language we can hear the arguments that traditional elites have always used against parvenus—that their positions
have been obtained too recently.[19]

To place this dispute in context, it must be pointed out that the
family whose social status was inherited had acquired a noble title
less than fifty years before; furthermore, the father of the girl—and
of her objecting brother—was a parvenu who had married into a
socially superior family. The brother's charge failed to stick, and the
partners in the marriage were declared to be equals, but not before
both the Council of the Indies and the crown had been dragged into
the dispute.[20]

Claims to greater precedence or social honor were sometimes
delicately brought up as doubts stemming from the lack of information on the other family. In one case a woman who had been married to a rich Iberian-born merchant said there was little known
about her son's fiancée's family. The family was from Sonora—a region, the mother pointed out, inhabited by wild and barbarous Indians.[21] This careful innuendo put the girl's family on the defensive
without the other family's hands having been sullied by picking up
the mud it intended to sling.

One of the most famous cases of argument by insinuation involved Don José Gerónimo Villar Villamil. Holder of a hundred-
year-old entail that consisted principally of a huge, decaying house,
once one of the grandest in Mexico but now only a few years away
from being declared unfit for human habitation, Don José objected
to his son's intended marriage partner on the grounds that there was
insufficient information on her social status. Her family, it was true,
did not have a century-old entail to its name. But the claim that there
was insufficient information on her heritage was simply absurd. She
was the daughter of a town councilman, therefore Spanish and of
superior social position. Regarding her personal desirability, it need
only be said that she was none other than the legendary, gifted María
Ignacia Rodríguez, also known as la Güera Rodríguez, later described by Alexander von Humboldt as the most beautiful woman
on two continents.[22]

For the most part, the elite of colonial Mexico opposed marriages
because of differences of honor as precedence and status, not because of differences of race. The small (28 percent) but interesting
group of cases in which racial differences were raised was only

slightly larger than the 22 percent of cases alleging racial differences between 1690 and 1779, despite the existence of legislation making racial inequality the grounds for exercising a parental veto. The reasons for even a relatively small group of cases alleging racial difference among the elite of New Spain originated in the unusual racial composition of eighteenth-century Mexico. By the end of that century, even a number of the leaders of colonial Mexico were not of pure Spanish blood. By the time of independence, 16 percent of those who held noble titles—counts, viscounts, or marquises— were acknowledged to be of racially mixed origin.[23] Once accepted into the elite, these castas were denominated Spaniards, regardless of color of their skin or the texture of their hair. By the end of the colonial period, the term "Spaniard" thus had two meanings. It could indicate physical appearance, but it could also signify elite social position regardless of physical appearance.

Families making objections to marriages on racial grounds used both direct and indirect approaches. The indirect attack focused on illegitimacy, a specter rooted in a centuries-old Mexican tradition of miscegenation. Because in the sixteenth and seventeenth centuries liaisons between the races occurred predominantly outside of marriage, being of racially mixed parentage usually meant being illegitimate. As a result, many of the ordinances of the seventeenth century that really aimed at preventing racially mixed persons from holding office or entering certain professions were worded to exclude the illegitimately born. Illegitimacy thus became a synonym for being racially mixed, and was so understood by the sophisticated jurists of the seventeenth century, including the celebrated Juan de Solórzano.

Although the epithet had lost much of its venom by the late eighteenth century, it was still employed in that sense by several families opposing marriages under the terms of the Pragmatic. One father who was accused of social inequality on the grounds of illegitimacy had been given up for adoption. To counter the argument that he was unequal, he responded that a note indicating he was of pure Spanish blood had been pinned to his clothes; this evidence terminated the discussion of illegitimacy as evidence of social inequality. The father understood well that the accusation had been an attack on his racial background, and he responded with the appropriate information.[24]

Several creole families, however, were directly accused of racial inferiority. Because of the degree of racial mixing that had occurred in the preceding two centuries, it was more likely that intermarriage would take place with someone of complex racial heritage; there were few fully black people living in central Mexico in 1779.[25] This meant that when a family was accused of descent from blacks, it had to look back through several generations, searching the record books, family memories, and the community's recollections in order to prove that their pedigree was untainted by a black ancestor. They sometimes uncovered memories that they would have preferred to forget.

Perhaps the most ironic contest took place between two families in Campeche in 1787. The boy's father objected to the match because the girl was illegitimate. He hinted at but did not actually accuse her of black ancestry. The girl was revealed instead to be the illegitimate daughter of one of the region's most prominent families, born during the heir's engagement to a Spanish woman whom he subsequently decided not to marry, and adopted and raised by her father's mother. When, despite this evidence, the boy's father still refused to accede to the match, the fiancée informed the court of what she had known all along: that the man objecting to her presumed racial background had married the mulatta daughter of the hog slaughterer of Ixmal. His wife, in fact, was the direct descendant of a slave, the footman of the bishop of Yucatán.[26] The attack on the girl's status reflected the insecurity of his own position.

Rarely was the accusation of inferior racial status based on physical features alone. In one instance, however, a prominent landowner in the valley of Mezquital opposed his daughter's marriage to the son of a well-to-do merchant and part-time official of the Royal Treasury simply because the merchant's son looked black. On the basis of the family's appearance, the tribute collector had twice tried to put them on the tribute list, once seven years before the engagement and again only two years before. In both instances the merchant had appealed to the tribute tribunal in Mexico City and had succeeded in having his wife and children removed from the lists. To an outside observer, as the tribute collector was, the family looked mulatto.

The parish records confirmed what appearances had suggested. The boy's father's christening record listed him a morisco. Only

something had happened to the record between the time it was set
down and the time it was examined in the matrimonial dispute: a
knife had been taken to the designation "morisco," only partly removing the entry, and the word "Spaniard" written over in a different hand and ink. The christening records of the boy's mother,
María Nicolasa Salgado, had been similarly altered. The entries for
four of María's older brothers and sisters were untampered with,
and the parents were described as "moriscos." On the records of
three children, including María's own, the racial designation had
been partly or completely erased. On María's record, however, it
was still possible to read the original writing that stated she was a
morisca. Evidence of the altered baptismal certificates plus testimony from ten witnesses were the landowner's bases for arguing
that the merchant's family was descended from blacks and therefore
unequal to his own.

But another picture of María Nicolasa Salgado's racial heritage
emerged from her husband's arguments before the tribute tribunal
in the 1780's, arguments that were also based on records of María
Nicolasa's family. In 1724 the Salgado family had managed to obtain
a royal permit to bear arms, a social privilege normally reserved to
Spaniards, and occasionally granted to elite mestizos or Indians, but
completely forbidden to blacks. The 1724 privilege established the
family as mestizos, declaring that their dark complexion originated
with a great-grandmother who had been an Indian cacique. The
pursuit had been reconfirmed several times between 1724 and the
time of the dispute, and it was therefore established that this dark-
complexioned family had enjoyed continuous social prominence for
nearly half a century. Many witnesses were willing to declare that
María Nicolasa Salgado, the mother of the young man who was in
love with the landowner's daughter, was and had always been considered Spanish—that is, she had always been accorded elite social
status.

Two sets of records and memories were contradictory. The Sal-
gados' ancestry clearly had to include blacks, for how else could one
account for their appearance? But in 1724 the family had carefully
sorted out those of their antecedents who fitted the pattern of acceptable social mobility—the Indian ancestor to account for the dark
skin, the Spanish ancestors to account for the lightening—and legitimated their social standing. Any black ancestors, who had ob-

viously played an important role in their heritage, were glossed over.[27] The family thus altered their racial heritage to fit their social position.

Neither the local court nor the Audiencia accepted the argument that race was a matter of physical appearance. Both rejected the landowner's claim of substantial social disparity. The evidence, of physical appearance as well as the tribute lists and birth records, labeled an invalid indicator of race. The social standing that the Salgado family had enjoyed in the valley of Mezquital for over fifty years was a superior index to the family's race.

When, as often happened, there was no direct physical evidence, black ancestors had to be traced back across several generations. One dispute involved two wealthy landowning families in the Quecholac region of Puebla. The case centered on efforts to establish the racial identity of the great-great-grandmother of the young woman, María Luisa Romero. Although it is hard to take seriously a debate over substantial social inequality based on the race of one woman born over a hundred years before, the participants clearly did so.

Those opposing María Luisa's marriage claimed that her great-great-grandmother, Benita Arellano, was the illegitimate daughter of a black or mulatta servant called Nana Tules, who had worked for the chief constable of Acatzingo.[28] However, parish records in the town where Benita was born suggested that she was not a mulatta but rather the child of a Spanish mother and a dark—Indian or mestizo—male. Such a union did not conform to the stereotype of interracial sex (Spanish male with lower-status female), nor did it fit the code of gender-linked honor that held a woman disgraced for having an out-of-wedlock baby, much less a racially mixed child. Both sides in the case ignored the evidence. Those opposing the marriage did not find the confirmation necessary under the Pragmatic of Benita's black ancestry. Benita's descendents did not care for the obvious conclusion that their ancestor was the out-of-wedlock offspring of a Spanish woman and an Indian or mestizo male.

The next generation portrayed Benita's parentage and racial identity differently. In 1738 one of Benita's sons decided to enter the priesthood. Since sacerdotal ministry was forbidden to blacks but open to descendants of other racial groups, the son presented witnesses who declared that he was the descendant of mestizos and Spaniards. These witnesses labeled Benita not a mestiza but the daughter of a mestiza and a Spaniard, and therefore one step closer to being Spanish in the culturally sanctioned pattern of social mobility. Furthermore, they reversed the sexual roles by stating that Benita was the illegitimate daughter of a Spanish male and a mestiza. Reality was thus altered to conform to prevailing beliefs about interracial sex and the code of sexual honor.

In the late eighteenth century, those opposing María Luisa's marriage took the story one small step further, by transforming Benita from the daughter of a Spanish male and a mestiza into the offspring of a Spaniard and a black. The fundamental alteration to the story of Benita's parentage had been made by Benita's own descendants in the second generation; eighteenth-century witnesses merely embroidered on the already changed story.[29] The opposing family's suspicion that the Romeros were covering up something in their background was well founded, but they had not covered up a black ancestress.

Moreover, the real issue in this case was not the parentage of the historically remote Benita Arellano but an incident from the more recent past: the persons opposing the marriage had lost an inheritance battle to María Luisa's grandfather some years before. Objecting to her race was merely the pretext to be used for settling a grudge. Indeed, even when parents argued for moral inequality or differences in status, their objections were frequently quite far removed from the motives and social conflicts that had actually provoked the prenuptial conflicts. Several of the cases outlined in this chapter make this clear. The underlying objections to marriage partners were in fact fairly evenly divided among three categories: economic disparities, differences in social status within the Spanish community, and pursuit of personal grudges or matters of temperament. Together these factors accounted for just over 80 percent of the cases appealed to the Audiencia and the Council of the Indies.[30] Economic disparities and status differences, rather than descent from slaves, were what the upper levels of eighteenth-century Mexican society believed to be the principal social distinctions.

Parents making use of the Pragmatic to prevent marriages were not the only ones who failed to follow the letter of the law. The judges charged with enforcing it also ignored its provisions. For example, the Audiencia and the judges of the Council of the Indies held to the newly emergent ideas about honor in finding sexual misconduct by a woman to be adequate proof of her substantial social inferiority. Their decisions on other issues tended to favor certain kinds of arguments over others. On economic differences they ruled inconsistently. On the one hand, they maintained that economic differences were not valid reasons for objecting to a marriage, particularly if the least well off party was a fortune-hunting peninsular. On the other hand, if besides economic differences there was a difference of race, they accepted the combination as a valid motive for preventing a marriage.[31]

The strictness of the Pragmatic's definition of social inequality in terms of descent from slave ancestors constituted an assertion that significant social inequality existed only between races and that within races there was social equality. But the practical reality of eighteenth-century Mexican social distinctions was far more complicated than the law's rhetoric suggested. In the resolution of the prenuptial conflicts it became evident that the elite of colonial society who sat in judgment did not really believe that a Spanish silversmith's daughter was the social equal of a marquis's son or even of the son of a town councilman. Nor did they hold that the son of a Spanish surgeon or of a successful estate administrator was the equal of a regional political chief's daughter. For the elite of colonial New Spain, the reality of social differentiation lay in far more subtle social distinctions.

One consequence of using race as the sole means of expressing substantial social inequality was to exaggerate the extent of equality within racial groups; another was to exaggerate the extent to which racial differences were the critical markers of social distinctions between groups. In contrast to the wording of the legislation, in the judgment of these high colonial officials a wealthy mulatto family was the equal of a wealthy Spanish family. A mulatto or a descendant of mulattoes was unequal to a Spaniard only if he was poor. The trend in decision making was that economic differences tied to racial differences, rather than racial disparity alone, constituted substantial social inequality.

In the early part of the eighteenth century, race mixing occurred faster than at any previous time. By the final decades of the century significant numbers of the racially mixed had become well-to-do;

wealth and influence were no longer reserved for the pure Spanish. As a result, the highest court in the New World, the Audiencia, refused to define race on the basis of physical appearance or biological heritage, but defined it rather on the basis of social standing. One who was wealthy, whatever his physical appearance, was "Spanish"; "race" was only useful as an index of social status if it was not tied to great wealth or influence. If physical appearance was at odds with social status, social status took priority.[32]

The liberties that both parents and judges took with the Pragmatic make it clear that the law's use of descent from slaves as the determinant of social inequality had grave shortcomings. Its concentration on racial expressions of social inferiority excluded consideration of the relation of honor to status, exaggerated equality among Spaniards, and, above all, overestimated the extent to which slave ancestry remained the critical marker of social inferiority. These shortcomings stemmed from the unforeseen conflict between long-standing Hispanic ideas about the foundations of social distinction and two recent historical circumstances: the increasing mixture of races and the growing awareness of differences of wealth and power among Spaniards.

The ideas of inequality embodied in the Pragmatic were fundamentally complicated by the historical fact of race mixture. The distinction between descendants of Indians and descendants of slaves, however clear in theory, had become hopelessly muddled in the real world of New Spain by the late eighteenth century. Over the centuries, the numerically larger Indian population had mixed with descendants of slaves to produce a group of people in New Spain who were known collectively as *castas* but about whom the Spaniards had never made any effective social distinctions. Nonetheless, late eighteenth century Mexican thinking about social differences was rooted in a historical tradition in which the different statuses occupied by slaves, Indians, and Spaniards constituted the fundamental distinctions of colonial society. To admit the blurring of distinctions between the descendants of Indians and the descendants of slaves would have required a major rethinking of the critical social differences as well as the creation of another language for talking about social inequality.

Indeed, a whole new series of names was invented in the eighteenth century to describe the racially mixed, but these were too late to have any significant social impact. Racial difference was the only language available to express substantial social differences, and it was inadequate to the task.

Colonial society's inability to express its growing cognizance of social disparity—specifically differences in economic and social status—resided in the fact that although money was becoming the central guarantor of social status, race rather than money was the dominant metaphor for social inequality. That economic differences were not accepted as the real source of social inequality had to do with cultural tradition. While concern with money and property in making marital arrangements grew in the eighteenth century, the cultural heritage that rejected money making as "vile interest" was still strong. Vile interest was certainly at stake, but to acknowledge it as the *origin* of social distinction was still impossible.

Another reason for the Pragmatic's definition of social inequality in terms of race was the absence of a clear alternative. The classic Spanish (and European) language of social distinctions, of nobility and tribute payers, was not applicable to late eighteenth century American reality. Obviously, the older European terminology, which was used to describe a system of only two groups, could not apply in New Spain, where the offspring of Spanish and Indian unions, regardless of their poverty or illegitimacy, were exempt from tribute payments; using the classic Hispanic categories would have meant calling a large body of poor and marginal mestizos "nobles." Furthermore, the distinction between noble and plebeian had never been made within the Mexican Spanish community itself, in which actual members of the titled nobility were only a minority of the wealthy, powerful, and influential. Using this second interpretation of the category of noble would have meant leaving out many leading families.[33]

The absence of linguistic convention forced the Spanish aristocracy to try a variety of distinctions, including, as mentioned, the return to the medieval concept of status as connected with the priesthood and the military. None was adequate to the task of defining or symbolizing the wealthy and powerful. The most valiant efforts to create distinctions of greater and lesser rank within the non–tribute payers ("nobility") were unsatisfactory because the precise object to which "greater" or "lesser" referred could not be articulated. To speak of greater and lesser wealth or power was still not a cultural possibility.

Thus the Pragmatic's definition of social inequality was determined by the colonial heritage that the significant social distinctions were racial. In other words, "race" remained the dominant cultural metaphor for social difference despite the fact that race had increasingly less to do with social differences. Like the language of social inequality within the elite, where the titled nobility included only part of the class of wealthy and powerful, so too the language of race differences described only one part of the lower social groups.

The disparities that aristocratic eighteenth-century Mexican families were struggling to express were the inequalities of power, wealth, and prestige. But by the end of that century, there did not exist a word or a language to express these differences. The search for a language rooted in traditional historical distinctions was ultimately unsuccessful because the differences that society found significant were based on a new and entirely different economic and social order. The word that finally did emerge in the nineteenth century was a term that could be used to describe inequalities of status, position, and wealth: "class." The efforts of the eighteenth-century aristocratic families are instructive in that they show a group forging a self-conscious identity for itself by struggling to express the distinctions it considers important in a world in which the language of such distinctions does not yet exist. It is this process of creating a separate, self-aware identity that a subsequent generation would label the start of "class consciousness." For the late eighteenth century, however, the word "class," as a marker of distinctions of rank within society, did not exist. It would remain for the nineteenth century to create that meaning.

In 1803, the Spanish crown abandoned its effort to maintain race as the primary definition of social inequality. Parents were granted the right to prevent the marriages of their sons under the age of twenty-five and their daughters under twenty-three without having to state their reasons, whether social, racial, or economic inequality, resentment, a grudge, or greed. In recompense, persons over those ages were allowed the freedom to marry whomever they chose. Two years later this freedom was restricted for the upper reaches of

Spanish society, who were forbidden to marry descendants of slaves even as adults. The latter restriction produced practically no litigation in New Spain; far more problematic was the institution of what was in effect an absolute parental right to veto marriages. The legitimacy of parental vetoes was part of an emerging belief about marriage; the prohibition of interracial marriages belonged to a dying vision.[34]

The framers of the Pragmatic were also mistaken about the role parents would play. They had viewed parents as responsible adults who would act not only dispassionately but also in the best interest of their children or their families. In this they were wrong. Greed, personal grudges, and the whims of difficult personalities were responsible for over a third of all oppositions to marriage. Far from eliciting behavior protective of young people and their interests, the Pragmatic brought out the worst in parents, allowing them to vent the frustrations of their own thwarted ambitions on their children. Their language in the petitions drips with hypocritical concern for social stability that scarcely masks their essential pettiness, egotism, and bitterness. If children could be tempted into rash marriages in the first burst of passion, their elders could be equally tempted to prevent marriages out of pique, jealousy, or a desire for revenge. The Pragmatic of 1803 was an open invitation for such passions to reign unchecked.

The remaining two-thirds of the parents, not impelled by greed, grudges, or arrogance, were motivated by concern for their own social prestige, and based their objections on differences of wealth, income, or social status. The widespread use of the 1778 Pragmatic for the defense of social prestige indicates the power of the new definition of honor as social status or precedence and the vastly greater social importance attached to such considerations than to the more traditional view of honor as moral integrity or virtue.

A radical alteration had occurred in the dominant discourse of colonial Hispanic society. What social institutions had once labeled unjust interference in the choice of a marriage partner—parental vetoes based upon the inequality of partners—were now labeled legitimate, and actions they once intervened vigorously to prevent, they now sanctioned. Changes in cultural values and institutional practices shifted normative approval in prenuptial conflicts from couples to parents along with the increasing acceptance of the once-condemned motivation of self-interest and rational calculation in choosing a spouse. The principal elements of honor as virtue— keeping marriage promises and protecting feminine reputations— were ideals of an increasingly remote past: honor as status was becoming the dominant creed. In short, the emerging eighteenth-century discourses about marriage and the authority of parents in relation to it dramatically altered the conventions of the earlier period. What has often been viewed by historians as an explicitly "traditional" characteristic of marriage emerged in New Spain as a result of changes associated just as explicitly with the modern era. Only much later, in the nineteenth and twentieth centuries, would the "traditional" parental control of marriage be relaxed and children once again, albeit in a totally different cultural environment, be free in society's view to pursue their own marriage choices, as they had been in an entirely different social context in the sixteenth century.

Conclusion

Marriage and family relations with respect to marriage in Spanish colonial Mexico had a distinctive character and an unusual evolution. In the sixteenth and seventeenth centuries the cultural values relating to patriarchal control over marriage that were embodied in the ideas and practices of the institutions of social control differed, often dramatically, from those of other European societies. Further, although between the seventeenth and eighteenth centuries the underlying assumptions about parental control of marriage changed greatly in both Western Europe and colonial Mexico, the direction of the changes was very different; in European societies the bonds of patriarchal control over marriage loosened, just as they were tightening in Mexican society. The dominant ideological position of sixteenth-century Hispanic institutions about the parental role in marriage choice emphasized paternalism, "to guide children toward the good," as one writer expressed it, and discouraged parents from taking an authoritarian role. Institutional ideology on the same subject in the eighteenth century encouraged the exercise of authoritarian control especially by fathers—that is, classic patriarchal control over marriage choices.

The contrast between Mexican and "traditional" European society arises from several critical differences: the nature of arranged marriages, attitudes toward motives of interest, the requirement for parental consent to marry, the relationship between capitalism, individualism, and patriarchal control of marriage choices, and the decline of honor. In this Conclusion, we will review the major findings of this study by placing them in comparative perspective. Whereas the first two dimensions of comparison concern so-called "traditional" society in colonial Mexico, the latter three address Mexican society in a process of transition to the modern era.

Europe is indeed an ideal counterpoint for such comparisons. The preponderance of research on families in early modern France, England and its colonies, and to a lesser extent Germany has produced a generalized image in contemporary scholarship of a "traditional" patriarchal family that was transformed into the modern family during the nineteenth and twentieth centuries.[1] Hispanic society, and the New World version of it upon which this study is focused, is perceived, rightly or wrongly, as a highly conservative society, and it has therefore been readily assumed to fit the "traditional" pattern. Since nearly all the limited research on the Latin American family has dealt with the second half of the eighteenth century, the question of a transition from an earlier perspective has not arisen, hence there has been no reason to challenge the adequacy of the generalized view of the "traditional" family as applied to the Hispanic world.[2] But the issues that arise from an analysis of colonial Mexican prenuptial disputes, when juxtaposed to European materials, permit a revised and more subtle view of what the "traditional" European family was generally like.

The Nature of Arranged Marriages

Marriage arranged by parents rather than chosen freely by their children has been presumed to have been frequent in precapitalist societies in Western Europe, including Spain. Arranged marriages, it has been further presumed, were more common among the elite than among other social groups. All the prenuptial conflicts in this study, however, which occurred among the elite and relatively well-to-do, resulted from freely chosen rather than arranged marriages.[3] Clearly, arranging marriages was not, even among the well-to-do, a rigidly established custom or one strongly supported by institutions such as the church. But if not all marriages even among the well-to-do were arranged, how often were marriages freely chosen?

The prenuptial conflict cases themselves cannot be the basis of a general statement about Mexican society because they represent only a minority of all marriages. The evidence concerning the frequency of arranged marriages is equally problematic, since it consists mainly of occasional literary references and a few notable examples from wealthy or powerful families.[4] The literary evidence is ambiguous at best, since material can be cited to suggest that both freely chosen and arranged marriages predominated. That some marriages among the very well born were arranged is incontestable, but it is not possible to generalize from this evidence to a majority of marriages. The evidential base is simply too narrow.

Perhaps more important than the question of evidence is the pitfall of the arbitrary division of marriages into arranged marriages and those made by choice. Not all marriages can be so simply categorized. For example, if parents or a go-between arranged for a meeting between their daughter and a likely suitor, did this constitute an arranged marriage? The meeting is arranged, but so too are many of the meetings by which even modern couples meet their future spouses. The important question is whether young people had a choice, or a right to accept or reject the mate proposed for them, or whether the parents had the unchallengeable authority to impose their selection on their children. If parents routinely tried to choose marriage partners for their offspring but lacked the authority to impose their choices, as they did in colonial Mexico, these marriages could not occur without the consent of couples. This was a very weak form indeed of arranged marriage, which in most historical discourse has been strongly associated with the exercise of authoritarian power within the family. Marriages were not arranged by the imposition of parental power but were negotiated, with children's wills taken into account, as we have seen in this study, and this in the midst of the most "traditional" phase of colonial Mexican history.

The moral literature of the Golden Age as well as community responses and ecclesiastical actions in specific sixteenth- and seventeenth-century Mexican conflicts show clearly that imposed marriages were widely regarded as improper and worthy of sundering if the couples resisted. The final choice of a spouse, it was believed, properly resided with the couple themselves.

This attitude toward marriage contrasts sharply with the teachings and practices of Protestant communities throughout Western Europe in the sixteenth century. Protestant teachings maintained that ultimate control over the choice of a marriage partner rested with the parents rather than with the couple. Parents had a right to veto any marriage proposed to them, and they were also free to arrange marriages for their offspring. In Protestant and Catholic communities alike, negotiations between parents and children were probably more common than conflict. But when differences in marriage choices were unresolvable in Protestant communities, the parents, not the children, were the ones who had the ultimate authority. Similar attitudes prevailed in Catholic France, where parents' veto over marriage choices was firmly established in civil law and enforced by civil courts. Although isolated examples can be found of couples marrying by choice in both French and Protestant communities, the authority sanctioned in official discourses rested not with children but with their parents.[5]

The Motives of Interest and Love

A general impression to be gained from the historical evidence so far advanced by scholars is that marriages in the early modern world were loveless as compared with the standard of our own era's attitudes about marriage for love.[6] Historians Lawrence Stone and Jean-Louis Flandrin, describing marriage in England and France, both affirm that marriages were made not for couples but for families, and primarily for material considerations and social prestige.[7] In describing marriages in England between 1500 and 1660, Stone writes: "Marriage [was] primarily a contract between two families for the exchange of concrete benefits, not so much for the married couple as for their parents and kin—considerations subsumed by contemporaries under the single rubric of 'interest.' This tended to be the predominant motive at the top and also toward the bottom of the social scale."[8]

Flandrin makes a virtually identical statement about France: "Marriage . . . had as its function, not only among kings and princes, but at all levels of society, to ally two families and to allow them to perpetuate themselves, more than to satisfy the love of two young people." Further, "Even in peasant marriages material considerations and considerations of social prestige were fundamental to the choice of a spouse."[9] As both historians describe, interest was the primary consideration in marriage and was normatively approved as a legitimate motive for marriage.

Another historian, David Hunt, has argued that although love did play a role in marriage in seventeenth-century France, it was a secondary one, and legal as well as cultural forces were arrayed against it.[10] The conflict between marriage for love and marriage for interest runs through recent historical scholarship and through generations of novels as well, from Henry Fielding's *Tom Jones* to Thomas Mann's *Buddenbrooks*, and it pervades the novels of Jane Austen, Honoré de Balzac, and John Galsworthy. In sixteenth- and seventeenth-century Spain, as in colonial Mexico, a powerful ecclesiastical tradition reinforced by the Hispanic Counter-Reformation's rejuvenation of the teachings of Thomas Aquinas established love as an expression of man's rational faculties, and an expression of individual will. Consequently, marriage for love enjoyed positive and indeed normative support not merely from popular sources but also from within the dominant institution of social control, the Catholic Church. This positive valuation of marriage for love, both official and popular, allied to the extraordinary power of church officials in regulating marriage created a climate in which marriage for love was not only possible but was protected and defended. Both the ecclesiastical protection and the defense of marriage for love set Hispanic society apart from other European societies in the sixteenth and seventeenth centuries.

Certainly there were some marriages for gain in colonial Mexico as elsewhere, but sixteenth- and seventeenth-century Hispanic society, influenced by this same religious tradition, did not share in the general European normative approval of interest motives. Using financial incentives to foster and prevent marriages was normatively condemned, and material interests, frequently attributed to parents, were often challenged as malicious. Although this normative antipathy to interest did not, as we have seen, endure the changes of the eighteenth century, together with ecclesiastical protection and defense of marriage for love, it differentiates Hispanic and other European societies in the sixteenth century regarding the role of parents in the decision to marry.

The Requirement for Parental Consent to Marry

Requirements for parental consent to marriage varied across the map of sixteenth-century Western Europe. In general, Protestant religions required parental consent. Where secular control of marriage prevailed (whether Protestant or Catholic), parental control over marriage was also affirmed. In Swiss and German Protestant lands as well as in Catholic France, parental consent to marry was mandatory under civil law, often with the encouragement and approval of religious authorities. Anglican England and Catholic Spain, however, demanded only the consent of the parties and made no formal provision for parental consent.[11] The differences between these two countries and religions raise the question of why most areas and religious doctrines required parental consent and these two did not.

On the one hand, both Anglican England and Catholic Spain allowed ecclesiastical authorities to continue to control marriage and prenuptial conflicts. It may well be argued that the similarity between Catholic Spain and Anglican England represented a common adherence to a religious tradition: the medieval Catholic idea that marriage consisted in the consent of the parties, and that parental consent was not required. Anglican and Catholic theology differed fundamentally over the question of papal authority, not over central doctrines such as free will, the nature of salvation, the sacraments, and the role of bureaucratic authority and tradition.[12]

However, the similarity between Catholic Spain and Anglican England extended only to the absence of a formal doctrine of parental consent. Why did Catholic Spain create a series of institutional measures to protect individual wishes from untoward interference, while Anglican England merely omitted the requirement for parental consent to marry? This question returns us to the contrast with which this book began, between the fictional tale of Romeo and Juliet and the experience of their real-life Mexican counterparts, Gerónimo and Juana.

Why Spain went further than England in children's marriage choices can be answered in one of two ways. First, the Council of Trent had revitalized Catholic tradition in Spain and provided a new series of remedies that could be used to protect children from malicious parental interference. There was no similar move by religious authorities in England to establish means of protecting individual will to marry; an existing tradition was merely continued. Second, and perhaps more important, cultural attitudes regarding motives for marriage were quite different in the two countries. In sixteenth- and seventeenth-century England, both love *and* interest were culturally acceptable motives for marriage.[13] There did not exist the kind of sharp dichotomization between the culturally expected motives of parents and children that characterized Spanish society. In Spain, children were seen to marry for love and as a pure expression of will, and this was virtuous, while parents were seen to interfere from a personal or familial motive of interest, which constituted an unjust challenge to the will of couples. This clear-cut opposition, between the generally approved position of couples and the criticized position of interfering parents, justified the church's intervention in prenuptial conflicts. The English allowed for a more ambiguous mixture of motives between love and interest in marriage disputes. Since moral wrong did not lie definitively with parents nor right exclusively with children, institutional interference to maintain moral standards of conduct regarding marriage choices was unnecessary.

The major differences in extent and legitimacy of parental authority over marriage choices among the major Western European powers in the early modern era thus depend on the religious and institutional constraints on the one hand, and cultural attitudes toward the motives of passion and interest in marriage on the other. Where secular control of marriage prevailed (whether Protestant or Catholic), parental control over marriage was affirmed. Furthermore, those areas that viewed marriage for gain or social status as an implicitly or explicitly acceptable motive for marriage also supported parental authority over marriage choices.[14] Early modern French and German societies regarded marriage for gain as a social desideratum, as did English society of the same era, albeit ambivalently. Only in the system of Hispanic values enforced by the Catholic Church was love (as the expression of will) set overtly above considerations of interest. Even here, however, approval of interest as a motive for conduct reshaped attitudes toward the roles of parents and children in marriage choices by the mid-eighteenth century.

Capitalism, Individualism, and the Rise of Patriarchy

The most common historical thinking that guides narratives about the history of the Western family posits a long, dramatic shift brought about by forces of capitalism such as market discipline, an entrepreneurial spirit, the freeing and commodification of labor, and a concern with means-ends efficiency. Despite various qualifications and challenges, the basic image still depends on the polar opposites of a traditional cultural order giving way to a contrasting modern one. Even the most detailed and thoughtful accounts of the family, such as Lawrence Stone's on England, follow this general framework, and the debates about the early modern family in specific cases (for example, as between Stone and Alan MacFarlane) are based at least as much upon the value of the basic schema (that is, continuity as against discontinuity, in the society before and after the stimulus of change) as upon the quality of evidence. While this study, which has posited certain striking changes in parent-child relationships regarding marriage choices in colonial Mexico, does not depart radically from the usual outline, it does provoke critical reflection upon two of its assumptions: that of traditional patriarchy giving way to the more egalitarian family, and correspondingly, that of a pervasive traditional authority in social life being superseded by an equally pervasive individualism.

In this study, what resembles modern individualism as well as what resembles traditional authority occur *together* in social forms both before and after the impact of capitalism. The Catholic Church's acceptance of freedom of choice in marriage, the condition which for historians like Edward Shorter and Lawrence Stone epitomizes the modern family, occurred in what historians have considered an archetype of the traditional social order—sixteenth-century Spanish society, under an authoritarian religion noted for its unequivocal denial of individual freedom of conscience. This study has shown that there is no inherent incompatibility in the denial of personal autonomy or individualism in one sphere—interpretation of faith and doctrine—and its acceptance in another—the choice of a spouse. The protection of personal choice of a marriage partner in colonial Mexico owed its origin not to a pervasive ideological individualism, but to classic canon law and to cultural ideas about the expression of personal will as love, and the importance of honor.

With respect to the changes in the family wrought by the growth of early capitalism, we see that recognizably modern forms of the family embody within them features that appear to be the epitome of a traditional order. Indeed, in colonial Mexico the introduction of a capitalist economic ideology, interacting with the other complex cultural changes described in earlier chapters, altered the qualified paternalism influencing marriage choices of the sixteenth and seventeenth centuries toward the more authoritarian patriarchal control of marriage of the eighteenth century. Capitalism, or more accurately the changes in attitudes about control of property and acquisitiveness that accompanied capitalism, provided for the reevaluation of the role of fathers by stressing the significance of their economic function and by strengthening their authority as a consequence of their management not only of the immediate family's well-being but also of its ambitions within new realms of economic activity.

To be sure, in medieval Castile the authority of fathers was well established. Referred to as *patria potestas*, it was defined as adhering in both parents, although fathers were given a special role. It originated both with natural reason (because children are born of parents) and with law (because children will inherit the parents' property). *Patria potestas* was legitimized by the priority of generation—of age and experience—inheritance, and Roman tradition.[15] With the advent of new thinking about the importance of economic power, parents argued that their control of money, and thus of participation in the market and commerce, was the central condition legitimating what was essentially their enhanced political power over their dependents.

Since in traditional Catholic teaching, self-seeking had been linked to immorality, and acquisitiveness to greed, parents' ambitions for gain or status were unlikely to be considered proper justification of their authority over marriage choices. But as interest gained priority over will as a legitimate motive for marriage in the course of the eighteenth century, it became a justification for the exercise of paternal authority in the choice of a spouse. Invoking the idea that will expressed an unstable emotional state, parents argued that more reliable aspirations, such as the self-seeking that underlay the free market, were needed in order to ensure that marriage decisions were made responsibly. Thus in the eighteenth century, paternal authority over marriage choices was reinvented in a more authoritarian way than before, and new sources of legitimacy were found to buttress the early modern form of patriarchal authority.

Even the definition of individualism, the ideological emblem of the modern or modernizing social order, might be qualified in light of the fact just demonstrated that patriarchal authority over marriage choices was itself fostered by the appearance of mercantile capitalism in colonial Mexico. The standard historical outline posits a link between capitalism and individualism, and the standard argument is that the self-seeking mentality engendered by capitalism spread into noneconomic areas of life, and the wish to be free emerged as romantic love.[16] Furthermore, in the upper classes in particular, the spirit of capitalism liberated young people from parental control of marriage, as an entrepreneurial bourgeoisie became accustomed to dealing with the world in an autonomous and self-reliant way, and thus made possible a different approach to marriage.[17] What we find for colonial Mexico, however, is that the love ideal of the precapitalist period became increasingly subordinated to the passion of interest and that the freedom of dependent children to choose mates became more, not less, constrained. What, then, is an appropriate context for understanding the presumed dominance of individualism as it relates to marriage choices in the face of a situation in which a very traditional looking phenomenon is also fostered by capitalist ideology?

Obviously, individualism was an ideology that was far from uniform and was limited by factors of gender, age, and class. It was by no means a generic and universal attribute of all those who lived in capitalist social orders. Individualism as the ideology informing capitalist economic institutions applied most saliently to the main actors in those institutions, namely adult males. The virtues of individualism were expressed as success in the context of the male-dominated enterprises of commerce, finance, and manufacturing. Furthermore, individualism was associated with the adult males of a particular class—the emerging bourgeoisie as it developed in various national and colonial situations. Here, individualism was in fact male individualism founded implicitly upon exclusions by gender and age. In its application to marriage choices during the late colonial era in Mexico specifically, individualism for some members of the family, notably the eldest male members, amounted to patriarchal authority, and for women and children it was irrelevant. The individualism that had engendered the freedom children enjoyed regarding marriage choices in the "traditional" period had disappeared.

Although the general schema of historical change does indeed apply to the subject of this book, it does so in a qualified way. The ironies revealed in long-term changes characterizing prenuptial disputes in colonial Mexico suggest the need for a flexible, considered application of the schema in evaluating research on Western family history. Apparent differences and similarities of multiple social dimensions are thoroughly mixed and juxtaposed within and between periods that are often lumped in two heaps as traditional versus modern. Parental authority, for example, is evident before and after a period of change. What changes, what makes a difference, are the contexts of cultural meaning in which the essential continuity of something so basic as parental authority is framed. Capitalism itself is the global, albeit complex, grand dynamo of change in the schema; yet when it is understood locally and case by case, it takes on the diverse hues of the specific societies to which it applies. Thus, invaluable as it is as a framework for family history, the influential schema we have discussed is most useful when tested against local situations where it reveals through fine-grained and sophisticated comparisons a diversity of variations, feature by feature.

The Decline of Honor

As recent anthropological studies have noted, honor as a matter of personal reputation or virtue has been subordinated to a primarily socioeconomic meaning of the concept in contemporary Mediterranean communities. The standard of honor is now associated most strongly with economic markers of social status, as inhering in one who is a person of property and who is free from the necessity of manual labor.[18] The priority of socioeconomic or status dimensions of honor marks a definitive shift from the era in which the poor but respectable man of honor was a staple of ordinary life and fiction. In colonial New Spain, the intertwined bases of the older concept of honor as virtue—men's promise keeping and the protection of feminine reputations for sexual honor—began to decline in significance in the seventeenth century and continued to do so into the eighteenth. The waning of honor as virtue and its realignment with socioeconomic markers of status have persisted to the present.

The demand for an end to "unequal" marriages in Mexico originated with a group of colonial aristocrats—wealthy merchants and bureaucrats—who desired to establish clear boundaries of status, a change that entailed a reinterpretation of honor. Why did they choose to do this, and why did their concerns become so pressing in the middle of the eighteenth century?

Marriages across boundaries of status are perceived in many societies as perhaps the greatest threat to maintaining such distinctions and consequently are the focal point of the staunchest efforts to fortify and defend those boundaries. The heightened aristocratic preoccupation with status distinctions in eighteenth-century Mexico stemmed from the decline of an older system of social categories and the overlapping but separate emergence of a new one. The older system of social distinction was founded upon differences of race and depended on social taboos against interracial marriage (tacitly permitting, however, nonmarital unions between the races). Nonetheless, by the middle of the eighteenth century the occurrence of interracial marriage among the well-to-do and prominent who aspired to aristocratic values was threatening the integrity of their group. At the same time, an emerging system of social distinction within the Hispanic community, based openly upon wealth and social position, was being created by the unprecedented social mobility of the eighteenth century, which was itself the result of new discoveries of bullion, expanding urban markets, and emerging opportunities of freer trade. Why these aspirations of status had not appeared before, notably during the comparable economic boom of the sixteenth century, is worth considering.

For the sixteenth-century Spaniard in Mexico, the definitions of social status were firmly linked to the mother country and predicated on an eventual return there. A noble title, a town council seat, or even an elaborate house in Spain were sought after as validations of newly attained social position. By the eighteenth century, the socially mobile Spaniard's aspirations were more firmly linked to the colony. Although the highest officials of the colonial bureaucracy and church retained their ambitions for power and position in Spain, most Spaniards in Mexico no longer looked automatically for ultimate status reward in Spain, but instead were oriented to the locally evolving system of privileges.

Hence more was at stake for aristocratic families than ever before. Mexico was increasingly a society in which distinctions of status within the Spanish community mattered, and mattered a great deal.

The emergent differences of class appeared as upwardly mobile persons of other racial identities were breaking out of their places in the long-standing set of social categories that had also imposed itself on racial groups in colonial Mexico. It was a society, too, in which the most important categories of status had always encompassed racial distinctions, but in which these categories were now increasingly inadequate to describe differences of actual economic or social standing in a racially diverse population.

This same group of colonial aristocrats was also the source of the self-interested demand for parental, specifically patriarchal, authority over marriage. Although these aristocrats employed patriarchal authority in part to preserve boundaries of status and to define an emerging concept of class, the explicit ideological expression of patriarchal authority originated in the vacuum created by the gradually eroding faith in the stability of personal will, which in turn undermined the previously assumed sense of obligation created by marriage promises.

The social sanctions surrounding honor as virtue had been the dams that held the personal emotions of love and will in check. The penalties for breaching the code of honor—loss of respect and standing—reinforced the sense of responsibility associated with acting out of the emotion of love. As the penalties lessened, personal desires were released from their social constraints and took on the appearance of uncontrolled emotions. The idea that these emotions were socially disruptive appeared when a new idea about the foundations of social stability began to gather momentum. If among late eighteenth century Spaniards in Mexico, social stability resided more self-consciously in the defense of boundaries of status, then the desires leading to marriage that might cross or erode those distinctions were socially disruptive and in need of control.

Although some historians have linked these developments to the growth of individualism, such was not the case in Mexico. It may be that declining checks on the demand for individual gratification, such as the male's ability to seduce a woman without suffering devastating consequences, initiated the move away from honor as promise keeping; but the ultimate blow to that concept came when "family interests"—the desire of certain elders to avoid entangling alliances with less wealthy or prestigious families—overrode considerations of honor. Traditionally, honor had been linked to a moral responsibility for having seduced a woman, or to the pressing need for a family to remedy by marriage a daughter's loss of sexual honor (even if to a man who was ineligible in terms of property or status). In other words, the simple willingness to place individual gratification ahead of family interests did not lead to a diminution in the importance of sexual honor in Mexico. Rather, it was changes in the basis of relationships among families that did so.

Honor as virtue involved protecting the reputation of families regarding the sexual honor of their women. Honor as status signified protecting the position and rank of upper class families. In both instances what was being sought was the protection of the reputation of a family, but what was meant by familial reputation had a significantly different meaning in each case. The placing of one family's interest in protecting its class and property ahead of another family's concern with protecting its women's reputation led to the ultimate waning of honor and the increase in suits over broken promises to marry that New Spain experienced in the eighteenth century. The diminishing power of honor as moral virtue to compel marriage across boundaries of status and wealth was accompanied by the enhanced importance of social status, money, and property in marital arrangements, and with greater priority given to considerations of social class than to moral responsibility.[19] The chief conflict in colonial Mexico was not between families and individuals, but among families over the priority of two types of honor: honor as a concept of moral worth and honor as a standard of class and property.

Changes in values are never uniform and rarely affect all levels of society equally. At the end of the colonial period some members of the ecclesiastical hierarchy and even some of the aristocracy still rejected what had become the prevailing position on the valuation of interest and property. Transitions in social and cultural values often lack the kind of clear chronological definition that historians of political or economic change can expect. Yet the effects of such transitions are perhaps most starkly communicated by the contrast between the language of one period and that of another. In the eighteenth century, when for the first time choice of a marriage partner on the basis of one's own wishes was regarded disdainfully, an aristocratic Mexican father complained that his son had promised to marry, "forgetting obedience to his parents, moved only by his liking."[20] Lost to this eighteenth-century father who railed against his sons's motivation of "liking" was the sentiment of Miguel de Cervantes, who expressed the values of Hispanic culture two centuries earlier: "The laws of forced obedience oblige us to do a great deal; but the force of liking obliges us even more."

Reference Matter

Notes

For an explanation of the citation forms of the prenuptial cases, see the Bibliographic Note (p. 309). The following abbreviations are used in the Notes:

AGI   Archivo General de Indias (Seville)
AGN Archivo General de la Nación (México)
AHN Archivo Histórico Nacional (Madrid)
AP   Archivo Parroquial del Sagrario Metropolitano (Mexico City)
Documentos en proceso—Documents in process of cataloging
exp.   *expediente* number
Mat   Matrimonios

Introduction

1. AGN, Mat 61, exp. 12.

2. Age is one of the minor differences. Gerónimo was about eighteen, two years older than the fictional Romeo, and Juana was about sixteen, two years older than Juliet.

3. The judge's formal title was provisor and vicar general of the archdiocese of Mexico. As vicar general he exercised the delegated power of the ordinary (the bishop or archbishop), and consequently he had greater authority than judges of other ecclesiastical courts.

4. The term marriage opposition as used in this study differs from its definition in church law. Under canon law, a marriage opposition is a formal denunciation of a legal bar to a proposed but not yet contracted marriage. I use the term in a broader sense to include actions as well as formal denunciations, and actions taken in or outside church courts. For a complete

description of church law, see Adhemar Esmein, *Le mariage dans le droit canonique*, 2d. ed. rev. and enl. by Robert Génestal (Paris, 1929), 1: 449, 469–72.

5. AGN, Civil 1559, exp. 1; Civil 2150, exp. 1; Civil 2241, exp. 7.

6. Some of the key proponents of this notion are Edward Shorter, *The Making of the Modern Family* (New York, 1975); Lawrence Stone, *The Family, Sex, and Marriage in England, 1500–1800* (New York, 1977); and Jean-Louis Flandrin, *Families in Former Times: Kinship, Household, and Sexuality*, trans. Richard Southern (Cambridge, Eng., 1979). See also Michael Mitterauer and Reinhard Sieder, *The European Family: Patriarchy to Partnership from the Middle Ages to the Present* (Chicago, 1982).

7. Jack Goody terms this model "an ethnocentric version of ameliorative evolutionism" in *The Development of Family and Marriage in Europe* (New York, 1983), p. 2; see also Alan MacFarlane, "*The Family, Sex, and Marriage in England, 1600–1800*, by Lawrence Stone," *History and Theory*, 18 (1979): 103–26; and Steven Ozment, *When Fathers Ruled: Family Life in Reformation Europe* (Cambridge, Mass., 1983), p. 177.

8. Linda Pollock, *Forgotten Children: Parent-Child Relations from 1500 to 1900* (Cambridge, Eng., 1983); Alan MacFarlane, *The Family Life of Ralph Josselin* (Cambridge, Eng., 1970); Jay Mechling, "Advice to Historians on Advice to Mothers," *Journal of Social History*, 9 (1975): 44–63; Kathleen M. Davies, "Continuity and Change in Literary Advice on Marriage," in R. B. Outhwaite, ed., *Marriage and Society: Studies in the Social History of Marriage* (New York, 1981). Another reaction is to argue that no fundamental change took place, as do Ralph A. Houlbrooke, *The English Family, 1450–1700* (London, 1984), and Alan MacFarlane in *Marriage and Love in England: Modes of Reproduction, 1300–1840* (Oxford, 1986).

9. In different and occasionally antagonistic ways, both Lawrence Stone and Alan MacFarlane argue for the importance of a doctrine of individualism in establishing independence of parental control over marriage, but they disagree on the timing. Stone sees independence of parental control arising from "affective individualism," which emerged in the late 17th and early 18th centuries; MacFarlane sees the basis in individualism, and particularly individual property rights, which he traces back to the 13th century. Both assert that this doctrine was critical to English marriage patterns. See Stone, pp. 221–69; and MacFarlane, *Marriage and Reproduction*, pp. 119–47, 338–40.

10. Pollock, *Forgotten Children*, examines a group of English diaries; MacFarlane's *The Family Life of Ralph Josselin* is based upon a single diary. Large sections of Ozment's *When Fathers Ruled* also rely on a single diary, that of Herman von Weinsberg. For the use of correspondence, see Miriam Slater, *Family Life in the Seventeenth Century* (London, 1984). For the use of

catechal literature, see Gerald Strauss, *Luther's House of Learning: Indoctrination of the Young in the German Reformation* (Baltimore, 1978), pp. 90–101. For the use of handbooks of model letters (in addition to biography and diaries), see MacFarlane, *Marriage and Reproduction*.

11. For use of demographic methods, see Stone, pp. 603–20; Daniel Scott Smith, "Parental Power and Marriage Patterns in Hingham, Massachusetts," *Journal of Marriage and Family*, 35 (1973): 419–28; and the critique offered by David Levine, "For Their Own Reasons: Individual Marriage Decisions and Family Life," *Journal of Family History*, 7 (1982): 255–64. For anthropological approaches, see Martine Segalen, *Love and Power in the Peasant Family: Rural France in the Nineteenth Century* (Chicago, 1983); and John Gillis, *For Better, For Worse: British Marriage, 1600 to the Present* (N.Y., 1985).

12. For an argument defending the use of diaries, see Pollock, pp. 68–91. See also Sara Heller Mendelson, "The Weightiest Business: Marriage in an Upper-Gentry Family," *Past and Present*, 85 (1979): 126–35; and Miriam Slater, "A Rejoinder," ibid., pp. 136–40.

13. This point is made by Houlbrooke in *English Family*, also by John Gillis, "Affective Individualism and the English Poor" (review of Stone's *Family, Sex, and Marriage*), *Journal of Interdisciplinary History*, 10 (1979): 121–28.

14. Michael MacDonald's *Mystical Bedlam* (Cambridge, Eng., 1981), relies on the patient records of a 17th-century English physician.

15. See, for example, Mechling, "Advice to Historians"; Davies, "Continuity and Change"; and Houlbrooke, *English Family*.

16. Although this is White's critique of Foucault, I believe it also applies to most of the literary critics, historians, and philosophers influenced by Foucault. Hayden White, "Foucault Decoded: Notes from Underground," *Tropics of Discourse* (Baltimore, Md., 1978). Recent efforts to address the problem of change in discourse include William Sewell, *Work and Revolution in France: The Language of Labor from the Old Regime to 1848* (Cambridge, Eng., 1980); François Furet, "The Revolutionary Catechism" (trans. Elborg Foster), in Furet, ed., *Interpreting the French Revolution* (Cambridge, Eng., 1981); and Lynn Hunt, *Politics, Culture, and Class in the French Revolution* (Berkeley, Calif., 1984). The best theoretical treatment to date of change in discourse is Raymond Williams, *Marxism and Literature* (Oxford, 1977).

17. During the 16th century and most of the 17th, marriage license applications from the secular parishes of Mexico City were handled by the diocesan notaries. By the end of the 17th century, the burden of record keeping had grown so great that most of the applications were transferred to notaries in separate parishes. Prenuptial conflicts and marriages between persons from different parishes continued to be forwarded to the diocesan notaries. The amount of documentation used for this study was so massive

that I kept careful count of the number of applications only while reading the Archivo del Provisorato. When I used this archive it contained 5,138 marriage license applications and produced 36 percent of the conflicts. Since the Archivo seemed to produce conflicts at roughly the same rate as the other documentation from the archdiocesan court, I estimated the total extant applications in this source at 14,272 with an additional 2,000 from the parish archives, making a total of 16,272. This, of course, is only an estimate. I have chosen to call this data marriage license applications because in fact they are requests to the ordinary for his permission (*licencia*) for the local priest to marry the couple or announce the banns. The term "información matrimonial" was adopted for these records only in the 18th century and therefore it is anachronistic for 17th-century records, as well as less descriptive of their content than "marriage license applications." For further details see the Bibliographic Note.

18. See, for example, Michael M. Sheehan, "Choice of a Marriage Partner in the Middle Ages: Development and Mode of Application of a Theory of Marriage," *Studies in Medieval and Renaissance History*, n.s., 1 (1978): 1–33; Michael M. Sheehan, "The Formation and Stability of Marriage in Fourteenth-Century England: Evidence of an Ely Register," *Medieval Studies*, 33 (1971): 228–62; Thomas Max Safley, *Let No Man Put Asunder* (Kirksville, Mo., 1984); and James F. Traer, *Marriage and Family in Eighteenth-Century France* (Ithaca, N.Y., 1980). Two exceptions are Gene Brucker, *Giovanni and Lusanna* (Berkeley, Calif., 1986), which relies upon only a single case, and Verena Martinez-Alier, *Marriage, Class, and Colour in Nineteenth-Century Cuba: A Study of Racial Attitudes and Sexual Values in a Slave Society* (Cambridge, Eng., 1974). I began systematic study of prenuptial conflicts in 1976 for my dissertation, "Parents Versus Children: Marriage Oppositions in Colonial Mexico, 1610–1779" (University of Wisconsin-Madison, 1980); a similar thesis later that year was Ramon Gutiérrez, "Marriage, Sex, and the Family: Social Change in Colonial New Mexico, 1690–1846" (University of Wisconsin-Madison, 1976). Despite its title, Daisy Rípodas Ardanaz's excellent *El matrimonio en Indias: realidad social y regulación jurídica* (Buenos Aires, 1977) is primarily a study of colonial legislation and church regulation of marriage with occasional and unsystematic use of social documentation. A similar study dealing with Brazil in the colonial era is María Beatriz Nizza da Silva, *Sistema de casamento no Brasil colonial* (São Paulo, 1984).

Chapter 1

1. For example, the plows used throughout Spanish America are Andalucian and Extremaduran in origin; the horizontal spinning wheel originated in southern Spain, as did many of the techniques of folk and even fine

pottery making. Funerary and popular religious practices from southern Spain appear throughout Spanish America, to the exclusion of practices from the north. George Foster, *Culture and Conquest: America's Spanish Heritage* (New York, 1960), pp. 1–20, 227–34.

2. See two works by Peter Boyd-Bowman: *Patterns of Spanish Emigration to the New World* (Buffalo, N.Y., 1975), pp. 6, 23, 28, 55, 72, 81–83, and *Indice geobiográfico de mas de 56 mil pobladores de la América Hispánica*, 1 (México, 1985): ix–xxxviii; also Hernan Cortés, *Five Letters of Cortés to the Emperor*, trans. J. Bayard Morris (New York, 1928), First Letter, pp. 23–25.

3. James Lockhart, *Men of Cajamarca* (Austin, Tex., 1972), pp. 43–64.

4. James Lockhart and Enrique Otte, *Letters and Peoples of the Spanish Indies* (Cambridge, Eng., 1976), pp. 43–46, 67, 131–35; Lockhart, p. 53.

5. Lockhart and Otte, pp. 148–49; Boyd-Bowman, *Patterns*, p. 72.

6. Lockhart and Otte, pp. 174–85.

7. Ibid., pp. 17–38, 86–113.

8. Boyd-Bowman, *Patterns*, pp. 24, 48–49, 76. From 1520 to 1579, one-half to two-thirds of all merchants who emigrated to the New World were from Andalucia, mostly from Seville.

9. Quoted in Lockhart and Otte, p. 198.

10. Ibid., p. 255.

11. Ibid.

12. James Lockhart and Stuart Schwartz, *Early Latin America* (Cambridge, Eng., 1983), p. 105.

13. Ibid., p. 152; Cristiana Borchart de Moreno, *Los mercaderes y el capitalismo en México, 1759–1778* (México, 1984), pp. 235–38. Although Seville continued to dominate the transatlantic trade, by the middle of the 16th century its grip on the world economy had been broken and Amsterdam had replaced Seville as the center of the world economy. Immanuel Wallerstein, *The Modern World System* (New York, 1974), p. 199. With this shift, the dominant role of Sevillian merchants in the American trade declined, and new American-based companies sprang up.

14. Lockhart and Schwartz, p. 163.

15. Jonathan Israel, *Race, Class, and Politics in Colonial Mexico, 1610–1670* (New York, 1975), pp. 79–94. This tension was sometimes the source of contemporary satire, such as in the work of Mateo Rosas de Oquendo, cited by Fernando Benítez, *The Century After Cortés*, trans. Joan MacLean (Chicago, 1965), pp. 22–32, also pp. 74–86.

16. Wallerstein, pp. 352–53.

17. The reasons for this drastic drop have been the subject of heated debate. Some argue that the harshness of Spanish treatment caused the Indians to die in unprecedented numbers; the more commonly accepted view is that the Indian population was decimated by diseases brought by Spanish and

African immigrants. See Sherburne Cook and Woodrow Borah, *The Aboriginal Population of Central Mexico* (Berkeley, Calif., 1960), p. 88; and Rudolph Zambardino, "Mexico's Population in the Sixteenth Century: Demographic Anomaly or Mathematical Illusion?" *Journal of Interdisciplinary History*, 11 (1980): 1–27. Another estimate is provided by William T. Sanders, "The Population of the Central Mexico Symbiotic Region, the Basin of Mexico and the Teotihuacán Valley in the Sixteenth Century," in William Denevan, ed., *Native Populations of the Americas in 1492* (Madison, Wisc., 1976), pp. 98–101.

18. "Un blanco, aunque monte descalzo a caballo, se imagina ser de la nobleza del pais." Alexander von Humboldt, *Ensayo político sobre el reino de la Nueva España* (México, 1966), lib. 2 cap. vii, p. 90.

19. The quotation in full is as follows: "Pero en ninguna parte halla dispuesto, ni introducido que en las provincias de las Indias se reparten estos oficios por mitad entre nobles y plebeyos, como suele hacerse en muchos lugares de España, porque esta división de Estados no se practica en ellos; ni conviene que se introduzca." Juan Solórzano Pereira, *Política Indiana* [orig. ed. 1647] (Madrid, 1972), lib. 3 cap. 33 no. 48, also lib. 5 cap. 1 no. 10.

20. Accurate population figures are elusive, but rough estimates suggest that the archdiocese of Mexico by the mid-17th century was only 1.3 percent Spanish, 2 percent black, and nearly 97 percent Indian. In Mexico City, however, at the heart and center of the archdiocese, Spaniards made up over 10 percent of the inhabitants and Indians less than half. No precise figures are available on the black population, but one estimate puts it at around 35 percent; the remainder of the city's population was a tiny fraction of racially mixed origin. Gonzalo Aguirre Beltrán, *La población negra de México*, 2d ed. (México, 1972), pp. 212–14, 219.

21. See, for example, Solórzano, *Política Indiana*, lib. 2 cap. 30 nos. 18–21, 55.

22. For the lack of prohibitions on intermarriage, see Daisy Rípodas Ardanaz, *El matrimonio en Indias: realidad social y regulación jurídica* (Buenos Aires, 1977), pp. 7–60.

23. Patricia Seed, "Social Dimensions of Race, Mexico City, 1753," *Hispanic American Historical Review*, 62 (1982): 569–606; John K. Chance, *Race and Class in Colonial Oaxaca* (Stanford, Calif., 1978); Magnus Morner, *Race Mixture in the History of Latin America* (Boston, 1967); Lyle McAlister, "Social Structure and Social Change in New Spain," in Howard F. Cline, ed., *Latin American History: Essays on Its Teaching and History* (Austin, Tex., 1967), vol. 2.

24. In Mexico City, for example, mestizos were more apt to be unskilled laborers like their Indian forefathers, while mulattoes were more likely to

be domestic servants as their black progenitors had been. Seed, pp. 600–601.

25. Data on the castas from Aguirre Beltrán, pp. 221, 228. I differ with Aguirre Beltrán on the timing of the rise of the castas. Lacking accurate data from the mid-17th century, Aguirre Beltrán assumed that the rate of growth of the castas was constant during the 17th century. My own work on marriage patterns in the parishes of Sagrario Metropolitano, Santa Veracruz, and Santa Catarina Mártir points to the emergence of the castas after 1670; see "Mexican Miscegenation: A Preliminary Historical Inquiry," paper read at the International Conference on Quantification in History, Florianopolis, Brazil, November 1984. Similar conclusions based on different sources are also being drawn by Douglas Cope in a dissertation currently in progress at the University of Wisconsin-Madison.

26. Silvia Arrom, "Marriage Patterns in Mexico City, 1811," *Journal of Family History*, 3 (1978): 385. Elsewhere in New Spain, Indians were less likely to engage in concubinage than Spaniards or castas. Woodrow Borah and Sherburne Cook, "Marriage and Legitimacy in Mexican Culture," *California Law Review*, 54 (1966): 946–1008, esp. p. 963; Thomas Calvo, *Acatzingo: demografía de una parroquia mexicana* (México, 1973), pp. 50–54; Claude Morin, *Santa Inés Zacatelco (1646–1812)* (México, 1973), pp. 26, 73–77. At least, the fees charged the Indians were lower in the official list of fees called the *arancel*, which, though updated irregularly, preserved the pattern of different fees by race. See Solórzano, *Política Indiana*, lib. 4 cap. 3, no. 23; *Recopilación de las leyes de Indias*, lib 1 tit. 13 leyes 6, 7, 13; lib. 1 tit. 18 ley 10.

27. The data were collected from the Archivo Parroquial del Sagrario Metropolitano (Mexico City), *Libros de bautismos de castas*. In 1660 the ratio of illegitimate to legitimate births was 114 to 100. For Spaniards, the ratio was 56.6 illegitimate births for every 100 legitimate ones in 1640, 53.5 in 1660, 57.7 in 1680.

28. The comparisons are made with the 1628 marriage license applications in Mexico City from the three non-Indian parishes existing at that time, Santa Veracruz, Santa Catarina Mártir, and the Sagrario Metropolitano. The marriage pattern by race and nationality examined through the marriage records themselves for these parishes changed little until 1670, and it is not clear that the changes that began in 1670 were statistically significant. Overall, race could not be determined for one or both partners in about a third of the cases (34.5 percent), but marriages in which the race was indicated for one partner were included. Only the conflicts in which the race of neither spouse could be determined were excluded from the calculations. For additional information on slave marriages in Mexico City, see Colin Palmer, *Slaves of the White God: Blacks in Mexico, 1570–1650* (Cambridge, Mass., 1976), pp. 106–12.

29. There are very few censuses that contain information on occupations before the 18th century. The first complete census was made in 1793. Although the original copy of this census has been lost, a summary is available in AGN, Historia, vol. 523. The rough comparison is based upon this summary.

30. AGN, Mat 40, exp. 53 (1760).

31. The most comprehensive treatment of New World innovations is Rípodas Ardanaz, pp. 103–206, 223–57. An excellent general treatment of ecclesiastical attitudes toward Indians is Paulino Castañeda Delgado, "La condición miserable del indio y sus privilegios," *Anuario de Estudios Americanos*, 28 (1971): 245–335; see also his article "El matrimonio legitimo de los indios y su canonización," ibid., 31 (1974): 157–88.

32. J. H. Elliott, *Imperial Spain, 1469–1716* (New York, 1963), p. 106; Pierre Vilar, *Histoire de l'Espagne* (Paris, 1947), p. 29.

33. Other tactics used by Ferdinand and Isabella included royal appointees to supervise the municipalities, a viceroy to rule Aragon, Catalonia, and Valencia, and judicial reform which created a hierarchy of courts. Elliott, pp. 76, 81, 86–87, 91–95, 171–72.

34. Ibid., p. 106.

35. The independence of the ecclesiastical arm of government received its classical formulation in G. Castillo de Bobadilla, *Política para los corregidores y señores de vasallos en tiempo de guerra y para prelados en lo espiritual y temporal entre los legos* (1574), 2 vols., esp. vol. 1 lib. 2 cap. 15. This volume was often cited by canonists and royal jurists of the Hapsburg era. Nancy Farriss, *Crown and Clergy in Colonial Mexico, 1759–1821* (London, 1968), p. 88.

36. AGI, Audiencia of México, vol. 44, viceregal decree, Sept. 12, 1669; Audiencia of México, vol. 46, letter, viceroy to king, May 30, 1673. Philip II stated the aim forthrightly: "La governación temporal y la eclesiástica, y de las religiones ordenándose en lo que se pueden compadecer por unos mismos distritos procedería siempre con mas conformidad y correspondencia y ayudándoselas unos a los otros sería mayor el aprovechamiento y bien de la República así en lo espiritual como en los temporal." AHN, Codices 772-B, f. 93, lib. 1 tit. xi ley i.

37. A complete description of the Patronato system is in Farriss, pp. 15–38.

38. The crown nominated all post-pontifical dignities in metropolitan and cathedral churches, and the principal dignities in collegiate churches and those churches subject to consistorial action. *Universalis ecclesiai regimini* (1508), English translation in William E. Shiels, *King and Church: The Rise and Fall of the Patronato Real* (Chicago, 1961), pp. 110–12. The royal right to nominate to the lesser benefices was delegated to the viceroy in the first

half of the 16th century. *Recopilación de las leyes de Indias*, lib. 1 tit. 6 leyes 6, 26 (1552, 1553).

39. For a brief overview of Hapsburg and Bourbon appointment policies, see Patricia Seed, "The Colonial Church as an Ideological State Apparatus," paper read at the Sixth Congress of Americanists, 1981.

40. Pierre Imbart de la Tour, *Les origines de la Réforme*, 10th ed. (Melun, 1948), 1: 92–93, 104–10, 113–31; 2: 485. See also James F. Traer, *Marriage and Family in Eighteenth-Century France* (Ithaca, N.Y., 1980), p. 32.

41. Appeals from Valladolid went to Mexico, but those from Mexico went to Puebla, the nearest suffragan not subject to Mexico's jurisdiction. This pattern of appeals is still followed by Mexican ecclesiastical courts today. Crown supervision of the movement of information to the American churches was directed toward the same end. The crown required all papal bulls and briefs to be submitted to the Council of the Indies for approval before being sent to the New World. Although this procedure could have been used to extend royal control over church affairs, it appears to have been used largely to prevent the papacy from interfering in the decisions of the American ecclesiastical courts. Farriss, chaps. 2, 3.

42. Farriss labels this sytem "indirect control," pp. 15–83.

43. The distribution of cases between the date of the first surviving prenuptial conflict (1574) and the first major change in ecclesiastical policy (1690) is shown in the accompanying table. (There were 6 other cases from the mid-17th century on which the exact dates were indecipherable.) The distribution reflects those records that have survived flood, fire, war, and administrative neglect. One vicar general (the favorite nephew of a powerful archbishop) was eventually removed for incompetence; he appears to have kept few if any records. Other judges appear not to have taken care that the notaries recorded their decisions or even completed the marriage license applications. Ironically, the most complete records of the entire period are those of the great flood (1628–29), when the threat of imminent destruction apparently prompted efforts at preservation.

TABLE TO NOTE 43
Prenuptial Conflict Cases, 1574–1689

Period	Cases	Period	Cases	Period	Cases
1574–99	9	1630–34	50	1665–69	19
1600–04	4	1635–39	6	1670–74	37
1605–09	6	1640–44	43	1675–79	9
1610–14	24	1645–49	7	1680–84	13
1615–19	12	1650–54	9	1685–89	10
1620–24	29	1655–59	2		
1625–29	85	1660–64	9		

Chapter 2

1. Adhémar Esmein, _Le mariage dans le droit canonique_, 2d ed. (Paris, 1929), 2: 141–56, provides succinct summaries of the views of both Luther and Calvin.

2. Antonio Gramsci, _Prison Notebooks_, trans. Quentin Hoare and Geoffrey Nowell Smith (New York, 1971), p. 170 n. 71. For additional information on the concerns about free will in Catholic Spain, see Melquiades Andrés, _La teología española en el siglo XVI_ (Madrid, 1976), 2: 336–37.

3. Luther, Calvin, and Zwingli rejected marriage as a sacrament. George H. Joyce, _Christian Marriage: An Historical and Doctrinal Study_, 2d ed. (London, 1948), pp. 178–81; Natalie Zemon Davis, "Ghosts, Kin, and Progeny: Some Features of Family Life in Early Modern Europe," _Daedalus_, 106 (1977): 106–8. For a comparison of the two approaches in southwest Germany, see Thomas Max Safley, _Let No Man Put Asunder_ (Kirksville, Mo., 1984), pp. 31–32, 145.

4. Esmein, 2: 185–95; Gabriel le Bras, "Mariage," in A. Vacant and E. Mangenot, _Dictionnaire de théologie catholique_, vol. 10 (Paris, 1928), cols. 2234–42. The dominant tradition in canon law held that parental consent was not necessary for a marriage. No less an authority than Thomas Aquinas held that a daughter had a right to marry without her father's consent because she was a free person. Thomas Aquinas, _Summa Theologica_ (1267–73), Eng. trans. Fathers of the English Dominican Province (London, 1911–25), q. 45 art. 5 obj. 1.

5. Joyce, pp. 127, 129, 234–36; John Joseph Carberry, _The Juridical Form of Marriage_ (Washington, D.C., 1934), pp. 24–36, esp. p. 28. The decree was not promulgated in Great Britain, Scandinavia, Prussia, and Saxony, all largely Protestant areas. It was issued in Holland because the Dutch were still under Spanish (Catholic) rule at the time of Trent. Carberry (n. 6) mistakenly suggests that the decree was promulgated in France.

6. James F. Traer, _Marriage and Family in Eighteenth-Century France_ (Ithaca, N.Y., 1980), pp. 33–34; Esmein, 2: 283–85. Furthermore, the decrees of the Council were never accepted by the French crown despite numerous efforts toward that end. In 1615 an assembly of French clergy adopted the decrees of the Council, but the crown still refused to accept them, and after 1625 efforts to gain official acceptance in France were abandoned. Victor Martin, _Le gallicanisme et la réforme catholique: essai historique sur l'introduction en France des décrets du Concile de Trent, 1563–1615_ [orig. ed. 1919] (Geneva, 1975), esp. pp. 392–93.

7. Steven Ozment, _When Fathers Ruled: Family Life in Reformation Europe_ (Cambridge, Mass., 1983), pp. 6, 61; John Demos, _A Little Commonwealth_ (New York, 1970).

8. Ozment, p. 6; Martin Luther, "That Parents Should Neither Compel Nor Hinder the Marriage of Their Children and That Children Should Not Become Engaged Without Their Parents' Consent," *Luther's Works*, vol. 45, ed. Walther Brandt and Helmut T. Lehmann (Philadelphia, 1962), pp. 385–93; François Wendel, *Le mariage à Strasbourg à l'époque de la réforme* (Strasbourg, 1928), pp. 100–110; Lyndal Roper, "Going to Church and Street: Weddings in Reformation Augsburg," *Past and Present* 106 (1985): 97–98. Even Erasmus, who accepted the sacramentality of marriage, supported parental control over marriage. Emile V. Telle, *Erasme de Rotterdam et le septième sacrement* (Geneva, 1954), pp. 264–65, 290, 357–58, 388.

9. Philip II sent no less than 14 cédulas urging prelates, corregidores, and town councils to observe the decrees of Trent. Amalia Prieto Cantero, *Archivo General de Simancas: Catalog V Patronato Real* (Valladolid, 1946), pp. 275–308. Prior to the Council of Trent, Castilian civil law also prevented a family from disinheriting a daughter if they had tried to keep her from marrying in order to hold on to her inheritance. *Fuero Viejo* (1250, last revision 1377), lib v tit. 5 ley 2. After Trent, disinheritance was permitted only under very restricted conditions. If a daughter married beneath her class, and in secret, she could be disinherited, but not if she could show that her father either treated her badly or had tried to prevent her from marrying in order to hold on to her dowry. Martín de Azpilcueta (1492?–1586), *Manual de confesores y penitentes* (Valladolid, 1570), cap 24 nos. 2, 3; Manuel Rodríguez Lusitano, *Suma de los casos de conciencia* (Salamanca, 1597), cap. 132 no. 6. If a daughter *publicly* married someone beneath her station, the father was obliged to give her a dowry, even if he had not originally agreed to do so. Rodríguez, cap. 14 no. 4; Juan Gutiérrez (d. 1618), *Canonicarum quaestionum utriusque fori tan exterioris quam interioris anima* (Venice, 1609), lib. 2 pract. q. 4. no. 8. The Mexican canonist Alonso de la Vera Cruz stated that parents sinned against matrimonial liberty by attempting to disinherit their children. Vera Cruz cited by Daisy Rípodas Ardanaz, *El matrimonio en Indias* (Buenos Aires, 1977), p. 265. The ley de Toro no. 49 (reiterated by Philip II in 1563) allowed for disinheritance of children who married clandestinely, meaning outside the church and without witnesses. The definitive commentary on the Leyes de Toro is by Antonio Gómez, *Compendio de los comentarios extendidos por el maestro Antonio Gómez a las leyes de Toro* [orig. ed. 1572] (Madrid, 1795), pp. 246–48. Fur further discussion of the definition of clandestinity, see Chap. 5 n. 49.

10. Those favoring parental dictates over children's wishes included the Dutch-born William Estius who taught in France, Jean Platel, in France, Fernando Rebello, in Portugal, Adam Tanner, a German who taught in Munich, Vienna, and Prague, and Italians Prospero Fabani and Roberto Bellarmino. Francisco Gil Delgado, "El matrimonio de los hijos de fami-

lia," in *Revista española de derecho canónico*, 16 (1961): 345–78; also Vacant and Mangenot, eds., *Dictionnaire de théologie catholique*. Of this group only Bellarmino's work is known to have circulated in 17th-century Mexico, but the teachings of Bellarmino that circulated were those of *Una declaración copiosa de la doctrina cristiana*, in which Bellarmino argues for a position consistent with the actions of the 17th-century Mexican church. Three things are required for marriage, he says: the absence of impediments, the presence of a priest, and the consent of the parties, which "must be free and not forced by any great fear." For an English translation, see *An Ample Declaration of the Christian Doctrine*, trans. Richard Hadock (Douai, France, 1604), pp. 255–58.

11. Tomás Sánchez (1550–1610), *Compendium in totius tractus de s. matrimonii sacramento* (Lyons, 1626), "filius," no. 6. For the dominance of Sánchez's position on this issue in the Catholic Church, see Gil Delgado, p. 357. For how Sánchez was regarded generally by the 17th-century Roman curia, see John T. Noonan, *The Power to Dissolve: Lawyers and Marriages in the Courts of the Roman Curia* (Cambridge, Mass., 1972), chap. 1, esp. pp. 31–41. Sánchez's position is the one advocated by Thomas Aquinas, *Summa*, q. 47 art. 6.

12. Gil Delgado, p. 357 n. 54; Vacant and Mangenot, eds., *Dictionnaire de théologie catholique*. Before the Council of Trent there had been a variety of opinions on this subject in Castile, but a significant trend supported the autonomy of young people, including daughters, over their marriage choices. Luis Vives, for example, devoted most of a 1523 essay to establishing the moral characteristics desirable in a spouse and to describing in detail why parents should be guided by their daughter's inclinations and not force upon her what *they* wanted for themselves. *De la mujer cristiana* in *Obras completas* (Madrid, 1947), cap. XV, esp. pp. 1057–59.

13. One of the first non-Hispanic theologians to adopt Sánchez's position was the Belgian-born Jesuit Leonard Lessius, who became professor of theology at Louvain University early in the 17th century; his disciple and countryman Giles de Conink carried on his teachings. Other canonists supporting individual choice over a marriage partner gained popularity only in the second half of the 17th century. The majority of the works favoring marital choice by canonists of other nations were published in the second half of the 17th or in the early 18th century, the most famous of which is Alphonso Maria di Ligouri's *Theologia moralis* (Gil Delgado, pp. 345–78). Although Gil Delgado (and Rípodas Ardanaz, p. 262, following him) do not distinguish among the authors historically or by nationality, this distinction can be established by consulting Vacant and Mangenot, eds., *Dictionnaire de théologie catholique*. Two exceptions to the pattern are Milanese-born Martin Boncina and the English-born Benedictine Robert Sayer.

14. Azpilcueta (Martín de Navarro) is the best-known advocate of this position.

15. Jaime Baron y Arín, *Luz de la fe y luz de la ley* [orig. ed. 1716] (Madrid, 1732), pp. 501–4. Baron y Arín is perhaps the last well-known Spanish theologian to espouse the classic 16th- and 17th-century views on parental authority over marital and occupational choice. A popular mystic in his day and prior of the Dominican convent at Zaragosa, Baron y Arín wrote explanations of Catholic doctrine designed for the mass of educated lay people; he sought to make the abstract statements of principle in canon law concrete social realities of everyday life that could be understood by ordinary people. In so doing he rendered explicit the often implicit cultural norms that influenced 16th- and 17th-century interpretation of the canon law tradition. Before the 18th century, most books on this subject were addressed to priests or canon lawyers and generally omitted such detail.

16. Juan Rodríguez, *Prudente confesor y resolución de graves dificultades en la administración del santo sacramento de la Penitencia* (Valencia, 1645), pp. 49–51.

17. Enrique Villalobos, *Suma de la teología moral y canónica* (Madrid, 1682), trat. xiii, dif. 38 no. 3. The manual was first printed in Salamanca between 1620 and 1623. The edition cited is the thirteenth. Similar sentiments are in Antonio Machado de Chávez, *Perfecto confesor y cura de almas* (Madrid, 1646), lib. 3 mat. 10.

18. Baron y Arín, pp. 501–4. The tradition that parents must provide a daughter with a state at the right age goes back to the 13th-century Leyes de Partida. "Si el padre alongasse el casamiento de su fija, de manera que ella passasse de edad de veinte y cinco anos, si despues desto . . . se casasse contra voluntad de su padre, non podría el desheredarla por tal razón." Part. vi tit. vii ley 5.

19. Baron y Arín, p. 502.

20. Liñán y Verdugo in the 1620 *Guía de forasteros que vienen a la corte [Madrid]*, cited by Ricardo del Arco y Garay in *La sociedad española en la obra dramática de Lope de Vega* (Madrid, 1942), pp. 433–34; Baron y Arín, p. 502.

21. Doña Ana in *Querer más y sufrir menos* (edición Real Academia), vol. 9, jornada 3, p. 64.

22. Flora in *Persiles*, lib. 4 cap. 1.

23. Lisardo in *Nadie se conoce* (edición Real Academia), vol. 7, act 1, p. 686.

24. Lawrence Stone, *The Family, Sex, and Marriage in England, 1500–1800* (New York, 1977), pp. 283–86; Randolph Trumbach, *The Rise of the Egalitarian Family: Aristocratic Kinship and Domestic Relations in Eighteenth-Century England* (New York, 1978), pp. 97, 291; Jean-Louis Flandrin, "Amour et mariage au xviiiᵉ siècle," in Flandrin, *Le sexe et l'occident: évolu-*

tion des attitudes et des comportements (Paris, 1981), p. 83. A more detailed comparison of European ideas about the proper reasons for marriage is given in the Conclusion.

25. The presence of a hegemonic discourse does not preclude the existence of other discourses that are archaic, residual from a previous era, emergent, or novel. Raymond Williams, *Marxism and Literature* (Oxford, 1977), pp. 121–27. The challenge to historians is to distinguish the dominant from other discourses. For an example of an otherwise excellent work that fails to do so, see Rípodas Ardanaz, *El matrimonio en Indias*.

26. *Council of Trent*, sess. 24 chap. 1.

27. Drawing upon Roman law and the decisions of popes and councils since the 5th century, Gratian characterized the consent necessary for marriage as stemming from a person's free will (*libera voluntate*). Successors to Gratian defined two elements preventing free will: force and fear (*vis et metus*). Both invalidated a contract in Roman law, but only force had invalidated Roman marriage. In effect, Catholic canonists extended Roman notions of contract to the sacrament of marriage. John T. Noonan, Jr., "Power to Choose," *Viator*, 4 (1973): 419–34; Joseph Chatham, *Force and Fear as Precluding Matrimonial Consent: The Element of Injustice* (Washington, D.C., 1950), pp. 18–20, 27–65; Joseph Sangmeister, *Force and Fear as Precluding Matrimonial Consent: An Historical Synopsis and Commentary* (Washington, D.C., 1932), pp. 35–64; Michael Sheehan, "Choice of a Marriage Partner in the Middle Ages: Development and Mode of Application of a Theory of Marriage," *Studies in Medieval and Renaissance History*, n.s., 1 (1978): 1–33. The adoption of these principles by 16th-century Spanish canonists is discussed by Rodríguez, *Suma*, cap. 224 no. 3; Sánchez, *Compendium in totius*, "metus," no. 8.

28. Joyce, p. 82. The religious leader of the Puritans wrote, "There is in all children . . . a stubbornness and stoutness of mind arising from natural pride, which must in the first place be broken and beaten down; . . . For the beating and keeping down of this stubbornness, parents must provide carefully for two things: first that children's wills and willfulness be restrained and repressed. . . . Children should not know, if it could be kept from them, that they have a will of their own." John Robinson, *Of Children and Their Education* (1628), excerpted by Philip Greven in *Child-Rearing Concepts, 1628–1861* (Itasca, Ill., 1973). Such a complete denial of the child's free will was fundamentally incompatible with respect for the autonomy of children in the choice of a marriage partner. See also Lloyd de Mause, "The Evolution of Childhood," in de Mause, ed., *Childhood in History* (New York, 1974); M. J. Tucker, "The Child as Beginning and End: Fifteenth- and Sixteenth-Century English Childhood," in de Mause, ed., esp. pp. 246–51; Joseph E. Illick, "Child-Rearing in Seventeenth-Century England

and America," in de Mause, ed., esp. pp. 311–12. For Germany, see Gerald Strauss, *Luther's House of Learning* (Baltimore, Md., 1978), pp. 52–53. A slightly more mixed picture in France is presented by Elizabeth Wirth Marvick, "Nature Versus Nurture: Patterns in Seventeenth-Century French Child-Rearing," in de Mause, ed. Linda Pollock is critical of these views; see *Forgotten Children* (Cambridge, Eng., 1983), pp. 33–67.

29. Joyce, p. 82; Stone, pp. 166–78, 182–83. Edmund S. Morgan, *The Puritan Family: Religion and Domestic Life in Seventeenth-Century New England*, 2d ed. (New York, 1966), claims that 17th-century Puritans did not favor force in marriage, but the only source he can cite to support this contention dates from 1736 (Willard's *Compleat Body of Divinity*). As many historians, including Lloyd de Mause and J. H. Plumb, have noted, the 18th century marks a transition *away* from emphasis on force. See de Mause, "Evolution of Childhood," pp. 222, 224; and J. H. Plumb, "The World of Children in Eighteenth-Century England," *Past and Present*, 64 (1975): 64–95. Cotton Mather, writing in the first decade of the 18th century, favored psychological manipulation over force. For relevant excerpts of Mather's diary, see Greven, pp. 42–45.

30. Luther, "That Parents Should Neither Compel nor Hinder the Marriage of Their Children."

31. Rodríguez, *Suma*, cap. 224 no. 3, cites the agreement on this subject between two of the major Spanish theologians, Martín de Navarro (known as Azpilcueta) and Diego de Covarrubias. Sánchez, *Compendium in totius*, "metus," nos. 8, 9, 13, 15. The Roman court of appeals also recognized this distinction between counsel (reasonable methods) and coercion. See the decision dated Venice, May 25, 1622, cited by Noonan, *Power*, pp. 43–44.

32. Villalobos, trat. xiii, dif. 38 no. 3. Similar sentiments are voiced in the popular manual by Antonio Machado de Chávez, *Perfecto confesor y cura de almas* (1646), lib. 3, cap. x. Sentiments of this sort also appear in 16th-century guides, including Rodríguez, cap. 229 no. 6; Azpilcueta, cap. 15 no. 9; Luján, colloquy 1, part 1.

33. Baron y Arín, lib. 2 cap. 10, p. 503.

34. Ibid., cap. x, p. 502. Similar sentiments are expressed by Cervantes in *Quijote*, part 1, cap. 51.

35. These categories corresponded to the first three of six types of unjust interference established by Sánchez (1550–1610): (1) use of force (beatings, imprisonment), as well as threats to kill, maim, imprison, or murder; (2) the threat of disgrace, for example, cutting off the hair; (3) excessive efforts at persuasion or dissuasion; (4) reluctance to hand over an inheritance; (5) objections to economic differences between the two; (6) dislike ("no es de su gusto"). Tomás Sánchez, *De sancto matrimonii sacramento disputantionum* (Lugduni, 1621), vol. 3 disp. ix.

36. AGN, Archivo del Provisorato, caja 23 Nieto-Sándoral (1629).
37. AGN, Mat 113 #83 (1629).
38. AGN, Archivo del Provisorato, caja 21 Domínguez-Hernández (1620).
   39. AGN, Mat 64 #8 (1628).
   40. AGN, Mat 48 #122 (1628).
   41. AGN, Archivo del Provisorato, caja 21 Enríquez-Bello (1683).
   42. AGN, Mat 29 #55 (1634).
   43. AGN, Mat 5 #31 (1631).
44. Julio Caro-Baroja, "Honour and Shame: An Historical Account of Several Conflicts," in John Peristagny, ed., *Honour and Shame: The Values of Mediterranean Society* (Chicago, 1965), p. 85.
   45. AGN, Archivo del Provisorato, caja 25 Fernández Ortega–Tolosa (1641).
   46. AGN, Mat 64 #128 (1629); Mat 126 #74 (1640).

Chapter 3

1. For example, Don Gerónimo Lopez Ossorio described his relationship with Doña María de la Mota as follows. "Visto algunas veces a la dicha Doña María de la Mota en casa de Don Antonio de la Mota su padre, y de la dicha comunicación se cobraron afiliación y voluntad el uno al otro. Y trataron de contraer matrimonio. Y para ello se dierón palabra de casamiento." Declaration Jan. 17, 1628, AGN, Mat 48 #15. Other examples are Mat 28 f. 300v (1628); and Archivo del Provisorato, caja 15 Legazpi-Rivera (1630). For an example of the simple use of *gusto*, see declaration of Francisca, mestiza, Nov. 10, 1612, AGN, Mat 71 #9. The lengthier declaration of Alonso de Arellano contains his rationalization of his emotional preference: "De su libre y espontanea voluntad y gusto por concurrir en la dicha Doña María las partes y calidades que en tal caso se requieren y por ser doncella honrada, virtuosa, y bien nacida." Declaration Nov. 23, 1617, AGN, Mat 86 #59. Other examples are AGN, Mat 64 f. 185v (1628); and Archivo del Provisorato, caja 15 Legazpi-Rivera (1630), declaration by Doña Juana Rivera. Gonzalo Fernández de Oviedo, chronicler of Charles V, also described marriages for affection as "por gusto." J. de M. Carriazo, "Amor y moralidad bajo los reyes católicos," *Revista de archivos, bibliotecas y museos*, 60 (1954): 53–76, esp. p. 68. For the role of liking and attachment in modern ideas of love, see Zick Rubin's *Liking and Loving* (New York, 1973), and "The Measurement of Romantic Love," *Journal of Personality and Social Psychology*, 16 (1970): 265–73; also Alvin Pam, Robert Pltuchik, and Hope Conte, "Love: A Psychometric Approach," *Psychological Reports*, 37 (1975): 83–88.
2. The famous chivalric novels of northern France, for example, Chré-

tien de Troyes's Arthurian romances, and the chivalric poetry of southern France envisioned the object of love as a woman married to another man. So too did the writing of Andreas Capellanus, author of the most famous treatise on courtly love, *On Love*. The two famous exceptions are Chrétien de Troyes's *Erec* and Wolfram Eschenbach's *Parsifal*. Furthermore, few of the poets of courtly love addressed their verses to their *wives*. A poetic exception is the *Brévari d'Amour*, probably composed in the early 14th century by the Frenchman Matfre Ermendaud. Alicia C. de Ferraresi, *De amor y poesía en la España medieval: prólogo a Juan Ruíz* (México, 1971), pp. 164–65; Christopher N. L. Brooke, "Marriage and Society in the Central Middle Ages," in R. B. Outhwaite, ed., *Marriage and Society: Studies in the Social History of Marriage* (New York, 1981). Castilian writers, like those elsewhere in medieval Europe, also composed tales of adulterous courtly love, but several wrote love poems for their wives.

3. Adulterous love is fated in *El castigo sin venganza* of Lope de Vega, as well as in many of Calderón's tragedies. On the history of attitudes toward love, see Christine J. Whitbourne, *The Arcipreste de Talavera and the Literature of Love*, Occasional Papers in Modern Languages, University of Hull, pp. 10, 16; Yvette de Baez, *Lírica cortesana y lírica popular actual* (México, 1969), pp. 25, 35–36; and Ferraresi, pp. 125, 186. For the conflict between viewing love as imprisoning and love as an act of free will in the 15th century, see Diego de San Pedro, *Prison of Love* (1492), trans. Keith Whinnom (Edinburgh, 1979); and commentary by Peter N. Dunn, "Narrator as Character in the Carcel de Amor," *Modern Language Notes*, 94 (1979): 187–99. A now outdated study by Otis H. Green, *Spain and the Western Tradition* (Madison, Wisc., 1964), pp. 199–211, fails to distinguish between love and lust, as did nearly all 16th-century writers. "El amor es infinito," Cervantes observes in *La Galatea*, "si se funde en ser honesto, y aquel que se acabe presto, no es amor sino apetito." Lib. 1, in *Obras completas*, ed. Annel Valbuena Prat (Madrid, 1960), p. 632. Green's confusion between sexual passion and love leads him to ignore the diversity of evidence provided even by the literature he quotes. Gaspar Gil Polo's *Diana enamorado*, for example, states that love has no power over men except insofar as they place themselves in its power (p. 201). Green's discussion of Cervantes's treatment of love in the exemplary novels fails to note that the subject of Cervantes's criticism is sexual passion, not love. Nor does he note the praiseworthy way in which Cervantes treats young people who defy religious and social boundaries to marry for love. For a more sophisticated recent interpretation of the relationship Green tries to establish between reason and emotion, see David Jonathan Hildner, *Reason and the Passions in the Comedias of Calderón*, Purdue University Monographs in Romance Languages (Philadelphia, 1982), pp. 93–100.

4. Aquinas, *Summa Theologica*, part I, questions 79–82; emphasis added. The quotation is from q. 82, art. 5, reply obj. 1 (p. 143). Thomistic philosophy, with its attitude toward will as part of the rational faculty of man, was emerging as the dominant philosophy in 16th-century Spain. Two of the best-known neo-Thomists of the 16th century were Francisco Suárez and Tomás Sánchez. John Noonan traces the antecedents of a different ecclesiastical connection between love and marriage in medieval canon law in "Marital Affection in the Canonists," *Studia Gratiana*, 12 (1967): 481–509.

5. *Enmendar un daño a otro*, act 1, *Obras de Lope de Vega*, edición Real Academia (Madrid, 1916–30), 5: 297. Medieval literature, while not connecting love to will, displayed a similar ambiguity, exalting the goddess of love on the one hand, and treating her with disrespect on the other. Michael J. Ruggiero, *The Evolution of the Go-Between in Spanish Literature Through the Sixteenth Century* (Berkeley, Calif., 1966), pp. 25–32.

6. Miguel de Cervantes, *La Galatea*, lib. 2 p. 653. Green's *Spain and the Western Tradition* fails to note the emerging importance of the Thomist-inspired treatment of will (*voluntad*) in 16th-century writing and instead searches for esoteric examples of an older attitude toward will; see pp. 197–207.

7. Pedro Luján, *Coloquios matrimoniales*, (Alcalá de Henares, 1577), colloquy 3, 2d part. An important indicator of both the acceptability to a reading public and popularity of the advice offered is the number of editions. According to one authority there were seven editions of Luján's *Coloquios* published between 1550 and 1589. Antonio Manuel Palau y Dulcet, *Manual del librero hispano-americano*, 2d ed. (Barcelona, 1959), 7: 712. More editions were published, since the Biblioteca Nacional in Madrid also has an edition of 1591.

8. Similar ideas are found in the "Romances Amorosos" of the 17th-century Spanish-born Peruvian poet Juan del Valle Caviedes. Guillermo Díaz-Plaja, *Antología mayor de la literatura hispanoamericana* (Barcelona, 1969), esp. stanza xiv, p. 1073.

9. Archivo del Provisorato, caja 24 Rosas-Velásquez (1699); caja 40 Rosa–Juana Francisca (1708); caja 1 Rodríguez-Sánchez (1728). This usage of *amores* can also be found in literary sources, for example in Lujan's famous aphorism, "Todo casamiento por amores pocas veces deja de parar en dolores." For *mujer enamorada* see *Ordenanzas del Visitador de la Nueva España Tellos de Sándoval para la administración de la justicia 1544*, cited by Josefina Muriel, *Los recogimientos de mujeres* (México, 1974), p. 36.

10. The condemnation of sexual lust owed its origin to religious sentiment and Neoplatonic ideas about love popular during the Golden Age. Neoplatonism, disseminated in Spain through León Hebreo's *Dialogos de amor*, distinguished love of the body from love of the spiritual being. For examples see Lope de Vega's novels *El peregrino en su patria* (1603) and *La*

Dorotea (1632), as well as Cervantes, *Quijote*, part 1, cap. 24, and *La Galatea*, lib. 1, p. 632.

11. Justina Ruíz de Conde, *El amor y el matrimonio secreto en los libros de caballerías* (Madrid, 1948), pp. 152–76, 243; Joanot Martorell and Marti Joan de Galba, *Tirant lo Blanc*, trans. David H. Rosenthal (New York, 1984).

12. Ruíz de Conde, pp. 173–80, 195–97, 200; Angel Valbuena Prat, *La vida española en la edad de oro* (Barcelona, 1943), pp. 59–75.

13. Ricardo del Arco y Garay, *La sociedad española en las obras de Cervantes* (Madrid, 1951), pp. 257, 259. In the story about the Captive in *Quijote*, Cervantes has a Christian captive fall in love with the Moor Zoraida (*Quijote*, part 1, caps. 39–41). A similar tale occurs in Cervantes's play *Los baños de Argel*.

14. Tales of love meander through Cervantes's first novel, *La Galatea*, and two of his comedies, *La casa de los celos* and *El laberinto de amor*. It is also a theme in the exemplary novels *Las dos doncellas, La fuerza de sangre, La española inglesa*, and *La señora Cornelia*. Angel del Río, *Historia de la literatura española*, rev. ed. (New York, 1963), 1: 292–93, 311–12, 315–16.

15. *Lo fingido verdadero*, act 2.

16. For example, in *La esclava de su galán*.

17. Citations are to the version edited by Carlos Castillo, *Antología de la literatura mexicana* (Chicago, 1944), p. 65.

18. Edward Honig, *Calderón and the Seizures of Honor* (Cambridge, Mass., 1972).

19. Manuel Rodríguez Lusitano, *Suma de los casos de conciencia* (Salamanca, 1597), preface to cap. 13 no. 1; Luján, colloquy 1, 1st part. John Noonan argues that theologians valued married love more than anyone else in the Middle Ages. Although this view is controversial, if correct, it would suggest that the Hispanic approval of marriage for love was a continuation of a medieval tradition. *Contraception: A History of Its Treatment by the Catholic Theologians and Canonists* (Cambridge, Mass., 1965), pp. 254–57.

20. Juan Rodríguez, *Prudente confesor y resolución de graves dificultades en la administración del santo sacramento de la Penitencia* (Madrid, 1638), p. 48.

21. Jean-Louis Flandrin, "Amour et mariage au xviii⁰ siècle," in *Le sexe et l'occident: évolution des attitudes et des comportements* (Paris, 1981), p. 87.

22. Jean Hagstrum, *Sex and Sensibility* (Chicago, 1980). Several historians have found a correlation between the increase in literary attention to marriage for love and its occurrence in England. Lawrence Stone, *The Family, Sex, and Marriage in England* (New York, 1977), pp. 283–86; Randolph Trumbach, *The Rise of the Egalitarian Family* (New York, 1978), pp. 97, 291. Although Trumbach's starting date is slightly earlier than Stone's (c. 1720), he supports Stone's thesis concerning the increasing prevalence of marriage for love after 1780.

23. William and Malleville Haller, "The Puritan Art of Love," *Hun-*

tington Library Quarterly, 5 (1942): 255–56; Edmund S. Morgan, *The Puritan Family*, 2d ed. (New York, 1966), pp. 56–57, 79–86; James Turner Johnson, *A Society Ordained by God: Puritan Marriage Doctrine in the First Half of the Seventeenth Century* (Nashville, Tenn., 1970), pp. 15, 33; Kathleen M. Davies, "Continuity and Change in Literary Advice on Marriage," in R. B. Outhwaite, ed., *Marriage and Society* (New York, 1981), p. 65.

24. Frida Weber de Kurlat, "Amar, servir, y esperar de Lope de Vega y su fuente," in *Collected Studies in Honor of América Castro's Eightieth Year* (Oxford, 1965), pp. 435–45; Lope de Vega, *Caballero de Olmedo* (Madrid, 1970); Arco y Garay, *La sociedad española en la obra dramática de Lope de Vega* (Madrid, 1942), p. 630.

25. Anthropologist Julian Pitt-Rivers describes a similar idea among contemporary Andalucian peasantry, and suggests a possible reason for the unwillingness to acknowledge any other motive. "In contrast to the peasantry of Europe as they are generally described, the Andalucians are extremely romantic in their choice of a spouse. The marriage [sic] arranged by the parents for considerations of property are rare and are regarded ill"; also, "the notion of personal autonomy is expressed in a romantic attitude toward marriage which makes it disreputable to marry for money rather than love." Julian Pitt-Rivers, *The Fate of Schechem* (Cambridge, Eng., 1977), pp. 63, 91. The expression of such "disreputable" ideas is sometimes found in popular lyrics. See Margit Frenk Alatorre, "De la seguidilla antigua a la moderna," in *Collected Studies in Honor of Américo Castro's Eightieth Year*, esp. p. 100.

26. Luján, colloquy 1, 1st part.

27. Vives, cap. xv. For contrary opinions, see comments by the Bishop of Norwich (England) and the French writer Pierre-Joseph d'Orléans in the middle of the 17th century, cited by Jean-Louis Flandrin, *Families in Former Times* (Cambridge, Eng., 1979), pp. 135, 167–68.

28. This point is well made by Peter N. Stearns and Carol Z. Stearns, "Emotionology: Clarifying the History of Emotions and Emotional Standards," *American Historical Review*, 90 (1985): 813–36, esp. pp. 820–21.

29. Prelates who intervened in these cases could follow several general guidelines laid down by theologians and canonists for interpreting the meaning of "unjust interference." Officials of the Mexican church courts of the 16th and 17th centuries followed the list of six actions established by the great Golden Age Hispanic canonist Tomás Sánchez in *De sancto matrimonii sacramento disputationum* (1621), vol. 3, disp. ix. The two actions relevant to economic motives were (4) reluctance to hand over an inheritance, and (5) objections to economic differences between the two. See also Azpilcueta, *Manual de confesores y penitentes* (1570), cap. 22 no. 32; and Manuel Rodríguez Lusitano, *Suma de los casos de conciencia* (1597), cap. 229. Rodríguez also

discusses the agreement of the major 16th-century canonists on this point. All six categories were strongly rooted in Hispanic cultural heritage as well as in theological tradition. The objections to economic differences and reluctance to hand over an inheritance were related to the Hispanic moral condemnation of motives of gain.

30. AGN, Mat 126 #5 (1640).

31. AGN, Mat 10 #177 (1629). Another case concerned a pair of fifty-year-olds, Bartolomé Rubio and María Salas, a widow. The widow's children were adamantly opposed to her remarrying and had even threatened her life should she do so. With the assistance of two of their friends, a silversmith and a merchant who had witnessed these outbursts, the pair were able to spend the last years of their lives together. AGN, Mat 48 #50 (1628).

32. AGN, Mat 5 #64 (1633). Other cases include Archivo del Provisorato, caja 38 Lucio-Covarrubias (1581); Mat 90 fs. 195 ff. (1623); Mat 98 #119 (1672); Archivo del Provisorato, caja 13 Cano Montezuma–Bazán (1674).

33. AGN, Mat 10 #16 (1629).

34. AGN, Mat 28 #35 (1628).

35. AGN, Mat 85 fs. 55–56 (1621).

36. AGN, Archivo del Provisorato, caja 20 Anton-Cristina (1640).

37. AGN, Mat 126 #36; Mat 90 fs. 12 ff.; Mat 28 #93; Mat 75 #64; Archivo del Provisorato, caja 13 (1611).

38. This idea, common in contemporary popular American culture, was given its original sociological statement by Ernest W. Burgess, "The Romantic Impulse and Family Disorganization," *The Survey*, 57 (1926): 290–94, and has been echoed by dozens of other studies since, including William Goode's frequently cited "The Theoretical Importance of Love," *American Sociological Review*, 24 (1959): 38–47. For a critique, see William M. Kephart, "The 'Dysfunctional' Theory of Romantic Love: A Research Report," *Journal of Comparative Family Studies*, 1 (1970): 26–36.

39. AGN, Archivo del Provisorato, caja 20 Vargas-Villalobos (1620).

40. Ruth Pike, *Aristocrats and Traders: Sevillan Society in the Sixteenth Century* (Ithaca, N.Y., 1971), pp. 90–91, 104–9; William Taylor, *Landlord and Peasant in Colonial Oaxaca* (Stanford, Calif., 1972); David Brading, *Miners and Merchants in Bourbon Mexico* (Cambridge, Eng., 1971), p. 12.

41. Diana Balmori, Stuart F. Voss, and Miles Wortman, *Notable Family Networks in Latin America* (Chicago, 1984).

Chapter 4

1. Declaration of Francisco de la Vega, Aug. 3, 1622, AGN, Mat 81 fs. 137 v; Diego Pacheco, Jan. 5, 1629, AGN, Mat 10 f. 4; Nicolas Reyna, Mar. 9, 1629, AGN, Mat 10 f. 198.

2. *Arte nuevo de hacer comedias*, in *Obras escogidas* (Madrid, 1961), 1: 896; Liseo in *Los ramilletes de Madrid* (edición Real Academia), act 2, p. 484; Tello in *El galán de la Membrilla*, in *Obras escogidas*, 3: 898; Peribañez in *Peribañez y el comendador de Ocaña*, in *Obras escogidas*, act 3, p. 779; Cervantes, *Persiles*, lib. 1 ch 2.

3. *Porfiar hasta morir*, in *Obras escogidas*, act 3, p. 898.

4. The quoted passage is from Peter Dunn, "Honour and Christian Background in Calderón," in Bruce W. Wardhopper, ed., *Critical Essays on the Theater of Calderón* (New York, 1965), p. 65. See also Julian Pitt-Rivers, *The Fate of Schechem* (Cambridge, Eng., 1977), pp. 1–17.

5. The association of nobility with honor as virtue was dominant through much of Western Europe. For similar concepts in Italy, see Américo Castro, "Algunas observaciones acerca del concepto del honor en los siglos xvi y xvii," *Revista de filología española*, 3 (1916): 12–13; and Frederick Robertson Bryson, *The Point of Honor in Sixteenth-Century Italy: An Aspect of the Life of the Gentleman* (New York, 1935), pp. 1–26, 104–10. For France, see Ellery Schalk, "The Appearance and Reality of Nobility in France During the Wars of Religion: An Example of How Collective Attitudes Can Change," *Journal of Modern History*, 48 (1976): 20–24; and David Bitton, *The French Nobility in Crisis, 1560–1640* (Stanford, Calif., 1969), chap. 5. For England, see Lawrence Stone, *The Crisis of the Aristocracy, 1558–1641* (Oxford, 1965), p. 199; and C. L. Barber, *The Idea of Honour in the English Drama, 1591–1700* (Göteborg, 1957), chaps. 3, 12. The Spanish historian Antonio Domínguez Ortiz refuses to take this ideology seriously, but can only do so by commiting the anachronism of accusing 16th-century society of intentional "false consciousness." Antonio Domínguez Ortiz, *Las clases privilegiadas en el antiguo régimen*, 2d ed. (Madrid, 1979), p. 186.

6. Carlos in *La obediencia laureada* (edición Biblioteca de Autores Españoles), act 1, p. 168; Teodoro in *Ello dirá* (edición Real Academia), act 3, p. 66; Arco, *Cervantes*, pp. 254–55. For an examination of other aspects of honor in Lope, see Donald Larson, *The Honor Plays of Lope de Vega* (Cambridge, Mass., 1977).

7. John Peristagny, ed., *Honor and Shame: The Values of Mediterranean Society* (Chicago, 1965).

8. There is a burgeoning number of studies on urban illegitimacy in 16th- and 17th-century Spain pointing to astoundingly high levels of out-of-wedlock births by the standards of the rest of Europe. What is perhaps most astonishing of all is that this difference has gone largely unremarked by historians, especially considering the amount of ink spilled over the 18th-century rise in English and French illegitimacy rates to levels near the levels of Spanish society in the late 16th and early 17th centuries. One of the few historians to comment on the matter is Peter Laslett in his intro-

duction to Laslett, ed., *Bastardy and Its Comparative History* (Cambridge, Mass., 1980), in which he compares data from Talavera de la Reina with six English parishes with the highest level of illegitimacy in the 16th century. He makes no comment, however, on the irony of Spanish societies having the highest illegitimacy rates along with the most rigid ideology of prenuptial chastity. The European data on births upon which this comparison is founded are in ibid., p. 18. On Spanish illegitimacy rates, see Universidad de Santiago Compostela, *Actas de las I jornadas de metodología aplicada de las ciencias históricas*, vol. 3 (Segovia, 1975), especially articles by Teófanes Egido, Manuel Fernández Álvarez, José Manuel Pérez García, Baudilio Barreiro Mallón; also Adriano Gutiérrez Alonso, "Evolución de la demografía vallisoletana durante el siglo XVII," *Investigaciones históricas* (Valladolid), 2 (1980): 39–69; María del Carmen Anson Calvo, "Un Estudio demográfico con ordenadores: La parroquia de San Pablo de Zaragosa de 1600 a 1660," *Estudios del departamento de historia*, 1 (1976): 225–45; and Claude Larquie, "Étude de démographie madrilène: la paroisse de San Ginés de 1650 à 1700," *Mélanges de la Casa Velásquez*, 2 (1966): 225–55. At least one Spanish historian has commented on the very high levels of the late 16th century, when illegitimate births outnumbered legitimate births. Manuel Fernández Álvarez, "La demografía de Salamanca en el siglo XVI a través de los fondos parroquiales," in *Homenaje al Dr. D. Juan Regla Campistol* (Valencia, 1975), esp. pp. 349–50. Another historian, scandalized by the prospect of such high illegitimacy rates, altered the techniques for establishing legitimacy in order to achieve a level that was normatively acceptable. Elena Maza Zorilla, "Régimen demográfico de una villa castellana. La natalidad en Villalón de Campos durante los siglos XVI y XVII," *Investigaciones históricas* (Valladolid), 1 (1979): 71–97, esp. p. 91. Similar findings in Spanish America have noted even higher levels of illegitimacy among Spanish women. See Claude Mazet, "Population et société à Lima au XVI et XVII siècles: la paroisse de San Sebastian (1562–1689)," *Cahiers d'Amérique Latine*, 13/14 (1976): 53–100. My examination of the christening records of the central parish of Sagrario (Mexico City) between 1640 and 1700 shows illegitimate births to Spanish women fluctuating around 33 percent.

9. This was true even when there was no conflict or the couple had been arrested for concubinage. AGN, Archivo del Provisorato, caja 21 Gutiérrez-Castillo (1602); Pinelo-Trujillo (1606); Mat 85 #9 (1621); Mat 90 fs. 223–26v (1623); Mat 102 fs. 255–57 (1623); Mat 64 #28 (1628); Mat 5 #92 (1633); Mat 126 #37 (1640); Mat 19 #89 (1644); Archivo del Provisorato caja 13 Mendoza-Medina (1663); Mat 27 #52 (1672); jail—Mat 60 #94 (1605); Mat 126 #16 (1640); Archivo del Provisorato caja 5 Fernández Montiel–Ángeles (1640). In so doing, clerics of the Mexican church were actually adding a cultural consideration—protection of a reputation for

honor—to Sánchez's six reasons for the dispensing of banns (see Chap. 2 n.35).

10. AGN, Mat 19 #70 (1644).

11. AGN, Archivo del Provisorato, caja 23 Montezuma Navarrete–Velásquez. For information on the Montezuma clan, see Charles Gibson, *The Aztecs Under Spanish Rule: A History of the Indians of the Valley of Mexico, 1519–1810* (Stanford, Calif., 1964), pp. 423–26.

12. AGN, Mat 88 f. 339v; Mat 48 #122 (1628); Archivo del Provisorato, caja 15 Castañón–Crespo; Mat 10 #27 (1629); Mat 81 fs. 47–49 (1621).

13. In 1629, Tomás Menses came before the ecclesiastical magistrate with a problem. Antonia Gutiérrez, whom he had promised to marry, was pregnant but her brothers believed her to be still a virgin. To protect both of them from the "great scandal and troubles" that her brothers would inflict if they knew of her illegitimate pregnancy, Tomás asked for, and received, permission to marry her secretly. AGN, Mat 10 #210 (1629); Mat 85 #9 (1621).

14. AGN, Mat 90 #162 (1619); Mat 102 fs. 255–57 (1623); Mat 86 #71 (1620); Mat 88 fs. 27–28v (1629).

15. AGN, Mat 64 #4 (1628).

16. The following is a partial list of the types of threatened or actual use of criminal courts overcome by church intervention: imprisonment in jail or in a textile workshop (used most frequently by the owners of slaves), Mat 2 #14 (1674); Mat 19 #52 (1682); Archivo del Provisorato, caja 20 Banagan (1631); caja 15 Cruz (1630); Mat 85 #30 (1621); Mat 5 #31 (1631); Mat 48 #15 (1628); Mat 76 #45 (1612); Mat 5 #103; Mat 90 #162 (the father had him jailed for rape); Mat 29 #25 (1662); Archivo del Provisorato, caja 5 Anusari (1664); threatened Real Justicia, Mat 28 #104 (1628); Mat 29 #55 (1634); threatened exile, Archivo del Provisorato, caja 21 Vega (1645).

17. Michael M. Sheehan, "The Formation and Stability of Marriage in Fourteenth-Century England: Evidence of an Ely Register," *Medieval Studies*, 33 (1971): 228–62; idem., "Choice of a Marriage Partner in the Middle Ages: Development and Mode of Application of a Theory of Marriage," *Studies in Medieval and Renaissance History*, n.s., 1 (1978): 1–33; Juan García González, "El incumplimento de las promesas de matrimonio en la historia del derecho español," *Anuario de historia del derecho español*, 23 (1953): 611–42; Abelardo Levaggi, "Esponsales: Su régimen jurídico en Castilla, Indians y el Río de la Plata hasta la codificacíon," *Revista del Instituto de Historia de Derecho Ricardo Levene*, 21 (1970): 11–99. For an empirical example, see AGN, Mat 121 #96 (1729).

18. The discovery of something that would nullify a marriage was, of course, valid cause for termination of an engagement. Church canonists recommended several additional causes. Although the list varied slightly

among the canonists, there was consensus on the seriousness of the commitment and a number of the acceptable causes. Among the more important reasons given for terminating an engagement were leprosy or other incurable or contagious diseases, dismemberment, sudden reversal of fortune of the intended bride or groom, entering religious life, or either one having sexual relations with someone else. These serious reasons allowed one party unilaterally to break an engagement. Medieval canonist Panormitanus included a difficult temperament as grounds for dissolving an engagement. Some grounds were incorporated into the civil law of the Partidas. *Manual de confesiones y penitentes* (1570); Azpilcueta, cap. 22 nos. 22–26 (1555); Tomás Sánchez, *De sancto matrimonii sacramento* (1621); Machado de Chávez, *Perfecto confessor y cura de almas* (1646), lib. 3, part 1, trat. 8 (1646); García González, p. 636.

19. These preferences were reversed in the 18th century. Martínez-Alier, for example, finds status concerns overriding honor as virtue in mid-18th-century Cuba. Verena Martínez-Alier, *Marriage, Class, and Colour in Cuba* (Cambridge, Eng., 1974), pp. 113–19.

20. Such conflicts were 18.5 percent of all prenuptial conflicts in this period.

21. AGN, Mat 88 fs. 339ff.

22. AGN, Mat 71 #9 (1612); Mat 29 #65 (1631).

23. Four percent were marriages between Spanish males and casta females; 2 percent were between casta males and Spanish females.

24. AGN, Mat 19 #52 (1682).

25. AGN, Archivo del Provisorato, caja 23 Rivera-Berrica (1633); caja 20 Santillan-Rodríguez (1631); Mat 19 #52 (1682).

26. AGN, Mat 5 #32; attachment to children.

27. Only one such instance was encountered out of nearly 400 cases; AGN, Mat 28 fs. 214–19v (1628).

Chapter 5

1. Approximately three-fourths of all the dispensations in this period were granted because of unjust parental interference. The remainder covered a variety of miscellaneous reasons such as an urgent need to leave town suddenly on business, the imminent arrival of Lent, the serious illness and potential death of a common-law spouse, or to protect the honor of a Spanish woman. Examples of the first reason include AGN, Archivo del Provisorato, caja 21 Barrera-Pérez (1604); Mat 49 #133 (1628); Mat 64 #97 (1628); Archivo del Provisorato caja 35 Xacome-Reyes (1631); caja 5 Ortuño-Aranda; Clero Regular y Secular 66 fs. 39–41 (1636); Archivo del Provisorato, caja 15 Hierro-Bermeo (1671); Mat 111 #49 (1672); and Mat 5 #92 (1633). Examples of the second are Archivo del Provisorato, caja 12

Quiroz-Ramírez (1612); caja 15 Jiménez-Neira (1633); caja 15 Ledesma-Arfias and Vera-Salazar (1635); and caja 17 Velásquez-Arfias (1679). Examples of the third are Mat 5 #74 (1633); Archivo del Provisorato caja 15 Santana-Santiago (1633); Mat 5 #36 (1633); Mat 64 #133 (1628); Mat 5 #74, 93 (1633); Clero Regular 66 fs. 38–39; Mat 98 #15 (1672); Mat 90 fs. 59–60v (1675); Mat 96 #32, 38 (1680); and Mat 53 #20. Examples of protecting Spanish women's honor are given in Chap. 4 n. 9.

   2. Canon lawyers sometimes go to great lengths to differentiate secret marriages and dispensation of the banns when both have the same social effect, namely that the marriage takes place secretly and without any prior publicity. The only difference between the two is that *after* the marriage has taken place the participants in a secret marriage are still sworn to secrecy. Vincent Paul Coburn, *Marriages of Conscience: An Historical Synopsis and Summary* (Washington, D.C., 1944). Since before the marriage there is no practical difference between the two, I have used secret marriage in preference to "dispensation of the banns" because it is more understandable and accurately expresses the social effects of church practice.

   3. The announcement of the banns of marriage was made mandatory by the Council of Trent as part of the complicated negotiations to make the decrees palatable to the different political factions represented at the meeting. Gabriel le Bras, "Mariage," in Vacant and Mangenot, eds., *Dictionnaire de théologie catholique*, vol. 10, cols. 2232–42; Adhémar Esmein, *Le mariage dans le droit canonique* (Paris, 1929), 2: 177–79, 195–99; *Council of Trent*, sess. 24, chap. 1. On the origin of the bishops' power to dispense, see Esmein, 2: 356–75; and James B. Roberts, *The Banns of Marriage: An Historical Synopsis and Commentary* (Washington, D.C., 1931), pp. 38–39. Since this technique represented a threat to the French requirement for parental consent, French law forbade marriage by minors without banns and without parental consent. Esmein, 2: 199–200.

   4. AGN, Mat 10 fs. 343–45 (1584).

   5. Dispensation of banns was requested, but the request was denied, in approximately 12 percent of the cases. For noncorroboration of witnesses, see AGN, Mat 85 #20 (1621); for the church's suspicions, see pp. 84ff.

   6. AGN, Mat 5 #31 (1631).

   7. Twenty-one-year-old Diego de la Cruz and fifteen-year-old Cristina de Santiago landed in the municipal jail of Mexico City when Cristina's mother denounced them to the authorities for living together. One of their friends, an older unmarried Spanish woman, declared to ecclesiastical authorities that Cristina's mother was "endeavoring with great assiduity to have Diego de la Cruz sent to the Philippines or other exile so that this marriage does not take place." Another friend, the mestiza wife of a shoemaker, added that the mother's efforts to obtain Diego's exile "were being favored

by certain powerful people" and that it would be in the service of God to allow Cristina and Diego to marry. Officials of the church married them secretly in jail. AGN, Archivo del Provisorato, caja 15 Cruz-Santiago (1636).

8. Fernando and his half-brother Cristóbal had previously fought over their father's inheritance and their relationship had been marked by suspicion and mutual dislike ever since. AGN, Mat 7 #41 (1631).

9. AGN, Archivo del Provisorato, caja 23. In 1629, despite the viceroy's opposition, church officials married his gentleman-in-waiting, Don Gabriel Moscoso, to the wealthy widow of the head of the treasury. Church officials married them secretly without the viceroy's knowledge or consent. AGN, Mat 88 f. 268 ff; also Mat 122 #52 (1672).

10. AGN, Mat 90 fs. 12–13v; Mat 79 #90.

11. For the history of this technique in English ecclesiastical courts, see R. H. Helmholz, *Marriage Litigation in Medieval England* (Cambridge, Eng., 1974), pp. 170–71.

12. The year before, Gerónima's father had successfully prevented the marriage. His opposition was founded in their economic inequality: Juan was poor, and his daughter wealthy. AGN, Mat 5 #91 (1633).

13. For example, Matrimonios, AGN, vol. 5, #91 (1633); vol. 7, #63 (1634); Documentos en proceso (1641).

14. Custody was also occasionally employed in prenuptial disputes for other reasons, such as the lack of suitable housing. AGN, Archivo del Provisorato, caja 97 Puebla-Reyes (1663). Church officials also attempted to use the *depósito* more generally to prevent women from engaging in sexual activity. This action, of course, was not designed to protect a woman's liberty (as in prenuptial conflict cases), but rather was meant to prevent her from enjoying her freedom under the guise of protecting her honor. Recognizing the inherently punitive motives behind this action, women avoided this type of *depósito* whenever possible and efforts at "protection" rapidly degenerated into the punitive sequestration that they were intended to be. Josefina Muriel, *Los recogimientos de mujeres* (México, 1974).

15. When twenty-one-year-old Ana María Herrera Vargas and twenty-five-year-old Alonso Delgado decided to marry in 1628, Ana María's parents vehemently opposed the match and prevented her from appearing in church court. Upon her fiancé's petition, Ana María was removed from her parents' home by royal officials and placed in temporary custody with the friends who had earlier witnessed her solemn promise to marry. AGN, Mat 48 #122 (1628).

16. Doña Ursula Velarde in 1668 was ordered not to take her slave Antonia Ignacia out of Mexico City while the banns were being read. She was free to sell Antonia if she wished in the meantime, but only to a resident of

Mexico City. AGN, Archivo del Provisorato, caja 28 Riveros-Antonia (1668). A nearly identical case is caja 28 Olanos-Cruz (1672).

17. Of the total of 379 opposed marriages, the outcome could not be determined for 40 marriages (12 percent of the cases). These were therefore excluded in the final count of the number of successful and prevented marriages.

18. In 1663, mestiza María eloped with a young Indian, Domingo Reyes. After spending time with him during the elopement, María decided that he was not the man she wanted to spend the rest of her life with and the marriage was called off. AGN, Archivo del Provisorato, caja 97 (1663). Nicolasa Encarnación, a free mulatta, terminated her relationship with Diego Santos, a free black, because of her mother's opposition to the match, saying she did so not out of fear but out of affection for her mother. AGN, Archivo del Provisorato, caja 15 Santos–Nicolasa Encarnación (1686).

19. Twenty-two-year-old Antonia Castañón, who lived in Cuernavaca, became enamored of a Spaniard named Juan Crespo, employed by the royal mint. At Juan's request, Antonia was brought to Mexico City and placed in temporary custody by the chief judge of Mexico City. There she not only denied that she had promised to marry Juan but also refused to admit that she even knew him. Juan persisted, but to no avail. When her father died fourteen months later, Antonia promptly left Cuernavaca for Mexico City, where she told church officials that she had been intimidated into denying knowing Juan, and that now that the father was dead, she was eager to marry. The ceremony was held shortly thereafter. AGN, Archivo del Provisorato, caja 17 Crespo-Castañón (1647); a similar case is caja 26 Cruz–Ursula Francisca (1641). Few young people had such serendipity, and young women who were so frightened they would not even acknowledge acquaintanceship with their fiancés were usually prevented from marrying.

20. For example, AGN, Mat 28 #69; Archivo del Provisorato, caja 30 Orduña–Cuella y Tovar (1665).

21. AGN, Mat 48 #2 (1628).

22. AGN, Mat 76 #8 (1612); Archivo del Provisorato, caja 5 Esguerra (1630).

23. It should be noted that the figures for Spanish men and Spanish women are calculated separately by sex. The figures given for castas are based on the number of marriages, not on the number of persons (male and female). Since the Spanish figures are based on sex and the casta figures on marriages, adding them together would be like summing up the proverbial apples and oranges. Separate calculation on the basis of sex is as follows. Casta men were 24 percent of the total but 44 percent of those whose marriages were halted. Casta women were 28 percent of the total but 48 percent

of those whose marriages were halted. The remainder of the men's and women's races could not be determined. Figures are from AP, Sagrario Metropolitano, Mexico City, *Libros de matrimonios de españoles, Libros de matrimonios de castas.*

24. AGN, Archivo del Provisorato, caja 5 Ortega-Mendoza (1685). Church officials would not dispense the banns when a slave was about to be taken out of town by his master, although they would perform this service for a Spaniard. Contrast examples in note 1 this chapter with AGN, Clero Regular 66 fs. 50–52 (1636).

25. AGN, Archivo del Provisorato, caja 20 Felipa-Lisea (1686).

26. Elena de Agüero, the mulatta slave of influential municipal official Don Diego Zarate, sought to marry Ignacio Reyes, a free mulatto for four years. In August 1640, with no more powerful backers than a slave man and his mestiza wife and Ignacio's declaration that he was willing to go wherever her master ordered her to live, the church court judge of Mexico City ordered their secret marriage in spite of the opposition of a powerful municipal official. AGN, Mat 126 #95 (1640); Mat 126 fs. 19–20 (1640).

27. It should also be remembered that such opportunities were available for urban slaves, and were far less likely to be available for slaves residing in rural areas.

28. Esmein, 1:93–97.

29. Ibid., pp. 227–30, 235.

30. Ibid., pp. 229–434 passim.

31. For the evolution of these principles in canon law, see ibid., pp. 1–98.

32. Ibid., pp. 370–434. For examples of the use of these impediments to dissolve marriages see, for example, AGN, Mat 81 fs. 62–78 (1621).

33. The list of impediments vitiating consent also included two other categories called "errors"—mistaken belief about a person's condition (ignorance of slave status), or mistaken belief about the person (generally covering fraud or misrepresentation of the person's identity). These "errors" could not be used by others to oppose a marriage because they were accepted as impediments only if the deceived party alleged that the other party had misrepresented himself or herself. Esmein, 1:344–70. For an example of such a case from the Mexican archdiocesan archive, see AGN, Mat 85 fs. 260–395 (1743). Error was not used for opposition to a marriage in prenuptial conflicts in the Mexican ecclesiastical courts.

34. Esmein, 1:227, details, pp. 236–334. Puberty was assumed to be age twelve for girls, fourteen for boys.

35. Ibid., pp. 370–434. The bond of affinity was created by sexual intercourse either in or outside marriage. For instance, a man who had sexual

relations with a woman had a first-degree bond of affinity with her sister. For the history of this impediment, see George H. Joyce, *Christian Marriage* (London, 1948), pp. 537–44.

36. Between 1563 and 1564 the Council of Trent made minor changes in the canonical impediments subject to Protestant attack—consanguinity, affinity, *cognatio spiritualis* and *legalis*, public honesty, and solemn vows. Esmein, 2: 141–56, 290–98, 265–70, 273–77; *Council of Trent*, sess. 24 chaps. 2, 3, 4, 5. Their substance, however, was reaffirmed in the face of such criticisms.

37. On rare occasions these postnuptial announcements were omitted.

38. AGN, Mat 31 #63, declaration Mar. 26, 1674.

39. See allegations from the father between Mar. 26 and Apr. 17, 1674, AGN, Mat 31 #63; Esmein, 1: 270–74.

40. AGN, Mat 31 #63. A two-hour debate among the physicians and surgeons preceded their acceptance of the commission to investigate from the ecclesiastical judge.

41. Such actions were not forbidden under canon law. A constitution of Pope Sixtus V addressed to the papal legate in Spain on June 22, 1587, allowed third parties to allege impotence. Esmein, 2: 306–7. Also, the young man's disfigurement was mentioned in other instances without becoming a cause for dispute. Report by master surgeon Bartolomeo Callejón Salmerón on the condition of Francisco Xavier Infante, aged 50, Nov. 4, 1764.

42. AGN, Mat 31 #63. See allegations and responses, Apr. 3, Apr. 10, and Apr. 17, 1674.

43. Esmein, 1: 282–83. Esmein, 1: 259–96, discusses the history of these procedures. All the methods proposed by lawyers for both sides were adaptations of procedures laid down in medieval canon law for accusations of impotence.

44. The total of seven judges was not fortuitous. Seven was the number of witnesses that medieval canon law, borrowing from a Germanic tradition, had adopted as the necessary number of corroborators of a case of impotence after a marriage had been contracted. The head of the ecclesiastical court adhered strictly to the seven-expert rule in the investigations and in the findings, although neither the circumstances of this case nor this particular application of the seven-witness rule had been foreseen in canon law. AGN, Mat 31 #63, Auto del Provisor, Apr. 21, 1674.

45. AGN, Mat 31 #63, report by Dr. Nicolas Méndez Olaeta.

46. AGN, Mat 31 #63, July 30, 1674.

47. AGN, Mat 31 #63, Auto del Provisor, Aug. 14, 1674.

48. AGN, Mat 28, #81 bis fs. 214–19v (1628).

49. *Council of Trent*, sess. 24, chap. 6; Esmein, 2: 283. The correct formal definition of the impediment of clandestinity is the failure to observe the

formalities of marriage. Tomás Sánchez, *Compendium in totius*, "clandestinum" no. 1; Thomas Alexander Lacey, *Marriage in Church and State* (New York, 1912), p. 83; John Joseph Carberry, *The Juridical Form of Marriage* (Washington, D.C., 1934), p. 3. The official Vatican organization established to interpret the decrees of the Council decided in 1587 that "clandestinity" signified only the lack of certain formalities—marriage without the priest and witnesses. Esmein, 2: 198–99. In French church courts, however, the word *clandestinité* historically meant without parental consent, a meaning not shared with other Romance languages, and not accepted as official church doctrine. Unfortunately, several historians have presumed that the French meaning had broader significance in church law, for example, Jean Gaudemet, "Législation canonique et attitudes séculières a l'égard du lien matrimonial au xvii siècle," *XII Siècle*, nos. 102–3 (1974), pp. 18, 20; and Beatrice Gottlieb, "The Meaning of Clandestine Marriage," in Robert Wheaton and Tamara Hareven, eds., *Family and Sexuality in French History* (Philadelphia, 1980).

50. Two earlier canonists, Gratian and Panormitanus, had argued that the violence in abduction could be against parents. Sánchez said this was not true because parental consent was not required for marriage. Esmein, 2: 280–85. Sánchez's position was adopted by the Mexican church. See ecclesiastical commentary, AGN, Mat 29 #25.

51. AGN, Mat 29 #25 (1662). Examples of ecclesiastical protection of eloping couples from parental interference can also be found in Mat 5 #91 (1633); Mat 7 #63 (1634); and Documentos en proceso (1641).

52. Esmein, 2: 284–85.

53. Ibid., p. 285.

Chapter 6

1. For much of the 16th and 17th centuries, levels of illegitimate births had been considerably higher among the slaves and the racially mixed population. In the central parish of Mexico City, for example, in 1650 over half of all births to racially mixed and black mothers were illegitimate. During the second half of the 17th century (to 1700) the number of illegitimate births to black and racially mixed mothers declined, from 55–60 percent of all births to approximately 40 percent. AP, Libros de Bautismos de Castas, Libros de Bautismos de Españoles, 1640–1710. Tomás Calvo has noted a similar decline in Guadalajara at the same time, and attributes it largely to the decreasing proportion of slave mothers. It is not possible to determine whether this was also true of mothers in Mexico City because the records make no distinctions between black and casta women, and ecclesiastical notations of mothers' names make record linkage virtually impossible. Tomás Calvo, "Family and Parish Register: Guadalajara in the Seventeenth Cen-

tury," paper read at the Congress of Americanists, Manchester, England, 1982.

2. For some of the few instances of the use of *real auxilio* for prenuptial conflicts in rural areas, see AGN, Mat 90 fs. 431–36 (1724); and Mat 41 #21 (1735).

3. The practice of dispensing banns to protect a woman's reputation for sexual honor became less automatic around 1670, and less frequent in the years that followed, but it was not until 1690 that the practice became extremely rare. For examples of the exceptions, see AGN, Mat 1 #55; Mat 60 Urquiza-González (1699); Mat 50 #22 (1705); Mat 96 #59 (1706); Mat 47 #68 (1744); Mat 69 #75 (1766); and Mat 123 #49 (1779). Since 1690 marks the virtual end to both secret marriages and royal police assistance, it also marks the first dramatic increase in the number of marriages prevented. The distribution of cases between 1690 and the effective implementation of the Pragmatic in 1779 is shown in the accompanying table. The exact date was indecipherable in 5 cases (out of 270).

4. AGN, Mat 50 #22 (1706). Sexual relations are frequently called "fragilidad humana" in both prosecutions for concubinage and lawsuits over broken marriage promises.

5. See above note 3, also AGN, Mat 14 #38 (1705). Church officials restored the practice of dispensing banns in the 1740's, but under quite different conditions. A growing number of couples adopted the custom of marrying when near death, either out of repentance or to secure the inheritance rights of their offspring. By 1740, church officials were once again permitting marriages without publicity, but only for deathbed marriages. The lack of publicity in these circumstances was due to a lack of time rather than to a need for secrecy. Manuel Pérez, *Farol Indiano* (México, 1713), p. 62. Dispensations continued to be granted occasionally for other reasons, such as allowing a couple to receive the nuptial blessing before the start of Lent. Examples include AGN, Mat 4 #26, #27 (1758); and Mat 69 #38 (1770).

6. Another reason for the church's slowness to depart from tradition

TABLE TO NOTE 3
Prenuptial Conflict Cases, 1690–1779

Period	Cases	Period	Cases	Period	Cases
1690–94	22	1720–24	3	1750–54	10
1694–99	6	1725–29	21	1755–59	13
1700–04	10	1730–34	10	1760–64	18
1705–09	21	1735–39	18	1765–69	34
1710–14	7	1740–44	11	1770–74	27
1715–19	13	1745–49	4	1775–79	17

here may have been concern for the legitimation of the child. For examples of enforcement of marriage promises, see AGN, Archivo del Provisorato, caja 17 Aranda-Jirón (1694); caja 1 Trujillo-Carmona (1702); Mat 14 #38 (1706); and Archivo del Provisorato, caja 3 Sánchez-Montealbo (1726).

7. The phrase "vain pretexts" was that of an ecclesiastical judge, AGN, Mat 85 fs. 124–v. Later examples include vol. 15 #8 (1765); vol. 53 #4 (1710); Archivo del Provisorato, caja 3 Sánchez-Montealbo (1726); and Mat 35 #2 (1738).

8. For example, AGN, Mat 90 #162 (1619); vol. 102 fs. 255–57; vol. 86 #71 (1620); Mat 48 #36, #39 (1628); vol. 88 fs. 27–28v (1629).

9. AGN, Mat 19 #2 (1671).

10. AGN, Mat 11 #49, Mat 13 #21. For examples of 17th-century jailings see Mat 65 #75 (1669); Mat 2 Rodríguez-Asunción (1674); Mat 125 #2 (1683). Contrast, for example, the action of the church court in 1620 (Mat 86 #71) with that of the same court in 1773 (Mat 13 #21). In the first case the man was not permitted to leave jail until he married. In the second, he was released, rearrested, and only threatened with prison.

11. Historically, marriages made in jail were controversial. One of the first Mexican canonists, Alonso de la Vera Cruz, regarded such marriages as invalid. During most of the colonial period, however, prevailing opinion followed Tomás Sánchez, who held that such marriages were valid and such pressure licit. Pérez, *Farol indiano*, trat. V, cap. 2, nos. 7–9.

12. Ibid., trat. V, cap. 2. It was only with the decreasing satisfaction of priests with the consequences of such marriages that clerical opinion shifted. An extensive later expression of this position can be found in the statements of the Promotor fiscal, AGN, Mat 54 #74 (1780).

13. For a description of the difference between *ex oficio* and *ex parte* suits, see John Stanley Purvis, *An Introduction to Ecclesiastical Records* (London, 1953), p. 65.

14. AGN, Archivo del Provisorato, caja 31 Bobadilla-González (1729). A nearly identical case is Mat 85 fs. 116–20v (1760).

15. AGN, Archivo del Provisorato, caja 9 Santa Cruz–Patricia (1727).

16. The proportion of prenuptial disputes involving the wealthy increased from half of all cases between 1574 and 1689 (N = 389) to over 70 percent between 1690 and 1779 (N = 270).

17. AGN, Archivo del Provisorato, caja 3 Farno-Aduña (1776). Similar cases are caja 1 Villaseñor-Montano (1770); Mat 85 #51 (1760); and Mat 110 #7.

18. AGN, Mat 103 fs. 413v, 415v (1749). Other examples of pleas of conscience included Mat 106 #23 (1734); Mat 50 Salinas-Gómez (1762); Mat 105 #30 (1771); and Mat 36 #72 (1771).

19. AGN, Mat 103 fs. 413–v (1749); Archivo del Provisorato caja 10 Covos Mojíca–Martínez (1751); Mat 41 #14 (1768); Mat 99, f. 1.

20. AGN, Archivo del Provisorato, caja 30 Zuñiga-Colchado (1699).

21. Lawrence Stone, *The Family, Sex, and Marriage in England, 1500–1800* (New York, 1977), pp. 629–30.

22. It was not the young men who could ill afford to bear the costs of marriage who were involved most often in these suits, but a disproportionate number of well-off (see note 16 above). Also, although some have argued that economic activity fluctuated widely, alternating between stagnation (1670–95, 1715–30) and rapid growth (1695–1715), the changes in attitudes toward honor proceeded in a single, consistent direction. See John Coatsworth, "The Limits of Colonial Absolutism: The State in Eighteenth-Century Mexico," in Karen Spalding, ed., *Essays in the Political, Economic, and Social History of Colonial Latin America* (Newark, Del., 1982).

Chapter 7

1. AGN, Mat 85 fs. 124–25v.

2. AGN, Archivo del Provisorato, caja 7 Valdez Topete–Flores (1702).

3. AGN, Archivo del Provisorato, caja 20 Núñez Merio–Artiaga Velasco (1704); a similar case is caja 31 Arze-Richarte (1779).

4. AGN, Archivo del Provisorato, caja 19 Iturria-Huerta (1768).

5. Interestingly enough, Protestant theologians who denied the right of children to choose their own marriage partners introduced anger and temporary insanity as legitimate grounds for terminating an engagement. Such categories were more easily manipulated by parents and were probably adopted for this reason. At the same time, Protestant theologians also denied all the impediments that protected individual consent. François Wendel, *Le mariage à Strasbourg à l'époque de la réforme* (Strasbourg, 1928), pp. 99–100.

6. AGN, Mat 46 #26 (1777). The father in this case was a wealthy peninsular merchant and influential member of the mining tribunal (*consulado*). For details on his activities, see Cristiana Borchart de Moreno, *Los mercaderes y el capitalismo en la ciudad de México: 1759–1778* (México, 1984), pp. 231, 237, 246, 258, 272.

7. The trends that these cases were selected to illustrate began early in the 18th century and were to continue through the end of the century. Overt arguments for patriarchy, which began at mid-century, did not eliminate parents' efforts to deny their children's independent will but simply carried it the next step further. When this occurred, parents used claims for disregarding the child's obviously independent will as part of the set of arguments further supporting patriarchy.

8. AGN, Civil 2251 exp. 5 (1791) fs. 11-v; see also Mat 85 fs. 205-v (1743).

9. Literary portraits of go-betweens can be found in medieval literature

also, for example Juan Ruíz's *Trotaconventos*. Michael J. Ruggiero, *The Evolution of the Go-Between in Spanish Literature Through the Sixteenth Century* (Berkeley, Calif., 1966). Other examples of servant go-betweens include AGN, Mat Indiferente, Negrete-Hernández (1715). A neighbor was blamed for being the force behind another marriage promise in AGN, Mat 103 #79, f. 369 (1749).

10. AGN, Archivo del Provisorato, caja 46 Sánchez–Castillo Altamirano (1728).

11. AGN, Mat 41 #7, #8 (1768).

12. AGN, Mat 9 #5 (1770).

13. AGN, Archivo del Provisorato, caja 46 Sánchez-Castillo Altamirano (1728); caja 3 López Arteaga–Román (1728); Mat 41 #14 (1768); Mat 9 #5 (1770).

14. AGN, Archivo del Provisorato, caja 7 Herculano-Benítez (1735); caja 9 García-Pérez (1735); Mat 85 #62 (1743); Mat 85 fs. 205–8 (1743); Mat 83 fs. 28–29v, 66–67v (1747); Mat 103 #79 (1749); Mat 105 #9 (1756); Mat 105 #9 (1756); Archivo del Provisorato, caja 3 Baptista-Roldán (1758); Mat 85 fs. 116ff (1760); Mat 79 fs. 245ff (1766); Mat 46 #26 (1777).

15. AGN, Archivo del Provisorato, caja 29 Díaz-Serrano (1768).

16. AGN, Mat 36 #72 (1771). Other examples of priests urging consideration of obligations of conscience include Mat 40 #39 (1760), and Archivo del Provisorato, caja 1 Rodríguez-Sánchez (1728).

17. It is worth noting that the average age at first marriage of young people involved in conflicts was slightly older in the later period, 1670–1779, than in the earlier period, 1574–1689. In the first period, the average age of men was twenty-four, and of women, nineteen. In the second period the average ages were twenty-four and a half (men) and twenty (women).

18. AGN, Mat 93 fs. 139–49 (1726).

19. AGN, Civil 1913 exp. 6 fs. 26–27. For subsequent adoption by couples of this term see Mat 125 #15 (1788).

20. AGN, Civil 1844 exp. 1 f. 18.

21. Eighteenth-century examples of the use of *gusto* and *voluntad* include AGN, Matrimonios, Indiferente, Cuevas–García (1717); Mat #105 (1719); Mat 84 fs. 430–36 (1725); fs. 412–15 (1725); Mat 93 fs. 139–43 (1726). Early 18th-century continuation of this understanding of *amores* can be seen in AGN, Mat 78 f. 43 (1726); Archivo del Provisorato, caja 1 Rodríguez-Sánchez (1728). For the use of *amores* to mean sex, see AGN, Mat 48 #122 (1628); Archivo del Provisorato, caja 24 Rosas-Velásquez (1699), caja 40 Rosa–Juana Francisca (1708); and Mat 107 #1.

22. For the Spanish meaning of *amor*, see Academia Española, Madrid, *Diccionario de la lengua castellana*, 3d ed. (1791); Juan Corominas, *Breve diccionario etimológica de la lengua castellana*, 3d ed. (Madrid, 1973). For *amor* in

conflict cases, see AGN, Mat 34 #76 (1766); Mat 41 #7–8 (1768); Mat 73 #4 (1773); Mat 107 #1 fs. 20 (1776); and Mat 123 #49 (1779). The trend in usage continued into the 19th century. In 1801, Josefa Vicente Romero complained that Don Juan Dios Estrada had "con aquellas halagunas razones sofisimas y encarecimientos que aparentan los apasionados o pretendientes enamorados, logró de mi cuerpo lo mas acendrado y apreciable que podía apetecer su desordenado apetito." AGN, Archivo del Provisorato, caja 2.

23. The shift is registered etymologically as well. In contemporary Spanish dictionaries the second meaning of *amor* (sing.) is passion, which is still the primary meaning of the plural *amores*. The first meaning still suggests an inclination toward the good that attracts our will. Although love was not wholly redefined as passion, the word *amor* gradually altered to mean an inclination that attracts the will. Today, however, the relationship between love and will is lost, and "will" and "consent," the linguistic choices of 16th- and 17th-century couples, are now considered obsolete synonyms for "love." Eduardo Echegaray, *Diccionario general etimológico de la lengua española* (Madrid, 1887), 1: 291; Real Academia Española, *Diccionario de la Real Academia* (Madrid, 1970).

24. AGN, Civil 2107 exp. 1.

25. AGN, Archivo del Provisorato, caja 1 Buitron-Peláez; Civil 2107.

26. This notion appears to have originated with Edward Shorter, *The Making of the Modern Family* (New York, 1975), p. 149, and has been subsequently adopted by other historians including Ramón Gutiérrez, "From Honor to Love," in Raymond Smith, ed., *Kinship and Ideology in Latin America* (Chapel Hill, N.C., 1984).

27. One father's attorney replied that parents may not maliciously impede the marriage, but they may do so justly. By justly he meant in accord with the parents' interests. AGN, Mat 36 #72 (1771).

28. AGN, Civil 1913 exp. 4f. 77v.

29. AGN, Mat 30 #46 (1759).

30. AGN, Mat 46 #26 (1777).

31. AGN, Archivo del Provisorato, caja 30 Zuñiga–Colchado Villaseñor (1699).

32. AGN, Archivo del Provisorato, caja 10 Covos-Martínez (1750).

Chapter 8

1. For the 18th-century Spanish meanings, see Academia Española, Madrid, *Diccionario*, 3d ed. (1791); and Juan Corominas, *Breve diccionario*. In Roman law, interest meant compensation due a creditor because of a loss suffered by lending. Twelfth-century Scholastics contrasted interest with usury, which was forbidden, but 16th-century critics such as Martin Luther

maintained that interest and usury were the same. See Benjamin Nelson, *The Idea of Usury: From Tribal Brotherhood to Universal Otherhood* (Chicago, 1969), pp. 33, 89, 233; John Noonan, *The Scholastic Analysis of Usury* (Cambridge, Mass., 1957), pp. 105–6, 117; and Bartolomé Clavero, "Interesse: traducción e incidencia de un concepto en la Castilla del siglo XVI," *Anuario de historia del derecho español*, 49 (1979): 19–57. For the broader meaning of interest in the early modern era, see Albert O. Hirschman, *The Passions and the Interests: Arguments for Capitalism Before Its Triumph* (Princeton, N.J., 1977).

2. Cervantes, *Quijote*, Part I, caps. ix, xi.

3. The critique can be found as early as Plato and Aristotle.

4. Hirschman, *Passions*. For a flawed account of this process in France, see Bernard Groethuysen, *The Bourgeois: Catholicism vs. Capitalism in Eighteenth-Century France* [orig. ed. 1927] (New York, 1968), pp. 191–239. Groethuysen reduces human beings to the incarnation of ideas, hence there are no separate groups of bourgeoisie with conflicting interests, only *the* bourgeoisie; no conflicts within the church, only *the Church*.

5. Richard Herr, *The Eighteenth-Century Revolution in Spain* (Princeton, N.J., 1958), pp. 120–27. The Spanish nobility tended to invest in maritime and wholesale commerce, mining, and estate manufacturing, especially metallurgy, armaments and munitions, paper, glassware, and textiles. William J. Callahan, *Honor, Commerce, and Industry in Eighteenth-Century Spain* (Boston, 1972), pp. 16, 19.

6. Eli F. Heckscher, "Mercantilism," *Encyclopedia of the Social Sciences* (1938), pp. 333–39. For comments on traditional Spanish ideas, see Peggy K. Liss, *Atlantic Empires: The Network of Trade and Revolution, 1713–1826* (Baltimore, Md., 1983), pp. 50–56.

7. Clarence Haring, *The Spanish Empire in America* (New York, 1947), chaps. 16 and 17, characterizes the economic relationship between Spain and its colonies as mercantilist from the start, but he points out that such policies failed to develop successfully until the 18th century. Stanley J. and Barbara H. Stein, *The Colonial Heritage of Latin America* (New York, 1970), pp. 99–101, refer to Spain's earlier relationship to her colonies as "an essentially late medieval commercial system, a sort of mercantilism in one port," and call the 18th-century development "proto-economic nationalism" (pp. 46, 88). Since, following Heckscher, I see economic nationalism as the major aim of 18th-century mercantilist policies, my use of "renascent mercantilism" here and the Steins' "proto-economic nationalism" are substantially the same. Enrique Semo, *Historia del capitalismo en México* (México, 1973), cites Marx's argument that mercantilism and the expansion of world markets contributed significantly to the rise of capitalism and describes this era of Mexican history as one of "embryonic capitalism." See also Eduardo

Arcila Farías, *Reformas económicas del siglo XVIII en la Nueva España*, 2 vols. (México, 1974).

8. Heckscher, "Mercantilism"; Liss, *Atlantic Empires*. For a related point, see John TePaske, "Spanish America," *International History Review*, 6 (1984): 515.

9. Callahan, p. 12, esp. n. 51; José Antonio Maravall, "Espiritu burgués y principio de interés en la ilustración española," *Hispanic Review*, 47 (1979): 291–325.

10. Callahan, pp. 1–2, 9, 11, 15.

11. Ibid., p. 41.

12. Ibid.; Charles C. Noel, "Missionary Preachers in Spain: Teaching Social Virtue in the Eighteenth Century," *American Historical Review*, 90 (1985): 866–92.

13. Callahan, pp. 38–40, 43. For further information on Calatayud, see Albert Baudrillant, ed., *Dictionnaire d'histoire et de géographie ecclésiastique*, vol. 2 (Paris, 1949). The clergy of New Spain were similarly affected in the decisions regarding marriage conflicts. Some acceded to the new beliefs that parental motives of gain were not illegitimate, while others held strictly to the more traditional denunciations of avarice. Although Callahan (p. 72) sees the effort to modify traditional values as largely unsuccessful, I believe that such efforts profoundly affected marriage policy in the 18th century by making it easier for dynastic families to consolidate and for "interest" to play a key role in matrimonial decisions.

14. Barbara H. and Stanley J. Stein question the extent to which Spanish policies can actually be credited with the increase in silver from America or the improvement of Spanish trade with American colonies ("Concepts and Realities of Spanish Economic Growth," *Historia Ibérica: economía y sociedad en los siglos XVIII y XIX*, 1: 103–19). However, they clearly establish the importance of new ideas about encouraging entrepreneurial development (p. 105).

15. R. J. Shafer, *The Economic Societies in the Spanish World (1763–1821)* (Syracuse, N.Y., 1958), pp. 24–45.

16. "Contact with British wares and tenets of political economy and with Anglo-American premises and products was . . . mounting." Peggy Liss, "Creoles, the North American Example, and the Spanish American Economy, 1760–1810," in Jacques Barbier and Allan J. Kuethe, eds., *The North American Role in the Spanish Imperial Economy, 1760–1819* (Manchester, Eng., 1984), p. 15. See also Joyce Appleby, *Economic Thought and Ideology in Seventeenth-Century England* (Princeton, N.J., 1978), pp. 242–79.

17. For Spain see Maravall, "Espiritu burgués," and for New World Spaniards see Eduardo Arcila Farías, "Ideas económicas en Nueva España en el siglo XVIII," *Trimestre económico*, 14 (1947): 68–82. Arcila points out

how both mercantilist and free trade ideas were sometimes argued by officials of the Royal Treasury and the merchant guilds of Mexico City and Vera Cruz. He also indicates the novelty of ideas about the public good in the writings of these officials.

18. They also affected the colonial state, but the subject is controversial. Books dealing with the impact of state policies on the economic structure of New Spain, in addition to works cited above, include two works by David Brading: *Miners and Merchants in Bourbon Mexico* (Cambridge, Eng., 1971), and "El mercantilismo ibérico y el crecimiento económico en la America Latina del siglo XVIII," in Enrique Florescano, ed., *Ensayos sobre el desarrollo económico de México y América Latina* (México, 1979); and John Coatsworth, "The Limits of Colonial Absolutism: The State in Eighteenth-Century Mexico," in Karen Spalding, ed., *Essays in the Political, Economic, and Social History of Colonial Latin America* (Newark, Del., 1982).

19. AGN, Archivo del Provisorato, caja 40 Ríos–Orozco Godines (1706); a similar incident is caja 3 Pérez Marañón–Jiménez de Cisneros (1779). A further indication of changed attitudes toward economic threats comes from a mother who opposed her son's marriage on the grounds that he lacked the money to maintain a wife, arguing further that this was a "rational" objection to the marriage. AGN, Mat 30 #36 (1759); Civil 1474 Fernández-Bravo (1764).

20. AGN, Civil 1913 exp. 4 f. 77v.

21. AGN, Mat 36 #72 (1771). It is possible to argue that the Enlightenment was responsible for the new exaltation of calculation in human affairs, but the argument seems farfetched, mainly because, although both the Enlightenment and patriarchal arguments emphasize the role of reason, the kind of reason is quite different. The Enlightenment exalted *individual* reason and was very skeptical of the notion of superior reason by virtue of authority. Mirabeau and Voltaire, who had themselves been victimized by abusive parents who proclaimed the superiority of their ambitions over those of their offspring, specifically condemned the reason of patriarchal authority. In other words, Enlightenment thinkers attacked the system of parental authority that the parents in these cases were seeking to establish.

22. AGN, Archivo del Provisorato, caja 3 Bautista-Roldán fs. 88v–89 (1758). There was not in fact much church opinion at the time to support this claim. See notes 7, 19, and 20, Chap. 12, for a more detailed discussion.

23. AGN, Mat 41 #16 (1768).

24. AGN, Archivo del Provisorato, caja 3, Pérez Marañón–Jiménez de Cisneros (1771).

25. AGN, Archivo del Provisorato, caja 24 Lascano (1771).

26. AGN, Mat 36 #72 (1771).

27. AGN, Mat 103 fs. 377–467 (1749).

28. The doctrine of normative patriarchy also gave slave owners a kind of authority they had never enjoyed before. Although ecclesiastical enforcement of marriages between slaves or blacks in the 17th century had often been lackadaisical, the church had still observed a certain degree of respect for individual liberty to marry, even among slaves. This vanished in the second half of the 18th century. Slaves were now required to present a license from their master before they were allowed to marry, whereas in the 17th century, not only had such licenses been unheard of, but many slaves were married against the express wishes of their owners.

29. The actual numbers of fathers or male relatives changed little between the 17th and 18th centuries. In the first as well as the second period men were the source of the opposition half of the time. More importantly, the rhetoric altered, even though the numbers did not change, at least initially.

30. Medieval civil law required parental permission and punished *daughters* for marrying against parental wishes. *Fuero Juzgo* lib. iii tit. 1 ley 2; *Fuero Viejo de Castilla* lib. v tit. v leyes 1, 2 modified by the *Fuero Real* lib. iii tit. i ley 5, *Leyes de Partida*, part. 6 tit. vii ley 5. The distinction between sons and daughters was also maintained by classical canonists, for example, Tomás Sánchez, *Compendium totius tractus*, "filius" no. 1. The requirement that *sons* have parental permission was part of the unprecedented affirmation of patriarchy in the late 18th century. A similar development occurred in 18th-century Brazil. See Maria Beatriz Nizza da Silva, *Sistema de casamento no Brasil Colonial* (São Paulo, 1984), pp. 117–20.

31. *Ordenanzas Reales de Castilla* lib. v tit. vi ley 1, lib. v tit. 1 ley 2; *Fuero Juzgo* lib. iii tit. 1 leyes 2, 7; lib. v tit. v ley 2. The *Fuero Juzgo* (lib. iii tit. 1 ley 2) frowned upon mothers, brothers, or other relatives helping a daughter marry whom she wished against her father's wishes. The Spanish Visigothic code accorded mothers greater authority over children than did other Germanic codes of the era, according to Paul Gide, *Étude sur la condition privée de la femme* (Paris, 1885), pp. 316–17.

32. AGN, Archivo del Provisorato, caja 3 Pérez Marañón–Jiménez de Cisneros (1779). For additional information on the family, see Brading, *Miners and Merchants*, p. 274.

33. AGN, Archivo del Provisorato, caja 3 Pérez Marañón–Jiménez de Cisneros (1779).

34. Lawrence Stone, *The Family, Sex, and Marriage in England, 1500–1800* (New York, 1977), pp. 152–53; Gerald Strauss, *Luther's House of Learning* (Baltimore, Md., 1978), pp. 116–23. The analogy between political and familial authority undoubtedly made Protestant doctrines very appealing to secular rulers, and perhaps explains its rapid acceptance among the German princes.

35. Both Stone and Strauss use functionalist arguments. Strauss also argues that the nuclear family became the focus of attention possibly because of the transition from extended to conjugal forms. The existence of a transition (except perhaps among the elite) has been largely discredited in the work of Peter Laslett, ed., *Household and Family in Past Time* (Cambridge, Eng., 1972).

36. In 1783 wives who favored a child's marriage that their husbands opposed were forbidden by the crown to give the child an inheritance out of their own money, "para obviar los perjuicios que acarrea la falta de subordinación de la mujer al marido . . . que las mujeres reconozcan la autoridad de su consorte como cabeza de las mismas familias." The authority being supported was not parental but specifically patriarchal: "Real Cédula aclarando dudas sobre el cumplimiento de la Real Pragmatica, referiendo a matrimonios." Richard Konetzke, ed., *Colección de documentos para la historia de la formación social de Hispanoamérica, 1493–1810* (Madrid, 1953), 3: 527–29.

Chapter 9

1. For example, AGN, Archivo del Provisorato, caja 40 Posada–Díaz Mayorga (1715); caja 20 Verdura-Posadas (1695), Núñez Merlo–Artiaga Velasco (1704); Mat 90 fs. 431–36v (1724) establishes the presence of equality between two mulattoes.

2. AGN, Archivo del Provisorato, caja 3 fs. 88v–89 Bautista-Roldán (1758).

3. AGN, Mat 103, fs. 377–467 (1749).

4. Ibid.

5. "No siendo ni extraño ni lo primero en el Mundo que la imbecilidad del sexo debajo de la palabra de casamiento se abandonó a las importunas soliciaciones de un hombre decente y con facultades para remediarla [*sic*]. . . . Don Joaquín quien como cristiano y caballero [es] obligado por todo derecho, natural, divino y positivo a repararle su honor y cumplirle la palabra." AGN, Mat 103, f. 414–414v (1749).

6. AGN, Mat 103, fs. 413–v.

7. Joaquín "trata el casamiento . . . prefiriendo el bien espiritual de su alma a el gusto y vanidad de su parentela." fs. 414–414v. Pitt-Rivers noted the contrast between the Puritans and Andalucians. Among the Puritans, "possession [of money] . . . became an end in itself as a sign of Grace. . . . The conflict between honor-precedence and honor-virtue was resolved in favour of the former." See Julian Pitt-Rivers, *The Fate of Shechem* (Cambridge, Eng., 1977), p. 36. A similar resolution of the conflict was argued by members of the 18th-century aristocracy of New Spain.

8. AGN, Mat 30 #46 (1759); AGN Mat 103 f. 415 (1749).

9. AGN, Mat 73 #41 (1770).

10. AGN, Mat 30 #46 (1759); Mat 46 #26 (1777); Mat 36 #71 (1773).
11. AGN, Mat 41 #16 (1768). [Emphasis added.]
12. AGN, Mat 43 #25 (1755).
13. AGN, Mat 41 #16 (1768); Mat 123 #49 (1779).
14. William J. Callahan, *Honor, Commerce, and Industry in Eighteenth-Century Spain* (Boston, 1972), pp. 11, 13, 30.
15. See declaration of priest of Toluca, May 21, 1768, in AGN, Archivo del Provisorato, caja 29 Díaz Peralta–Serrano; Pitt-Rivers, p. 36.
16. AGN, Mat 21 #68 (1774); Mat 123 #49 (1779); Archivo del Provisorato, caja 19 Iturria-Huerta (1768); caja 10 Jimeneo–Bueno y Alcalde (1763); Mat 41 #36 (1769). The struggle to redefine social status in terms that ultimately related to financial standing had begun.
17. AGN, Civil 1474 (1764).
18. AGN, Archivo del Provisorato, caja 29, Navarro-Ortíz (1768).
19. Some representative works include Franklin Ford, *Robe and Sword* (Cambridge, Mass., 1953); Davis Bitton, *The French Nobility in Crisis, 1560–1640* (Stanford, Calif., 1969); Carolyn Lougee, *Le Paradis des Femmes: Women, Salons, and Social Stratification in Seventeenth-Century France* (Princeton, N.J., 1976); Ellery Schalk, *From Valor to Pedigree: Ideas of Nobility in France in the Sixteenth and Seventeenth Centuries* (Princeton, N.J., 1986); and Lawrence Stone, *The Crisis of the Aristocracy, 1558–1641* (Oxford, 1965).
20. Some historians attribute the rise in interracial marriages to the proliferation of intermediate racial categories: others say it was an increase in unions between persons of closely related ethnic or racial categories. Both arguments hold that the fundamental social and racial boundary defined by marriage remained intact until the end of the colonial period. The data from the Sagrario suggest, however, that not only were the categories more numerous, but all groups were marrying outside their group more than before, and not merely into adjacent categories.
21. AP, Sagrario, *Libro de matrimonios de españoles*, ibid. *de castas*, 1640–1822.
22. AGN, Mat 99 fs. 329–v, 354, 383v.
23. AGN, Mat 99 fs. 354v, 355–56, 386–87.
24. AGN, Mat 99 fs. 393–v. For an entirely different resolution to a similar case in the 17th century, see Archivo del Provisorato, caja 37 Salazar-Sepúlveda (1668).
25. AGN, Mat 36 #71 (1773).
26. This figure is an approximation based on the following information. Interracial marriages by Spanish women still constituted only about 30 percent of all interracial marriages. Yet 60 percent of the opposed interracial marriages involved Spanish women and men of Indian or African ancestry.
27. AGN, Mat 121 #28 (1744).

28. AGN, Archivo del Provisorato, caja 17 Aranda-Xirón (1694).

29. AGN, Archivo del Provisorato, caja 40 Posada–Díaz Mayorga. In another instance, when relatives wished to prevent a marriage to a young mulatto male they presented the young woman with an attractive alternative. AGN, Archivo del Provisorato, caja 20 Manuel Antonio–Mexía (1693).

30. AGN, Archivo del Provisorato, caja 40 Posada–Díaz Mayorga (1715); Mat 93 fs. 139–49 (1726); Mat 115 #61 (1726); Mat 85 fs. 97–99v (1731); Mat 54 #39 (1763).

31. AGN, Mat 83 fs. 345–50v (1731). Questioning the racial status by the family was also sometimes a means of provoking doubt about a person, and was simply a delaying tactic. AGN, Mat 35 #12 (1736); Clero 134 f. 171–v (1766); Mat 107 #1 (1776). It was only when a Spanish woman married a man from a lower racial status that the church's concerns about interracial marriage were triggered.

32. Part of this insecurity was manifested in the increasing preoccupation with the marriages of daughters. Between 1584 and 1689, only half of the oppositions came from the woman's family or guardians. Between 1690 and 1779, over 70 percent of the objections originated on the woman's side; a dramatic increase.

33. Assimilation was also furthered by the Catholic Church's traditional policy that marriage was subject primarily to the wills of the parties involved, which rendered established families largely unable to keep their children from marrying the offspring of families of lower social and racial origins. Preventing such marriages was not impossible, since during the 18th century the royal courts had become an alternative forum for parental opposition, but the church's persistent adherence to its policy permitted many such marriages to take place against the express desires of the families.

34. AGN, Mat 9 #5 (1770). Another protest based on the fact that the other person was a mestizo is Archivo del Provisorato, caja 9 Arena Santa Cruz–María Patricia (1727). Similar phenomena may have occurred elsewhere in Spanish America, as Jaime Jaramillo Uribe suggests. See "Mestizaje y diferenciación social en el Nuevo Reino de Granda en la segunda mitad del siglo XVIII," *Anuario Colombiano de historia social y de la cultura*, 2 (1965): 21–48.

35. AGN, Archivo del Provisorato, caja 18 Guerrero-González (1715).

36. In 1733, the Inquisition's notary appeared before the church court in Mexico City to protest his son's effort to marry a mulatta named Micaela Fernández. The son had tried unsuccessfully to marry her seven or eight years before; the father believed that the reason the marriage had not taken place earlier was that Micaela had cast a spell on his son. The notary's wife

had taken apart a pearl in the center of the coral rosary Micaela had given the son as an engagement present and found it to contain yellow powder and a tangled bunch of hair with some tiny bones. She took these out of the pearl and replaced them with a medal of Saint Gerónimo. The church court responded that the allegation of witchcraft appeared to be nothing more than an attempt to impede the marriage because of the racial disparity. Spells were not a barrier to marriage, the judge remarked, as long as full liberty to consent was shown. AGN, Mat 120 #8.

    37. AGN, Mat 71, Ugarte-Jaimez (1753).

    38. AGN, Archivo del Provisorato, caja 4 Juan Cristóbal–Rivas (1761).

    39. AGN, Archivo del Provisorato, caja 19 Fernández de la Peña–Rodríguez (1768).

    40. The only exception was an estate owner who accused his son of trying to marry the daughter of an Indian whom he characterized as a barbarian. AGN, Mat 50, Salinas-Gómez (1762).

    41. AGN, Mat 50 #69 (1778).

    42. AGN, Mat 9 #5 (1770); Mat 121 #1 (1771).

    43. AGN, Mat 105 #30 (1771).

    44. AGN, Mat 30 #46 (1759).

    45. AGN, Mat 36 #72, petition June 27, 1772.

    46. AGN, Mat 9 #5, cuaderno 2, Oct. 18–Nov. 3, 1770.

    47. AGN, Mat 41 #16, petition July 14, 1768. For other examples see Archivo del Provisorato, caja 1 Villaseñor-Montano (1770).

    48. AGN, Mat 41 #14 (1768).

    49. This had not always been the case. In the 17th century the distinctions between racial groups had been more clear-cut, and lighter parents had objected to their offspring marrying darker men and women. By the 18th century, such differentiation was increasingly difficult and the darker families often had the additional advantage of wealth.

    50. In 1774, a poor but honorable Spanish woman reduced to living in the Hospicio de Pobres (a residence for the poor), complained about the marriage of her fifteen-year-old daughter to José Mariano Cuestas, an artisan whom she labeled as *chino* or *lobo* (a black-Indian mixture). The daughter had left home several different times to live with her lover, and once when this happened the mother had them arrested for concubinage. Shortly after the arrest, his family, who liked the daughter, arranged for the two to marry. The banns were about to be read when the girl's mother wrote a letter to the church court judge complaining that destructive consequences would follow from such a marriage. He was not her daughter's equal, being of low rank, as well as lazy, poorly employed, and unable to support a wife. Furthermore, she alleged that her lineage would be stained by such a match. Finally she changed her mind and decided to allow the

marriage to proceed, perhaps in the expectation that a son-in-law, however poorly employed, might be willing to contribute to the support of his poor mother-in-law. The church court judge did not seem much concerned about the mother's desire to protect her daughter's Spanish status, for he indicated that the differences in race were probably compensated for by the similarity in class position, since the young man's family was better off than the girl's was. AGN, Archivo del Provisorato, caja 6 Cuestas-Serrano (1774). In another case the young man feared his fiancée's guardian's objections based on race, but the guardian appeared not to mind. Mat 69 fs. 212–18 (1770).

Chapter 10

1. Julian Pitt-Rivers, *The Fate of Shechem* (Cambridge, Eng., 1977), pp. 3–4, 30–31; AGI, Audiencia de México, vol. 40, ramo 1, letter, king to viceroy, Jan. 24, 1665; letters, viceroy Mancera to king, Jan. 24, 1665, and Dec. 2, 1665.

2. AHN, Codices, 727-B, "Auxilio" Reales Cédulas Dec. 1, 1543, Jan. 19, 1544, Jan. 10, 1561, May 7, 1571; *Recopilación de las leyes de Indias*, leyes 12, 13 lib. 1 tit. 10; Juan Solórzano, *Política Indiana* (1647), lib. IV cap. 22 n. 4. When the uncle of Eugenia Suárez cut off her hair to dishonor her and then locked her up in his house to prevent her marrying Gregorio Herrera, the royal governor of Mexico City posted a bearer of the standard of justice outside the uncle's house to see that she was released to the custody of the church notary. AGN, Mat 75 #90 (1620).

3. AGI, Audiencia de México, 707, letter, archbishop to king, Nov. 2, 1660.

4. AGI, Audiencia de México 707, letter, archbishop to king, Nov. 2, 1660, Real Cédula Oct. 13, 1660 (México); AHN, Codices, 727-B, "Auxilio" Real Cédula May 16, 1678 (Panamá), May 31, 1712 (Charcas). For the prompt response of royal officials in the early part of the century, see AGN, Mat 98 #52 (1612); and Archivo del Provisorato, caja 15 Saucedo-Martín (1612). Later examples include AGN, Archivo del Provisorato, caja 34 Hernández-Torres (1670); caja 30 Quiñones-Paez (1670); Mat 2 #37 (1671); and Mat 29 #26 (1672).

5. AHN, Codices, 727-B, "Auxilio" Real Cédula May 16, 1678 (Panamá), May 31, 1712 (Charcas). Even the cost of having the ecclesiastical constable remove a woman for temporary custody was out of the reach of many. AGN, Clero 34 f. 216-v (1768). The importance of the constable's fees is alluded to in AGN, Mat 115 #58 (1726). For a list of the fees of officials in Madrid, see AHN, Consejos, vol. 20165 leg. 18. For the cases to which the church began to restrict itself, see AHN, Codices 729-B, Real Cédula Apr. 22, 1660.

6. AGN, Archivo del Provisorato, caja 42 Carmona-Frías (1679); case #59, caja 12 Lara-Elías (1689); case #17, caja 15 Cruz-Rojas (1674); Santos-Nicolasa Encarnación (1686); caja 5 Ortega-Mendoza (1685); Mat 29 #25 (1672).

7. AGN, Mat 53 #16 (1710). For Spanish elopement practices, see Verena Martínez-Alier, "Elopement and Seduction in Nineteenth-Century Cuba," *Past and Present*, 55 (1972): 91–129.

8. AGN, Mat 85, fs. 116–20v. Other rural areas obtaining royal police assistance in the early 18th century include Zultepec (1706) Mat 14 #28; Cuernavaca (1709) Mat 24 #1; and Tecualoya (1743) Mat 85 #62.

9. In one case, the parents were neither insolent nor scornful but coolly pushed aside the church's threats of excommunication. On April 14, 1728, church officials in Cuautitlán ordered the parents of Doña María Castillo Altamirano to permit her to make a declaration of her matrimonial intentions. On April 16 her father refused, saying María was in Mexico City. The church responded the following day by ordering the father to bring her from Mexico City to church court. He ignored the church's order, so the next day the judge of Cuautitlán turned to her mother and ordered her to allow her daughter to declare under pain of excommunication. On April 20 the request was repeated, also unsuccessfully. On April 26 her mother was asked again, and this time she too responded that María was in Mexico City. The next day the church threatened to make good its excommunication order for María's father. When the threat was repeated the following day to María's mother, she politely but firmly resisted the church officials' demands. On May 3 the church magistrate announced that he would excommunicate them at High Mass the next day. Four more days passed before the parents of María Castillo allowed her to appear before an ecclesiastical magistrate. Well over three weeks had passed, more than sufficient time for the parents of María Castillo to pressure their daughter to change her mind about marrying. AGN, Archivo del Provisorato, caja 46, Sánchez-Castillo (1728).

10. AGI, Indiferente General 2889, "Razón de las determinaciones tocantes a si se han de proponer para obispados mayores sujetos mitrados en otros."

11. For most of the 17th century, the power of the council had been curtailed because of the hegemony of the king's favorite. When that epoch ended, the council moved to restore its jurisdiction over American affairs by establishing a system of regular promotions and appointments in the ecclesiastical hierarchy.

12. Analysis based on data supplied by Mariano Cuevas, *Historia de la iglesia*, 5 vols. (México, 1946–47), 4: 113–20. See also Francisco Sosa, *El espiscopado mexicano* (México, 1877).

13. AGN, Mat 47 #68 (1744).

14. AGN, Mat 89 fs. 221ff (1728); Mat 118 #84. Other secret marriages include AGN, Clero 52, fs. 289–91 (1693); and Mat 84 fs. 412–15 (1725). For 17th-century enforcement in Mexico, see AGI, Escribanía de Cámara 954, 955, 957, 958. Periods of enforcement in the first half of the 18th century include 1720–22 and 1737–39. After 1750, sales of exemptions ceased and the penalties for marrying a woman from the district became more stringent. See Mark Burkholder and D. S. Chandler, *From Impotence to Authority: The Spanish Crown and the American Audiencias* (Columbia, Miss., 1977), pp. 41, 46, 96, 131. Picado Pacheco wound up being fined only 3,000 pesos, twelve years after his marriage took place. AGI, Audiencia de México 1121, Anexo al consulta de 24 febrero 1740. For a history of the legislation and the sometimes torturous means of avoiding it, see Daisy Rípodas Ardanaz, *El matrimonio en Indias* (Buenos Aires, 1977), pp. 317–49; and Richard Konetzke, "La prohibición de casarse los oidores o sus hijos e hijas con naturales del distrito de la Audiencia," in *Homenaje a Don José María de la Peña y Cámara* (Madrid, 1969), pp. 105–20.

15. AHN, Codices, "Auxilio" Reales Cédulas Nov. 30, 1743, Feb. 25, 1767; and Francisco Antonio de Elizondo, *Práctica universal forense de los tribunales de España y las Indias*, 4 vols. (Madrid, 1783), tomo III, p. 388.

16. Max Weber, *Economy and Society*, ed. Guenther Roth and Claus Wittich, 2d ed. (Berkeley, Calif., 1978), pp. 975, 1002.

17. AGN, Mat 42 #1 (1688). On female "retreats," see Josefina Muriel, *Los recogimientos de mujeres* (México, 1974).

18. AGN, Archivo del Provisorato, caja 1 Ursana-Machuca (1738).

19. Viceroy Carlos Francisco de Croix (1766–71) observed: "Hay muchos padres que tiene hijos de mala conducta, y creyendo que la patria potestad alcanza a destinarles a su arbitrio, practicaba el presentarlos por un memorial al virrey, para su aplicación a la tropa o destino a presidio, y por lo regular piden se les remita a Filipinas, creyendo hagan fortuna, *y respecto no tener los padres semejante arbitrio*, y que en algunos pudende haber distinto motivo del que representan, y en otros ser tan ligero que no merezca castigo, he tomado providencia . . . para que averiguando la conducta del hijo y padre . . . no castigar al inocente." [Emphasis added.] *Instrucción del Virrey Marquis de Croix que deja a su sucessor Antonio María Bucareli* (México, 1960), pp. 84–85; James F. Traer, "The French Family Court," *History*, 59 (1974): 212. Despite Croix's caution, however, the abuses continued.

20. For example, in addition to cases described in the text, see AGN, caja 4 Espinosa-Cordero (1738); Civil 1474 Ibarra-Bilbao (1752); Archivo del Provisorato, caja 14 Pérez-Ávila (1755); Mat 30 #46 (1759); and Mat 36 #72 (1771).

21. AGN, Mat 71, Martínez-Rivadeneira (1743).

22. AGN, Mat 41 #21 (1735); also AGN, Mat 20 #52; Documento en proceso (Hernández-González), Mat #105 (1719); Mat 50 #69 (1778); Michael Scaradaville, "Crime and the Urban Poor: Mexico City in the Late Colonial Period" (Ph.D. diss. University of Florida, 1977), p. 194.

23. AGN, Civil 1474, Peláez-Espindola (1778).

24. AGN, Clero 34, fs. 441–43 (1776).

25. Signs of increasing circumspection by religious officials were apparent as early as the 1670's. In 1672, church officials ordered the banns read for a marriage the viceroy opposed, when just fifty years earlier they had permitted secret marriages in similar circumstances. AGN, Mat 122 #52 (1672).

Chapter 11

1. From 1690 until 1715, the rate of marriages prevented or probably prevented by parents was 24.3 percent (N = 70); from 1715 until 1779, the rate was 36.4 percent (N = 200). The overall level of parental success for the period 1690–1779 was 34.5 percent (N = 270).

2. AGN, Mat 11 #18, #19 (1701).

3. AGN, Mat 120 #30 (1731); Mat 78, fs. 38–43v (1726); Mat 12 #139 (1755).

4. For a striking example of this, see AGN, Mat 120 #1 (1710).

5. AGN, Mat 108 #35 (1723).

6. For an extensive commentary on this problem, see AGN, Mat 54 #2 (1753).

7. On one occasion in 1725 the church notary went to the home of Gertrudis Pavón Medina in Mexico City to ask her if she still wished to marry. When he set foot inside the door he noticed her father becoming livid with rage. Fearing for Gertrudis's safety as well as his own, he took her out of the house himself, without a court order, and placed her in temporary custody. AGN, Mat 84, fs. 430–36. Personal initiatives of this sort were rare, however, and the proximity of relatives threatening to do damage was often an effective deterrent. AGN, Mat 14 #28 (1706); Mat 118 #10, #11.

8. The substance of diriment impediments has been little altered even in the 20th century. This is partly if not entirely attributable to the fact that civil rather than canon law is the dominant force in regulating marriage in the modern era. Only two changes, both relatively minor and neither of importance to our argument, were made between the Council of Trent (1563) and the start of the 19th century. A constitution of Pope Sixtus V in 1587 extended the impediment of impotence to men who had merely been rendered infertile by an operation (Adhémar Esmein, *Le mariage dans le droit canonique*, 2: 306–8). In 1749, Pope Benedict XIV declared null the marriage of unbaptized persons to baptized persons (ibid., pp. 299–300). As Esmein

points out, the practice of nullifying such marriages had been common in several areas of the world since the 16th century, and the degree of innovation in the decree was comparatively minor.

9. No formal list of prohibitive impediments was ever agreed upon by canonists or church councils, including the Council of Trent, even though they were at least as old as the diriment impediments, having been mentioned for the first time in the 4th century (Esmein, 1: 228–29, 320–21, 437–38). See, for example, Thomas Aquinas, *Summa Theologica*, part. 3 q. 50 art. 1. The only prohibition to receive attention from church officials at Trent was the one that had been attacked by the Protestant reformers, namely, the Catholic custom of barring marriage during Advent and Lent. Not surprisingly, church officials affirmed this as a prohibitive impediment. Esmein, 1: 320–21.

10. Covarrubias, *Opera*, 1: 156. "Sic sponsus prohibetur cum alia quam sponsa contrahere matrimonium, et tamen si contrahat matrimonium tenet." Cited by Esmein, 1: 154.

11. AGN, Mat 121 #96 (1729); Mat 40 #52 (1738); Mat 99 fs. 251ff. (1743); Archivo del Provisorato, caja 4 Delgado-Ortega (1744); Mat 83 fs. 1–247v (1747); Mat 103 fs. 377–467 (1749); Mat 50 Salinas-Gómez (1762); Archivo del Provisorato, caja 14 Alberto Antonio–Gutierrez (1752); Archivo del Provisorato, caja 46 Luz–Cruz y Martínez (1762); Mat 79 fs. 168–95 (1766); Archivo del Provisorato, caja 29 Navarro-Ortíz (1768); Mat 86 fs. 349–58 (1770); Mat 86 fs. 178–231 (1770); Mat 105 #30 (1771); Archivo del Provisorato, caja 24 Lascano (1771); Mat 121 #1 (1778).

12. AGN, Mat 86, fs. 178–230v (1770).

13. For example, Mat 72 #50 (1765); Clero Regular y Secular, 197 #18 (1769); Mat 105 #30 (1771).

14. Examples of traditional spousal cases are AGN, Archivo del Provisorato, caja 23 Aresa-Salazar (1674); caja 23 José de los Ángeles (1686); caja 1 Cruz-Alarcón (1702); caja indiferente Ariola-Durán (1707); caja 40 Bilbao-López (1708); caja 1 González Soto–Catalina Ángeles (1709); Reparas-Río (1723); caja 1 Bayo-Velásquez (1727); caja 31 Baez-Sánchez (1729); caja 14 Lanza Traílla–Villaseñor (1754); caja 14 Joaquín N–Becerra (1756); caja 1 Cepeda–Ruíz (1764); caja 10 Orihuela-Solis (1765); caja 8 Castro-Espinosa (1765); caja 19 Velasco Tabor–Ortíz (1768); caja 14 Villanueva-Téllez (1773).

15. AGN, Mat 36 #72 (1771).

16. See, for example, R. H. Helmholz, *Marriage Litigation in Medieval England* (Cambridge, Eng., 1974), pp. 113–15.

17. Helmholz, p. 115, argues that four or five months was not a long period for the resolution of ecclesiastical suits, but his criteria for this allegation are unclear and his definition of "long" is imprecise. Mexican

church courts in the 17th century gave definitive periods for response and held the parties to them despite allegations of even diriment impediments. AGN, Mat 2 #36 (1672); Mat 76 #8 (1612).

18. For the range of motives see AGN, Mat 121 #90 (1729); AGN, Mat 85 fs. 219–48 (1743); Mat 83 fs. 1–247v (1747); Mat 103 fs. 377–467 (1749); Mat 43 #25 (1755); Mat 30 #56 (1759); Mat 40 #39 (1760); Mat 72 #50 (1766); Mat 41 #78 (1768); Mat 86 fs. 178–231 (1770); and Mat 86 fs. 349–58 (1770).

19. For another example of family pressure, see AGN, Mat 30 #46; and Archivo del Provisorato, caja 47 Torres-Pascuala (1765).

20. The exception is AGN, Archivo del Provisorato, caja 14 (1752).

21. AGN, Mat 50, Salinas-Gómez (1762). A similar case is Mat 72 #50 (1765).

22. In 1774, in the hot sugar and cattle ranching region of northern Guerrero, the daughter of a powerful family became engaged, not to the owner of one of the region's great estates, but to an estate administrator. Her family opposed the match vehemently and gracelessly. Not only did they threaten and punish her, but her mother had the exceedingly bad taste to shout at the church court judge. As a result, Doña Francisca Román was ordered in temporary custody by the church court over her family's objections and in spite of a major disturbance they caused at the time of her removal. With Francisca safely protected, the announcement of the forthcoming marriage was made from the pulpits on Sunday. Stymied in their attempts to prevent the marriage, the family called upon a cousin whom Francisca had been interested in several years before. The cousin appeared before the judge and declared that he had a prior existing promise to marry Francisca, and that the marriage to the estate administrator should be called off. In one of the few instances of prompt ecclesiastical response, the judge of Mexico City to whom this problem was forwarded declared that the validity of the prior engagement rested on the existence of canonical impediments. If the cousin to whom she had been engaged was within the prohibited degrees of kinship, then the earlier engagement was to be declared invalid and she was free to marry the estate administrator. AGN, Archivo del Provisorato, caja 3 López de Arteaga–Román (1771). For an example involving a diriment impediment, see AGN, Mat 30 #46 (1762).

23. There are a few instances of spontaneous ecclesiastical intervention as late as the 1720's. In 1727 when the local ecclesiastical judge of Cuernavaca—one of the relatives opposing a woman's match—refused to place her in temporary custody, the church in Mexico City sent a special commissioner to Cuernavaca to settle the matter. AGN, Archivo del Provisorato, caja 1 Marticorena-Jiménez. Also, in 1726 banns were dispensed in Oaxaca because the (unidentified) owner of some money would be displeased. Ar-

chivo del Provisorato, caja 6 Ortega-Franco (1726). For the distinction between *de parte* and *de oficio* suits, see Chap. 6.

24. The success rate for parents was over 36 percent.

25. Mat 9 #5 (1770). For additional details on such procedures in subsequent Spanish law, see Juan García González, "El incumplimiento de las promesas de matrimonios en la historia del derecho español, *Anuario de historia del derecho español*, 23 (1953): 611–42.

26. AGN, Mat 41 #36.

27. Other egregious illustrations of the use of force include AGN, Mat 85 #65 (1743); and Archivo del Provisorato, caja 1 Posadas–Botellos Mobellan (1742).

28. Richard Konetzke, ed., *Colección de documentos para la historia de la formación social de Hispanoamérica* (Madrid, 1953), 3:401.

Chapter 12

1. In some areas, traditions lingered on for centuries after their original reasons for being had disappeared. In the 17th century, for example, the formal barriers to marriage, rooted in an amalgamation of German and Roman law and crystallized in the Middle Ages, were used to decide the validity of objections to marriage.

2. AGN, Archivo del Provisorato, caja 7 Sánchez-Olivera (1715).

3. AGN, Archivo del Provisorato, caja 64 Ibarguen-López (1719–20).

4. Tomás Sánchez, *De sancto matrimonii sacramento disputationum* (1621), lib. IV, disp. vii, nos. 5–8; disp. vi, no. 16; Machado de Chávez, *Perfecto confessor y cura de almas* (1646), lib. 3 trat. x. For a definitive analysis of the doctrine of reverential fear, see Joseph Sangmeister, *Force and Fear as Precluding Marital Consent: An Historical Synopsis and Commentary* (Washington, D.C., 1932). For an interesting case history of how canon law on reverential fear was adapted to another culture, see Roch Francis Knopke, *Reverential Fear in Matrimonial Cases in Asiatic Countries: Rota Cases* (Washington, D.C., 1949). George H. Joyce, *Christian Marriage: An Historical and Doctrinal Study* (London, 1948), p. 81, argues that the dominant position was argued by Azpilcueta, and the less influential position by Sánchez.

5. Some time in the second decade of the century, a young Indian woman named Micaela from a town near Cholula in the province of Puebla wanted to marry. Her parents favored an Indian from the capital of the province and persuaded her that it was her moral obligation to agree to the marriage, but then Micaela became enamored of a chief of her own town and decided to marry him. The first man still wanted to marry her, however, and tried to prevent her from marrying the chief. Micaela argued that her parents had used "reverential fear," or their moral power, to force her to accept the first man against her will. When the principal judge of the

church court in the province of Puebla decided in favor of the first man, Micaela appealed to the ecclesiastical judge of Mexico City, who agreed that her parents had used "reverential fear" to force her to marry and that the first engagement was therefore void; thus she became free to marry the man she wanted. The reaction of the ecclesiastical hierarchy in this case was mixed. On the one hand, the judge of the court in Puebla did not see the intimidation as invalidating the contract, whereas the principal judge of the Mexico City court adopted the dominant ecclesiastical tradition in rejecting the use of reverential fear. AGN, Mat 13, fs. 243–398.

6. Benedicti Papa XIV, *Bullarium* tom. 1 (Rome, 1749). I am indebted to Cynthia Kaldis for the translation.

7. Biblioteca Nacional, Madrid, José Javier Tenebra y Simanes, "Consulta que se me hizo sobre si el cura o qualquier juez eclesiastico puede o debe impedir los matrimonios . . . desiguales." Tenebra was the parish priest for the town of Tecamachalco and a frequent (unsuccessful) aspirant for the cathedral chapter in Puebla. It is worth noting that the canonical support for Tenebra's assertions is extremely flimsy. There is one cite to an epistle of Saint Ambrose, a description (not a prescription) of Roman marriage practices by a 9th-century pope, one reference to a forged papal letter (cited by a subsequent pontiff), and a reference to the provincial council of Cologne (1536), which also cites as its authority the papal forgery. Tenebra's evidence thus boils down to one epistle by a minor church father, a 9th-century description, and one forged canon. Considering that Tenebra, in the records of nearly ten centuries of the church's jurisdictional control over marriage, could only find a single epistle, a description, and a forgery to buttress his position, one can say that he had very little support indeed in the canonical tradition. His passing references to scripture and contemporary practices of sees of Constance and Naples are even weaker arguments, since only canonical prescriptions governed such decisions. See note 21 below.

8. Response of Promotor Fiscal to petition of Gertrudis Miranda, July 14, 1768, alleging, "No hay capitulo canónico que desponga ser necesario el consentimiento de los Padres para el Matrimonio de sus hijos." AGN, Mat 41 #16.

9. This is clear in the response cited in ibid.

10. AGN, Archivo del Provisorato, caja 6 Aguilera Paloma–Vega (1750) (removed for reverential fear).

11. AGN, Mat 115 #58 (1726); Mat 11 #56; Mat 52 fs. 479–84 (1767); Mat 66 #45; Mat 54 #39; Mat 109 #100 (1752); Mat 1 #36; Mat 108 #35 (1723); Mat 120 #18 (1733), #30 (1731); Mat 11 fs. 180, 196 (1770). There were also hundreds of instances of women being questioned about their liberty to declare prior to the proclamation of the Pragmatic. For 1770, for instance, some examples include Mat 85 #1, 12, 15, 30, 42, 43, 46, 49, 50; Mat

104 f. 226, 243, 255v, 282, 288, 315, 395, 437; Mat 69 f. 34, 61, 112v, 118, 204, 209, 266, 312, 320v, 372, 396v.

12. AGN, Mat 13 #48, Mat 60 #60 (1712) (desists for fear).

13. The basic work on the actions of Charles III vis-à-vis the Catholic Church is Nancy Farriss, *Crown and Clergy in Colonial Mexico, 1759–1821* (London, 1968), pp. 87–196; for Abad y Queipo's commentary see p. 171.

14. Ibid., pp. 93–94.

15. The principal agent of this controversy was a self-important but incompetent creole bureaucrat named Antonio Joaquín Rivadeneira, whose two-volume report on the proceedings of the Fourth Provincial Council was greeted with contempt by the supreme body, the Council of the Indies. What the bureaucrat thought was great learning was nothing more than a compendium of information from the popular encyclopedias of the day, and a disgrace not only to himself but to the council. The legal adviser to the council remarked on "the disgraceful and shameful ignorance with which [Rivadeneira] after interjecting himself in what was not for his inspection, touched on many points without understanding even the terms of the discussion. [He further] committed the grave disrespect of wanting to instruct the council with an indigestible appendix of specious impertinences taken from Ferrari's Library, the dictionary, and the encyclopedia, as if this Supreme Council need such assistance." He added further that the principal difference between the encyclopedias and dictionaries and Rivadeneira's commentary was that it was easier to find the material in the former. Biblioteca Nacional, Madrid, 19200, Antonio Joaquín Rivadeneira y Barrientos, "Compendio de todo lo trabajado durante el Concilio IV Mexicano." For the commentary by the fiscal de Peru, see Biblioteca Nacional, 4178, "Copia de varios ss. de la respuesta que el sr. fiscal Don Pedro de Piña y Mazo dio sobre el cuarto Concilio Provincial Mexicano," fs. 367–442. The quote is from fs. 338v, 340v-1.

16. The full text of the council proceedings was not published until more than a century later. *Concilio Provincial Mexicano Cuarto* (Queretaro, 1898).

17. Ibid., canon 10 lib. 4 tit. 1.

18. Ibid., canon 4 lib. 4 tit. 1. The archbishop of Mexico ceased granting secret marriages to protect feminine reputations for honor in 1690. See Chap. 6.

19. Ibid., lib. 4 tit. 1. In the wake of the Royal Pragmatic a Roman catechism was issued in Mexico and Spain which baldly stated that parental consent was necessary for marriage. The purpose presumably was to indoctrinate a new generation. See *Catecismo romano: compuesto por decreto del sagrado concilio tridentino para los parrocos de todas las iglesias y publicado por San Pío V*, trans. Lorenzo de Manterola (Pamplona, 1780), part. 2 cap. 7 no. 32.

20. Concilio Mexicano IV lib. 4. The original decree is as follows: "Ta-

metsi dubitandum non est, clandestina matrimonia, libero contrahentium consensu facta, rata, et vera esse matrimonia quamdiu Ecclesia ea irrita non fecit; et proinde jure damnandi sint illi, ut eos sancta Synodus anathemate damnat, qui ea vera, ac rata esse negant; *quique falso affirmant, Matrimonia, a filiisfamilias sine consensu parentum contracta, irrita esse, et parentes ea rata vel irrita facere posse*: nihilominus sancta Dei Ecclesia ex justissimis causis *illa* semper detestata est, atque prohibuit." [Emphasis added.] Council of Trent, sess. 24 chap. 1. The crucial "which" (*illa*) in the final phrase had historically been interpreted in the Hispanic church to mean only clandestine marriage, that is, without witnesses and a priest. The Mexican council's reinterpretation of this decree followed lines already established in France, where *illa* was reinterpreted to mean both clandestine marriages *and* marriages without parental consent. The Mexican council's lead in reinterpreting Tametsi was followed by royal officials in drawing up the Pragmatic. See note 26 below.

21. Joyce, pp. 117–18. For the spurious origin of the papal letter, see Vicente Coburn, *Marriages of Conscience* (Washington, D.C., 1944), pp. 6–7. The earliest attempt to introduce this justification in Mexico was in 1752. See note 6 above.

22. AGN, Mat 9 #5 (1770). For an example of a father defending the opposite point of view, see Archivo del Provisorato, caja 24 N-Lascano (1771); Mat 36 #72 (1771).

23. Farriss, pp. 35–38.

24. AGN, Mat 36 #72 (1771).

25. AGN, Mat 123 #49 (1779).

26. For the text of the Pragmatic, see Richard Konetzke, ed., *Colección de documentos* (Madrid, 1962), 3:406–13.

27. AHN, Consejos, libro año 1788, Real Cédula, Sept. 18, 1788, fs. 301–8. For additional commentary, see Real Academia de Historia (Madrid), Colección Mata Linares, vol. 18, fs. 384–85.

28. Daisy Rípodas Ardanaz, *El matrimonio en Indias* (Buenos Aires, 1977), pp. 289–300; José Mariluz Urquijo, "Victorian de Villava y la Pragmática de 1776 sobre matrimonios de hijos de familia," *Revista del Instituto del Derecho*, 11 (1960): 89–105; Gonzalo Vial Correa, "La aplicación en Chile de la Pragmática sobre matrimonio de los hijos de familia," *Revista chilena de historia del derecho*, 6 (1969): 335–62, esp. pp. 338–39.

29. "Real Cédula qu una junta de ministros exponga su dictamen sobre las providencias necesarias para evitar matrimonios desiguales." Konetzke, ed., 3:401–5.

30. Fevret, *Traité de l'abus* (1657), quoted by Adhémar Esmein, *Le Mariage dans le droit canonique* (1929), 1:86, 87. On the Thomistic origin of the distinction, see Esmein, 1:84–85, also Petro Fonitez, *Les diverses étapes de la laicisation du mariage au France* (Peripignan, 1972), pp. 73–74. Armed with

this useful distinction between a sacrament and a contract, the Council of the Indies then proceeded to lay out its objections to the 1741 papal encyclical, which had set strict guidelines for secret marriages but had insisted on the right of children to inherit from their parents. When the text of the encyclical was published in Spain, the royal reservation on this subject had been noted, as the framers of the Pragmatic well knew.

31. Gerónimo de Camargo, *Respuesta a la resolución de la junta de los eclesiásticos de Francia en razón de los principes de la sangre hechos sin el consontimiento del Rey* (Madrid, 1636).

32. The attempts by Spanish civil officials to make this novel legislation appear traditional are quite instructive on the creation of the myth of political "tradition." The junta de ministros which suggested the legislation attempted to legitimize their efforts by citing the practices of other Catholic nations of Europe, two minor 18th-century Italian canonists, and Spanish *civil* law and the Toledan councils from the early medieval era. See text in Konetzke, 3:404. They did not mention any of the major canonists who made 16th-century Spain the distinguished center of Catholic teaching, nor any other church teachings. The completed Pragmatic of March 23, 1776, intended for widespread publication, relied on the creation of a myth of a "national" tradition. It cited the *Fuero Juzgo*, lib. III tit. 2, and without specific reference to any subsequent legislation intimated that Spanish law had always followed this early precedent, when, in fact, it had not. Ibid., 3:407.

33. Max Weber, *Economy and Society* (Berkeley, Calif., 1978), pp. 226–27. "What is thought to be traditional is of more recent origin than people generally imagine it to be. . . . Indeed, there seems to be nothing which emerges and evolves as quickly as a 'tradition' when the need presents itself." Immanuel Wallerstein, *The Modern World System* (New York, 1974), p. 356. See also Eric Hobsbawm and Terence Ranger, *The Invention of Tradition* (Cambridge, Eng., 1983).

34. Konetzke, 3:623–25. Real Cédula, Mar. 8, 1787.

35. Medieval legislation had allowed for reconciliation and reinstatement of the inheritance. For the earlier legislation, see Chap. 2 n. 9. A similar but slightly different process was occurring in Brazil at the same time. See María Beatriz Nizza da Silva, *Sistema de casamento no Brasil colonial* (São Paulo, 1984), pp. 117–20.

Chapter 13

1. Latin American historians have often assumed the practices of the Pragmatic to be characteristic of the entire colonial period. The notable exception is Rípodas Ardanaz, who points out the emphasis on freedom to consent in ecclesiastical teachings on marriage in the centuries before the Pragmatic.

2. This definition was added to the Pragmatic when it was extended to America. For the text of the Pragmatic, see Richard Konetzke, ed., *Colección de documentos* (Madrid, 1962), 3: 406–13.

3. Solórzano, *Política Indiana* (1647), lib. 3 cap. 33 no. 48, also lib. 5 cap. 1 no. 10.

4. It was a Spanish jurist serving in New Spain who recommended the use of racial difference as the fundamental basis of social inequality. Daisy Rípodas Ardanaz, *El matrimonio en Indias* (Buenos Aires, 1977), p. 267.

5. Despite the strict prohibition against appeals to Spain, eight of the families also appealed either to the king directly (as the Count of Orizaba Valley did) or to the Council of the Indies. The figure of 46 cases represents all the cases that could be located using both the index to Civil (at Condumex) and the index to the Consultas of the Council of the Indies in the AGI. The distribution of cases by year of initiation is as follows: 1779–84, 7; 1785–89, 6; 1790–94, 14; 1795–99, 8; 1800–1804, 7; 1805–21, 4. Although a recorded decision could be found in only half the cases (10 upholding the family's opposition and 15 turning them down), parents were far more successful at preventing marriages because they simply added the Pragmatic to the repertoire of strategems to prevent a marriage. Parents employed inordinately long delays (often years) that led the couple to give up, and they appealed to church courts after being turned down in the royal courts. The result was that in over half (54 percent) of all the cases the parents prevailed (excluding cases for which no outcome was ascertainable). Eighteenth-century critics of the legislation who complained that the court upheld few oppositions focused their attentions too narrowly, on the decision alone, when the royal courts simply became one more voice among many ways of preventing marriages.

6. Rípodas Ardanaz (p. 305) suggests that most objections were racial, but I am skeptical about this assertion for two reasons. First, her conclusions are based on a superficial rather than a close reading of cases. Second, since the legislation required an allegation of racial inequality for parental opposition to be upheld, it would not be surprising that a number of parents and guardians briefly mentioned race at some point in their arguments in order to fulfill legal requirements, but dropped the matter quickly. A single mention of racial inequality in a 400-page case devoted to establishing differences of wealth and status should not be classified as an objection based on racial differences. To judge whether race actually was an issue for this study, I used all cases in which any effort was made to accuse the party of racial disparity.

7. AGN, Mat 73 #41 (1773).

8. AGI, México 2537 Consulta June 9, 1785.

9. AGN, Civil 1844, exp. 1 (1787).

10. For the importance of public acknowledgement of honor, see Julian Pitt-Rivers, "Honour and Social Status," in John Peristagny, ed., *Honour and Shame* (Chicago, 1965), p. 27.

11. AGN, Civil 1744 exp. 8 (1797).

12. Although the code of honor for men permitted young men a sexual freedom denied to women in colonial Mexico, it did impose some limits on their sexual conduct before marriage. One parent of a girl successfully prevented her marriage by arguing that her fiancé had exceeded the limits even of the double standard. The young man had seduced a servant girl and had defended his action by arguing that her morals, like those of all women of her social standing, were easily corruptible. The judge disagreed. It was not that servants were not corruptible, it was that the servant girl worked for another man. Eighteenth-century paternalism dictated that the servant girl's morality was protected by her master. The young man had transgressed by taking what belonged to another man. As further evidence of this young man's undesirable sexual conduct, the same mother pointed out that he had had an illegitimate child by another woman in the same town and that his responsibilities to the child would be the source of repeated visits to the child's mother and a constant source of tension and jealousy for her daughter. The judge agreed, and declared the mother's objections reasonable and prevented the marriage. The double standard was clearly operative in this element of the judge's decision, since, had the young man been female, the illegitimate child would have been sufficient to make him an objectionable mate. For the judge to accept the mother's objections, she needed to show that the illegitimate child would be an emotional threat to her daughter and not a violation of honor. AGN, Civil 1913 exp. 4 (1793).

13. AGN, Civil 2107 exp. 2 (1780). "The father of the girl . . . in theory, must not be allowed to become aware that his daughter is being courted. When the father appears, the lovers separate. He pretends not to notice them . . . until the young couple decide to get married." Julian Pitt-Rivers, *The Fate of Schechem* (Cambridge, Eng., 1977), p. 63.

14. AGN, Civil 2150 exp. 1; Civil 1559 exp. 1 (1785). Most of the father's fortune came from his marriage to the wealthy widow of the corregidor of Mexico City, Doña Francisca Ugarte. She had died, and under Spanish inheritance law the son was entitled to his share of his mother's estate at marriage. Although the father failed to acknowledge any financial motive for interfering, the necessity of turning over a substantial portion of his capital to his son was a likely source of his opposition.

15. This deference may be granted to someone who has something that members of the community covet but that is in short supply and held only by a few members. Classic honor by contrast is far more democratic, since it can be enjoyed by nearly everyone within a community. See the essay by

Max Weber, "Class, Status, and Party," in *Max Weber: Essays in Sociology*, ed. H. H. Gerth and C. Wright Mills (New York, 1946), pp. 180–95; and Edward Shils, "Deference," in Edward O. Laumann, Paul M. Siegel, and Robert W. Hodge, eds. *The Logic of Social Hierarchies* (Chicago, 1970), pp. 420–48.

16. For a discussion of these terms in Spanish definition of social status, see José Antonio Maravall, *Poder, honor y elites en el siglo XVII* (Madrid, 1979), pp. 201–14.

17. AGI, México, 40 Consulta May 24, 1803.

18. AGN, Civil 2107 exp. 2, 7 (1791). Other claimants to social honor also used this allegation. See AGN, Mat 17 #11 (1781).

19. For another kind of attack on someone enjoying military status see Civil 248 exp. 2.

20. AGI, México 140 Consulta 24 May 1803; Doris Ladd, *The Mexican Nobility at Independence, 1780–1826* (Austin, Tex., 1976), pp. 201–2.

21. AGN, Civil 2107 exp. 7 fs. 80–88v (1783).

22. AGN, Civil 1913 exp. 5 (1794).

23. There are no definitive studies of the racial composition of the elite as a whole, but reliable information is available on one part of this elite, the titled nobility. Ladd, p. 21.

24. AGN, Civil 130 exp. 1 fs. 5–7 (1802); Solórzano, lib. 2 cap. 30, nos. 20, 21.

25. Mexico, and indeed most of Spanish America, differed from Cuba in this respect. In the late 18th century, Cuba was becoming a slave society as a result of the importation of massive numbers of slaves to work on sugar plantations. The racial difference described by the Pragmatic—the separation of descendents of slaves—became the one significant social distinction in 18th- and 19th-century Cuba, whereas it did not apply in most of Spanish America. For the history of the Pragmatic in Cuba, see Verena Martínez-Alier, *Marriage, Class, and Colour in Cuba* (Cambridge, Eng., 1974).

26. AGN, Civil 1913 exp. 1 (1787). For a commentary on this as a strategy of responding, see Rípodas Ardanaz, p. 313 n. 174.

27. AGN, Civil 2251, exps. 2–4 (1791).

28. Illicit relations between a slave and her owner were common in the 17th century. Since Nana was a form of address used for wet nurses or nannies, sexual and racial images were merged. The story may have been reasonable in light of historical tradition of race mixture, but plausibility is not a criterion of truth. Furthermore, the arguments about descent from a distant black ancestress came wholly from the testimony of 18th-century witnesses who reported rumors they had heard about Benita's physical appearance or birth. Sources historically contemporary with Benita provided a different picture of her racial origin and identity.

29. AGN, Civil 1844 exp. 1 (1787).

30. For examples of grudges see AGI, México 1137, May 5, 1794; AGN, Civil 248 exp. 2 (1806); Archivo del Provisorato, caja 1 Buitron Pelaez (1788). For personal dislike see Civil 1586 exp. 11 (1802–3). Another intrafamily dispute, Civil 2251 exp. 6 (1794), was argued as a difference in race. Others are: grudge against grandfather, Civil 2251 exps. 2–4, 9 (1791), also Civil 1844 exps. 1, 1 bis (1787); bad relationship with wife, AGI, México 1132, Consulta Feb. 27, 1783; father temperamentally impossible, Civil 2107 exp. 1 (1780); threatens daughter with knife, Civil 1913 exp. 6 (1795).

For economic motives see AGN, Civil 1554 exp. 23 (1785–86); Civil 1499 exps. 1, 2 (1785–86); Civil 1913 exp. 8 (1798); AGI, México 1140, Dec. 11, 1801; woman lacked a substantial dowry, Civil 2169 exp. 3 (1796); man lacks money to support a wife, Civil 1590 exp. 8 (also gambling) (1782–83); Civil 1499 exp. 5, 6, 6 bis, 10 (1791–92); AGI, México 1135, Consulta Apr. 15, 1791; fortune hunter, Civil 2199 exp. 4 (1783); desire to hold on to an inheritance, AGN, Civil 2268 exp. 7 (1814), Civil 2251 exp. 7 (1795), Civil 2150 exp. 1 (1785); AGI, México 1135, Consulta Nov. 6, 1790.

For differences in social status within the Spanish community, see AGI México 1140 Consulta May 24, 1803; AGN, Civil 130 exp. 1 (1817), Civil 1499 exp. 14 (1801); Civil 259 exp. 2 (1791); AGI, México 1139, July 15, 1799; differences between servant on family estate and owner of ranch, AGN, Civil 1913 exp. 8 (1798); holder of dwindling entail, Civil 1913 exp. 5 (1794); AGI, México 1139 Consulta July 15, 1799; Civil 2107 exp. 2 (1791); Civil 2251 exp. 5 (1795); peninsular snobbery, Civil 1576 exp. 3 (1788); Civil 2107 exp. 7 (1783); Civil 1913 exp. 1 (1787).

For sexual honor see Civil 366 exp. 1 (1801–4); honor as a woman's immorality, Civil 1744 exp. 8 (1797); young man lacks honor, Civil 1913 exp. 4 (1793); woman's father condemned to jail, AGI, México 2537 Consulta June 9, 1785. For a catalog of some of the other reasons offered elsewhere in Spanish America, see Rípodas Ardanaz, pp. 310–13.

31. The bishop of Buenos Aires remarked that judges "frequently [passed down] opposite sentences and decisions in the same matter and in identical cases." Remark quoted by Rípodas Ardanaz, p. 284. Since a bishop could not have had access to the documents upon which the royal judges made their decision, his opinion could only be based upon impressions, and was undoubtedly related to his role as a prominent Latin American critic of the legislation.

32. The lack of a relationship between color or physiognomy and race had been observed before this. AGN, Mat 87 fs. 15–20 (1763).

33. Juan Solórzano's remark was that "esta división de Estados [entre nobles y plebeyos] no se practica en ellos [las Indias]; ni conviene que se introduzca." *Política Indiana*, lib. 3 cap. 33 no. 48, also lib. 5 cap. 1 no. 10; Ladd, p. 21.

34. For the Pragmatic of 1803, see AHN, Consejos, Libro año 1803 fs.

1597–1601. Subsequent modifications are f. 1603, Libro año 1804 f. 1787. For commentary, see Rípodas Ardanaz, pp. 273–74.

Conclusion

1. For the geographic concentration of work in family history, see the previously cited books on the European family by Shorter, Stone, Flandrin, Safley, Pollock, MacFarlane, Traer, Ozment, Levine, Trumbach, and de Mause, and on the Anglo-American family by Morgan, Demos, and Daniel Scott Smith. Other works on the Anglo-American family include Philip Greven, *Four Generations: Population, Land, and Family in Colonial Andover, Massachusetts* (Ithaca, N.Y., 1970); idem, *The Protestant Temperament: Patterns of Child-Rearing, Religious Experience, and the Self in Early America* (New York, 1979); Kenneth Lockridge, *A New England Town: The First Hundred Years* (New York, 1970); Daniel Blake Smith, *Inside the Great House: Planter Life in Eighteenth-Century Chesapeake Society* (Ithaca, N.Y., 1980); and Michael Gordon, ed., *The American Family in Social-Historical Perspective*, 2d ed. (New York, 1978). A bibliography published in 1980 showed that 40 percent of family history was written about the United States, France, and England. Lawrence Stone, "Family History in the 1980's: Past Achievements and Future Trends," *Journal of Interdisciplinary History*, 12 (1981): 51–87. For a household economic approach, see Michael Anderson, *Approaches to the History of the Western Family* (London, 1980); and Louise Tilly and Miriam Cohen, "Does the Family Have a History?" *Social Science History*, 6 (1982): 131–79.

2. The exception is Rípodas Ardanaz's excellent study of the ecclesiastical teaching and legislation on marriage in Spanish America. She does not, however, systematically examine either historical change or social practice in the colonial era and therefore does not draw conclusions about the historical transformation of institutional practices and popular attitudes toward parental control of marriage.

3. Parents played a critical role in the process, but this was no guarantee against an opposition. In one case the parents of both the boy and the girl had come to an agreement about the marriage, only to have it fall apart at the last minute when the couple were about to leave for the altar. The anger and efforts to block such marriages were as ferocious as those in which the selection had been made wholly contrary to family wishes. References to a parental role in negotiations include AGN, Mat 98 #84 (1612); and Archivo del Provisorato, caja 21 Rodríguez-Godó (1645). John Gillis describes how 16th-century English peasant couples made their own matches which were then ratified by family agreements. "Peasant, Plebian, and Proletarian Marriage in Britain, 1600–1900," in David Levine, ed., *Proletarianization and Family History* (New York, 1984), pp. 129–62, esp. pp. 131–33.

4. For example, Bartolomé Bennassar, *The Spanish Character* (Berkeley, Calif., 1979). The evidence of arranged marriages is mixed even among the high-ranking Spanish aristocracy. See J. de M. Carriazo, "Amor y moralidad bajo los reyes católicos," *Revista de archivos, bibliotecas y museos*, 60 (1954): 66–72. On arranged marriages in Spain, see Paula Sutter Fichtner, "Dynastic Marriage in Sixteenth-Century Hapsburg Diplomacy and Statecraft: An Interdisciplinary Approach," *American Historical Review*, 81 (1976): 243–65.

5. Edmund Morgan mentions isolated incidents in Anglo-American Puritan communities, and even Martin Luther describes one such instance. Edmund S. Morgan, *The Puritan Family* (New York, 1966), p. 151; Steven Ozment, *When Fathers Ruled* (Cambridge, Mass., 1983), p. 199 n. 185 citing Luther. On balance, however, normative weight rested far more with parents in 16th-century Protestant communities, despite arguments to the contrary. Ozment, for example, maintains that Protestant children had informal and legal alternatives for combating parental efforts to override their "mature" wishes in the choice of a spouse, but the evidence he offers suggests that such means were sharply limited and far more problematic than in colonial Mexico. Parental consent was required, and in Protestant areas parents could and did manage not only to prevent marriages before they took place, but to annul marriages that had already occurred, an impossibility under Catholic law. Ozment, p. 177, 37–39. See the critique by Lyndal Roper, "Going to Church and Street," *Past and Present* 106 (1985): 98. Furthermore, 16th-century German Protestant parents had legal standing to contest their children's marriages, something that was not true in 16th- and 17th-century Mexico; also, 16th-century Protestant courts permitted parents to disinherit children for marrying a "dishonorable" person, a privilege Spanish Catholic parents did not unqualifiedly enjoy until the final years of the 18th century.

6. Edward Shorter, *The Making of the Modern Family* (New York, 1975), pp. 148–50; Lawrence Stone, *The Family, Sex, and Marriage in England* (New York, 1977), pp. 282–87. The contrast between the "romantic love complex" and "settled affection" (for example, Stone, pp. 282, 316–17) is criticized as a neo-Freudian *moral* judgment by Irving Singer, *The Nature of Love*, 2d ed. (Chicago, 1984), 1: 23–38, esp. p. 37. Singer argues that the "romantic love complex" does not describe the phenomenon; he questions the desirability of love based upon contemporary ideas about ethical choice and presents his own interpretation. Singer, 2: 283–302.

7. A different pattern is described by an anthropologist who studied the peasantry of Andalucia, Spain, where the majority of the Spanish immigrants to Mexico originated. "In contrast to the peasantry of Europe as they are generally described, the Andalucians are extremely romantic in their

choice of a spouse. The marriages arranged by the parents for considerations of property are rare and are regarded ill." Julian Pitt-Rivers, *The Fate of Shechem* (Cambridge, Eng., 1977), pp. 63, 91.

8. Stone, pp. 271–72. Arranged aristocratic marriages in London are described by Vivien Brodsky Elliott, "Single Women and the London Marriage Market: Age, Status, and Mobility," in R. B. Outhwaite, ed., *Marriage and Society* (New York, 1981), pp. 84, 90. Elliott's perspective on the motives for marriage among the lower classes differs slightly from Stone's. She sees marriages by London servants as self-chosen rather than parentally controlled, but affirms that economic motives played a considerable role despite the lack of parental influence over selection. Pp. 89–91.

9. Jean-Louis Flandrin, "Amour et mariage au XVIIIᵉ siècle," in Flandrin, *Le sexe et l'occident* (Paris, 1981), p. 83. Jean Gaudemet expresses the same views in "Legislation canonique et attitudes séculières à l'égard du lien matrimonial au xvii siècle," *XVIIᵉ Siècle*, nos. 102–3, pp. 18, 26. See also Robert Muchembled, "Les nobles artésiens à l'époque de Philippe II," *Revue d'histoire moderne et contemporaine*, 22 (1975): 231–61.

10. David Hunt, *Parents and Children in History: The Psychology of Family Life in Early Modern France* (New York, 1970), pp. 58–67.

11. Alan MacFarlane has recently argued that the absence of a requirement for parental consent was a unique characteristic of English marriage patterns, grounded in a distinctive Anglo-Saxon individualism that was different from the cultural values of countries with a tradition of Roman law and *patria potestas*. However, since Catholic Spain and her colonies shared the tradition of Roman law and *patria potestas* yet failed to adopt a requirement for parental consent, this cannot account for the difference. MacFarlane, *Marriage and Reproduction in England* (Oxford, 1986), pp. 338–40. Furthermore, even in England, both Quakers and Puritans required parental consent. This suggests that the Anglican church's refusal to adopt such a requirement arose in great part from its self-conscious decision to steer a middle course between Protestantism and Catholicism. Anglicans remained close to Catholic conceptions of marriage, by calling it Holy Matrimony, for example, while at the same time adopting the formal Protestant position that it was not a sacrament. Horton Davies, *Worship and Theology in England from Cranmer to Hooker, 1534–1603* (Princeton, N.J., 1970).

12. The Anglicans did not have the same need as the German Protestants to establish the family as a vehicle for the teaching of doctrine because the similarities between the new religion and the old were more salient than the differences. The Puritans and Quakers, whose theological presuppositions differed substantially from those of Catholicism, encouraged the role of fathers as the doctrinal teachers within the family in an effort to combat both Anglican and Catholic orthodoxy.

13. MacFarlane, *Marriage*, pp. 148–73. MacFarlane oversimplifies his own case in a subsequent chapter (pp. 174–208), however, by extensively citing instances of approval of marriage for love without giving corresponding play to the existence of other motives that he earlier acknowledged.

14. Engels argued that the essential connection was between freedom in testamentory disposal of property and freedom of marriage choice. He argued that in the countries where paternal inheritance is secured to the children by law and they cannot be disinherited (Germany and countries with French law), children are obliged to obtain parental consent to marriage. In countries where parents have full freedom in testamentary disposal of property, parental consent to marriage is not legally required. Frederick Engels, *The Origin of the Family, Private Property, and the State* (New York, 1972), p. 136. Engels's assumption of a connection between patriarchal control of marriage and control of inheritance is challenged by the Spanish case, however, since under Castilian law children were forced heirs of their parents' property and yet there were no requirements for parental consent.

15. *Las Siete Partidas* (1256), part. 1 tit. 17 ley 1. In medieval law, however, the authority of the father had been trimmed from its broader Roman significance as head of a household full of slaves and servants, to an understanding of *patria potestas* as the authority of parents over their legitimate and adopted children. Part. 1 tit. 17 ley 3.

16. Shorter, pp. 259–64: Louise Tilly, Joan Scott, and Miriam Cohen, "Women's Work and European Fertility Patterns," *Journal of Interdisciplinary History*, 6 (1976): 447–76.

17. Stone, pp. 664, 258–61. Stone also lists (pp. 239–44) a convincing series of other explanations for the decline of patriarchal authority in England, including the strict settlement and political distrust of absolutism. John Gillis has recently suggested that the ties between the couple and community were not as decisively severed as Stone appears to argue, and that the conjugal couple has remained an ideal. Gillis, *For Better, for Worse* (New York, 1985), passim.

18. David Gilmore, "Anthropology of the Mediterranean Area," *Annual Review of Anthropology*, 11 (1982): 175–205; J. Davis, *The People of the Mediterranean: An Essay in Comparative Social Anthropology* (London, 1977). Slightly divergent earlier views include those of Verena Martínez-Alier (*Marriage, Class, and Colour in Cuba*, 1974), who attributes the importance assigned feminine sexual honor to the degree of rigidity in the social structure (pp. 120–23); and John Campbell, *Honour, Family, and Patronage* (New York, 1964). More usual are the views expressed by Jane Schneider, "Of Vigilance and Virgins: Honor, Shame, and Access to Resources in Mediterranean Societies," *Ethnology*, 16 (1971): 1–24.

19. Both types of cases also involved a conflict between the aims of an individual and the aims of a group, but the culturally significant content of those aims was completely different. In the first period, the conflict was between the aims of parents for economic, social, or political benefit and those of couples for carrying out commitments of honor; in the second, individual conscience was thrown squarely against parents' demands for status.

20. AGN, Mat 36 #72 (1771).

Bibliographic Note

The two basic sources for this study—marriage applications and lawsuits over proposed marriages—come from two different types of archives: parish records from Mexico City and the archive of the provisor and vicar general of the archdiocese of Mexico. Much of the colonial Mexico City parish archives as well as the colonial archive of the provisor and vicar general were seized as a result of the Reforma, the mid-nineteenth-century political movement that attacked the privileges of the church, including clerical control of marriage. It was indeed the seizure of these archives and their eventual transfer to the National Archives that made this study possible, for in Spain and most other Latin American countries the control of similar archives remains in private hands, hence fundamentally inaccessible.

In the wake of the Reforma, three types of documentation were seized, each relating to a part of ecclesiastical power that the government sought to eliminate: chantries, clerical control of marriage, and the ownership of real property by convents and monasteries. For the most part, these materials were kept separate: the archive of the provisor and vicar general became the core of Matrimonios, and the records relating to real property ownership by convents and monasteries became Templos and Conventos and Bienes Nacionales. Because marriage applications from the city of Mexico had been kept by diocesan notaries until the close of the seventeenth century, these, too, were seized when the archive of the vicar general was taken, and eventually they also became part of Matrimonios.

When Alejandra Moreno Toscano became director of the National Archives in 1977, she embarked on a program to reorganize existing documentation and allow public access to material that had previously been unobtainable. Toward that end she began a program of reclassifying several thousand volumes of the seized ecclesiastical material located in a "dump" category called "Indiferente." Over the next six years, thousands of pages of parish records and diocesan archives were placed in boxes mostly labeled Archivo del Provisorato. The addition of these more than doubled the volume of material that had been available when I began my research in 1976. (A small portion of the reclassified records from the original Indiferente are still in Indiferente boxes, and since I completed my research in 1983 a few scattered documents have continued to turn up.)

During most of the period of my research, there were neither indexes nor guides of any kind to most ecclesiastical records, and often neither foliation nor *expediente* numbers to the documentation I was using. I was therefore obliged to read every record I encountered, including all the volumes of Matrimonios, the entire archive of the Provisor and Vicar General rescued from Indiferente, and all the miscellaneous records scattered through the smaller *ramos* constituted out of the three categories of seized church records. The reasons for reading some of these other ramos stem from the history of these records in the archives.

The task was further complicated by the fact that not all the original categories were strictly maintained when the National Archives first classified the seized records. For example, the ramo called "Obras Pías" is an anomalous amalgamation of the private convent archive of the Bethlemite Fathers and part of the records of the Jesuit academy of San Pedro y San Pablo. Also, because the judges sometimes substituted for each other in emergencies, some diocesan marriage records appeared in the records of the chantry court and vice versa. Even though the spillover was relatively small, I went through all the smaller related ramos such as Clero Regular y Secular, Capellanías, and so on, after I had finished reading Matrimonios and the Archivo del Provisorato. By this time I had read thousands of parish marriage records and hundreds of lawsuits and had long ceased finding any material that challenged or altered the outline of my analysis of the history of prenuptial conflicts. After examining the first hundred volumes of Bienes Nacionales and finding nothing different from what I had already seen, I decided to leave aside the remaining odd marriage applications and conflicts (which I estimated would add no more than a third more cases to the documentation already collected).

The citation form in this book reflects the changing stages of archival organization. When I began, even the volumes of Matrimonios were neither paginated nor listed by expediente number. When these were added, I returned to the material to add the page or expediente number. I have preferred expediente number when both were available, but this was not always the case. The section formerly known as Indiferente and now largely called Archivo del Provisorato has been put into boxes and is as yet unnumbered. References to this material are therefore by box number, last names of the two principals, and year. Also, because I participated in the earliest reclassification of colonial ecclesiastical documentation when the archive was still at Tacuba, I have a few citations to material that had not yet been placed in the Archivo del Provisorato when I finished research. Where possible I have added the Provisorato numbers, but sometimes I have simply cited this material as Documentos en proceso (de catalogación).

For the eighteenth century, I also examined the records of the secular courts that held jurisdiction over prenuptial conflicts after 1779. Most of the corregidor's court records from Mexico City appear to have vanished (with the exception of a part of one year), so I concentrated on the extant information in the appeals court (the Audiencia), which I was able to locate by means of the index available at Condumex. Since several of the most eminent Spanish families also took their cases to the king, I examined these as well at the Archivo General de Indias in Seville.

The numbers of conflicts uncovered for each of the periods reflect the increasing restrictiveness of access to institutions for resolution of prenuptial conflicts. For the earliest period, 1574–1689, access to church officials was relatively easy and cheap, and the greatest number of cases (389) date from this period. For the next period, 1690–1779, when access to church officials became increasingly costly and difficult, the preserve of upper level families, the number of cases drops to 270. For the final period, 1779–1821, there is an even greater concentration upon the elite—46 families from the summit of colonial society. This concentration of the elite reflects what I believe to be the intentions of the legislation governing prenuptial conflicts, that is, the Royal Pragmatic on marriage. I believe that this legislation, despite its proclamation of equality of treatment for all save descendants of slaves, was specifically directed at the concerns of elite families, hence it is these families that this section studies. Although church officials did make some attempt to sidestep the restrictions on ecclesiastical intervention in prenuptial conflicts, their efforts were characterized by the same ambivalence they had had in the years immediately prior to the Pragmatic, and I therefore decided not to include any examination of these records in this book.

Although records of prenuptial conflicts form the core of the study, I also believed that it was necessary to examine the background against which they occurred, that is, the pattern of marriages in the population with the greatest percentage of conflicts in the court, namely Mexico City. I therefore also examined the microfilmed parish registers of Mexico City obtained by the Church of Jesus Christ of Latter-Day Saints with the cooperation of Mexican church officials. Examining the marriage records of every fifth year for the extant diocesan Spanish and Indian parishes in Mexico City during the sixteenth and seventeenth centuries, I discovered useful information regarding patterns of illegitimacy and interracial marriage. For the eighteenth century, I examined the marriage records of all the parishes every twenty-five years (the main parish of the Sagrario every five), and also the marriage applications for those parishes that had previously been handled by the diocesan notaries. The microfilmed applications did not turn up evidence of prenuptial conflict, since conflicts as well as special situations were forwarded by local priests to the vicar general for resolution.

Additional information on church-state relations and ecclesiastical writings on marriage came from the Archivo Histórico Nacional (Madrid), the Bibliotecas Nacionales of Madrid and Mexico, the British Museum, and the Library of Congress.

Index

98, 107, 140; attitudes toward race, 157; loss of church independence, 166–67, 169, 175, 192, 195; state restructuring of church appointments, 166–67, 169, 195; church fostering of secret marriages for state officials, 168–69; Bourbons as cause of church decline, 169; replacement of church courts with royal courts, 170, 174, 176, 201; use of exile and imprisonment, 171–72; use of criminal and municipal courts, 173–74, 176; royal intervention in Fourth Mexican Provincial Council, 194–96, 199, 203; church pressured to accept parental control, 200; issuance of the Pragmatic, 200–203

Concepción, Felipa, 82

Concubinage: defined, 27; legitimation of, by marriage, 72–73, 147; as miscegenation, 146; view of church on, 148; prevention of marriage on account of, 170, 173, 210; arrest for, 175, 195. *See also* Illegitimacy

Conquistadors, 18

Córdoba, María de, 164–65

Cortés, Hernán, 17ff

Council of the Indies, 166–67, 169, 195f, 202f, 207f, 214, 219f

Council of Trent: and marriage, 32–36, 40, 53, 203, 232; as rejoinder to Protestant criticism, 32, 110; subversion of, by French, 34–35; and free will, 50, 110, 232; banns made mandatory by, 75–76; Mexican church adoption of, 79; formulation of impediment of abduction, 89; and parental consent, 131, 201; and status inequality, 139

Count of Campomanes, 126

Court, ecclesiastical, *see under* Catholic Church

Covarrubias, Diego de, 36, 181

Creoles, 21, 27, 69, 81, 154, 167, 216

Cristóbal, Juan, 153

Culture, 9, 240; crystallization in New World, 18, 20–21; children's choice,

5, 11, 39, 42, 134, 192, 234; patriarchal control, 11, 227; doctrine of free choice, 32, 36, 46, 234; disapproval of coercion, 41–46; beliefs concerning marital motives, 47–48; concept of love, 48, 50, 52, 234; antipathy toward marriage for gain, 53–58, 60, 124; sexual honor, 56, 68, 71–72, 225; attitudes toward parental motives, 59, 123–24, 134, 173, 224–25; tradition of honor, 60–62, 68, 74, 90, 234; importance of promises, 68, 71–72, 225; church as supportive of, 80; as source of impediments, 84; Mexican compared with French and English, 90, 232–33; erosion of concept of love, will, and honor, 108–11, 123; attitude toward wealth, 124, 134, 204, 222–23; and mercantile capitalism, 125–26, 128, 234; emergence of aristocratic distinctiveness, 136; as shifting in priorities, 188; cultural values attacked, 190; parental arguments rooted in, 208; pattern of social mobility sanctioned by, 219; race as metaphor for social differences, 222–23

Delgado, Alonso, 44

Díaz, José, 165–66

Dualde, Luisa, 45

Emigration, to New World, 18–21

England, 51; compared with Hispanic world, 3, 7, 20, 228, 232–33; views on love, 53, 231, 233; as trading partner, 128; views on prenuptial disputes, 145; views on marriage motives, 230–33; views on parental consent, 232

Enríquez, José, 44

Esquivel, José María, 85–88

Family history: revisionist views, 6, 234; comparative views, 7, 228, 234; methodological approach, 8–9; lan-

224–25, 237, 239–40; reinterpretation of, by nobility, 237–39

Ibañez, José Mariano, 187–88
Illegitimacy: associated with racially mixed, 25, 146, 215, 222, 275; among blacks and castas, 26, 97–98, 216; among Spanish women, 63, 97, 266–67; as incentive for marriage, 64; as consideration for church action, 68; legitimization of children, 73; and illegitimate mothers, 138–39; as indication of social inequality, 210, 215; prevention of marriage for, 216, 218; double standard applied to, 219. *See also* Concubinage
Impediments, 84–91 *passim*, 112, 139, 153, 180–87, 190, 197–98
Indians: marriages of, 17, 25–26, 28, 82, 146, 148, 152–53, 217–18; status of, 22–24; compared with blacks, 24–25, 155, 206, 217; prenuptial conflicts involving, 26, 217; exempt from Inquisition, 29; distinct from Spanish in honor, 97; illegitimacy of, 146; protection of Spanish women from, 150; increase in wealth of, 150, 221; difficulty of differentiation by race; 155, 221; exempt from social inequality definition, 206; exempt from tribute payments, 222. *See also* Castas; Mestizos; Mulattoes
Inquisition, 29, 148, 195
Interest: defined, 123–25; growing legitimacy of, 123–24, 128–31, 134, 186, 225; effect of capitalism on, 125–27, 134, 235–36; depicted in literature, 126–27; in relation to love, 128–30, 230, 233, 236; in France and England, 230, 233; in relation to will, 233, 235

Jiménez, Cristobal de la Chica, 72–73
Jiménez Cisneros, Doña María Ana, 133
Jirón, Lugarda, 149

Jovellanos, Gaspar de, 143

la Güera Rodriguez, 214
Ladrón de Guevara, Antonio, 144
Ladrón de Guevara, Baltasar, 168
Language: as historical tool, 9–10, 240; of marital motives, 48, 50–51, 117, 119, 128, 130f, 206; *amor*, 119–20; used by crown, 201–2; describing black descent, 206; of status and social inequality, 208, 212, 221–23; of racially mixed, 221, 223; as evidence of parental hypocrisy, 224
León y Heredia, Don Pedro, 155
Letón, Doña Antonia, 182–83
Lisea, Matias, 82
Lope de Vega, 38–39, 49, 51, 53, 61–62, 71, 118
López Carrasco, Doña Joaquina, 4–5, 211
Lora, Doña Thomasa de, 98–99
Love: attitudes toward, 6, 12, 49, 53, 64, 109–10, 230–31; as motive for marriage, 39, 48, 59, 134, 230–31, 233; as expression of will, 47–48, 50, 53, 74, 117–18, 120, 123, 134, 231, 233–34, 239; tradition of courtly love, 48–49; in literature, 48–52, 231; teachings of Thomas Aquinas on, 49, 118, 231; in France and England, 53, 230–31; women's desires regarding, 53; versus marriage for gain, 53; as complement to honor, 61, 74; as unreliable emotion, 118–20, 123; priority of interest over, 128–30, 236; emergence of romantic love, 236
Luján, Pedro, 49–50

Machiavelli, 124
Machuca, Ana María, 170–71
Madrid, Diego de la, 174–75
Marriage: free will in, 5, 32–37, 39–42, 47, 59, 74, 196; parental authority over, 5, 35, 106–7, 109, 128, 131, 134–35, 177, 196–98, 223, 233; effect

of capitalism on, 6, 8, 233–37; historians' views of, 6–7, 230, 234; cultural attitudes toward, 12, 17–18, 50–54, 59, 74, 110–11, 177, 190, 192, 224; authority of church over, 17, 28, 30, 33, 68, 84, 90, 96–97, 140, 161, 167–77 *passim*; interracial marriage, 17, 25–26, 72–74, 81–83, 145–57 *passim*, 193, 205–6, 214–19; status distinctions in, 25, 136, 153, 212, 214; marriage conflicts of wealthier classes, 27; doctrines of church on, 31–40, 47, 89, 110, 131, 139, 174, 194, 196–97; Council of Trent on, 32–36, 40, 53, 75–76, 89, 131, 139, 201, 203, 232; Protestant views of, 33–35, 39; in France, 34–35, 53, 89, 171–72, 230; parental consent in, 35–39, 89, 131, 202, 206, 231–32; in literature, 38–39, 48–51, 74; parental veto over, 40, 130–31, 134, 138, 140–41, 192, 195, 198–99, 202, 224, 230; use of force in, 41, 174, 188, 191, 196; motives for, 47–49, 59, 74, 95, 131; attitudes toward marriage for gain, 48, 53–55, 59, 74, 111, 122–25, 128, 231–32; love as marital motive, 48, 51–53, 74, 118–19, 123, 134, 233; in England, 53, 230, 232; motives for opposition to, 55–59, 74, 95–96, 123–24, 131, 138–41, 145–57 *passim*, 219, 224; inequality and, 57, 138–45, 156, 193, 209–10, 217–20; premarital pregnancy, 63; sexual honor in, 64–65, 105, 139, 156, 225; pledge in, 65–66, 100, 109–11, 122, 180, 225; church's overriding of criminal proceedings concerning, 68, 76–77, 80; across socioeconomic boundaries, 69, 71–72, 145–57 *passim*; equality of honor in, 70, 74, 136, 139, 214; relationship of honor, love, and will in, 74, 233; use of secret marriage, 75–80, 98–99, 129, 168–69, 178–80, 192; definition of banns of marriage, 75–76; of lower-

level groups, 81–83, 88–89, 146–47, 149–53; impediments in, 84–89, 139; "vain pretexts" and, 111–12; erosion of love and will in, 109–10, 118–19, 122–23, 128–30, 134; growing legitimacy of interest, 122–25, 128–30, 134, 222; judgment replacing will in, 131; rule by father in, 132; antagonistic concepts of, 132; emergence of aristocratic distinctiveness in, 136; legislation regarding, 137, 157, 206; European view of, 145–46, 227–28, 231–32; changing balance of power in, 161, 169–70; by proxy, 172; change in declaration of intent in, 179–80; privatization of, 180, 184–88, 190; church support for equality in, 193, 197; status replacing will in, 194, 199–200, 240; Fourth Mexican Council and, 196; loss of honor as social inequality in, 208; creation of double standard in, 209–10, 220; status as honor over virtue, 214, 224–25; age limits on parental control of, 223; forbidden with slaves and upper levels, 223–24; arranged marriages, 228–30. *See also* Marriage oppositions; Prenuptial disputes

Marriage oppositions: defined, 4; records of, in Mexico, 27; interest and, 20, 55–56, 58–59, 207–8, 210, 217, 220, 224; economic inequality as basis for, 57, 138–42, 144; opposition to servant and slave marriages, 58; complexity of motives for, 59, 70, 95–96; equality of families and honor in, 70, 74; race as basis for, 74, 146–50, 152–53, 156–57, 206–7; use of royal police in, 78, 164–66, 168, 179; use of impediments for, 84–89; French handling of, 89, 171; loss of weapons to combat, 105–6, 178, 180; parental vetoes in, 131, 192, 195, 198; threat of excommunication in, 164–65, 179; use of state power in, 170–76 *passim*; use of imprisonment

of church, 162, 169, 176–77; parental success in, 177–78, 224; elimination of secret marriage in, 178; privatization of engagements, 180, 184, 186, 188; as private affairs, 184–88; as evidence for arranged marriages, 228. *See also* Marriage; Marriage oppositions

Protestantism: compared with Catholicism, 32–35, 37, 40, 229–32; on predestination and free will, 33, 110; on marriage, 33–35, 37, 40–41, 198, 229–33; on parental authority, 39–41, 229–33; as sanctioning force, 41; on love, 53

Ramírez, Diego, 45
Ríos, José Luis, 129
Rivadeneira y Mexica, Doña Manuela, 171–72
Rivera y Portes, Tomás, 73
Rodríguez, Juan, 78–79
Rodríguez, María Ignacia, 214
Rodríguez de Zuanavar, Don Jacinto, 147
Roldán, María Rosalia, 148
Romeo and Juliet, in Mexico, 1, 2–3, 6–7, 39, 232. *See also* Juana Herrera and Gerónimo Valverde
Romero, María Luisa, 218–19
Royal Pragmatic, *see* Pragmatic
Ruíz, Doña Catalina, 77
Ruíz, Mateo, 155
Ruíz, Pedro, 45
Ruíz de Alarcón, Juan, 21, 52–53

Sagade Buqueiro, Mateo, Archbishop, 161–62
Salazar, Margarita, 148
Salgado, María Nicolasa, 217
San Antonio, Juana de, 170
Sánchez, Nicolás, 114
Sánchez, Tomás, 36, 41, 89, 256–64 *passim*, 268f, 275, 277, 284, 295
Sandoval, Doña Sebastiana, 43–45
Santa Cruz, Matias, 104

Santo, Blas, 142
Sigüenza y Gongora, Carlos, 21
Slaves: castas exempt from slavery, 25; opposition to marriage of, 58, 81–83, 216, 223–24; separated from Spaniards by honor, 97, 206; illegitimacy of, 97; as scapegoats, 114; church as protector of, 140; marriage with Spaniards, 146, 149, 151–53, 185; growth in wealth of, 150, 152, 221; ancestry of, 153, 155, 206; as definition of social inequality, 206, 221. *See also* Blacks
Solórzano, Juan, 23
Sor Juana Inés de la Cruz, 21
State, *see* Church and state
Status: importance of, in New World, 19, 21–23; of Indians, 22; noble-plebeian distinction, 23; of blacks, 23, 155; of racial groups, 24, 155, 157, 188, 220–23, 239; in marriage, 25, 72, 188, 193, 238; and honor, 62, 69f, 137, 140f, 157, 188, 193, 200, 208–11, 214, 224, 240; condemnation of, 124; and wealth, 128, 143, 145; groups of rising and declining status, 137; erosion of boundaries of, 146–51, 153, 155, 157, 238; loss of, in sexual control, 150, 156; crisis of status insecurity, 150–51, 155–56; position of church on, 198; new language for, 208, 212–13, 222; medieval symbols for, 212–13, 222; as parental motive, 224; rewards for, 238; growth in importance of, 238–40

Tavira, María de, 57
Téllez Malpica, Ana Josefa, 187–88
Tenebra, Don José, 192–94
Tineo, Don Felipe, 168
Toledo, Viceroy Antonio, 161–62
Tolosa, Doña Francisca, 45
Trent, *see* Council of Trent

Ursana y García, Bernardo, 170–71

Library of Congress Cataloging-in-Publication Data

Seed, Patricia, 1949–
 To love, honor, and obey in colonial Mexico: conflicts over
 marriage choice, 1574–1821 / Patricia Seed.
 p.   cm.
 Bibliography: p.
 Includes index.
 ISBN 0-8047-1457-6 (cloth): ISBN 0-8047-2159-9 (pbk.)
  1. Marriage—Mexico—Mexico City—History. 2. Marriage—
Parental consent—Mexico—Mexico City—History. 3. Marriage—
Religious aspects—Catholic Church. 4. Mate selection—Mexico—
Mexico City—History. 5. Mexico—Social conditions—To 1810.
I. Title.
HQ728.S37 1988
306.8'1'097253—dc19   88–2374

∞ This book is printed on acid-free paper